Adjustment, Employment & Missing Institutions in Africa

THE EXPERIENCE IN EASTERN & SOUTHERN

D0537634

wo week

Adjustment, Employment & Missing Institutions in Africa

THE EXPERIENCE IN EASTERN & SOUTHERN AFRICA

EDITED BY
WILLEM VAN DER GEEST & ROLPH VAN DER HOEVEN

INTERNATIONAL LABOUR OFFICE
GENEVA
in association with
JAMES CURREY
OXFORD

International Labour Office, CH-1211 Geneva 22, Switzerland
in association with
James Currey Ltd, 73 Botley Road, Oxford OX2 0BS, United Kingdom

Copyright © International Labour Organization 1999
First published 1999

ISBN 92–2–110858–9 (ILO)

ISBN 0–85255–161–4 Paper (James Currey)
ISBN 0–85255–162–2 Cloth (James Currey)

British Library Cataloguing in Publication Data

Adjustment, employment & missing institutions in Africa :
the experience in Eastern & Southern Africa
1. Labor economics – Africa, Southern 2. Labor economics –
Africa, Eastern 3. Labor market – Africa, Southern 4. Labor
market – Africa, Eastern 5. Africa, Southern – Economic
conditions 6. Africa, Eastern – Economic conditions
7. Africa, Southern – Economic policy 8. Africa, Eastern – Economic policy
I. Geest, William van der II. Hoeven, Rolph van der
III. International Labour Office
331'. 09676

1 2 3 4 5 03 02 01 00 99

Typeset in 9/10½pt Palatino by Saxon Graphics Ltd, Derby
Printed in Great Britain by Villiers Publications, London N3

Contents

I
The Need for an Institutional Approach
to Structural Adjustment in Africa

1 Introduction & Overview
WILLEM VAN DER GEEST & ROLPH VAN DER HOEVEN

2 Africa's Adjusted Labour Markets: Can Institutions Perform?
ROLPH VAN DER HOEVEN & WILLEM VAN DER GEEST

A REVIEW
3 Adjustment, Employment & Labour Market Institutions in Sub-Saharan Africa
WILLEM VAN DER GEEST & GANESHAN WIGNARAJA

II
Adjustment, Employment
& Labour Market Institutions
COUNTRY EXAMPLES

8 Malawi
EPHRAIM CHIRWA & WYCLIFFE CHILOWA

LIST OF FIGURES & TABLES

Appendix tables

Notes on Contributors

Ephraim Chirwa is a Senior Lecturer at Chancellor College, University of Malawi in Zomba, Malawi. He has done research on the market structure and performance of the Malawian banking sector as well as on the divestiture programmes taking place as part of Malawi's adjustment programmes.

Wycliffe Chilowa is a Senior Research Fellow of the Centre for Social Research, University of Malawi in Zomba, Malawi. He has done extensive research on the impact of adjustment policy reforms on low-income households in Malawi, using various survey methods. He has a Ph.D from the University of Essex, United Kingdom.

Willem van der Geest (co-editor) has undertaken research and written on the welfare and income-distributional effects of public investment strategies, the modelling of food policies in sub-Saharan Africa, the constraints on economic and trade diversification in least developed countries and issues of structural adjustment. He previously worked at the ILO, Geneva, as Project Manager in the Employment and Training Department and is currently Director of the European Institute for Asian Studies in Brussels. He has a Ph.D. in Economics from Cambridge University.

Rolph van der Hoeven (co-editor) has researched and published extensively on planning for basic needs, on poverty analysis and monitoring, on the social aspects of privatization, on employment planning and employment strategies, and on structural adjustment and policy reforms. He has been the Economic Adviser to UNICEF and currently works for the Employment and Labour Market Policies Branch of the ILO responsible for structural adjustment and employment policies. He has a Ph.D in Economics from the Free University of Amsterdam.

Gerrishon Ikiara is a Senior Lecturer at the University of Nairobi, Kenya and a specialist on the Kenyan economy. He has contributed widely to the country's economic policy debates and published on issues of Kenya's industrialization strategy, on various aspects of the adjustment programmes adopted in Kenya, in particular agricultural marketing, and on the political economy of policy reforms. He chaired the wages council for security and protection workers.

Godfrey Kanyenze is a staff economist of the Zimbabwe Congress of Trade Unions (ZCTU). He has contributed actively to the ZCTU's alternative adjustment strategy (*Beyond ESAP*) and on issues of economic adjustment in Zimbabwe. He has a D.Phil in Economics from the University of Sussex, United Kingdom.

Ephraim Kaunga was formerly a Senior Lecturer at the Department of Economics, University of Zambia, a Permanent Secretary of the National Commission for Development Planning and an Executive Director of the holding company of the state mines ZIMCO; he was closely involved in the process of its divestiture. He currently lives and works in Zimbabwe. He has a Ph.D in Economics from the State University of New York.

Njuguna S. Ndung'u is a Lecturer in the Department of Economics, University of Nairobi, Kenya, specializing in quantitative policy analysis. He has researched and published on the dynamics of the inflationary process in Kenya, on price and exchange rate dynamics and on the impact of structural adjustment on low-income peasant households. He has a Ph.D in Economics from the University of Gothenburg.

Venkatesh Seshamani is a Professor of Economics at the University of Zambia and has done research and published extensively on issues of economic recovery and the structural transformation of African economies, as well as issues of research methodology. His contributions to the Zambian economic policy debate include analyses of public expenditure, social services delivery and safety nets.

Germina Ssemogerere is a Senior Lecturer and former Head of the Department of Economics, Makerere University, Uganda. She has researched and published on domestic resource mobilization, export diversification and exchange rate adjustment. She is a member of Uganda's task force on Poverty Reduction and of the National Forum. She has a Ph.D in Economics from Duke University, United States.

Ganeshan Wignaraja is Chief Programme Officer, Export and Industrial Development Division, Commonwealth Secretariat, London. He has researched and published on technological capability and external competitiveness. He has a D.Phil in Economics from the University of Oxford.

Foreword

Despite the application of structural adjustment programmes across Africa for over a decade and a half, their impact on livelihoods and employment remains hotly debated – and for good reason. There is considerable agreement that Africa's economic and social structures need to change in order to pull people out of poverty and provide them with decent employment opportunities. However, there is much concern about the way in which adjustment programmes are prepared and implemented – without duly taking account of the legitimate aspirations and perspectives of the majority of the population and striking the right balance between economic and social concerns.

This was recognized by the international community at the World Summit for Social Development, held in Copenhagen in 1995. Commitment 8 of the Declaration and Programme of Action is pertinent here:

> ... we commit ourselves to ensuring that when structural adjustment programmes are agreed they include social development goals, in particular eradicating poverty, promoting full and productive employment, and enhancing social integration ...

This commitment reflects closely the earlier concerns expressed by the constituents of the International Labour Organization at an ILO High-level Meeting on Employment and Structural Adjustment, held in 1987. Since then, adjustment programmes have changed and nearly all programmes today have a social component.

Most African countries have implemented several adjustment programmes, and one notices significant improvements. Currencies can be bought freely and are no longer overvalued, markets have been liberalized, interest rates have become positive in real terms, state-owned enterprises have been privatized, and new legal frameworks are changing the rules of the game. In various countries, per capita growth rates have become positive after long stretches of negative growth. Yet these gains are fragile, as has been acknowledged by the World Bank (*Global Economic Prospects 1998*). Moreover, there remains a strong feeling among the people of Africa that their situation has not improved, despite the often drastic measures implemented.

This volume by Willem van der Geest and Rolph van der Hoeven discusses the adjustment context in eastern and southern Africa. It notes that there is more consensus about the goals of adjustment than in the past, but finding the right balance between economic and social policies remains the key challenge. In particular, one needs to acknowledge the importance of institutions, especially labour market institutions, for achieving credible design and implementation of the programmes. Economic crisis and the early generation of adjustment programmes have led to decreasing capacity of labour market institutions either to provide appropriate structures to reach a national consensus through social dialogue or to support more effective implementation of the programmes.

The findings in this volume are informed by subregional and country analyses, and have been discussed at several national and subregional tripartite seminars at which many useful suggestions were voiced. These are reflected in the book. This research forms part of the ILO's action programme on 'Structural adjustment, employment and the role of the social partners' and has greatly benefited from a grant from DANIDA.

Werner Sengenberger
Director, Employment and Training Department
International Labour Office

Acknowledgements

This book is one outcome of a project, 'Structural Adjustment and the Role of Labour Market Institutions: A Capacity Building Project', which was jointly financed by DANIDA and the ILO. The project's objectives were to research and document the impact which structural adjustment programmes are having on the labour markets in selected African countries (Kenya, Uganda, the United Republic of Tanzania, Zambia and Zimbabwe), and to analyse how trade unions, employers' organizations and other labour market institutions in these countries could take a proactive approach to economic adjustment. Such an approach would seek to safeguard employment which is needed for the long-term growth and development of these countries, while at the same time identifying new economic opportunities and devising strategies for households and enterprises to take advantage of these. Five national seminars took place, namely in Kampala, Uganda (February 1996), organized jointly with the Economic Policy Research Centre, Kampala (EPRC); Lusaka, Zambia (April 1996), organized jointly with the ILO Area Office in Lusaka; Nairobi, Kenya (April 1996), organized jointly with the Institute for Policy Analysis and Research (IPAR); Dar es Salaam, United Republic of Tanzania (July 1996), organized jointly with the Economic and Social Research Foundation (ESRF) and the ILO Area Office; Harare, Zimbabwe (July 1996), organized jointly with the ILO's Southern Africa Multidisciplinary Advisory Team (SAMAT) and Dateline Southern Africa. A desk review was undertaken in the case of Malawi, and a sub-regional seminar took place in Kampala in September 1996. Researchers, government officials, employers and trade union representatives presented their findings and views at these seminars.

Rolph van der Hoeven chaired the Project Steering Committee at the ILO, comprising Ditero Saleshando and Robert Kyloh of the Bureau for Workers' Activities, and Akanino Etukudo of the Bureau for Employers' Activities, as well as Peter de Rooy of the Bureau for Multibilateral Funding. Willem van der Geest was the Task Manager of the project, responsible for organizing the seminars mentioned above and providing guidance in the preparation of the country case studies.[1] Useful comments by members of the Steering Group in the course of the project are gratefully acknowledged; the authors of the country case studies have made an important contribution by looking into the issues afresh and with great interest.

Furthermore, thanks are due to Thomas Bwalya, Pierre Dhonte, Lawrence Egulu, Ishrat Husain, Godfrey Kanyenze, Fred Opio, and George Ruigu who provided useful comments on the proceedings of the Kampala seminar. We would also like to thank Werner Sengenberger, Gek-Boo Ng, Eddy Lee, Vremudia Diejomaoh, Peter Peek and Peter Richards for their encouragement, support and comments at various stages of our work. Martijn Schrijvers, ILO intern, and Smitha Barbattina provided able research assistance for which we are very grateful. Secretarial support by Susan Porter, Christine Alfthan and Anne Drougard is also gratefully acknowledged.

[1]Reports of all the seminars are available upon request. The proceedings of the Kampala seminar are published in the Employment and Training Paper series (Paper No. 3), *Adjustment, Employment and Labour Market Institutions in Sub-Saharan Africa: An Emerging Consensus on Consultative Policy Design?*, by W. van der Geest and R. van der Hoeven, ILO, Geneva, 1997.

I

The Need
for an Institutional Approach
to Structural Adjustment in Africa

1 Introduction & Overview

WILLEM VAN DER GEEST & ROLPH VAN DER HOEVEN

Introduction

Sub-Saharan Africa's economic and social plight continues to arouse controversy, although less so than in the past. There now seems to be a consensus among politicians, academics, representatives of non-governmental organizations (NGOs) and others that economic changes are necessary for the region's growth rate to improve and to start making a dent in the increasing number of poor people in Africa. Secondly, although less universally accepted, there is the notion that Sub-Saharan African countries need to be better integrated in the world market and to take part in the process of globalization. As Gerry Helleiner puts it "Everyone is talking of "globalization". Some hail it; others fear it. In Africa, however, the question is more typically "why isn't there more of it?" Discussion of Sub-Saharan African prospects often features concern over its "marginalization" in the global economy as African shares of global trade and investment continue to decline' (Helleiner, 1997). And Paul Collier argues that 'the only international economic sphere on which Africa has remained non-marginal is aid' (Collier, 1995).

Many analysts point to absent or patchy implementation of macroeconomic and sectoral policies, together with the lack of well functioning markets, as a major cause of Africa's marginalization and the subsequent increase in poverty and slow employment creation (see Sachs and Warner, 1997).

The latter is undoubtedly true. The evidence we have been able to collect for East and Southern African countries clearly shows a general trend, namely, that the labour force in Africa is growing faster than the rate of jobs created, leading to an increased informalization of the economy. In most of the countries considered in this volume less than 10 per cent of the labour force works in the formal sector, as compared with 20–40 per cent at the end of the 1960s. In looking at the cause of this we feel that it is not so much the absence of reform policies, but rather their patchy implementation. However, we see the poor implementation as the result not so much of missing markets but of *missing institutions*. In effect, in many Eastern and Southern African countries institutions have been lacking to implement economic policy reform properly or to provide the necessary supply response to such policies. Indeed, the absence or weakness of institutions determines the appropriateness of the policy measures. For example, as part of their economic reform policies many countries in the region have reduced the number of public sector workers, but the supply response in the rest of the formal sector has been too weak to compensate for the decline in public sector employment; hence the continuation of the informalization of employment. Likewise, Africa's educational and training institutions seem to have difficulty in providing the appropriate skills for restructured markets, despite various attempts to make educational and training systems more market-oriented.

Furthermore, in order for labour market institutions to flourish properly a general acceptance by the social partners of such institutions is needed. We find this lacking in all countries of the sub-region. Economic reform policies are seen more or less as directives coming either from abroad or from a planning or finance ministry. Those who have to implement the policies often feel uninvolved and irrelevant. This is perhaps one of the most important reasons why it remains difficult to implement economic reform policies in Africa.

This volume therefore provides some further reflection on the problem of Africa's missing institutions. Chapter 2 spells out in detail the issues raised above, indicating that in all Eastern and Southern African countries bold attempts to liberalize markets have been made, but that the effects on employment have been limited. It then discusses from a theoretical point of view how the lack of institutions, of demo-cratic policy-making and of consultation among major social groups has weakened the implementation of reform policies.

After briefly reviewing the structure of African labour markets, Chapter 3 provides an overview of some African labour market institutions. It specifically discusses developments in institutions concerned with wage setting, training and social emergency funds and the role of employers' and workers' organizations in these institutions as well as in trying to build a general consensus around the reform programmes. The chapter ends with a number of recommendations for labour market institutions in Eastern and Southern African countries.

Part 2 of the volume deals with the specific situation in five case-study countries.

An overview of the country studies

Gerrishon Ikiara and Njuguna Ndung'u analyse, in the case of *Kenya,* whether trade unions, employers' organizations and other labour market institutions have taken a proactive approach to economic adjustment. Kenya embarked on structural adjustment programmes (SAPs) in the early 1980s but their implementation was slow and ineffective throughout the 1980s. Analysis of the impact of SAPs on the labour market is therefore limited by the short period of the analysis, i.e. 1991 to 1995. SAPs in Kenya were not very well conceived: during the period 1980–84 the government vaguely introduced SAPs but not much happened, while during the period 1985–91, the government increasingly accepted SAPs but their implemen-tation remained very poor. Implementation of the programmes is not an inde-pendent variable, nor merely a matter of political commitment, but is also a function of institutional gaps and weaknesses.

Consequently, in 1991, the donors suspended external development assistance to Kenya because the agreed economic reforms were not being implemented at the required pace. For example, out of the 255 parastatals in Kenya, only 8 had been privatized. The reforms required in 1991 included external trade liberalization; foreign-exchange liberalization; privatization; and creating an 'enabling envi-ronment' for investors, both local and foreign. The political tensions in Kenya have made it impossible to create such an environment.

Qualitative and quantitative changes in the labour market took place during adjustment. The evidence shows that real wages have declined dramatically. However, even before the SAP's firm implementation, real wages were not rising. The consensus was that these reductions could not simply be blamed on the SAPs and that the real determinants of wage levels, such as demographic shifts, changes in skills and productivity, investment levels and structure, had also moved unfavourably. Job security had substantially fallen and become virtually non-existent for the majority of people in the labour force. But decline in job security and lower wages have not led to much employment creation.

Germina Ssemogerere observes that although SAPs in *Uganda* had begun formally in 1987 in the form of a stabilization phase – the Economic Recovery Programme – serious implementation of structural adjustment programmes only started in 1990. Up to the present, no comprehensive employment policy framework has been in place to trace the responses of labour markets to adjustment. But a massive underutilization of labour is noticeable. Ssemogerere notes that on average each person works only 3 hours a day and that most of those retrenched still need to be redeployed. Furthermore, self-employment is the largest component of total employment (about 80 per cent) but there is very little information on it. Incomes remain unequally distributed. The lowest quartile of households (about 40 per cent of the population) receive only 8.8 per cent of the total income.

By looking at different segments of the Uganda labour market a better picture can be gained of how it has responded to adjustment. The study discusses adjustment in the context of a diversified peasantry. The rural labour market is segmented into three components: (i) self-employed smallholders (below 12 hectares); (ii) small-holders and small estates using hired labour; and (iii) large estates. Each of these has responded quite differently to the adjustment programmes. Under adjustment, the share of the international price received by producers, especially for coffee, improved because of the elimination of inefficient public marketing. However, for the first segment of smallholders, who comprise the largest share of the agricultural sector, export commodities represent only a small share of their production: most of their products are for own consumption or for the local market. Ssemogerere notes that, although the marketed surplus of food crops is small, it provides around 20 per cent of farm income. The evidence appears to indicate that the improvement in the share of international prices accruing to these small farmers has had only a limited impact in terms of their income. Moreover, the market liberalization took place at a time when the international price of coffee had collapsed.

Ssemogerere observes hostility on the part of the government vis-à-vis the trade unions which refuse to agree to downward wage flexibility. In her opinion, however, there can be a number of advantages in acknowledging the role of organized labour as it can play a constructive role in human capital formation, can enhance discipline at the workplace, and can encourage safety standards at work, all of which lead to the formulation and enforcement of appropriate labour contracts. She therefore argues that trade unions ought to be encouraged, through an appropriate policy framework for industrial relations, to work in partnership with employers in the liberalized market environment. The government therefore needs to establish a labour market policy which widens the conceptual framework of adjustment. The policy-making process should also be increasingly democra-tized. This can be done through broad-based consultation; in Uganda the expe-rience of the National Forum has been encouraging. It has become clear that such a National Forum needs support and capacity-building in order to formulate alter-native programmes.

Venkatesh Seshamani and Ephraim Kaunga observe that, after years of policy reversals and a stop-go policy with respect to macroeconomic management, *Zambia* has been taking its structural adjustment programme more seriously since the MMD government came to power. There has been a liberalization of interest rates through the auctioning of Treasury bills as well as liberalization of the exchange rate, while tariffs have been reduced and trade liberalized. The government withdrew from the domestic agricultural marketing system and extensive fiscal reforms were introduced, with a 'stop-payment' system of public expenditure since 1993/94. By these measures, Zambia managed to bring its inflation rate down from a very high level of 190 per cent in 1991 to around 5 per cent in 1995.

However, the real question is whether Zambia has actually achieved the objectives of its adjustment programme. The answer to this question is more nuanced since GDP per capita has gone down and the GDP growth rate has been negative throughout the period of adjustment, while real earnings have declined and real wages are very low – well below what one might call a 'living wage'. Furthermore, the available figures show that more people are getting poorer. For example, 71 per cent of the population were below the poverty line in 1992, with further increases likely, compared with 60 per cent in 1980. There has also been an increase in the use of child labour; recent estimates put the number of child workers as high as 1.5 million (mostly in the informal sector). Nor have other social indicators (such as life expectancy and child mortality) improved. The implications of all this for employment are that many people have lost their jobs and that the unemployment rate is very high, only partly due to the retrenchment of civil servants.

Seshamani and Kaunga conclude that the government had embarked on a two-pronged approach to structural adjustment, seeking to combine measures to restore macroeconomic stability with measures to reduce the negative social impact of the programmes by means of targeted social interventions through safety nets and social funds. Although it could be said that some measure of success has been achieved with regard to the former, the latter has almost completely failed. According to Seshamani and Kaunga, the government has given insufficient priority to the badly needed social expenditures and capacity-building in the social sector and is urging the creation of appropriate labour market structures where shareholders in the adjustment process can voice their grievances.

In his chapter on *Zimbabwe*, Godfrey Kanyenze emphasizes the distinction between tradeables and non-tradeables and the need to shift resources to the production of tradeables. He cites devaluation as one way of moving resources to the production of tradeables. He makes a distinction between real production wages and real consumption wages. In the tradeables sector, real production wages have fallen more than in the non-tradeables sector. Nevertheless, the growth and expansion of employment as predicted by the orthodox adjustment model have not materialized. Wages are the main source of income for urban households; therefore the decline in consumption wages explains, to a considerable extent, the increase in poverty. Simultaneously there has been a massive expansion of the informal sector.

It is difficult to assess whether it was the Economic Structural Adjustment Programme (ESAP), the drought that hit Zimbabwe, or the high debt problems that caused the deceleration of growth. In Zimbabwe the problem was not only one of implementation, but also of the *design* of the programme. On the design of ESAP, Kanyenze notes that there was very little consultation about the programme. As a consequence, there has been a focus on achieving financial targets rather than addressing the problems of capacity and inequity in the distribution of resources, such as land, working capital, etc. Kanyenze recommends that the government should pursue an employment-intensive growth strategy. To do so it should ensure proper co-ordination and harmony of labour market policies and a Labour Market Commission (LMC) should be established to improve the administration. The LMC should be based on the close and active participation of social partners, and the

Manpower Planning and Development Act, 1984 should be reviewed. Furthermore, the capacity for policy analysis, formulation and implementation of the representative organizations of employers and workers should be strengthened. The education and training system should be geared towards employment creation, among other measures through decentralization and the setting up of semi-autonomous institutions to promote private sector participation in human resource development, especially in the provision of firm-specific skills.

As Ephraim Chirwa and Wycliffe Chilowa point out, *Malawi* has been implementing structural adjustment programmes for a very long time; it was amongst the first to adopt such programmes in the early 1980s. International and domestic trade liberalization, agricultural sector reforms, public sector restructuring and privatization and financial sector reforms have been undertaken. Despite these structural reforms, the evidence shows that the policies as implemented have failed to take the economy back to the pre-adjustment levels.

Adjustment programmes have led to limited employment opportunities. The authors note that the rate at which the economy is absorbing the growing labour force has fallen by 69 per cent between the pre-adjustment and the adjustment periods. This took place even though the real wages, in an inflationary context, decreased dramatically. Reforms in the labour market are recent and have largely been prompted by the democratization process in the transition from a one-party state to a multi-party era. Nonetheless, labour market institutions have flourished and have become very proactive as a result of structural adjustment programmes and the democratic environment.

As will become apparent from the country experiences (Chapters 4 to 8), structural adjustment policies have a considerable impact on labour market institutions, and conversely development of these institutions can contribute to a better implementation of adjustment.

References

Collier, P. (1995) 'The Marginalization of Africa', *International Labour Review*, Vol. 134, No. 4–5, September.

Helleiner, G. (1997) 'Africa in the Global Economy', Toronto University, May (mimco).

Sachs, J.D. and Warner, A.M. (1997) 'Sources of Slow Growth in Africa', *Journal of African Economics*, Vol. 6, No. 3.

2 Africa's Adjusted Labour Markets: Can Institutions Perform?

ROLPH VAN DER HOEVEN & WILLEM VAN DER GEEST

Introduction

In order to better appreciate the interaction between adjustment policies, employment and labour markets, this chapter starts with an overview of the evolution of adjustment policies, followed by some general considerations arguing that the results of adjustment policies often depend as much on the initial conditions in which a country finds itself as on the policies themselves. This is further elaborated in the next section where the issue of growth, employment and adjustment is discussed in more detail.

The following section presents a brief overview of adjustment and employment changes in the case-study countries which are discussed in more detail in Part II of this book. Factors determining economic growth, employment creation, wage development, and human capital formation are evaluated in the context of changing international parameters. On the basis of this evaluation, some conclusions are drawn as to what can be learned from the adjustment experiences, arguing that there is need for a different interpretation of adjustment policies taking into account much more than hitherto the existence and functioning of institutions responsible for growth and employment creation. The final section provides some examples from the literature on the role of labour market institutions in the process of development and change.

The changing nature of adjustment programmes

Structural adjustment programmes can be defined as a set of policy changes or reforms which combine short-run stabilization measures and longer-run adjustment measures. These measures are applied either sequentially or simultaneously; they often overlap and different elements of the programme have different objectives.

The set of stabilization policies usually consist of the following elements:

- fiscal policies aimed at reducing public budget deficits through tax increases as well as reduction of public expenditures;
- monetary policies reducing the money supply either directly or by means of interest-rate policy;

- wage and price policies to control inflation in support of the above policies (orthodox programmes) or partly replacing them (heterodox policies);
- exchange-rate policies to reduce balance-of-payment deficits.

Structural adjustment programmes contain policies to make product and factor markets operate more smoothly by eliminating 'obstacles' by means of removing price controls and subsidies through a process of liberalization. One key element is the reform of trade policies to strive for freer trade. Further, restructuring the public sector and privatizing publicly owned enterprises in order to reduce the fiscal deficit and make enterprises more profitable are also part of a structural adjustment programme.

The above description makes it clear that it is much more difficult to delineate adjustment policies than it is to delineate stabilization policies. For example, one could question to what extent a change of trade policy regime is part of 'normal' policy and to what extent it is part of an adjustment effort. It is here that the classification as to what is and is not part of a structural adjustment programme becomes complicated. It might therefore be useful to discuss briefly the evolution of adjustment policies over time in order to understand better what it is all about.

Since the inception of structural adjustment policies, four generations of adjustment policies can be distinguished:

The *first generation* of adjustment programmes was aimed at *stabilizing the economy* following internal or external shocks. The major thrust of these programmes was to utilize the same instruments as industrialized countries had been applying all along since the 1950s to combat balance-of-payments deficits. Key measures included containing fiscal deficits by reducing government expenditure, making real interest rates positive, applying wage restraint for public sector workers and, to the extent possible, for private sector workers coupled with a real devaluation of the currency to stimulate exports and discourage imports. Reliance on these policy instruments characterized programmes of the early 1980s which were designed, especially in Latin America, to deal also with the growing debt crisis which the problems in Mexico in 1982 had made manifest.

A *second generation* of adjustment programmes, dealing more explicitly with issues of growth and capacity, was introduced in the mid-1980s. This second generation came to the fore because policies merely emphasizing stabilization in the economy did not succeed, in most cases, in bringing about growth. At best, the balance-of-payments gap was reduced. As a consequence, several countries undergoing stabilization programmes were caught in a vicious circle of slow or negative growth and large debt-service payments, which inhibited consumption and investment growth and compressed imports. Fairly early on in the 1980s, it had been realized that adjustment programmes would succeed only if they took into account concerns for growth beyond merely attempting to stimulate the export sector through devaluation. Initially it was thought that growth could be stimulated by liberalizing the economy. Restrictive policy regimes created distortions in product, capital and labour markets which hampered a free flow of products and production factors, which in turn would hamper growth. However, later on, more attention was given to investment and an increase in productivity, as it became clear that liberalization of markets, at times when stabilization policies were carried out, meant that growth opportunities were delayed. At best, stabilization laid the basis for improved growth in the future, but estimates of the turn-around of the economy were extended from 1–2 years in the early 1980s to 4–8 years in the latter half of the decade. The International Monetary Fund (IMF), for example, introduced an Enhanced Structural Adjustment Facility (ESAF) for poor countries which allowed them to receive support over a period of up three years with repayment stretched out over a period of ten years, in contrast to its regular credit tranches which were to be reimbursed over a period of 1 to 2 years.

A *third generation* of adjustment programmes started to focus explicitly on *social concerns*. In response to the ILO's High-Level Meeting on Employment and Structural Adjustment in 1987 and UNICEF's plea for 'Adjustment with a Human Face', the World Bank introduced its 'Social Dimensions of Adjustment' programme in 1988. This brought to the fore the notion of social safety nets and compensatory programmes in order to help or to compensate those groups whose living standards were adversely affected by the adjustment policies and who were facing a decline in living standards, either because of a decline in government services or because of increased unemployment. Since the 1990s, most adjustment programmes contain some form of social safety net, although there is still a great deal of discussion on whether social safety nets also provide the poor, and those worst affected by adjustment programmes, with sufficient tools to overcome poverty on a sustainable basis.

A *fourth generation* of adjustment programmes therefore deals not only with the effects of adjustment on people and institutions, but is trying to go further by *seeking to include people and institutions as actors*, thereby promoting participation and consultation. To what extent this is actually happening in practice is, however, still a matter of great controversy. The reasons for renewed attention to participation and consultation were that adjustment programmes had been designed mainly by central banks, ministers of finance and international agencies, and were based on the earlier conception (especially during the first generation) that adjustment would be a 'quick fix', setting countries back on the track towards sustained growth once and for all. However, at the time when adjustment programmes came to include concerns about growth and social development, the drafting of the Policy Framework papers, setting the stage for adjustment, were still dominated by those who were responsible for stabilization, and excluded those responsible for development and social policies. It was therefore deemed important to bring adjustment programmes back into the realm of national policy-making with the objective of economic and social development, not only for the people but also by the people. To achieve this was amongst the central concerns of the World Summit for Social Development which took place in Copenhagen in March 1995.

The Bretton Woods institutions are currently trying to apply the third generation of adjustment policies, often by combining growth-oriented programmes with so-called compensatory programmes. Even in those cases where the governments, with the support of the international financial institutions, are seeking to implement a third generation programme, considerable tension exists between the rhetoric and the actual policies. The Bretton Woods institutions have acknowledged the need to move to the application of the fourth generation of programmes. However, as they themselves readily admit, they find it difficult to do this.

Structural adjustment policies have been dominating economic and social policy-making for quite some time and determine the policies of multilateral and bilateral donors to a considerable extent. Table 2.1, for example, indicates the percentage of total disbursements by the World Bank, the largest multilateral donor, which are devoted to structural adjustment loans for five Eastern or Southern African countries which are discussed further in this volume. As can be seen from the table, structural adjustment loans form the majority of the disbursement by the World Bank Group. For Zambia, Malawi, Kenya and Uganda, this has been the case since the end of the 1980s, and more recently also for Zimbabwe. Structural adjustment

Table 2.1   *Disbursement for adjustment lending as a percentage of total World Bank disbursements, 1988–96*

Country	Fiscal year 1988	Fiscal year 1992	Fiscal year 1996
Kenya	44.2	53.0	42
Malawi	23.8	41.1	40
Uganda	55.8	52.1	38
Zambia	16.0	88.8	64
Zimbabwe	–	52.4	26

Source: World Bank, 1993; 1997; selected findings from OED evaluations.

programmes are still leading most of the policy-making in these and other countries, although the nature of the programmes has changed.

Stabilization and adjustment policies, employment and poverty: Some general considerations

Since stabilization policies are more narrowly defined and constitute an integral element of almost all adjustment programmes, we shall look first at the theory regarding the effects of stabilization policies on employment and poverty. The instruments mostly applied are fiscal and monetary policies, coupled with wage policies and devaluation (the latter are sometimes also labelled as switching policies). Fiscal and monetary policies which deflate the economy as part of a stabilization programme aimed at reducing the absorption in the economy tend to lower growth rates or have resulted in a decline in the national income. (Kenya and Zimbabwe are examples here.) The simulation models applied by Mohsin Khan of the IMF (Khan, 1990) point to an effect of reduced growth for usually one or two years. How do such deflationary policies affect employment and poverty? If one assumes that employment elasticities and income distribution do not change in the short run, then a deflationary programme, by definition, reduces employment opportunities and increases poverty in the short run. How much depends not only on the amount of deflation but also on the parameters which describe the employment and income inequality functions of the particular economy. A first approximation is that stabilization policies decrease employment opportunities and increase poverty (a slowdown of growth means fewer people at work). However, it is difficult to maintain the assumption that income distribution remains unchanged during a process of stabilization, since the very policy instruments applied in the stabilization process change the parameters describing the distribution of the various components of income, such as income before tax (wages, profit, rents), income after tax and net incomes which include the imputed benefits of public services (Ndulu, 1992). The shape of the demand function for employment may also change but it is usually assumed that this does not happen in the short run; the labour intensities and the sectoral growth patterns change significantly only over the medium to long term.

However, some authors (e.g. Sahn, 1992) argue that poor people do not take part in the formal economy and especially do not make much use of government services. Hence, they argue that the poor are less (either negatively or positively) affected by stabilization policies than non-poor groups which profit much more from public services. Hence, stabilization policies, and especially the fiscal contraction, result in a more equal tertiary income distribution. These views are questioned, however, by many observers, who note that the level of public services for low-income households has declined (e.g. in health, education and economic infrastructure).

In general it is accepted that the deflationary component of stabilization policies results in increased poverty, although its intensity depends both on the relative weight and intensity of the policies adopted and on the initial conditions, as Khan (1993) has demonstrated. Khan (p. 15) classifies countries into *four groups* characterized by the *degree of efficiency* (that is, having basically the right policies and institutions to adapt to world market conditions and changes, and hence a positive growth of labour and/or total factor productivity) and by *the degree of egalitarian structure* (that is, a fair distribution of income and assets).

In an *efficient egalitarian country* a balance-of-payments deficit which requires adjustment is typically caused by an external shock or by an overheating of the economy. In such a situation the correct answer is often a quick stabilization policy of a deflationary nature, which will result in a temporary increase in unemployment and a temporary drop in real wages. The efficiency of the economy will quickly allow for recapturing the world market and the egalitarian system will keep a hold on the increase of poverty. However, few countries fall into this category.

A larger number of countries fall into the *efficient inegalitarian* group. In this group a stabilization and deflationary policy will increase poverty and unemployment and several groups of the population will be worse off after the policy. Institutional and policy changes are needed to reverse this situation. The deflationary elements of the structural adjustment programmes should be scrutinized for their poverty-enhancing impact. Corrective measures should be taken by retargeting public expenditure, by the provision of compensatory programmes to the group of citizens most affected and by an alteration of production patterns and ownership structures so that poorer groups such as peasant farmers and small-scale industries can improve their production and productivity.

A third group of countries falls into the category of *inefficient egalitarian economies*. In this situation adjustment programmes ought to concentrate on long-term structural changes and changing incentive structures and institutions for economies to react better to world market signals. Stabilization programmes in this situation will not bring about a resumption of growth, putting the egalitarian system under strong pressure and often causing its breakdown, thus placing countries often in the fourth category of countries.

The fourth category consists of countries which combine an *inefficient and inegalitarian system*. Most African countries fall into this group although some belong rather to group 2 (Zimbabwe) or group 3 (United Republic of Tanzania in the early 1980s). The main challenge for countries in this group is a resumption of growth and a reduction of inequality allowing the whole population to benefit from growth. It is in this group of countries that adjustment programmes often break down and emphasis on stabilization and deflationary policies will frequently fail to lead to the desired results. Countries need simultaneously to remove structural impediments which lead to inefficiency and which prevent egalitarian development. Adjustment policies should therefore be part of an overall and continuous development process which combines adaptation to foreign competition, and industrial and agricultural policies for small and large-scale producers with programmes of land redistribution and investment in human capital.

The major effect on poverty and employment as part of the stabilization package, however, is not expected to result only from the deflationary package but also from the switching package, i.e. devaluation of the national currency which changes the price ratio between tradeable and non-tradeable products. The theory is somewhat ambivalent about the outcome (Demery and Addison, 1993). The difficulty lies with the interpretation of the theory in practice. Firstly, the definition of tradeables is not always clear. Secondly, the production and consumption patterns of the poor cannot easily be mapped on the category of tradeables and non-tradeables. The complication is well explained in Jamal and Weeks (1993) and Stewart (1995). Stewart argues that initial conditions determine whether or not switching policies lead to more employment and poverty reduction. In the absence of growth, employment, income distribution and thus poverty are likely to worsen following devaluation in economies:

(i)   specializing in mineral exports or agricultural products whose production is unequally distributed;
(ii)   where urban poverty is high in relation to rural poverty;
(iii) ˙ where there is a large oligopolistic modern sector, specialized in import-substituting production – this will affect urban incomes in particular.

Employment, income distribution and the poverty situation are most likely to improve where:

(iv) tradeables are labour-intensive relative to non-tradeables (i.e. in economies specializing, especially at the margin, in labour-intensive manufactures or labour-intensive agriculture);
(v)   rural poverty is high in relation to urban poverty, and rural incomes (and tradeable production) are fairly evenly distributed.

African countries can be found primarily in categories (i), (iv) and (v).

Thus, the *a priori* assumptions on the relation between stabilization policies, employment and poverty rest on the combined effect of fiscal policies (in general, negative), monetary policies (usually negative), wage policies (usually negative) and devaluation (negative or positive depending on the specific situation). Combining these effects, it can be argued that stabilization policies usually decrease employment opportunities and increase poverty, at least in the short to medium run.

The effect of *adjustment policies* on employment and poverty is more difficult to judge. For example, the effect of privatization on poverty or of a shrinking in public sector employment depends very much on whether, for example, retrenched civil servants belong to poor groups or not, whether they can find other jobs, and whether the privatization process will result in a decline in the tax burden for the poor and free up resources for the creation of productive employment. Also, the effect of deregulation cannot be predicted in advance. If deregulation reduces rent-seeking by wealthy and influential groups and this results in lower prices of products consumed by ordinary workers and the poor, then adjustment policies can contribute to a decline in poverty. However, if deregulation results in the creation of private monopolies, then its effect on the poor may be negative. The poverty effects of adjustment policies therefore depend much more on the initial social and economic setting in the country undergoing adjustment and on the type of adjustment policies applied in the same way as we described earlier the categorization by Khan (1993).

Adjustment, economic growth and employment

As indicated in the introduction, attention in structural adjustment policies has shifted to long-term concerns. One of the reasons for shifting the emphasis to longer-term structural adjustment policies was the recognition that in the case of Africa an important element in reducing poverty is for countries to grow faster. Even to achieve no further increases in the total number of the poor under assumptions of unchanged income distribution would require growth rates which most African countries find difficult to attain. Table 2.2 provides an overview of some required growth rates in countries in Southern and Eastern Africa, given different scenarios of population growth.

Earlier publications (Cornia *et al.*, 1992; Horton *et al.*, 1994) have shown that the impacts of SAPs on the demand for labour and employment can be manifold and of a varied nature. An overview of the relationships between the various components of the SAPs and employment is given in Table 2.3 below. It shows how the economy-wide effects of adjustment on goods and services markets may affect the demand for labour. It is imperative to distinguish at least two possible scenarios with respect to the growth of output and value added for each policy component:

(i) *moderate and rapid growth* of GDP (at least 1 per cent above population growth), which would afford an average real per capita income growth of 1 per cent or above; and

(ii) *slow growth, stagnation or declining growth* (below the threshold for moderate growth) which would cause a negative growth of average real per capita income.

How these two scenarios will 'translate' into direct and indirect demand for labour will depend on the nature of the technical change which is taking place during adjustment. Technical change may be labour-saving or capital-saving. However, much of the technical change which is sought for SSA's manufacturing and service sectors will be labour-saving, in particular because of the present low productivity in these sectors. Hence, in order to assess the employment impact of the various components of the SAPs it would be plausible to assume that moderate and rapid growth scenarios are likely to be accompanied by labour-saving technical change. Utilizing these assumptions Table 2.3 formulates some hypotheses about the short to medium-term impact of employment under the different growth scenarios.

Table 2.3 suggests that the overall employment impact of adjustment, in the short to medium term, would be unpredictable in the case of the high growth scenarios (it may be positive or negative). The outcome would depend on whether the positive employment creation of the competition-enhancing components exceeds the likely negative impact of most of the institutional change-oriented components. The institutional policy reforms, increasingly centre stage of the adjustment programmes during the 1990s, would tend to reduce employment, with the possible

Table 2.2 *Minimum rates of GDP growth needed to prevent rising numbers of poor under different population growth scenarios*

Country	Target GDP growth rate			Actual GDP growth	
	Scenario population growth				
	2%	2.5%	2.8%	1981–91	1986–91
Kenya	4.1	5.2	5.8	4.8	5.8
Malawi	4.7	5.8	6.5	4.6	4.8
Uganda	4.4	5.5	6.2	4.6	6.5
Zambia	11.5	14.4	16.1	0.5	1.9
Zimbabwe	4.2	5.3	5.9	3.5	4.3

Source: Demery et al., 1994.

Table 2.3   *Output-employment relationships during adjustment (short to medium term)*

	Scenario I: High to moderate growth (With moderate or rapid technical change)	Scenario II: Moderate to negative growth (With slow or no technical change)
Adjustment programme components:		
Competition-enhancing components		

1. International, *including:*
   – Trade liberalization
   – Real exchange rate adjustment and currency convertibility
   – Foreign ownership and FDI
	positive employment effect	zero or negative employment effect

	positive employment effect	zero or negative employment effect

2. Domestic, including:
   – Domestic trade deregulation
   – Financial sector reform		

Sub-total	**positive**	**zero to negative**
Institutional change-oriented components		
1. Privatization	positive or negative employment effect	zero to strongly negative employment effect
2. Civil service reform	zero or negative employment effect	strongly negative employment effect
3. Induced labour market flexibility	positive, zero or negative employment effect	negative employment effect
Sub-total	**ambiguous**	**zero to strongly negative**
Overall employment impact	**may be positive or negative**	**zero to strongly negative**

exceptions of privatization and induced labour market flexibility in a high growth context. The extent of employment creation would depend on the degree of labour-saving technical and institutional changes during adjustment. Whether the competition-enhancing components of the programme would increase (net) employment would depend on the relative magnitudes of growth and labour-saving technical change. For an overall increase of employment, the positive effect of the employment creation (primarily in the private sector) would have to outweigh the negative effects of the loss of employment due to institutional changes (primarily in the public sector). The low to negative growth scenarios will tend to reduce employment and (net) labour-saving technical change will make this outcome even more likely. Output-employment elasticity estimates may show the extent to which these effects are working; separate estimates of such elasticities before and during/ after adjustment would indicate whether the output-employment relationships have changed significantly during adjustment. Moreover, Table 2.3 points to the importance of productivity changes and technology during adjustment as determinants of the employment impact.

Even if the labour intensity within the economy does not change during adjustment, maintaining the same overall level of employment will require that employment in the non-public sector will have to grow at a rate equal to the rate of loss of public sector employment, but weighted by the relative size of the two sectors. Hence, starting from an initial situation with a relatively large share of employment in the public sector, a rapid contraction of this sector would require that the growth of non-public employment should be increasing quite fast, merely to achieve a stationary level of employment. Labour-saving technical change will require a further acceleration of the non-public employment growth rate merely to maintain the same level of employment opportunities. In the SSA context a stationary level of employment opportunities could not be considered a desirable outcome. The growing problems of unemployment, underemployment and involutionary development of a growing informal sector under adjustment (more people to do the same job) will be discussed in the various case studies.

Examining the broad employment and distributional effects can overlook the *intra-group* distributional consequences, which can hamper long-term development. As Palmer has argued, there are good reasons for believing that women have suffered more than men from the adverse impact of adjustment policies in many countries. The change in policy stance to one of fiscal restraint and an open competitive economy has had the effect in many cases of shifting costs from the state to women. Health service and local infrastructural cutbacks have made social reproduction more difficult, with women substituting more of their labour to cover the deficit of state provision. In many places urban unemployment has risen as old industries have declined, while new ones have not grown strong enough. The new urban poverty has forced many women into greater participation in the labour force for extremely low remuneration. Lack of public provision, and the rigidity of the gender division of labour in social reproduction, have combined to jeopardize standards of childcare, health and family welfare (Palmer, 1995).

Many rural areas have experienced greater incentives to export primary products. The extra effort required to increase such exports has interacted with gender-typing of tasks leading to greater increases in work for women than for men. This was often in addition to a more onerous burden of social reproduction work. New production incentives have tended to give male heads of household reason to appropriate and redirect household resources, including women's labour. In Uganda for example, the wife decides in 76 per cent of the cases on the outflow of grain from food storage, but the husband decides in 72 per cent of the cases on the marketing of grain (see Chapter 5). The forced redeployment of resources to production of export cash crops would not only have added to the stress on women but could have led to long-term social costs in the form of disinvestment in the health and education of children. Any exacerbation of gender asymmetries of rights and obligations would worsen allocative inefficiency and raise long-term social costs (Palmer, 1995). It remains important to realize that broad employment and distributional figures can mask a worse situation, which provides all the more reason to be suspicious of the employment and distributional consequences of adjustment policies.

Adjustment and employment changes in selected Eastern and Southern African countries: Overview and lessons

Policy reform in five countries
Table 2.4 provides qualitative information regarding the timing and intensity of adjustment for the five countries in this survey. The table suggests that the precise patterns and sequences of adjustment were quite different across the countries, notwithstanding similarities in the external conditions which they faced, their institutional set-up and their economic policies. The two aspects of adjustment policy reform which were adopted early in the programmes were domestic trade deregulation and exchange-rate adjustment. In these countries a significant part of the

Table 2.4   *Timing and intensity of implementation of policy reforms*

| Country | Competition-enhancing policy reforms | | | | | Institutional-change oriented policy reforms | | |
| | International | | | Domestic | | | | |
Period started and speed of implementation	Trade liberalization	Exchange rate adjustment	Foreign ownership and FDI liberalization	Domestic trade deregulation	Financial sector reforms	Privatization enacted	Civil service reforms	Labour market flexibility induced
Kenya	Late	Early	Late	Early	Early	Late	Late	Early
	Fast	Fast	Slow	Slow	Fast	Slow	Slow	Slow
Malawi	Early	Early	Early	Early	Late	Late	Late	Late
	Slow	Slow	Slow	Slow	Slow	Fast	Slow	Slow
Uganda	Late	Early	Early	Early	Early	Late	Early	Late
	Slow	Fast	Fast	Fast	Slow	Slow	Fast	Fast
Zambia	Late	Late	Late	Early	Late	Late	Late	Late
	Slow	Slow	Slow	Fast	Slow	Fast	Fast	Fast
Zimbabwe	Late	Late	Late	Late	Late	Late	Late	Early
	Slow	Slow	Slow	Fast	Slow	Slow	Slow	Slow

Notes: Early: Policy reforms introduced during 1980s. Late: Policy reforms introduced since 1990. Slow: Very limited changes in first 3 years of implementation. Fast: Substantial changes within 3 years of implementation.

domestic marketing environment was in the hands of the small-scale private wholesale and retail sectors, and public marketing boards were phased out relatively fast during the 1980s. Examples of this were marketing of coffee in Uganda and wholesale marketing of food in Zambia and Zimbabwe. Kenya's cereal produce board, however, was an exception in this regard, as it continued to receive government support in the 1990s (see Chapter 4 on Kenya). In the area of exchange-rate adjustment, a policy of maintaining a competitive real effective exchange rate (coupled with liberalizing access to foreign exchange) was adopted in most countries, though at different speeds.

The institutional change-oriented measures, such as privatization, civil service reform and inducing labour market flexibility through deregulation, became more important in the 1990s. Civil service reforms, once adopted, were carried out in a rapid fashion (particularly in Uganda). However, privatization of state-owned enterprises has not been implemented rapidly in most SSA countries. This may be seen as a response to the widespread concerns about the weakness of SSA stock exchanges, the high probability of the emergence of private monopolies and the possible negative consequences which the privatization may have for the welfare of consumers of goods and services (see Adam, 1994). The timing and speed of implementation differed considerably between countries, partly reflecting the different initial conditions. However, even this relatively homogeneous group of five countries has adopted the policy reforms with varying speeds and in different sequences. One reason explaining this varied pattern of implementation of policy reforms may be that the benefits and gains of reforms remain unpredictable and uncertain. In this situation governments, often pressurized by the international financial institutions, adopt specific policy reforms without a coherent and strategic overview. This causes sluggish implementation as well as policy reversals, as observed in the cases of Kenya, Malawi and Zambia discussed below.

Table 2.5 presents the macroeconomic outcome indicators for the five countries before and during/after adjustment policy reform. What emerges is a picture of successful reduction of public deficits, but obtained at the cost of slow or sluggish macroeconomic growth (except in Uganda). The counterfactual scenario (would it have been worse without the adjustment policy reform?) has not been established

Table 2.5   *Macroeconomic indicators during implementation of adjustment policy reforms*

Country	Growth of GDP per capita (%)			Overall fiscal deficits (% of GDP)			Trade deficits (% of GDP)		
	Before	During/ after	% change	Before	During/ after	% change	Before	During/ after	% change
Kenya	−0.5	−1.1	−0.6	−7.3	−2.3	+5.0	−2.1	+1.3	+3.4
Malawi	2.5	−0.7	−3.2	n.a.	n.a.	–	−14.2	−11.3	+2.9
Uganda	−1.5	3.2	+4.7	−5.2	−5.2	0	−2.3	−16.5	−14.2
Zambia	−3.2	−1.7	+1.5	−14.4	−1.6	+12.8	−1.3	−6.0	−4.7
Zimbabwe	0.3	−2.2	−2.5	−8.2	−5.0	+3.0	−1.0	−5.6	−4.6
Africa[a]	−0.7	0.1	0.3	−6.4	−5.2	+1.2			

Notes: 'Before' refers to the average for the period 1981–86 except for Malawi where it is for 1973–79. 'During/after' refers to average for 1991–93. 'Trade deficits' are for goods and non-factor services and GDP is measured at constant market prices. [a]Median growth rates for 1981–86 and 1987–91 for 29 SSA countries.

Sources: World Bank (1994, p. 138); *World Tables* 1995; *IMF Financial Yearbook*; Economist Intelligence Unit.

with any certainty. Nevertheless, it is clear that the *macroeconomic outcomes which were realized are quite unsatisfactory*. Of the five countries reviewed here, only one has, for any sustained period of time, realized a 'high' GDP growth performance exceeding population growth by more than 1.5 per cent (Uganda, since 1990), while two displayed a positive GDP per capita growth rate. Moreover, the growth performance *during* the adjustment period 1991–93 appears to be lower than that realized prior to the implementation of the adjustment policy changes for some of the countries (particularly Kenya and Zimbabwe).

Experience in recent years
We shall briefly review the economic and social development in these countries in order to substantiate some of the earlier general points.

Macroeconomic experiences. We first look at some elements contributing to *economic growth*. Regarding *gross domestic investment* (Appendix Table 2.1) we notice different patterns. Kenya's investment ratio remained more or less stable during the 1980s, dipped in the early 1990s and then returned to its 1980 level. However, the *domestic savings rate* (Appendix Table 2.2) remains volatile, which makes the process still unsustainable. Uganda's investment ratio is realizing an upward trend but is also mainly propelled by foreign inflows as its domestic savings ratio, although increasing, remains low. Zambia's investment ratio is extremely low and erratic, and so is its domestic savings rate. Foreign inflows have not changed this picture very much. Zimbabwe, interestingly, had high savings rates and somewhat lower but stable investment rates. In the early 1990s investment rates rose, but have since declined. Zimbabwe's domestic savings rates have decreased following adjustment loans and emergency aid. Malawi's investment ratio had already declined in the mid-1990s against a low or negative gross domestic savings rate. These points are elaborated further in the case-study chapters below.

The large deficits in the *current account balance* before official transfers (Appendix Table 2.3) reflect the increase in foreign inflows during the periods of structural adjustment, but were generally lower in 1996 than in 1990–1. Most countries made considerable progress in reducing the *overall public deficit* (Appendix Table 2.4). Regarding GDP growth, one can notice an improvement in Uganda. The situation remained erratic in Kenya, Malawi, Zambia and Zimbabwe in the mid-1990s, but had improved somewhat in 1996 (Appendix Table 2.5). Have the economies become more open? In most countries we notice that exports as a percentage of GDP have increased, except for Zambia and Malawi where the export share has remained erratic (Appendix Table 2.6). Figures unfortunately do not allow us to observe whether structural changes have caused the composition of exports to change to increase the share of manufacturing, thereby reducing the dependence on agricultural products whose prices fluctuate to a greater extent. Although adjustment policies seem to have increased openness in the area of trade, they have not yet succeeded in attracting direct foreign investment, the percentages of which have been as low as in the past (Appendix Table 2.7).

Changes in employment patterns. The *consequences for employment and wages are more difficult to gauge*, as statistics in these areas, as with social statistics in general, are often difficult to come by. One of the major aims of structural adjustment policies in most African countries is a reduction of public sector employment. The statistics indeed indicate that public sector employment both in absolute numbers and as a percentage of the labour force has decreased since early 1990 for all countries. The *changes in public sector employment* in Kenya, Uganda, Zambia and Zimbabwe, as well as in the United Republic of Tanzania (hereafter referred to as

Table 2.6 *Public sector employment under adjustment, 1980–95*

Country		1980	1986	1990	1993	1994
Kenya	CGE	254.5	297.6	325.4	317.1	–
	TPSE	471.5	574.6	700.1	685.4	688.4
	TPSE/FS %	46.9	48.9	49.5	46.5	45.8
	TPSE/LF %	8.3	8.6	8.9	8.0	7.7
	FS/LF %	17.6	17.6	18.0	17.1	16.9
		1980	1985	1991	1993	1995
Tanzania,	CGE	223.9	261.8	319.5	326.4	279.4
United	TPSE	442.4	480.1	500.3	510.0	459.4
Rep. of	TPSE/FS %	73.3	75.8	53.6	50.0	50.5
	TPSE/LF %	5.4	5.5	5.0	4.8	4.1
	FS/LF %	7.4	7.2	9.2	9.6	8.1
		1982	1985	1990	1991	1995
Uganda	CGE	191.2	–	269.0	214.9	148.0
	TPSE	271.2	–	406.1	368.9	302.0
	TPSE/FS %	–	–	37.1	34.9	30.5
	TPSE/LF %	–	–	6.4	5.0	3.9
	FS/LF %	–	–	17.2	14.5	13.3
		1980	1985	1989	1992	1994
Zambia	CGE	148.3	–	110.6	141.0	131.7
	TPSE	272.3	–	–	332.0	298.9
	TPSE/FS %	58.4	–	–	61.8	59.7
	TPSE/LF %	17.2	–	–	12.8	10.8
	FS/LF %	29.4	–	–	20.7	18.0
		1980	1986	1990	1993	1995
Zimbabwe	CGE	717.7	90.8	94.9	88.0	86.0
	TPSE (est.)	125.0	194.9	221.8	213.0	206.0
	TPSE/FS %	12.4	18.5	18.6	17.2	17.9
	TPSE/LF %	4.2	5.7	5.6	5.0	4.5
	FS/LF %	34.1	30.9	30.3	28.9	25.3

Key: CGE = Central government employment (thousands of workers).
        TPSE = Total public sector employment (thousands of workers).
        FS = Formal sector wage employment.
        LF = Labour force total.

Source: ILO-WEP data base; ILO yearbooks; various national estimates.

Tanzania) are summarized in Table 2.5, combining employment data from national and international sources. The table illustrates the increase in public employment during the 1970s and early 1980s, as well as the subsequent decline since 1990 (in absolute and relative terms). In the context of the growing labour force, the share of total public sector employment in the 'formal sector' declined. In Tanzania, Kenya and Zambia, approximately half of the formal sector employment was in the public sector, whereas for Uganda and Zimbabwe the percentages were respectively 20 and 30 per cent. However, the decrease has not been compensated by concomitant increases in private sector (formal) employment; as a consequence the share of formal sector employment as a percentage of the labour force has decreased in the countries under consideration. All five economies, which are considered to be among the better performers in Africa (World Bank, 1994), have become more infor-malized. In countries where information was available the *share of wage employment in tradeables* decreased in Kenya and Zimbabwe and remained stable or increased slightly in Zambia (Appendix Table 2.8). Furthermore, the *structure of formal employment* has not changed very much. In Kenya employment in manufacturing has increased somewhat but in the other countries even the absolute numbers have declined or stayed more or less the same (Appendix Table 2.9).

Wages. One could argue that high wages might have prevented increases in manufacturing employment. But this is not the case. *Manufacturing wages* are lower in the 1990s than in the 1980s (Appendix Table 2.10). The data illustrate the decline of real wages in the countries reviewed here, although the point in time when the decline started and the magnitude of the fall differ across the countries. Zambia's average earnings in manufacturing and the non-agricultural sector as a whole have been declining since the late 1970s; their 1992 real value was only about one-third of the 1977 value. In Kenya private as well as public sector wages have declined since 1987 and real wages fell by approximately 50 per cent. In Zimbabwe manufacturing wages as well as average non-agricultural wages have declined sharply since 1990—a fall of approximately 30 per cent in the subsequent three years. Taking into account the devaluation of the currency in all five countries, manufacturing wages in dollars have *decreased* considerably. The general pattern of declining wages is confirmed by the plummeting of the *minimum wage* (Appendix Table 2.11). Except in Zimbabwe, the minimum wage has lost its meaning as a floor in the wage structure. Its collapse is a further indication of the increasing flexibility of the labour markets in many African countries.

Human capital development. Countries show a mixed performance on human capital development. *Gross primary school enrolment* increased in Malawi from 60 per cent in 1987 to over 100 per cent in 1994, and in Zambia to about 90 per cent. It declined in Uganda, Kenya and Zimbabwe. However, in the latter country, this may be due to the catching-up effect since gross enrolment ratios above 100 indicate that older children above the age-range still attend primary school (Appendix Table 2.12). Zimbabwe and Uganda showed slight declines in *gross secondary school enrolment*, Zambia some increase and the figures remained rather low in Malawi and Kenya (Appendix Table 2.13). In most countries, education expenditure per capita declined, which has resulted in a deterioration in the quality of education. Declines are large in Kenya and Zambia (Appendix Table 2.14). *Health expenditure per capita* also decreased in most countries (Appendix Table 2.15).

External environment. What has been the external environment against which these countries have been adjusting? First, all five countries except for Kenya had to face *adverse terms of trade*, partly the consequence of the inability to diversify exports (Appendix Table 2.16). Secondly, *debt service/export ratios* have remained incredibly high. In some cases the ratios have been declining, not because exports have increased or overall debt levels have decreased but mainly as a consequence of debt rescheduling arrangements (Appendix Table 2.17). In effect, *long-term debt as a percentage of GDP* has been increasing for all countries up to 1994 (Appendix Table 2.18). Of the long-term debt, *the multilateral debt* has increased considerably (Appendix Table 2.19), partly reflecting the situation of the multilateral institutions being the lenders of last resort. Given the size of the multilateral debt, current discussions regarding writing off or rescheduling part of this debt are of paramount importance.

Lessons

As the previous section has indicated, the case-study countries adopted consid-erable reform measures, which led to a reduction of their public sector deficit. Also their exchange-rate systems became more liberalized, with full or virtual unifi-cation of the system in Kenya, Zambia, Zimbabwe and Uganda (Dhonte *et al.*, 1994). Some slight improvement in growth could also be noticed; in many cases, however, it was barely larger than the population growth for 1991–93 (GDP per capita was negative in Kenya, Zambia and Zimbabwe, erratic in Malawi but positive in Uganda). In some countries exports increased. However, despite the various adjustment programmes little structural change took place. The experi-ences of the countries studied fit a more general pattern of marginalization throughout Africa. In all countries, direct foreign investment has remained small and debt/GDP ratios have increased, with an even larger increase in multilateral debt. As one observer put it, 'This [aid] is the only aspect in which Africa is not marginalized from the world markets' (Collier, 1995). The marginalization of Africa is well reflected in the employment and wage data we were able to assemble. These confirm the decline in public sector employment, which is insufficiently matched by an increase in private formal sector employment, thus leading to an informal-ization of the economy.

What kind of lessons can we learn from this sobering collection of data in the countries studied? Do they imply an open rejection of all adjustment policies? Or do further adjustments and deeper reforms need to be made in order to stay on course, as some commentators want us to believe? To answer this question one perhaps needs to look beyond adjustment and seek explanations of and solutions to Africa's marginalization and its lack of foreign financial inflows.

In the past a lack of foreign inflows could be explained by an anti-enterprise attitude on the past of African governments, but the reform process, including the free convertibility of currencies, has removed much of the anti-private sector bias in policy-making. Another explanation of the absence of foreign investments might have been the high price of labour, making exports and especially labour-intensive exports uncompetitive on the world market. However, as indicated already, labour markets have shown enormous wage flexibility and African wages, taking account of the depreciation of the currencies, are amongst the lowest on the world market (ILO, 1995).

What, then, might have caused foreign investors to bypass most African countries including not only the countries examined in detail here but also a country like Ghana, which has applied, perhaps for the longest period of all African countries, the various elements of a structural adjustment programme?

Several reasons can be advanced (see e.g. ILO, 1995; Collier, 1995). One reason is the fear of policy reversals. Since policies undertaken under structural adjustment programmes are often induced by the international financial institutions, foreign investors fear that the reform policies may be undone once the adjustment programme is finished. Nigeria's, and to a lesser extent Kenya's, erratic trade liberalization policies in the 1980s are good examples of this. Another frequently noted problem is that, although the policies pursued may be on the right track, institutions to implement the policies are often lacking. Privatization without an independent judiciary and competent accountancy practices may well lead to a system of crony capitalism, which favours neither workers nor honest entrepreneurs.

The need for labour institutions for adjustment policy reform

It is increasingly realized that, for policies to be credible and to be workable, *institutions* are needed to shape such policies. These institutions will provide mechanisms to decide on possible trade-offs between different groups, some of which may be hurt and others of which will benefit, to monitor the proper implementation of the policies, and to provide some binding constraints to make frequent and erratic policy reversals not an easy option for policy-makers.

These are, of course, difficult tasks for institutions. There might be some correlation between the existence of institutions to undertake these tasks and the levels of economic development, but that is by no means straightforward. Countries (like Turkey or Argentina) with a relatively high level of GDP lack such institutions or have institutions which cannot fulfil such tasks, while other countries (like Botswana or Mauritius) seem to be able to make their institutions perform such multiple roles.

Przeworski and Limongi (1993) maintain that democracy is a necessary but not a sufficient condition for institutions to perform such functions, and that the true nature of democracy is to have institutions where classes with different opinions and different interpretations of economic development can argue with each other and find a basis for compromise. Savvides (1995), in explaining economic growth in Africa, finds that 'in addition to economic variables, we find the degree of political freedom to be a significant contribution to economic growth' (p. 449). Democracy thus provides a basis for accepting institutions which foster consensus building and can at the same time provide constraints on policy implementation such that 'the ship of state is not moving up and down the waves without a strong rudder'.

In discussing the need for economic growth in Africa and the relevance of 'new growth theory models' Aron (1995: 108) argues that 'An important feature of these models is the attention accorded to the powerful influence of legal, financial and other institutions as factors in growth, and the social considerations which may impinge on the characters of these institutions'. Furthermore, 'The empirical growth models lend strong support to the role of state institutions in developing human capital, providing and maintaining infrastructure, facilitating research and development, promoting political stability and importantly in making consistent macro economic policy and sticking to it'. Brautigam (1996) gives a vivid account of the lack of institutions and professional societies of accountants, lawyers, and so on, which provide these institutions with the necessary carrying capacity in the society.

However, the inclusion of institutions as a major variable in explaining economic growth leads to the so-called dilemma of 'path dependency', to the extent that initial conditions influence the growth path of a country leading to a situation where institutions cannot develop because countries do not grow sufficiently, and they do not grow sufficiently because they lack proper institutions. As various authors have shown, the so-called new growth theories still do not deal easily with these issues, since policy recommendations frequently take the form of macroeconomic stability, trade reform, etc. (van der Hoeven, 1995; Aron, 1995; Taylor, 1997), but fail to address the question of how to overcome the institutional bottlenecks. Problems of how economic reform and economic adjustment can change institutions are therefore unresolved.

The question thus becomes, how do adjustment policies influence the development of institutions, and more importantly how should adjustment policies be changed in order to allow the creation or development of institutions in the direction described above?

By giving primacy to 'correct' policies, and urgency to implementing the 'correct' policies, many structural adjustment programmes have neglected the question of whether the existing institutions were capable, technically as well as politically, of preparing, implementing and sticking to such a set of macroeconomic policies. Moreover, 'correct' policies have often destroyed existing and frequently ill-functioning institutions. As Aron argues, 'The act of completely destroying institutions with a view to beginning a new set of institutions, may simply bring about a permanent loss in capacity and massive postponed adjustment costs' (1995: 112). The deterioration of working conditions in various civil services in Africa is indicative of a virtual destruction of institutional capacity in certain African countries and makes the implementation of reform policies *more* difficult (Brautigam, 1996).

Rodrik (1996: 11), in a recent overview of economic reform policies, writes:

> One of these concerns [which need clarification] concerns the distinction between (a) macro economic policies aimed at economic stability, such as fiscal, monetary and exchange rate policies and (b) liberalization policies aimed at structural reform and growth, such as the removal of relative price distortions and the reduction of state intervention … maintaining the distinction reminds us that the consensus on what constitutes appropriate structural reform is based on much shakier grounds than is the consensus on the need for macro economic stability.

In explaining successful reform policies in terms of both economic and employment growth, Rodrik (1996: 11) singles out countries which during the reform process have developed capable institutions and continues:

> It is reasonable to suppose that at least part of the explanation has to do with some of the special initial conditions that the East Asian countries showed prior to their economic trade off. Two such conditions stood out … a much better educated labour force than would have been expected on the basis of their income [and] perhaps more importantly, in all of them the distribution of income and wealth around 1960 was exceptionally equal by cross-country standards.

Governments did not need to contend with powerful income groups and did not need to apply ad hoc redistributive policies but could concentrate on development and supervising the bureaucracies.

There is thus considerable evidence that economic reform processes need institutions which can deal with trade-offs, human capital development, income redistribution and the social consequences of adjustment while providing a positive climate for growth. The need for stronger institutional development implies, according to North (1995: 25):

(a) Political institutions will be stable only if they are supported by organizations with an interest in their perpetuation. Therefore an essential part of political/economic reform is the creation of such organizations.

Box 2.1 A taxonomy of labour institutions

1. The nature of employment contracts – the rules, both formal and informal, which govern hiring of workers, firing, working conditions, the length of the working day; the duration of such contracts, the nature of control over work which they imply; the extent of protection and of security. More generally, this fundamental labour institution refers to the nature of jobs, as socially defined entities involving rights, obligations, and social position.

2. The mechanisms for controlling and regulating employment contracts – state regulation (administrative or legal) or collective negotiation, or sets of values or norms held by the parties concerned. The nature of the machinery for enforcement and adjudication (such as the labour inspectorate, labour tribunals). This may also include social forms of control, e.g. through indebtedness or the threat of force.

3. The organization and representation of labour: trades unions, trade or craft associations, etc., and the areas over which they have control or influence, the ways they are organized and function. This may include whether they are unitary or fragmented, their linkage with other (e.g. political) institutions, the range of their activities.

4. The organization and representation of employers: employers' associations, business or enterprise associations and the areas over which they have control or influence, the ways they are organized and function.

5. The institutions of the labour market itself – the dominant procedures for job search and rules for access to jobs of different types, the systems for information – hiring halls, employment exchanges, newspaper advertisements, or alternatively particularistic networks of contacts and intermediaries. Discrimination, screening and selection procedures and institutional constraints on mobility may come in here.

6. The methods by which wages are paid (in cash and in kind, directly or as fringe benefits, piece or time rate, the frequency and reliability of payment, regulated by contract or discretionary).

7. The process of wage fixing: regulatory bodies, procedures, rules to be followed; negotiation and conciliation procedures; reference points and minima, their levels and the processes by which they are determined.

8. Training and skill institutions – the mechanisms for the acquisition of skills and credentials for labour market access; thus the formal and informal education and apprenticeship systems. The recognition of skills and qualifications – their acceptability as credentials for job access; and the systems for learning on the job.

9. The organization of jobs within the firm – the nature of occupational hierarchies and job progression within internal labour markets, criteria for promotion or for dismissal, the operation of work groups and the division of labour; systems for motivation and the operation of 'corporate culture'; the ways different types of firm organize labour use (small and large, formal and informal …).

10. The structure of ownership and control over production, and in particular the rules governing the spheres of influence of workers and owners of capital or land: joint decision-making procedures, co-operative or worker-managed organizations, tenancy and the rules governing its functioning.

11. The social and state regulation of self-employment – the rules governing conditions of work, access to the means of production and to markets; the prevalence of indirect or hidden wage relationships in self-employment, e.g. in homeworking and other forms of subcontracting (to which the elements of item 1 above may apply). Property institutions are important here, particularly (but not exclusively) in agriculture.

12. Social security and income guarantee systems, the institutions for social insurance (health, unemployment …), the 'social wage' – provided by the State, by the enterprise, through institutionalized private systems, through informal private community or semi-feudal networks; the conditions imposed for access to benefits. The nature of family or community obligations to support the sick or unemployed.

Source: Rodgers, 1994.

(b) It is essential to change both the institutions and the belief systems for successful reform since it is the mental models of the actors that will shape choices.
(c) Evolving norms of behaviour that will support and legitimize new rules is a lengthy process and in the absence of such reinforcing norms polities will tend to be unstable.
(d) While economic growth can occur in the short run with autocratic regimes, long-run economic growth entails the development of the rule of law and the protection of civil and political freedoms.

A further question is to what extent the development of labour market institutions can contribute to a more effective institutional framework for reform policies.

Rodgers (1994) uses a broad interpretation of labour (market) institutions (see Box 2.1) which include the legal or customary background of contracts and agreements (points 1–2), the nature of representation of the various groups in the labour market (points 3–4), the 'proper' institutions of the labour market which regulate labour supply and demand and which guarantee the commitments of contracts (points 5–7), the institutions which contribute to an increase in the productivity of labour (point 8) and efficiency in the firm (point 9), the regulation of ownership (point 10), the institutions influencing self-employment (point 11) and the institutions governing social safety nets (point 12).

In neoclassical writings labour market institutions and regulations are often seen as hindering economic development. Most discussions on institutions, regulations and actions in the labour market tend to be negative.

However, there seems to be a changing trend among economists. Tzannatos (1996) in a recent World Bank study argues that in many cases labour market regulations have not hindered economic reform and that labour markets are quite flexible, despite regulations (a point also made by Velenchik (1997) in a recent survey of industrial change in Zimbabwe). Also Azam (1995) when describing a research agenda for Africa writes:

> Although minimum wage fixing legislation has a bad reputation among economists, like any artificial price fixing, it is worth further examination in the light of current theoretical research ... the minimum wage is not fixed exogenously and its effects thus depend drastically on the bargaining process that leads to its determination ... therefore the diversity of the roles it might play is extremely wide (p. 78).

Toye (1995) argues against dismantling existing labour market institutions and regulations too quickly and argues instead for wage employment and income policies which are 'macro' compatible and for labour market institutions which allow the solution of inherent conflicts. The basic idea of macro compatibility does point towards a superior policy-making process, which has proved itself capable, in fortunate circumstances, of reconciling the legitimate aspirations of labour with the limits on them imposed by the macroeconomic conjuncture. This process is variously known as 'social dialogue' or 'social compact'. 'Although in many developing countries existing labour regulations are still an impediment to productivity increases, *it does not follow from this* that deregulation of the labour market with unfettered discretion of employers over the conditions of labour is the objective at which adjustment programmes should be aiming' (p. 80).

A main objection to devoting more attention in economic analysis to institutions is 'that many of the institutional operations on which the framework focuses – for example the role of the State – can not be measured' (Harris *et al.*, 1995: 13). This seems to be an overpessimistic view. Analyses through case studies based on economic, historical and political analysis allow for assessments and some indirect way of measuring the working of institutions. Furthermore, as Toye has argued, the New Institutional Economics (NIE) can serve as a 'bridge' to mathematical neo-classicists for whom the path of economic historians and development specialists has shown a sustained tendency to diverge over recent years (cited in Harris *et al.*, 1995: 13).

In order to obtain a better understanding of the functions of some important labour market institutions, Chapter 3 will provide a survey of the literature and discuss in more detail institutions dealing with the representation of various groups, wage regulation institutions, institutions responsible for human capital and productivity increase and institutions providing social safety nets in the sub-Saharan African context.

References

Adam, C. (1994) 'Privatization in Africa' in van der Geest, W. (ed.) *Negotiating Structural Adjustment in Africa.* London: James Currey.

Aron, J. (1995) 'The Institutional Foundations of Growth' in Ellis.

Azam, J.P. (1995) 'Development Policy for Africa: A Research Agenda' in Berthelemey.

Berthelemy, J.C. (1995) *Within African Economies.* Paris: OECD.

Brautigam, D. (1996) 'State Capacity and Effective Governance' in Ndulu and van de Walle.

Collier, P. (1995) 'The Marginalization of Africa', *International Labour Review,* Vol. 134, No. 5.

Cornia, G., R. van der Hoeven and T. Mkandawire (1992) *Africa's Recovery in the 1990s: From Stagnation and Adjustment to Human Development.* London: Macmillan.

Demery, L. *et al.* (1994) *Poverty, Inequality and Growth.* Washington, DC: World Bank.

Demery, L. and T. Addison (1993): 'The Impact of Macroeconomic Adjustment on Poverty in the Presence of Wage Rigidities', *Journal of Development Economics,* Vol. 40, No. 2.

Dhonte, P. *et al.* (1994) *Economic Trends in Africa: The Economic Performance of sub Saharan African Countries.* IMF Working Paper 94/109. Washington, DC. International Monetary Fund.

Ellis, S. (1995) *Africa Now: Peoples, Institutions, Development.* London: James Currey.

Engberg-Pedersen, P. *et al.* (eds) (1996) *Limits of Adjustment in Africa.* London: James Currey.

Harris, J., J. Hunter and C.M. Lewis (1995) *The New Institutional Economics and Third World Development.* London: Routledge.

van der Hoeven, R. (1995) 'Structural Adjustment, Poverty and Macro Economic Policy' in Rodgers and van der Hoeven.

Horton, S., R. Kanbur and D. Mazumdar (eds) (1994) *Labor Markets in an Era of Adjustment,* Vols. 1 and 2. Washington, DC: World Bank, EDI Development Studies.

International Labour Office (1995a) *World Employment Report 1995.* Geneva: ILO.

——. (1995b) *World Labour Report 1995.* Geneva: ILO.

Jamal, V. and J. Weeks (1993) *Africa Misunderstood or Whatever Happened to the Urban-rural Gap.* London: Macmillan.

Khan, A.R. (1993) *Structural Adjustment and Income Distribution.* Geneva: ILO.

Khan, M. (1990) 'The Macroeconomic Effects of Fund-supported Adjustment Programmes', *IMF Staff Papers,* vol. 37, no. 2. Washington, DC: International Monetary Fund.

Mazumdar, D. (1994) 'Wages in Africa', Washington DC: World Bank (draft).

Mosley, P. (1994) 'Decomposing the Effects of Structural Adjustment: The Case of sub-Saharan Africa', in R. van der Hoeven and F. van der Kraaij eds. *Structural Adjustment and Beyond in Sub-Saharan Africa: Issues for Research and Policy.* London: James Currey.

Ndulu, B. (1992) 'Enhancing Income Distribution and Rationalizing Consumption Patterns', in Cornia et al.

Ndulu, B. and N. van de Walle (1996) *Agenda for Africa's Economic Renewal.* Washington, DC: Overseas Development Council.

Nelson, J. (1994) 'Organized Labour, Politics and Labour Market Flexibility in Developing Countries', in Horton *et al.*

North, D.C. (1995): 'The New Institutional Economics and Third World Development' in Harris et al.

Palmer, I. (1995) 'Public Finance from a Gender Perspective', *World Development,* Vol. 23, No. 11.

Przeworski, A. and F. Limongi (1993) 'Political Regimes and Economic Growth', *Journal of Economic Perspectives*, Vol. 7, No. 3.

Rodrik, D. (1996) 'Understanding Economic Policy Reform' *Journal of Economic Literature*, Vol. 34, No. 1 (March).

Rodgers, G. (ed.) (1994) *Workers, Institutions and Economic Growth in Asia*. Geneva: International Institute of Labour Studies.

Rodgers, G. and R. van der Hoeven (1995) *The Poverty Agenda: Trends and Policy Options*. Geneva: International Institute for Labour Studies.

Sahn, D. (1992) 'Public Expenditures in sub-Saharan Africa During a Period of Economic Reform', *World Development*, Vol. 20, No. 5.

Savvides, A. (1995) 'Economic Growth in Africa', *World Development*, Vol. 23, No. 3.

Stein, H. (1994) 'Theories of Institutions and Economic Reform in Africa', *World Development*, Vol. 22, No. 12.

Stewart, F. (1995) *Adjustment and Poverty, Options and Choices*. London: Routledge.

Ssesemogere, G. (1996) 'Employment and labour markets during adjustment in Eastern and Southern Africa: The case of Uganda'. Prepared for ILO workshop, 29 February 1996. Geneva, ILO (mimeo).

Taylor, L. (1997) 'The Revival of the Liberal Creed: The IMF and the World Bank in a Globalized Economy', *World Development*, Vol. 25, No. 2.

Toye, J. (1995) *Structural Adjustment and Employment Policy: Issues and Experiences*. Geneva: ILO.

Tzannatos, Z. (1996) *Labor Policies and Regulatory Regimes*. PSP Occasional Paper No. 11. Washington, DC: World Bank.

Velenchik, A.D. (1997) 'Market Power, Firm Performance and Real Wage Growth in Zimbabwean Manufacturing', *World Development*, Vol. 25, No. 5.

World Bank (1993) *Adjustment Lending in Sub-Saharan Africa*. Washington, DC: World Bank.

—— (1994) *Structural Adjustment in Africa: Reforms, Results and the Road Ahead*. Washington, DC: World Bank.

—— (1995a) *World Development Report 1995. Workers in an Integrating World*. New York: Oxford University Press.

—— (1995b) *Labour and the Growth Crisis in Sub-Saharan Africa*. Washington, DC: World Bank.

—— (1997) *Adjustment Lending in Sub-Saharan Africa – An Update*. Washington, DC: World Bank.

Appendix 2.1: Adjustment experiences in selected Eastern and Southern African countries: Some illustrative tables

Table A2.1   *Gross domestic investment, 1987–96 (% of GDP)*

Country	1987	1988	1989	1990	1991	1992	1993	1994	1995	1996
Kenya	24.3	25.0	24.7	24.2	21.0	16.9	17.6	18.6	19.2	19.3
Malawi	15.7	18.7	21.2	19.1	20.1	18.8	12.2	13.2	15.2	17.6
Uganda	9.7	10.8	11.1	12.7	15.2	15.9	15.2	14.7	16.4	16.7
Zambia	12.7	11.1	10.8	17.3	11.0	11.9	10.4	13.8	13.0	11.9
Zimbabwe	17.2	21.8	18.9	23.2	25.0	25.5	21.2	20.0	17.5	17.9

Source: World Bank, *African Development Indicators*, 1997

Table A2.2   *Gross domestic savings, 1987–96 (% of GDP)*

Country	1987	1988	1989	1990	1991	1992	1993	1994	1995	1996
Kenya	19.2	19.7	17.3	19.0	19.7	16.4	22.5	21.3	12.9	16.9
Malawi	13.3	9.2	4.7	9.4	12.4	0.1	−4.2	−2.4	2.1	10.9
Uganda	−0.1	0.6	1.0	0.6	0.7	0.4	1.1	4.1	7.4	6.3
Zambia	16.5	18.2	3.8	17.8	14.5	6.4	8.6	10.0	5.9	6.5
Zimbabwe	21.4	26.9	21.5	23.4	19.5	13.6	19.5	18.1	14.8	18.4

Source: World Bank, *African Development Indicators*, 1997

Table A2.3   *Current account balance, excluding net capital grants/GDP, 1987–96 (%)*

Country	1987	1988	1989	1990	1991	1992	1993	1994	1995	1996
Kenya	−7.7	−8.0	−10.0	−8.0	−4.3	−4.0	1.2	−0.2	−5.4	−1.2
Malawi	−5.2	−8.2	−14.0	−7.8	−11.5	−20.0	−16.8	−17.9	−15.5	. .
Uganda	−2.2	−4.5	−6.9	−10.0	−13.5	−11.8	−11.8	−7.8	−7.9	−8.6
Zambia	−15.3	−7.1	−5.6	−11.8	−15.2	−23.7	−13.2	−10.7	−13.7	−11.4
Zimbabwe	0.0	0.8	−1.2	−3.8	−8.3	−15.3	−5.6	−5.5	−5.6	−1.8

Source: World Bank, *African Development Indicators*, 1997

Table A2.4   *Overall government deficit or surplus (including grants), 1987–96 (% of GDP)*

Country	1987	1988	1989	1990	1991	1992	1993	1994	1995	1996
Kenya	−0.2	−0.3	−0.2	−0.3	−0.2	−0.5	−0.4	−0.1	0.0	0.1
Malawi	−0.5	2.5	3.0	−1.4	−0.3	−7.8	−3.9	−6.3	0.9	−1.0
Uganda	−3.8	−3.9	−3.2	−4.4	−3.4	−7.3	−3.2	−3.8	−3.0	3.2
Zambia	−5.4	−9.3	−4.3	−8.3	−7.0	−2.5	−5.1	−5.8	−5.3	−4.0
Zimbabwe	−9.7	−8.5	−8.8	−7.3	−5.4	−6.2	−4.8	−5.7	−8.3	−7.6

Source: World Bank, *African Development Indicators*, 1997

Table A2.5   *Annual GDP growth, 1987–96*

Country	1987	1988	1989	1990	1991	1992	1993	1994	1995	1996
Kenya	5.9	6.2	4.7	4.2	1.4	−0.7	0.4	2.7	4.4	4.3
Malawi	1.1	3.1	0.6	8.8	6.2	−10.0	15.2	−12.9	13.5	16.1
Uganda	3.8	8.0	6.3	6.4	5.4	3.2	8.3	6.1	11.2	9.4
Zambia	3.1	5.3	−0.9	0.3	−0.4	0.1	2.4	−1.6	−3.1	4.3
Zimbabwe	−1.4	9.2	6.3	−1.4	5.6	−8.2	2.5	6.0	−1.8	7.4

Source: World Bank, *African Development Indicators*, 1997

Table A2.6 *Exports of goods and services, 1987–96 (% of GDP)*

Country	1987	1988	1989	1990	1991	1992	1993	1994	1995	1996
Kenya	21.34	21.88	23.05	26.18	27.35	27.05	42.14	38.88	33.29	33.00
Malawi	25.94	24.12	19.63	24.08	23.56	22.46	16.44	30.05	29.62	21.32
Uganda	8.25	7.57	7.95	7.24	7.46	8.76	7.06	8.74	11.78	11.86
Zambia	39.48	33.31	26.81	35.88	34.61	37.11	32.46	37.07	42.39	38.40
Zimbabwe	29.88	31.40	31.68	31.94	45.92	36.13	38.05	41.80	44.26	41.19

Source: World Bank, *World Development Indicators*, 1998

Table A2.7 *Foreign direct investment, net inflows, 1987–96 (% of GDP)*

Country	1987	1988	1989	1990	1991	1992	1993	1994	1995	1996
Kenya	0.54	0.00	0.75	0.67	0.24	0.08	0.03	0.05	0.36	0.14
Malawi	0.01	0.00	0.00	0.00	0.00	0.00	0.00	0.08	0.07	0.05
Uganda	0.00	0.08	−0.04	0.00	0.03	0.10	1.71	2.20	2.11	1.98
Zambia	3.29	2.50	4.10	6.17	1.01	1.41	1.59	1.77	2.03	1.71
Zimbabwe	−0.57	−0.29	−0.16	−0.18	0.05	0.27	0.50	0.60	0.61	0.83

Source: World Bank, *World Development Indicators*, 1998

Table A2.8 *Share of employment in tradeables, 1975–80 to 1988–92 (%)*

Country	1975–80	1981–85	1988–92
Kenya	40.8	35.6	33.3
Zambia	37.6	38.5	39.3
Zimbabwe	55.0	48.8	45.6

Source: ILO Yearbook, World Bank, *World Tables*, 1995

Table A2.9 *Manufacturing employment, 1987–96 (1990=100)*

Country	1987	1988	1989	1990	1991	1992	1993	1994	1995	1996
Kenya	91.7	96.0	96.2	100.0	100.6	101.4	103.1	105.3	109.1	. .
Malawi	87.1	83.0	85.2	100.0	88.7	94.6	91.1	102.8	. .	. .
Uganda	. .	. .	. .	. .	. .	. .	. .	. .	. .	. .
Zambia	100.6	100.8	101.8	100.0	98.1	. .	. .	75.4	. .	. .
Zimbabwe	93.1	99.1	100.7	100.0	102.0	119.6	93.7	90.9	86.4	88.7

Source: World Bank, *World Tables*, 1996, and UNIDO database, 1998.

Table A2.10 *Real wages in manufacturing, 1987–96 (1987=100)*

Country	1987	1988	1989	1990	1991	1992	1993	1994	1995	1996
Kenya	100.00	99.35	102.47	100.47	91.35	. .	. .	. .	. .	50.61
Malawi	. .	. .	. .	100.00	80.92	71.15	60.01	47.39	27.41	. .
Uganda	100.0	112.0	137.9	. .	. .	. .	. .	. .	. .	. .
Zambia	100.0	101.1	75.7	71.9	76.4	. .	. .	. .	. .	. .
Zimbabwe	100.00	104.12	104.02	106.02	100.24	85.38	73.98	75.94	76.06	75.31

Source: For Kenya, Malawi and Zimbabwe, *ILO Yearbook*; For Uganda and Zambia, World Bank, *World Tables*, 1996

Table A2.11 *Real minimum wage index, 1987–94 (1982=100)*

Country	1987	1988	1989	1990	1991	1992	1993	1994
Kenya	85.0	. .	78.0	85.0	74.0	64.0	59.0	55.0
Malawi	. .	. .	. .	. .	. .	. .	. .	. .
Uganda	33.3	928.7	61.9	75.1	78.1	65.6	. .	. .
Zambia	. .	102.0	. .	. .	. .	. .	. .	. .
Zimbabwe	. .	. .	. .	89.5	84.6	63.8	. .	. .

Source: Various national sources.

Table A2.12   *Gross primary school enrolment, 1987–95 (%)*

Country	1987	1988	1989	1990	1991	1992	1993	1994	1995
Kenya	98.0	96.0	98.0	95.00	. .	. .	91.00	87.00	85.00
Malawi	60.0	64.0	66.0	68.00	. .	85.00	90.00	135.00	. .
Uganda	76.0	80.0	. .	74.00	. .	73.00	. .	72.00	73.00
Zambia	97.0	97.0	95.0	98.00	. .	. .	. .	91.00	89.00
Zimbabwe	133.0	128.0	126.0	116.00	. .	. .	119.00	113.00	116.00

Source: World Bank, *World Development Indicators*, 1998

Table A2.13   *Gross secondary school enrolment, 1987–95 (%)*

Country	1987	1988	1989	1990	1991	1992	1993	1994	1995
Kenya	23.0	23.0	. .	24.00	. .	. .	25.00	25.00	24.00
Malawi	4.0	4.0	4.0	4.00	. .	4.00	2.00	. .	. .
Uganda	13.0	14.0	. .	13.00	. .	12.00	. .	11.00	12.00
Zambia	19.0	20.0	. .	. .	. .	. .	. .	28.00	. .
Zimbabwe	. .	51.0	52.0	49.00	. .	. .	44.00	45.00	47.00

Source: World Bank, *World Development Indicators*, 1998

Table A2.14   *Government expenditure on education, per capita in constant prices, 1987–95 (1990=100)*

Country	1987	1988	1989	1990	1991	1992	1993	1994	1995
Kenya	115.4	114.4	114.1	100.0	97.6	79.8	62.1	. .	. .
Malawi	108.1	112.9	. .	100.0	. .	. .	. .	. .	. .
Uganda	. .	. .	. .	. .	. .	. .	. .	. .	. .
Zambia	119.4	106.9	109.7	100.0	122.2	94.4	76.4	105.6	90.3
Zimbabwe	105.8	112.5	119.3	100.0	96.4	. .	. .	. .	. .

Source: World Bank, *World Tables*, 1996, and *African Development Indicators*, 1997

Table A2.15   *Government expenditure on health, per capita in constant prices, 1987–93 (1990=100)*

Country	1987	1988	1989	1990	1991	1992	1993
Kenya	120.4	112.5	114.7	100.0	96.6	80.6	65.7
Malawi	86.8	91.1	. .	100.0	. .	. .	. .
Uganda	. .	. .	. .	. .	. .	. .	. .
Zambia	157.6	178.3	102.7	100.0	121.3	71.0	65.3
Zimbabwe	84.0	94.0	95.0	100.0	. .	. .	. .

Source: World Bank, *World Tables*, 1996

Table A2.16   *Terms of trade index, 1987–96 (1987=100)*

Country	1987	1988	1989	1990	1991	1992	1993	1994	1995	1996
Kenya	100.0	103.8	97.5	93.2	102.6	102.4	120.1	171.3	151.9	150.3
Malawi	100.0	92.6	100.1	108.0	113.9	92.8	82.6	89.3	90.6	. .
Uganda	100.0	99.8	95.1	76.0	69.7	63.0	58.9	73.0	103.8	90.0
Zambia	100.0	122.0	64.5	83.3	71.1	53.5	52.2	50.4	52.0	47.5
Zimbabwe	100.0	102.9	93.6	86.7	95.3	80.6	81.3	77.8	82.3	85.5

Source: World Bank, *African Development Indicators*, 1997

Table A2.17   *Total debt service, 1987–96 (% of exports of goods and services)*

Country	1987	1988	1989	1990	1991	1992	1993	1994	1995	1996
Kenya	39.74	38.85	36.40	35.18	32.40	30.90	26.90	32.76	30.22	27.54
Malawi	37.45	30.86	30.89	29.35	24.91	24.89	22.40	20.59	27.20	18.59
Uganda	39.38	62.22	61.25	59.92	73.27	57.29	64.71	43.75	20.01	20.01
Zambia	19.04	15.25	14.46	14.87	47.32	29.30	34.68	31.40	186.29	24.58
Zimbabwe	32.29	28.47	22.38	23.15	23.12	32.00	30.64	25.41	23.52	21.25

Source: World Bank, *World Development Indicators*, 1998

Table A2.18   *Total external debt GNP, 1987–95 (%)*

Country	1987	1988	1989	1990	1991	1992	1993	1994	1995
Kenya	75.1	70.9	73.3	87.2	98.3	91.3	139.5	110.4	97.7
Malawi	124.4	106.3	96.4	87	78.3	93.3	92.4	161.5	166.8
Uganda	30.8	29.8	42	61.1	85.1	105.7	95.5	85.9	63.7
Zambia	346.1	206.8	187.6	241.5	245.1	244.9	203.7	205.5	191.3
Zimbabwe	55.2	43.9	44.3	49.6	54.9	78.4	79.9	80.4	78.9

Source: World Bank, *Global Development Finances*, 1997

Table A2.19   *Multilateral debt/total external debt, 1987–95 (%)*

Country	1987	1988	1989	1990	1991	1992	1993	1994	1995
Kenya	33.7	33.1	36.7	35.2	35	36.3	36.6	38.5	39.5
Malawi	59	62.3	64.4	68.2	71.8	74.7	79.1	78.9	78.8
Uganda	42.4	45.6	45.1	49.2	51.3	53.3	57	59.7	61.8
Zambia	18.5	17.6	18.4	19.5	20.6	22.7	25.9	30.1	31.9
Zimbabwe	18.2	20.1	20.4	19.6	21.2	24.1	31.1	34.3	33.1

Source: World Bank, *Global Development Finances*, 1997

3 Adjustment, Employment & Labour Market Institutions in Sub-Saharan Africa

WILLEM VAN DER GEEST & GANESHAN WIGNARAJA

Introduction

This chapter examines the empirical characteristics of sub-Saharan African (SSA) labour markets and how these have changed during the process of adjustment. It starts with an exploration of the timing and sequencing of the implementation of SAP-induced reforms and the resulting economic performance. Then the nature of the relationships between SAPs,[1] the demand for labour and labour market changes is reviewed in more detail. The principal empirical aspects of African labour markets examined here are: employment growth, real wage developments, productivity growth, human capital, training and the acquisition of technological capability. A novel feature of the chapter is the attempt to integrate the findings from national and sectoral labour market studies with the literature on the microeconomics of technical change. The latter is less known but sheds useful insights on the dynamics of labour markets during adjustment.

The chapter is organized as follows. The second section reviews some recent literature on the relationships between SAPs and the demand for labour. The next section assesses the empirical evidence on employment and the productivity of sub-Saharan Africa's labour markets. The fourth section establishes the linkages between adjustment and the changing *structure* of employment, followed by an examination of the changing *terms* of employment. The next section discusses industrial relations and the role of the social partners, while the seventh section provides some general findings from the case studies. The final section raises issues and questions for the country studies in Part II of this volume.

Adjustment and employment: Some recent research findings

What happened to employment and wages in SSA during adjustment? The literature on SAPs and employment in SSA is limited. This reflects problems of the lack of data on employment and real wage developments as well as an undue focus on the macroeconomic outcomes of the SAPs, using the standard indicators of GDP growth and fiscal and trade deficits as a percentage of GDP. In most cases, this

---

[1] The term structural adjustment programme (SAP) is used here as a generic term to describe the range of policy reforms undertaken as part of a structural adjustment programme.

literature has disregarded the meso-variables (including employment) which determine the distributional outcomes of adjustment.

One exception is the OECD Development Centre's study on *Adjustment and Equity*, which explicitly deals with the employment and distributional impacts of adjustment (synthesized in Bourguignon and Morrison, 1992). The authors of this synthesis of seven country case studies review the context of the disequilibria and crisis in which stabilization and adjustment measures are adopted, and analyse the changes in employment, incomes, living standards and poverty during adjustment. In summary, employment in the rural areas did not deteriorate during adjustment, given the slower growth of labour supply, whereas unemployment increased sharply in urban areas; this was usually reflected in an increase of informal sector activity. Agricultural incomes also moved favourably, in contrast to non-agricultural wage incomes. The extent to which overall household incomes declined under adjustment depended on the level of non-wage factor income (which includes self-employment and the informal sector) and the impact of the reduced provision of government services. Living standards did not fall across the board during adjustment; there was improvement in rural areas in Ghana but also sharp falls in urban areas in Côte d'Ivoire.

Another exception is Cornia, van der Hoeven and Mkandawire (1992), which analyses Africa's recovery prospects in the 1990s. The study compares the adjustment experiences of Burkina Faso, Niger, Tanzania, Zambia and Zimbabwe, and outlines alternative approaches for the 1990s and beyond. Three theoretical and practical explanations of the need for alternatives are offered: (i) the persistent failure to achieve modification of SSA's production and trade structures; (ii) the fragility of growth; and (iii) the persistent neglect of the human factor in adjustment and development programmes. The study brings together fragmentary evidence on the decline of employment as well as the fall in real wages during the 1980s (Cornia *et al.*, 1992, 20–26). It identifies smallholder agriculture and small-scale industry with its manifold forward and backward linkages and positive employment effects as the engines of growth, justifying this on the grounds that these farms and firms are characterized by:

(i)   a more equitable distribution of earnings;
(ii)   higher microeconomic efficiency in resource and labour use;
(iii) the ability to accelerate food production and food security;
(iv)   the ability to reduce food import requirements;
(v)   more comprehensive linkages between agriculture and non-agriculture;
(vi)   a less capital-intensive choice of techniques; and
(vii) a higher degree of technological self-reliance.

The study noted the importance of complementary measures of international support for Africa's long-term recovery which would include, amongst others, bilateral and multilateral debt write-offs.

Horton *et al.* (1994) specifically focus on labour markets under adjustment and include three country case studies from SSA – Côte d'Ivoire, Ghana and Kenya. The Côte d'Ivoire study utilizes household survey data for the period 1985 to 1989, complemented by some industrial sector statistics (available only for the formal wage sector). The impact of adjustment implies a fall of overall formal wage employment as well as a reduction in real wages. Some reallocation of labour towards other sectors did take place as well as a move of the labour force into agriculture. Hence, some labour market flexibility was observed. The Ghana case study is based on a detailed 1987–8 cross-sectional household survey. Although the analysis presented signifies a substantial improvement in the understanding of the functioning of the labour market in Ghana, the data do not allow any firm conclusions to be reached regarding the impact of adjustment on employment over time. The authors present details of economic activity and employment by age, sex and education; unemployment and underemployment in urban and rural areas; and a detailed account of earnings from labour. The estimated earning functions show the significant positive returns of education to the individual (especially of secondary education) and that significant earnings differences persist between (i) sectors of employment and (ii) households with a different employment status. Noting evidence of changing wage differentials and changes in the patterns of migration, it is concluded that '… a flexible labour market probably helped achieve the macroeconomic improvements observed in Ghana during the 1980s', even though other factors may have been more important (Horton *et al.*, 1994: 402).

Kenya's pattern of employment change during the 1980s appears to differ from that of other sub-Saharan African countries: the public sector continued to dominate formal sector employment, even though a major drop in real wages took place. The expansion of employment was primarily in the informal sector.[2] As the other case studies found, the returns to high and specialized skills, from the point of view of the earner, appear to be increasing during adjustment; the returns to 'higher education were larger in the 1986 survey than the 1977–78 survey' (*ibid*.: 449).

Key characteristics of sub-Saharan Africa's labour markets

The growing labour force and its employment profile
Quantitative information about Africa's labour markets (in terms of employment, wages, unemployment and underemployment, the size and development of the informal sector, etc.) is scant and likely to be subject to considerable margins of error. Its general characteristics may be summarized as follows:

(i)   SSA's population grew at 3.06 per cent per annum during 1990–95, and is projected to decline only slowly to 2.31 per cent per annum over the period 1995 to 2025. Although a major share of the population is in the agricultural sector, the rate of rural to urban migration is high and accelerating. Hence a fast growth of the urban labour force is to be expected. For example, in Kenya the urban labour force grew by 6 per cent per annum – twice its population growth rate.

(ii) The total labour supply in 1995 in SSA was estimated at 228 million persons, of which 38 per cent were female.[3] It is projected to increase to 258 million by 2000.[4] Over the thirty-year period 1995 to 2025 the total labour supply in SSA will increase at a rate above that for the previous thirty years 1965 to 1995.[5] In contrast, in other regions of the world labour supply growth rates are falling.

---

[2]Kenya's database compares favourably with that of many other countries, as estimates, though not without definitional problems, are available which document the growth of informal employment (see Chapter 4 for further discussion and analysis).

[3]Labour supply as estimated according to the ILO definition, which includes all persons in employment as well as the unemployed.

[4]Labour supply is expected to rise to 534 million by 2025. By that time, SSA will comprise one-seventh of the world's labour force; some 14 countries in SSA are projected to have a labour force in excess of 10 million each. Nigeria, Ethiopia, Democratic Republic of Congo, South Africa, Tanzania and Kenya taken together will have a labour force of over a quarter of a billion, i.e. the same as the whole of SSA in 2000.

[5]Apart from a few countries including Mauritius, South Africa and Zimbabwe.

This expansion of the labour supply primarily reflects the changing age structure of the population. Although a limited decline in the labour force participation rate is forecast,[6] this does not outweigh the lagged effects of the period of high and increasing population growth in SSA since the early 1980s.[7] The (net) rate of growth of labour force participation will eventually exceed the growth of the overall population: the labour force will continue to increase at a high rate, although population growth is decelerating in SSA. Figure 3.1 displays this graphically.

Household surveys have been undertaken to counter the weaknesses of statistics about the employment profile of SSA's labour markets. The statistics are marred by a number of problems:[8]

(i)   *conceptual* deficiencies because of using inappropriate international employment classifications;
(ii) *data* deficiencies regarding incomes and non-wage payments in the modern sector and remuneration from self-employment; and

Figure 3.1   *Population and labour force, sub-Saharan Africa, 1980–2025 (five-year averages; projections from 1990 onwards)*

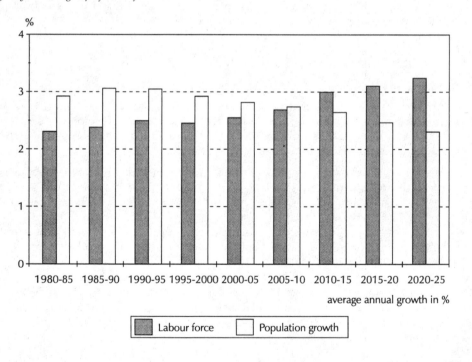

[6]The key assumptions with respect to labour force participation rates are that there is a decline in child labour (below 15 years of age), a lower participation rate of persons below the age of 19 on account of longer education, and lesser participation above the age of 55 in view of improved care for the elderly; these assumptions may be regarded as optimistic.

[7]The population growth of SSA increased from 2.94 to 3.06 per cent during 1980–95, at a time when population growth fell in all other regions of the world.

[8]For a review of the controversies in labour statistics see Chapter 1 of *World Labour Report* (ILO,1995c); for a discussion of definitional problems encountered in defining employment in one African country (Tanzania), see Bol (1995).

(iii) *analytical* deficiencies including non-representative sampling and incomplete processing of the data.

The employment profile of labour markets in SSA, based on a series of pilot household surveys carried out between 1986 and 1992 in the capitals of five West African countries as well as in Madagascar has been analysed by Lachaud (1994).[9] To address the *conceptual* deficiencies, Lachaud developed an employment typology which distinguishes the labour status of households on the basis of criteria reflecting protection, entry barriers to some types of employment and the amount of fixed and/or working capital controlled or owned. To avoid prejudging the characteristics of African urban labour markets in terms of oversimplified dualistic models of the formal-informal sector, the study examines the data through a cluster analysis, which groups households with the greatest similarity across a number of characteristics. The results of the six surveys indicate five distinct sub-groups, on the basis of the nature of employment contracts, which may be described as follows:

(i)   *protected wage employment*, governed by contracts of employment, legal constraints and with effective barriers to entry; it remains the largest group, comprising some 35 per cent of the total earners in the six pilot surveys;

(ii) *non-protected wage employment*, which is continuous and usually based on contracts of employment but which has low barriers to entry and hence is fiercely competitive; it comprises the second largest category, varying between 21 and 35 per cent of the total earners in the surveys;

(iii) *marginal self-employment* with low labour productivity and without established production premises or other capital, varying between 14 and 34 per cent of the surveyed earners;

(iv) *irregular employment* characterized by severe job insecurity, varying between 4 and 11 per cent of the earners surveyed;

(v)   *self-employment* with some, though limited, working capital and assets, typically working in small family units, comprising approximately 7 per cent of the earners surveyed.

Hence, between a quarter and a half of households derive their main income from the 'informal' sector in the urban areas, and this is reflected in the weak employment contracts – a fundamental labour institution poorly developed in this sector. In what follows, these general characteristics of Africa's labour markets – the rapid growth of its labour force, high rural to urban migration and a high degree of informalization of urban employment – will be complemented by a description of some of its micro characteristics, including productivity, training and human resource development.

Productivity growth
The importance of sustained productivity growth to an economy's dynamism and competitiveness is widely recognized in the literature on development (Syrquin, 1994). However, analyses of the determinants of productivity growth in Africa have been few. Studies on African developing countries (LDCs) are of two types: (i) studies attempting to estimate Total Factor Productivity (TFP) growth and labour productivity growth at the regional, national or sectoral levels using published data;

---

[9] The surveys were undertaken by the Institute of Labour Studies of the International Labour Office and covered altogether 2,705 earners in Abidjan in Côte d'Ivoire, Antananarivo in Madagascar, Yaoundé in Cameroon, Conakry in Guinea, Bamako in Mali and Ouagadougou in Burkina Faso.

and (ii) studies employing primary data collected from manufacturing enterprises in LDCs to investigate static productivity differences among enterprises. Each of these will be considered in turn.

Regional/national and sectoral productivity estimates. The TFP method involves estimating the contribution that the inputs, capital and labour, make to growth within a national production function framework. TFP, the residual from such an exercise, captures the efficiency with which these inputs are used.[10] The rate of TFP growth is taken as a proxy for technical change.

A World Bank study reports on trends in long-run total factor productivity (TFP) growth in several developing regions, including Africa, for the period 1960–87 (World Bank, 1991). It was found that SSA, along with Latin America, recorded a zero TFP growth. South Asia came next, with a growth of 0.6 per cent per annum followed by the Middle East and North Africa (1.4 per cent). East Asia came top with 1.9 per cent. For the 1995 *World Development Report* a comparison of the change in GDP per worker over time was made for 36 countries in sub-Saharan Africa; this was a broad indicator of changes in labour productivity at the national level. The adjustment period 1980–93 was compared with the period 1965–80. It was found that during 1980–93 GDP per worker had grown in 16 countries, whereas it had declined in some 20 others. Moreover, the rate of growth of GDP per worker in 1980–93 was below that of the earlier period for nearly all countries. Kenya, Tanzania, Uganda and Zimbabwe realized positive, though small, GDP per worker growth, Ghana experienced zero growth and Zambia faced a sharp decline in recent years (World Bank, 1995).

Various other studies provide national estimates of TFP growth as well as regional averages. Table 3.1 provides estimates by Syrquin (1994) of economy-wide TFP growth for Kenya and Tanzania and regional averages for East Asia, South Asia and Latin America for the period 1980–89. It also provides estimates by Cooper (1995) of manufacturing labour productivity growth, defined as real manufacturing value added per employee, for Zambia, Zimbabwe and South Africa in addition to the

Table 3.1   *Total factor productivity growth and manufacturing value-added growth in the 1980s*

Country/region	Economy-wide TFP-growth[a] (1980–89)	Growth of real manufacturing value added per worker (1980–90)[b]
Kenya	−0.5	1.4
Tanzania, United Rep. of	−1.6	−4.0
South Africa	n.a.	1.2[c]
Zambia	n.a.	0.5
Zimbabwe	n.a.	0.7
Average for East Asia	3.3	4.5
Average for South Asia	1.1	3.7
Average for Latin America	−1.1	1.1

Notes: (a) Total factor productivity growth estimates are from Syrquin (1994). (b) Real manufacturing value added (MVA) per worker estimates are from Cooper (1995). (c) 1972–90.

[10]The concept of total factor productivity growth is deeply rooted in the tradition of growth accounting. Growth accounting seeks to explain economic growth by analysing increases in physical capital and the labour force, adjusted for changes in composition and skills – the human capital factor. The contribution of each factor of production is estimated by multiplying its rate of increase by its share in national income. TFP growth, the proxy for technical progress, is found by subtracting the contributions of labour and capital from total growth. TFP growth is thus the residual from a growth accounting exercise.

others, for the period 1980–90. These data confirm that the TFP growth performance of Kenya and Tanzania was disappointing in the 1980s. The TFP growth rates of the two African economies (–0.5 per cent and –1.6 per cent respectively) are comparable to the average for the Latin American economies (–1.1 per cent) in the same period but well below the averages for South Asia (1.1 per cent) and East Asia (3.3 per cent). A similar conclusion can be reached using the manufacturing labour productivity estimates for the five African economies and the regional averages for Latin America, South and East Asia in the period 1980–90. Of the five African economies, Kenya (1.4 per cent) performs best in terms of manufacturing labour productivity growth, followed by South Africa (1.2 per cent), Zimbabwe (0.7 per cent), Zambia (0.5 per cent) and Tanzania (–4.0 per cent).

Another study by Nehru and Dhareshwar estimates TFP growth for developing and industrial countries for the period 1960 to 1987, using various alternative models (Nehru and Dhareshwar, 1994). It too finds that factor productivity growth in most countries of SSA has been negative. In its model specification human capital formation – measured as growth over time of the total number of years of schooling for the total population – proves to be a highly significant determinant of productivity growth. Taking into account this factor, the TFP growth is negative for virtually all countries in the region, with the notable exceptions of Kenya, Zimbabwe and Mauritius.[11] However, Nehru and Dhareshwar's estimates do not permit a reliable comparison of the levels of TFP growth realized before the adjustment policy reforms – during the period 1960–85 – with performance during/after adjustment from 1985 to 1995 (*ibid.*: 18).

Firm-level productivity studies. In a relatively recent development, several studies have attempted to estimate production functions for a single homogeneous industry in an African LDC (see Pack, 1993, for a discussion of the method). Amongst other things, this framework allows a comparison of the variation in realized productivity of individual firms with the best practice in the country (i.e. technical efficiency):

> It has been found that textiles, sawmilling, and other industrial activities in several African countries exhibit considerable intra-sector variation in TFP. Moreover, even the best local firms may fall far short of internationally realised productivity levels and a further fillip to domestic output can be obtained if all firms, both those locally efficient and those falling short of this standard, move toward international best practice (Pack, 1993: 7).

These findings on firm-level productivity differences in Africa are reinforced by research on technological capabilities at the firm level, which ranks inter-firm differences according to a common scoring system. The ranking attempts to integrate a variety of objective and subjective information into a comparable measure of a firm's capacity to use technology across a number of areas pertaining to the setting up, operation and transfer of technology. Studies of enterprises in Ghana, Kenya and Tanzania have been conducted after SAPs had been in place for a number of years.[12] The studies revealed that: (i) the levels of technological capability in African enterprises are below those of similar sized enterprises in other LDCs; and (ii) within African industry, there is a considerable variation in the technological capability scores realized by the firms.

---

[11]The study uses a cross-country comparative framework which imposes fixed parameters for the productivity of the amounts of labour and capital used in production. For the SSA sub-sample, a slope dummy variable is used, reflecting the structurally lower productivity of these factors, lowering the TFP growth estimates by –1.1 per cent.

[12]See Lall and Wignaraja (1997), Wignaraja and Ikiara (forthcoming) and Deraniyagala and Semboja (forthcoming).

In sum, the literature indicates that productivity achievements in SSA are well below the standards of other developing regions both at the national/industry level and the firm level. Within Africa, however, there is great variation in productivity attainments between countries and firms. Some countries, and firms within them, have higher productivity than the rest. A possible explanation for these differences in productivity achievement is the different level of human capital, which we shall discuss below, following a review of the changing structure of employment and real wage developments.

Adjustment and the changing structure of employment

The formal sector: Retrenchment in the public sector

Retrenchment of civil service and parastatal workers, recently implemented as part of adjustment programmes, is not a new phenomenon in SSA. The World Bank report on *Adjustment in Africa: Reforms, Results and the Road Ahead* addresses the question of public employment in the context of public sector management. It starts from the proposition that civil services are larger than needed, more costly than can be afforded and less 'effective and productive than they should be' (World Bank, 1994: 121). The study presents the impact of civil service reform programmes on employment during the period 1981–90 in ten selected countries and finds a retrenchment level of approximately 46,600 persons,[13] coupled with enforced/early retirement of 21,200 and the removal of 42,200 'ghost' employees (persons not working or non-existent) from the payroll.

Tanzania's 1994–5 retrenchments under the Civil Service Reform Programme have followed the exercises of 1975 and 1985. Past experience, as reviewed by Mamuya, indicates that the expected gains in terms of public sector net savings tend not to be realized (Mamuya, 1991). Actual retrenchment remained below its target for a variety of reasons:

(i)   implementation of the plans has tended to be slower than scheduled;
(ii) simultaneously with the retrenchment exercise, counteracting institutional changes were made which included the creation of new ministries (in 1975), the re-establishment of local government (in 1985) and the transfer of staff from the abolished parastatals back to line ministries, implying that staff levels were above those expected (also in 1985);
(iii) employers sought to retain staff (especially in 1975);
(iv) individuals successfully moved away from posts that were to be abolished to other ministries (in 1975 and 1985) or to local government (in 1985).

During both the 1975 and 1985 exercises in Tanzania the actual retrenchment was less than half the level recommended.[14] Compensation payments during 1985 totalled Tshs. 244 million, against anticipated annual gross savings of Tshs. 288 million (respectively $22 and $26 million). However, less than half of the intended number were actually retrenched. Hence, it may be inferred that the compensation payments amounted to between one and a half and two years of wage payments 'saved'.

The increased emphasis on adjustment measures oriented towards institutional change implies a much greater reduction of public sector employment levels in a

---

[13]Of these, 44,400 were in Ghana and included staff in district assemblies and in the education sector.

[14]About half of the target of 20 per cent of civil service staff was realized in 1975 and 47 per cent of the target in 1985; for details, see Mamuya, 1991: 22 and 39.

context of continued erosion of wage levels. During the recent 1994–5 retrenchment exercise in Tanzania, the target of retrenching 50,000 civil servants has indeed been more or less realized. Some 47,000 persons were removed from the payroll, 14,600 of them 'ghost-workers'. However, in line with previous experience, the wage bill has increased over the period of retrenchment due to high compensation rates. Uganda's public sector retrenched a total of 145,882 persons between July 1990 and July 1994, some 40,000 of whom were from the civil service itself, with the remainder drawn from temporary government staff, the education sector and the police. The army also underwent downsizing with the demobilization of 33,000 soldiers completed by 1995 and further reductions planned.

Cohen emphasizes the importance of public service reform for Kenya and analyses the political and economic constraints that hamper such reforms (Cohen, 1993). He notes that the determinants of the fast growth of public sector employment (6.5 per cent per annum during 1967 to 1991) were the changing role of the government, and fast population growth as well as political motives.[15] Notwithstanding this expansion of public sector employment, serious problems of inadequate administrative performance remained. Cohen lists the following signs of declining bureaucratic capacity: (i) weaknesses in the formulation of policies and programmes; (ii) non-retention of highly skilled professional and management staff; (iii) inadequate expenditures for operation and maintenance. Efficiency and morale within Kenya's civil service continued to deteriorate. Cohen argues that reduction of its size, elimination of duplication, increased allocations for operation and maintenance, pay reform and an effective fight against corruption are essential to counteract the twin problems of declining efficiency and low morale. However, the constraints to achieving success on these fronts are primarily political (Cohen, 1993: 466–76).

As part of an ILO-executed project on manpower planning, the likely employment effects of Zimbabwe's Economic Structural Adjustment Programme (ESAP) were projected through three scenarios (ILO, 1992). These employment projections were based on what appeared, with the benefit of hindsight, to be rather too optimistic assumptions regarding the output-employment elasticities during adjustment. The study assumed these to be constant on the basis of past time-series data. However, the evidence of the Zimbabwe experience would suggest that these elasticities declined during adjustment in a slow-growing economy; additional output did not require the same employment expansion as before. Hence the projections overestimated the employment creation during adjustment. Moreover, the growth of manufacturing output as well as the growth of exports were overestimated.[16] One lesson from this may be that research into output-employment relationships, as indicated above, needs to be undertaken.

---

[15]Ad hoc absorptions of staff by means of conversion to permanent status included: (a) public servants from the dissolved East African Community; (b) census enumerators and 'works paid' development project workers converted in 1979 and 1984 respectively; and (c) project and programme implementation staff at the district level. Furthermore, the government remained willing to act as employer of last resort, especially for unemployed school leavers and university graduates; a proliferation of advisory committees with independent staff and establishments took place and there were political motives in the creation of posts for reasons of patronage and ethnic balance.

[16]It was assumed that, even in a slow growth scenario, the reduction of civil service employment by 26,000, i.e. 24 per cent of the 1990 level, would be counteracted by major employment increases in education, manufacturing, tourism and commercial agriculture (respectively 12, 34, 13 and 20 thousand), leading to an overall increase in total formal sector employment of 8 per cent over the period 1990–95. To date, little of this employment growth has been realized.

The centrepiece of Zimbabwe's ESAP, as adopted in 1990, was a commitment to reduce the budget deficit through public expenditure reductions involving: (i) delaying or cancelling low-return public investments; (ii) reducing civil service employment (in the non-education sector) by some 24 per cent; and (iii) elimination of subsidies to loss-making public enterprises and parastatals. Government subsidies and advances to the marketing boards (trading in grain, dairy products, cotton and cold storage services) as well as various other parastatals, such as the railways and airways, were to be phased out by 1995, the final year of the ESAP, or even before. Notwithstanding the implementation of most of these measures, the public deficit reached a historic peak of 15 per cent of GDP at the start of the 1995–96 fiscal year.[17]

Formal sector: Growth in large-scale manufacturing industry?
A major debate is taking place between the World Bank and some academic critics regarding the effects of adjustment on Africa's manufacturing industry . The debate centres on the findings of the World Bank's *Adjustment in Africa* report (World Bank, 1994). Focusing on 29 African countries that initiated adjustment programmes in the 1980s, the report claims to have gone beyond previous Bank studies by providing: (i) comprehensive information on performance under adjustment; (ii) a detailed analysis of its effects on industry; and (iii) suggestions on ways in which programmes can be improved.[18]

To date the industrial response of individual African countries to adjustment seems to have been mixed. Interpreting adjustment largely in terms of stabilization, the study found that '… on the macroeconomic front, six of the adjusting countries had a large improvement in policies, nine a small improvement, and eleven a deterioration. As a whole, they cut their budget deficits … and reduced inflation to moderate levels' (World Bank, 1994: 3).[19] It went on to argue that there are payoffs to improving policies; it reported increases in the (median) export growth rate of 8 per cent and (median) industrial growth of 6 per cent for countries with the most improved macroeconomic policies, compared with a reduction of 0.7 per cent and an increase of 1.7 per cent, respectively, for countries with policy deteriorations (see Table 3.2). It argues that there is little systematic evidence to suggest that deindus-

Table 3.2 *Median industrial and export growth in sub-Saharan Africa under adjustment, 1981–91 (average annual growth, %)*

Country group	Industrial growth			Export growth		
	1981–86	1987–91	Median	1981–86	1981–91	Median
Large improvement in macroeconomic policies	−1.0	4.4	6.1	−0.3	6.7	7.9
Small improvement	2.1	5.0	2.8	2.5	4.3	3.0
Deterioration	0.5	3.6	1.7	1.3	0.6	−0.7
All countries (sample size 29)	1.4	4.1	2.5	2.2	3.6	2.0

Notes: Median refers to median difference between the periods.

Sources: World Bank (1994), Tables A.21 and A.22

---

[17]Budget speech 1995, Ministry of Finance, Harare, Zimbabwe.
[18]Previous work by the World Bank on adjustment in SSA industry includes Meier and Steel (1987). See Stein (1992) for a review of this work.
[19]According to the World Bank (1994, figure 2.3), the six star performers in terms of changes in macroeconomic policies are the following (listed in descending order): Ghana, Tanzania, The Gambia, Burkina Faso, Nigeria and Zimbabwe.

trialization has occurred in Africa following adjustment: on the contrary, the figures indicate an upturn in industrial and export activity in countries that have successfully adjusted. It concludes that, despite the progress achieved since the 1980s, African countries continue to lag behind East Asia in macroeconomic and industrial performance. Thus, it asserts that there is a need for more and further adjustment in the areas of trade, financial, privatization and agricultural policies to boost industrial and export growth.

In their review of adjustment in Africa, Mosley and Weeks (1994) argue that the World Bank study is flawed on statistical grounds. They reproduce the Bank's comparison between the six 'star African countries' (see Note 19) and other adjusting countries, add comparable data on 'non-adjustment lending countries' and perform statistical tests of the significance of the differences in performance between the various groups of countries. Paradoxically, they find that the non-adjusting group of countries perform *better* than the adjusting countries as a group and, in terms of investment performance, the countries classified by the Bank as having relatively poor macroeconomic management actually do better than the Bank's selected star performers. More important, they argue that:

> all the between-sample comparisons emerge as statistically insignificant; in particular, it is impossible to reject, at the 5 per cent or even the 10 per cent level of probability, the hypothesis that superior growth performance between 1987 and 1991 of those African countries which adopted what the Bank characterizes as 'better' macroeconomic policies arose from pure chance (Mosley and Weeks, 1994: 321).

Mosley and Weeks conclude that an effective adjustment strategy needs to incorporate policy measures to remove barriers to the expansion of aggregate supply in Africa. These would include establishing credit institutions which make collateral-free loans to small farmers and businessmen, promoting a green revolution in agriculture through fertilizer subsidies, using selective tariff protection to promote manufactured exports and developing new tax bases.

Critical reviews by Stein (1992, 1994) are particularly controversial. He argues that 'adjustment, as it is currently constituted in Africa, *is likely to be deindustrializing*' (Stein, 1994: 288, emphasis added). The performance of existing industries is likely to be affected negatively by increased competition from imports of consumer goods, rising interest rates and higher raw material prices for agricultural goods. Stein further argues that adjustment may not work in Africa because the neoclassical model underlying it misses fundamental 'structural causes of the industrial malaise in the region'. Among these structural causes, he lists the following: a losing battle on external accounts as a result of deteriorating terms of trade and high levels of multilateral debt, the absence of an entrepreneurial class to respond to new incentives with autonomous accumulation and limits on the open accumulation activities of visible minorities (such as the Asian population in East Africa). He concludes that alternative approaches to industrial adjustment in Africa should give more weight to structural issues. The weaknesses of his critique are its limited empirical assessment of industrial performance in countries under adjustment and its lack of attention to failures in the market for skills, technology, information and finance which hinder industrial development in SSA.

Lall also questions the underlying assumptions of the World Bank study (Lall, 1996). He argues that the analysis on which it is based neglects market failures in the process of developing technological capabilities; in particular, it does not address the fact that in the developing country context few firms have adequate knowledge of the possible industrial technologies, and they do not have equal access to these technologies. Their capacity to adopt technologies efficiently may entail great effort and cost. Specific supply-side-oriented policies are needed, and an exclusive reliance on competition to generate the much needed supply responses is unlikely to succeed.

Drawing on micro-level research into technological learning in LDCs, Lall argues that (i) the process of becoming efficient in African industry is slow, risky, costly and often prolonged and (ii) enterprises may face a range of market failures in both factor and product markets.[20] Among other things, the process itself has to be learnt and may involve technological externalities that require continuous interactions between firms and institutions focusing on engineering, training and research. In addition, capital markets which finance learning may be imperfect, due to moral hazard problems and information assymmetry between lenders and borrowers. Finally, firms may not invest in training because employees leave once they have been trained. All of these market failures tend to hinder the process of becoming efficient in African industry.

Lall concludes that policy reforms are necessary in Africa to remedy the industrial stagnation caused by haphazard interventions during periods of import substitution. But, under conditions of a multitude of market failures in Africa, he argues for a gradual approach to trade liberalization. This would permit industry to undertake costly relearning while adjusting to competition. Such gradualism would need to be complemented by the provision of adequate supply-side support (including the creation of general and specific skills and technological support systems for industry and aggressive promotion of foreign direct investment). Examples of such support may be adapted from the experience of East Asia, for example from Taiwan, China, but also from Mauritius.[21]

More fundamentally, critics claim that the theoretical model underlying the adjustment programmes is inappropriate and may result in misleading policy prescriptions for industrial development in Africa. The World Bank has yet to answer its critics: the debate over the impact of adjustment on Africa's industry is still far from an agreement or conclusion. However, what is clear is that little attention has been given by the Bank or its critics to the impact of adjustment on labour markets in Africa, especially regarding the question of the creation of new employment opportunities in the private (or newly privatized) enterprises.

The informal sector: Lateral expansion in stagnating markets
Although most observers agree that the informal sector has increased rapidly during adjustment, it is inherently difficult to document its changes with accuracy. A study by Mhone attempts to analyse the impact of structural adjustment on the urban informal sector of Zimbabwe, using a survey sponsored by the ILO. He found that at independence in 1980 the urban informal sector absorbed 'about 10 per cent

---

[20]This has been documented in the study of Ghana by Lall *et al.* (1994) and in recent studies of Kenya by Wignaraja and Ikiara (forthcoming), Tanzania by Deraniyagala and Semboja (forthcoming) and Zimbabwe by Latsch and Robinson (forthcoming). The results of these studies are reviewed in the following section.

[21]Since 1970, Mauritius has achieved an enviable transformation from a reliance on sugar plantations to becoming an exporter of manufactures and services. By 1995 its per capita income (US$ 3,380) puts it within the World Bank's category of upper-middle-income economies and well above the average for sub-Saharan Africa (US$ 490). The country's export success can be attributed to: an outward-oriented development strategy, which emphasized attracting foreign investment via EPZs; cheap, literate, bilingual labour (English and French-speaking); preferential access to the EU market as a signatory of the Lomé Convention; a reasonable concentration of entrepreneurs with international business experience; useful support from technology institutions (including the Mauritius Standards Bureau and the Export Processing Development Authority); and a low level of bureaucracy and a business-friendly economic environment (see Lall and Wignaraja, forthcoming).

of the labour force', whereas by the early 1990s this had risen to 'about 25 per cent of the labour force' (Mhone, 1995: 1). This growth has been determined by the relaxation of restrictive regulations following independence, the increased rural to urban migration and increased labour force participation, resulting in the urban informal sector accounting for 'almost as much employment as the formal sector' (*ibid.*: 2).

The informal sector survey covered 525 enterprises in the three main cities of Zimbabwe (Harare, Bulawayo and Gweru), capturing activities in both high and low density suburbs, as well as the central business districts, industrial areas and the peri-urban low income suburbs.[22] The three concepts used to analyse the changes in the role and status of the urban informal sector focused on efficiency, distinguishing between *allocative, technical* and *distributive efficiencies.*

The *allocative* efficiency concept analyses the use of the factors of production (capital, labour, land, etc.) across economic activities in the economy as a whole, and questions whether reforms of the policy environment increase the value added of the urban informal sector. Hence, allocative efficiency is to a considerable extent determined by the linkages between the formal and the informal sector, in particular through the markets for material inputs and the demand for outputs and services. The *technical* efficiency of the informal sector is a microeconomic concept, looking at the physical input-to-output relations within the enterprises themselves. Hence, it is measured in terms of productivity and monetary returns to factor inputs; optimality would be achieved when 'any change in the combination and utilization of resources would lower productivity or returns' (Mhone, 1995: 7). Finally, *distributive* efficiency refers to the implications of the policy reforms for the incomes and wages prevailing within the sector as compared with those in other sectors of the economy (or relative to an absolute norm, such as a poverty datum line).[23]

The impact on efficiency, distinguishing the three levels indicated above, may be summarized as follows (Mhone, 1995: 88–90):

> *allocative efficiency* was further reduced by the ESAP as the programme failed to resuscitate the (urban) formal economy, while exacerbating the informal sector's 'lateral expansion and involutionary growth.' Specific indicators are that ' large numbers of secondary school educated youths are increasingly absorbed in easy entry activities with low returns', and that the marginal productivity of new entrants is very low (p. 89).
>
> *technical inefficiency* was somewhat reduced, in particular for more complex activities and in specific locations (especially Gweru near the border); a 'marginal tendency' was noted towards an increasing division of labour; formalizing on-the-job training; adapting to changing competition by redesigning products, etc. (p. 89).
>
> *distributive inefficiency* was not reduced, as the sector failed to upgrade its activities or to seize opportunities downgraded in the formal sector; it is noted that ... 'the declines in economic welfare in the formal sector and the urban informal sector have been directly related and mutually reinforcing' (p. 90). However, the informal sector continues to play an important 'distributional function as an income-generating safety-net' (p. 90).

It is unlikely, however, that the urban informal sector will be able to fulfil the role of safety net to any significant extent in view of the quarter of a million labour market newcomers each year. More specifically, the ESAP did not include specific

---

[22]The survey was conducted in 1993 by lecturers and graduate students of the University of Zimbabwe. In addition to the enterprise questionnaire, supplementary data were collected regarding the household characteristics of owners and workers in the enterprises, the demand patterns which they face from households and industry and, finally, further data from those retrenched from formal employment.

[23]To make comparisons between the formal and informal sectors of the economy, and especially changes over time, requires a benchmark norm, such as the percentage of people in the sector below the poverty datum line.

actions to enable an accelerated expansion of the urban informal sector (Peters-Berries, 1993; Mhone, 1995).

A growing body of literature has analysed the development of the informal sector during adjustment, focusing on formal-informal sector linkages, the credit and financial constraints of the sector, the education and skills profiles and requirements of entrepreneurs and workers in the sector, gender aspects and the impact of the changing policy environment. Studies of Tanzania's informal sector noted its dependence on the formal sector and its importance for urban households as a source of income. ILO-sponsored research has examined the sector's potential for employment and income generation and the relationship between the State and the informal sector economy (ILO, 1991; 1993; Bagachwa and Lavanga, 1993). An employment policy advisory paper for Kenya emphasized the role of the informal sector in the creation of employment. It included proposals to accelerate small-scale and *Jua Kali* (sun-exposed) enterprise development through harmonization of regulation, credit and finance as well as infrastructural and institutional support (ILO, 1995b).

The changing terms of employment in sub-Saharan Africa

Real wage development under adjustment
The process of wage determination in Africa has been extensively studied in the literature on economic development. In pioneering work on the subject in the early 1950s, Lewis formulated a closed dualistic economy model to examine the process of modernization of a labour-surplus economy. In the 1960s, this work was given a neoclassical orientation by Fei-Ranis in the form of an open dualistic economy model and by Harris and Todaro in the form of a rural-urban migration model based on a lifetime income stream. Subsequent empirical applications of these models have been concerned with the developmental experiences of African LDCs (see Mazumdar, 1994 for surveys).

A common feature of most African economies is the existence of a large rural-urban wage gap. If the wage gap could be attributed to differences in factors such as the costs of training or the quality of labour, no market imperfection need be present. These factors, however, do not explain the bulk of the observed wage differences, and studies have focused on government policies in labour markets. The general pattern is that of a rural labour market for relatively unskilled labour in which wages for rural workers are approximately equal to their average productivity. The rural markets may be of a competitive nature with a large number of employers (mainly small farmers), an abundance of unemployed labour, adequate information on wage rates and considerable geographical mobility of labour. In contrast, non-competitive conditions prevail in urban labour markets for semi-skilled labour. This is attributed to government actions such as minimum wage legislation, as well as trade union organizations and the presence of high paying, enclave-type transnational corporations. These factors raise urban wages in the modern sector significantly above rural wage rates.

While the causes of the rural-urban wage gaps are still being debated, evidence indicates that the size of the gap is indeed quite substantial in several African countries. A recent study by Mazumdar (1994) provides the following estimates for 1988 of the ratio of average earnings in manufacturing to agriculture in several African countries: Botswana (3.4), Ghana (2.0), Kenya (2.6), Malawi (4.6) and Zimbabwe (4.3). Using the same ILO data sources, the ratios between (nominal) manufacturing and agricultural wages for 1991 were as follows: Botswana (2.1), Kenya (2.7), Ghana (0.9), Malawi (3.1) and Zimbabwe (4.8). Hence, under structural adjustment this indicator appears to have declined in some cases (Botswana, Ghana and Malawi), whereas it has increased in other cases (Kenya and Zimbabwe).[24] Mazumdar's observation that it is 'impossible to make generalizations which are even approximately valid for African economies as a whole' appears to continue to hold during adjustment in the 1990s (Mazumdar, 1994: 74).

Jamal emphasizes that both urban and rural African households tend to participate in the economy in highly diversified, multi-occupational ways, which he refers to as 'emergent straddling survival strategies' (Jamal, 1995: 3). He argues that the key assumption of the adjustment model, namely, that the relative prices need to change in favour of tradeables, much of which are agricultural export commodities, is inappropriate in the African context. He contends that a change in the relative economic fortune of one sub-sector of the economy (such as the export crop sub-sector, or the urban formal sector) may lead to only a limited *reallocation* of labour towards that sub-sector. It may, however, prompt a very considerable change in the private payments and remittance flows which occur continuously within households (or between households of the same clan, etc.).[25] One implication of the 'straddling' survival hypothesis is that migration flows are not determined by the individual's perception of rural/urban income differentials (as suggested by the Harris-Todaro framework), but that such migration is part of a strategy of the extended family to diversify and reduce dependence on any single source of income and economic activity. Falling real wages have therefore failed to stem rural/urban migration flows. This feature is central to Jamal's explanation of why SAPs adopted across SSA have not led to the intended acceleration of growth. Furthermore, he notes that the terms of trade losses experienced in many African economies during the 1970–90 period limited the scope for shifting relative prices in favour of agricultural export crops.

Other instances of major change, with its attendant instability and far-reaching effects on African labour markets, are:

- the rapid urbanization throughout Africa, with the urban population growing at more than twice the rate of the overall population;
- the rapidly declining importance of wage employment in the formal sector and the concomitant dramatic expansion of the informal sector, which by now provides more than 80 per cent of urban employment;[26]
- the rapidly falling real wages in the formal wage sector since the early 1970s; for example, monthly real wages in Sierra Leone in 1987 stood at less than 6 per cent of the peak wage level of 1970, whereas for Tanzania in 1991 they were 25 per cent of the peak in 1974. The urban formal wage for a one-person month could buy only three days of essentials in Sierra Leone and just two weeks in Tanzania.

Hence, the share of wages in the total income of urban dwellers has been reduced very sharply and an increasing share of household income, much of which is

---

[24]As indicated below, real manufacturing wages have declined in real terms in many African countries.

[25]Those experiencing a 'boom' would share some of the unanticipated windfall gains with those in less fortunate sectors. Such sharing is a mutual insurance which reflects, among other things, the expectation that the gains may only be temporary in a context of continued instability of prices, due to weather and climatic factors, transport bottlenecks, dramatic shifts in international commodity prices, etc.

[26]Jamal comments that 'never in history did such massive urbanization occur without a concomitant increase in formal sector employment'. The estimates presented are for Sierra Leone, Tanzania and Zambia and they assume that 45 per cent of the urban population is in some form of employment (Jamal, 1995: 13–14).

unrecorded, is derived from a variety of informal jobs. In the rural areas a similar pattern prevails.

Only a few studies have analysed wage behaviour at the firm level in adjusting economies in Africa (Knight, 1981; Knight and Sabot, 1983). This undoubtedly reflects the fact that the necessary information on the determinants of wages is difficult to obtain, often requiring the implementation of large and expensive firm-level studies. An exception is Jones (1994) who attempted to examine the determinants of manufacturing wages using data from a 1993 sample survey of 200 firms in Ghana.[27] He estimates an earnings function across enterprises in order to assess the following determinants of the levels of wage differences between firms: gender, apprenticeship, five variables describing educational achievements and five industry-specific dummy variables.[28] It was found that previous work experience and educational attainment were important determinants of the level of earnings realized in Ghanaian manufacturing during the period of adjustment.

We now turn to the issues of human capital and training under adjustment.

Human capital and training under adjustment
The frequent assertion that SSA has suffered from low productivity because of a shortage of skilled labour does not give much information about the nature and extent of the problem, nor does it shed much light on desirable and feasible policy recommendations. The overall productivity levels and their trends are poor if compared with other developing countries (see above). However, disaggregation does reveal strong as well as weak performances. Skill shortages, particularly in manufacturing industry, may occur because: (i) educated entrepreneurs and technically qualified workers are in short supply in a given country; (ii) enterprises invest too little in training; and (iii) enterprises lose skills as employees leave to join other firms or to establish their own enterprises. Evidence on entrepreneurial and technical education, the training of workers and labour turnover are reviewed in turn in order to provide a basis for policy recommendations on human resources development strategies and training in the SSA context.

Human capital. An eclectic approach to the causes of productivity growth in Africa suggests that, while greater outward orientation may contribute to raising productivity growth, the current conditions of early industrialization in Africa necessitate simultaneous attention to creating general and technical skills via education and training. This has been argued by among others, Cassen and Mavrotas (1997) and Lall and Wignaraja (1997). Without this skill creation, these analysts argue, the responsiveness of output to improved incentives is likely to be limited. They assert that considerable empirical evidence shows that industrial success in East Asia has been associated with education and training as well as outward-oriented trade policies.

This view is supported by micro-level evidence on productivity differences in Africa. An early study on Ghana used a range of variables, including the age of the firm, education levels of the workers and experience of the entrepreneur, to account for productivity differences. Interestingly, only the education level of the workers turns up as statistically significant (Page, 1980). This confirms the hypothesis that

---

[27]The survey was funded by the World Bank as part of its Regional Program on Enterprise Development (RPED).

[28]The education variables were the percentage of workers with primary schooling, with secondary schooling and with polytechnic diplomas. However, the percentage of workers with middle schooling or university education were not significantly related to the earning differentials between the enterprises.

worker education is an important determinant of industrial productivity. Other studies have focused more on managerial rather than worker skills to explain productivity differences. A study of Kenya and the Philippines suggests that in both countries the major cause of low productivity in factories is too large a diversification of products and consequently short production runs (Pack, 1988). It goes on to suggest that in many factories inadequate management skills also contribute to low productivity, compared with international best practice. A similar finding was reported by Abdouli in a cross-country study of productivity in several African countries (1989) which concluded as follows:

> it seems that technical performance is mostly affected by the quality of management in charge of decision making, and to a lesser degree, by the size of the enterprise itself (Abdouli, 1989: 27).

These results are confirmed by the literature on firm-level technological capabilities. Lall and Wignaraja (1997) attempted to account for the variation in technological capabilities in a sample of Ghanaian firms. Among other things, they found that there was a highly significant difference between the years of education of entrepreneurs of technologically competent and other firms. In terms of technical manpower, competent firms also had a significantly higher proportion of scientists, engineers and technicians in their workforces than other firms. Lall and Wignaraja concluded that human capital was a vital factor in accounting for differences in technological performance in firms under adjustment. However, enterprise training proved to be an important factor as well.

Some insights on the nature of entrepreneurial education and training in African-owned enterprises can be gained from a recent study covering 269 small enterprises in Tanzania, Mali, Malawi and Ghana (Parker et al., 1995). It found that entrepreneurs in small enterprises (6–49 employees) had more years of formal schooling than the general population, averaging 11.9 years in Malawi, 11.2 years in Tanzania, 10.2 years in Ghana and 6.7 years in Mali. However, only about 20 per cent of small enterprise owners in Tanzania and Ghana had some form of post-secondary education (such as a technical school), while in the other two countries the proportion was much smaller. This confirms that the levels of technical education amongst African entrepreneurs are comparatively low.

Such low levels of technical entrepreneurial education need not constitute a barrier to enterprise growth, provided that other employees within the enterprise are technically qualified. A separate study on 34 enterprises (large as well as small and medium-scale enterprises) in Ghana offers an insight on the employment of technical manpower at the firm level (Lall et al., 1994). It revealed very low levels of use of technical manpower; the employment of engineers in Ghanaian metal-working firms, for instance, was under 1 per cent of the total labour force. This may be compared with the figures for the employment of engineers in metal-working firms in India and Sri Lanka which were, respectively, 6.5 and 2.8 per cent. The comparison with the two Asian countries illustrates the extent of skill upgrading that may be needed if Ghanaian firms are to adopt more complex industrial processes. The Ghana study also showed that the employment of technical personnel tends to be concentrated in a few firms; nearly 60 per cent of the total number of engineers in the metal-working sector was concentrated in only 2 firms.

Enterprise training. Empirical evidence of firms in Asian LDCs has shown that, although various kinds of experience in production played some role in augmenting technological capabilities within firms, the effort to undertake explicit training was probably more significant. As technologies evolve, a continued process of job-specific training and retraining is required to supply the technical and managerial skills needed by process and product innovations. Increasing linkages between firms and training institutions, which result in a conscious transmission of information and skills, are also a vital feature of industrialization. Frequent contact with training institutions can provide a valuable input into technological development by undertaking activities with public goods characteristics and filling in for deficient markets. As SAPs imply the rapid liberalization of restrictions on imports of goods and services, increased competition from imports will result. Enterprise performance in an increasingly outward-oriented economy depends on the acquisition of technological capabilities to cut costs, improve productivity and upgrade quality. Formal education is essential for the acquisition of technological capabilities; it depends fundamentally on the training of the workforce. Active enterprise training is crucial for the acquisition of technological capabilities in African economies under adjustment.

Hence, we examine the available evidence on enterprise training in four African economies (Ghana, Kenya, Tanzania and Zimbabwe) which have introduced SAPs in the 1980s and early 1990s. Recent studies of the process of acquiring technological capabilities in enterprises during adjustment, using a similar questionnaire and interview method, investigated the extent to which training incidence had changed. Enterprise training incidence in manufacturing was defined broadly to capture both informal and formal training within firms as well as inter-firm linkages with institutions that provide training and other technical services. The latter has been neglected in most discussions of enterprise training in developing countries, but it is a vital component of human capital formation and productivity improvement at enterprise level.

Kenya adopted SAPs early in the 1980s, but limited progress was made in terms of trade policy reform during the decade. However, in the early 1990s, Kenya resumed its adjustment programme and implemented a series of sweeping trade policy reforms (see above). Information is available on enterprise training in Kenyan manufacturing from a survey conducted in February/March 1995 covering 41 firms in garments and engineering (Wignaraja and Ikiara, forthcoming). Table 3.3 provides some summary measures of enterprise training in two Kenyan manufacturing industries, garments and engineering, namely, the percentage of sales proceeds devoted to training, the percentage of employees sent on external training

Table 3.3 *Enterprise training under adjustment, Kenya, the United Republic of Tanzania and Zimbabwe, 1989 and 1994*

Country	% of sales spent on training, 1994	% of employees sent on external training at home and abroad		% of employees as traditional apprentices, 1994
		1989	1994	
Kenya (41 firms):				
Garments	0.13	0.27	0.47	19.6
Engineering	0.13	0.6	1.21	19.6
Tanzania, United Rep. of (61 firms):				
Garments	negligible	0	0	negligible
Engineering	negligible	4.1	4.5	negligible
Zimbabwe (33 firms):				
Garments	negligible	n.a.	0.4	0.9
Engineering	negligible	n.a.	3.9	3.8

Sources: Wignaraja and Ikiara (forthcoming) on Kenya; Deraniyagala and Semboja (forthcoming) on Tanzania; Latsch and Robinson (forthcoming) on Zimbabwe.

and the percentage of employees who were apprentices. The table also provides comparable information on Tanzania and Zimbabwe from enterprise studies conducted during the same period. The following conclusions may be drawn from the table. First, a high proportion of employee training in Kenya still occurs through the traditional African apprenticeship system: it covered 19.6 per cent of garment employees and 16.9 per cent of engineering employees in 1994. Secondly, the proportion of resources devoted to formal employee training in Kenyan firms is still very low (i.e. 0.13 per cent in both garments and engineering in 1994). Thirdly, the share of employees sent on external training courses increased slightly from 0.27 per cent to 0.47 per cent in garments during 1989–94 and from 0.60 to 1.21 per cent in engineering. In spite of the increase, these ratios are still quite low by the standards of other developing countries.

The Kenya survey also indicates few linkages with training and other institutions. Table 3.4 shows the percentage of firms using five main training institutions within each industry in 1989 and 1994. Of the 41 sample firms, 15 (i.e. 36.6 per cent) used an institution in 1994. This represents a notable increase over 1989 when only 6 firms (14.6 per cent) said that they had used an institution. However, the pattern of usage still remains highly skewed towards a single institution. The Kenya Bureau of Standards (KBS) is used by the largest number of firms in both industries; 30 per cent of garment firms and 33.3 per cent of engineering firms used the KBS in 1994. None of the other institutions were used by any of the garment firms in 1994, while the Kenya Industrial Research and Development Institute (KIRDI) and the Department of Engineering at the University of Nairobi were each used by 14.2 per cent of the engineering firms. The Jomo Kenyatta University of Agriculture and the Kenya Polytechnic were each used by only 4.8 per cent of the engineering firms. This indicated that Kenyan firms have recorded little improvement in training during adjustment.

Wignaraja and Ikiara's study confirms the findings of an earlier analysis of 40 enterprises in Kenya on the extent of formal training for workers as well as for technicians (Teitel, 1993). Of the 40 firms, 83 per cent said that they provided some form of on-the-job training for workers; however, most were vague on the exact nature and duration of such training. In addition, it was found that only 25 per cent of the firms had paid for training for technical personnel outside the firm – including studies towards a technical degree, management and computer training, production and tool room training as well as short seminars. The bulk of the training outside the enterprise was provided in the country rather than overseas. The study concluded that on-the-job and off-the-job programmes were weak in Kenyan enterprises.

Ghana, like Kenya, started its adjustment programme relatively early with the introduction of the Economic Recovery Programme in 1983. Ghana's trade reform

Table 3.4   *Percentage of firms using training and other institutions, Kenya, 1989 and 1994*

	KBS		KIRDI		Univ. of Nairobi, Dept. Engineering		J. Kenyatta Univ. of Agriculture		Kenya Polytechnic	
	1989	1994	1989	1994	1989	1994	1989	1994	1989	1994
Garments	10	30	0	0	0	0	0	0	0	0
Engineering	14.3	33.3	0	14.2	4.8	14.2	4.8	4.8	4.8	4.8

Note: Abbreviations, see text.

Source: Wignaraja and Ikiara (forthcoming). Information collected from a survey of 41 enterprises in garments and engineering.

effort was sustained and credible in the 1980s. Today, Ghana is widely acknowledged as having one of the most open trade regimes in Africa; indeed it is viewed as a potential newly industrializing economy (NIC) by some (World Bank, 1994a). Hence, one would expect that training efforts in Ghanaian firms are likely to have risen during adjustment. However, a study undertaken in mid-1992 covering 34 firms in four industries (garments, woodworking, food processing and engineering) (Lall and Wignaraja, 1997) found that formal training efforts in the sample firms were negligible. None of the garment firms sent employees on external training in 1991, while the share of employees sent by engineering firms was only 0.31 per cent, by food processing firms 0.24 per cent and by woodworking firms 0.19 per cent. The study observed that the bulk of the training in Ghanaian firms still took the form of traditional apprenticeships rather than explicit employee training, and that overseas training was limited to a few multinational affiliates which regularly sent employees abroad for training. It concluded that, contrary to expectations, Ghanaian firms have recorded little improvement in training during adjustment.

Tanzania may be considered a relatively late adjuster. Although an Economic Recovery Programme was initiated in 1986, significant trade liberalization did not take place until the late 1980s. However, trade policy reforms since then have been sustained and are regarded as credible; the World Bank credits Tanzania as scoring high on an index of changes in macroeconomic policy (World Bank, 1994: 260–61). A study undertaken in February/March 1995 involving 61 firms in garments and engineering sheds light on the nature of enterprise training (Deraniyagala and Semboja, forthcoming). As Table 3.3 shows, it did not find significant evidence of traditional African apprenticeship in the sample firms. At the same time, it found that formal training efforts were extremely limited in the Tanzanian firms. As in Kenya, the proportion of resources devoted to training was still negligible in 1994. In addition, the garment firms had not sent any employees on external training courses in 1989 or in 1994, while the share of employees sent by engineering firms increased modestly from 4.1 per cent to 4.5 per cent over the same period. There was little increase in the incidence of linkages with training institutions in Tanzania.

Zimbabwe adopted trade liberalization only in the early 1990s. A study undertaken in February/March 1995 involving 33 firms in garments and engineering illustrates the extent of firm-level training (Latsch and Robinson, forthcoming). The results of this survey are reported in Table 3.3. In contrast to Kenya, the Zimbabwean study found low levels of traditional apprenticeship in both industries in 1994 – 0.9 per cent of employees in the garments firms and 3.8 per cent in the engineering firms. But, similar to Ghana, Kenya and Tanzania, it found that formal enterprise-level training efforts were very low. The available evidence indicated negligible training budgets and low proportions of employees sent on external training in both sectors. The study further noted that the sample firms in both sectors had not significantly increased their contacts with the country's training institutions since adjustment. In some cases, declines in contacts were reported.

Some of the findings on enterprise training reported by Latsch and Robinson (forthcoming) are confirmed by a larger study involving 200 manufacturing enterprises in Zimbabwe carried out in 1993 (Gunning and Mbengegwi, 1995). The authors found that only 19 per cent of the enterprises had used one of the country's five main institutions in 1993. The Standards Association of Zimbabwe was the only institution used by the largest number of firms (i.e. 16.5 per cent). Interestingly, none of the firms said that they had sent their employees to the National University of Science and Technology for enterprise training.

More recently, in their survey of 45 manufacturing enterprises, Lall, Wignaraja, Robinson and Sellek (1997) also reported a low incidence of formal industrial training in Zimbabwe six years after the adoption of adjustment policies (see Table 3.5). Most firms relied heavily on on-the-job training and the traditional apprenticeship system rather than more formal types of skill formation. Out of 45 sample enterprises, only 33.3 per cent had in-house training programmes. In addition, few firms paid for employees to obtain technical training outside the firm (only 0.1 per cent of employees in the garments firms, 0.1 per cent in the wood products firms and 1.0 per cent in the engineering firms were involved in such training). The limited external training took place in local training institutes which typically lacked the capacity (equipment, workshops and trained faculty) to undertake skill formation geared to rapidly changing industrial technologies. There was hardly any evidence of more relevant overseas plant-based training in the sample firms. Thus, on the basis of these studies, there is little evidence to suggest that a significant improvement in training has occurred in the manufacturing sector in Zimbabwe during adjustment.

Finally, we consider some more general evidence from other African countries on the training incidence. A survey of 1,570 entrepreneurs in microenterprises in Niger, Nigeria, Senegal and Togo provides data on the types of training within enterprises (Birks et al., 1994). The study found that the bulk of the training in these African enterprises took the form of traditional apprenticeships, where a young entrant with little knowledge about a given profession learns by working alongside an experienced worker. The traditional African apprenticeship system is geared towards primary school leavers and involves little additional formal education. It is directed towards transferring relatively low-level manufacturing skills which do not alter much over time and do not require numerical abilities. There is no formal certification at the end of the apprenticeship period and the apprentices receive a wage well below the going market rate.

Thus, the evidence does not indicate a reduction in training in the manufacturing sectors of the four African countries; however, only slight improvements in training occurred in two of them (Kenya and Tanzania). Most of the change has taken the form of a decline in the coverage of traditional African apprenticeship. But formal training efforts have shown few signs of increasing. This could be one area where a proactive approach to Africa's adjustment by labour market institutions including employers and unions may be of particular importance.

Labour turnover. We now turn briefly to the influence of labour turnover on training. The Ghana study found that rates of labour turnover were variable, with metal-working and garments firms having a relatively high turnover of 8 and 6 per cent respectively (Lall et al., 1994). It also found that there was some propensity for the higher turnover rates to be concentrated in the smaller enterprises. The

Table 3.5   *Enterprise training and labour turnover, Zimbabwe, 1991 and 1996*

Industry	Number of firms with in-house training programmes	% of workforce sent on external training programmes	Worker turnover rates as % of employment	
	1996	1996	1991	1996
Garments (24 firms)	6	0.1	0.4	6.0
Wood products (9 firms)	4	0.1	0.3	5.9
Engineering (12 firms)	5	1.0	1.7	1.8

Source: Lall et al., 1997.

Zimbabwe study by Lall *et al.*, 1997 reported an increase in labour turnover rates between 1991 and 1996 (Table 3.5). The highest rates were in garments and wood products where labour demand was increasing. It noted that it was likely that the leakage of skills through turnover might have constituted a barrier to investment in training, but this needed to be ascertained through further investigation.

In sum, the available evidence points to the prevalence of three separate though related sources of skill shortages in Africa. Educated entrepreneurs and technically qualified workers are in short supply; enterprises invest too little in training; and enterprises lose skills as employees leave to join other firms or to establish their own enterprises.

Tripartite consultation and the role of trade unions and employers

Tripartite consultations under adjustment: Scope and limitations
We now turn to a review of the labour institutions dealing with the organization and representation of labour and employers. Tripartite consultation in sub-Saharan Africa was much written about and discussed in the 1970s, but dropped off the agenda of policy decision-makers during the 1980s and 1990s.[29] This partly reflects the process of policy decision-making in the economic reforms during the 1980s, which became increasingly 'closed' and characterized by limited, if any, consultation between the various interest groups, including employers' organizations and trade unions.

Many sub-Saharan African countries have ratified ILO Conventions: by October 1994, African countries had, on average, ratified some 27 Conventions. This may be taken as an indicator, albeit highly imperfect, of a country's commitment to the management of labour relations according to international principles. Conventions with direct implications for labour relations include those on the freedom of association and tripartite consultation;[30] the latter has been ratified by 12 countries in SSA.[31] Notwithstanding this formal commitment, the practice has been less exemplary, with state interventions 'aimed at controlling trade union activity' (ILO, 1994: 27). Others have registered concern at the 'tendency of our governments to negotiate structural adjustment programmes with both the IMF and the World Bank without involving or consulting their national employers' and workers' bodies or even the ministries of labour'.[32]

As we argued earlier, employers' organizations and trade unions can make significant inputs into the economic policy decision-making process, in particular where there are major policy reforms with uncertain outcomes. These inputs may be of a functional or a political nature. Functional inputs can be in terms of in-depth information about the functioning of segments of labour markets or regarding the likely impact which policy reforms may have on, for example, large-scale public and private enterprises.

---

[29]Across sub-Saharan Africa, a rudimentary structure for negotiation between organized labour and employers' organizations has existed since the 1920s (see, e.g. Mazumdar, 1994).

[30]These are the ILO's international labour Conventions Nos. 87 and 98 on, respectively, freedom of association and protection of the right to organize, and the right to organize and collective bargaining, and Convention No. 144 on tripartite consultation (international labour standards). For a comprehensive overview of international labour Conventions and their ratification, see ILO, 1995c: 108–9.

[31]These were Côte d'Ivoire, Gabon, Kenya, Malawi, Mauritius, Nigeria, Sierra Leone, Tanzania, Togo, Uganda, Zambia and Zimbabwe. Countries with a relatively limited commitment, as indicated by few ratifications, included Botswana and Zimbabwe with less than 10 ratifications each.

[32]The Secretary-General of the Pan-African Employers' Confederation speaking at an ILO-sponsored conference in 1992 (ILO, 1994).

The arguments for and against consultations between government, trade unions and/or employers' organizations reflect the limitations to consultations in a tripartite framework as well as the opportunities and benefits which these may have (Trebilcock, 1994). Potential benefits, drawing on the terminology used by Nelson (1994), are:

(i)   'corporatism' – for example, where trade unions and employers' organizations are able, through influencing their membership, to engage actively in negotiated settlements regarding wage demands, employment levels, training and productivity deals;

(ii) 'informational efficiency' – i.e. any implementation of adjustment measures and programme components requires in-depth knowledge of the microeconomic environment in which the measures are expected to generate positive impacts (now and later).

Hence, consultation as a part of the implementation process of SAPs could have a positive impact on productivity – and one much needed in view of the evidence reviewed above. The potential gains, resulting from increased efficiency, improved organization, restructuring of the sector and other changes in the macroeconomic and trade regimes, may be shared in a negotiated way between the various producers. To realize the potential productivity gains and move closer to 'best practice' requires co-ordinated actions; indeed, the parties are unlikely to realize such potential gains in isolation. As indicated above, training within enterprises constitutes one example of such a positive sum game. Consultation may serve to identify how policy reforms adopted at the macro-level can be made to generate the desired positive impacts at the decentralized micro-level of the enterprise or household-based production units (Moshi and Maenda, 1993).

The representativeness of the organizations involved is a key determinant of the extent of the possible gains. The effectiveness of consultation depends on which sub-groups of employers or workers the organizations represent and through which internal consultation processes. Finally, indirect gains from consultation may accrue to other members of the society (for example, the user of a service delivered, etc.). In cases of external benefits of tripartite consultation, some governmental actions in order to bring about the consultation may be desirable.

These potential benefits of consultations in bi- and tripartite frameworks have not been realized in the sub-Saharan African context under adjustment: effective formal or informal consultation hardly took place. One might enquire why the governments would prefer not to consult. The following are amongst the reasons noted by unions (OTTU, 1992; Egulu, 1995):

(i)   a 'fear of obstruction' of the adjustment programme;[33]
(ii)   a perceived 'non-representativeness' of the parties involved: unions and employers' organizations are not representative of the workforce (or the employers) as a whole;
(iii) the 'own' interest of the government as a large employer.[34]

---

[33]For example, if the reduction of employment is seen as 'inevitable' by those designing the programme, then there is little scope for a negotiated settlement.

[34]This may be increasingly important in the context of adjustment oriented towards institutional change, which includes reductions in public sector employment.

Impact of adjustment on trade unions

Gibbon's (1993) edited volume brings together a wide range of papers on the social and political aspects of economic reforms and structural adjustment in Africa.[35] Gibbon notes that the adjustment period has 'been marked by a growing assertiveness on the part of (some) civil society organizations', and presents evidence to this effect from Kenya and Zimbabwe in particular.

In Kenya relations between the state and civil institutions have responded to the increasingly important role of the dominant political party (KANU) during the 1980s. Different civil society organizations faced different fates, including deregistration, dissolution and 'beheading', sliding into slumber, reconstitution as patronage networks of KANU, co-optation into KANU and, lastly, heightened activism (Ngunyi and Gathiaka, 1993: 37). For example, the *matatu* (mini-bus taxi) owners' association was deregistered, as were the university's staff union and its student organization.[36] The authors describe the co-optation of the Central Organization of Trade Unions (COTU) as a 'spectacular instance of cooption of [a] mass organization by KANU' (*ibid*.: 41). By the end of the 1980s COTU had a total of 350,000 members – approximately 50 per cent of private sector wage employees. In 1989 KANU announced the affiliation of COTU to itself. This caused internal divisions within COTU, followed by splits culminating in the formation of a second 'national' congress and a new federation of workers. In the context of increasing pressure on KANU during the early 1990s on the part of international donors, including conditionality regarding KANU's intransigence with respect to political pluralism, COTU has emerged as a 'main source of opposition to structural adjustment' (*ibid*.: 48).

Political relations between the Government of Zimbabwe and the Zimbabwe Congress of Trade Unions (ZCTU), the apex organization of organized labour, have become problematic after a period of relative tranquillity in the early 1980s, as the state embarked on a 'project of cooptation' (Sachikonye, 1993: 255). This was fiercely resisted by the ZCTU in a context in which real wages in both the public and the private sector were falling and employment opportunities declining (see above). Collective bargaining and wage determination were among the key issues on which the ZCTU and employers' organizations agreed on bilateral consultation. As part of the ESAP the government committed itself to facilitating bilateralism within which employers and employees would negotiate agreements within Employment Councils. However, this intended governmental self-restraint was never practised. For example, in 1991 bilateral talks agreed wage increases at slightly below the inflation rate, which was a considerable improvement on the previous year. However, the government intervened in the wage-setting with a variety of arguments. For the public sector, it argued that local authorities' wage agreements fell under the purview of the government as an employer through its Ministry of Local Government; parastatal agreements were limited to the increases agreed for the civil service. For the private sector, the government advocated staggering the increased wage payments over several months, even though this was not part of the bilaterally negotiated agreements. In April 1992 the government tabled a Labour

---

[35]The study includes papers on Kenya, Lesotho, Tanzania and Zimbabwe.

[36]An example of a 'beheaded' organization was the Kenya Farmers' Association (KFA), which had previously built up a sole-agency monopoly position for the parastatal grain marketing board, NCPB. In the early and mid-1980s, new regional co-operative agencies were reconstituted to supply credit and inputs, which amounted to an expansion of KANU's patronage networks. The Civil Servants' Association, which sought to improve the professional performance of the civil service, was banned (Cohen, 1993).

Relations Amendment Bill, reversing the pledge of bilateral wage-setting. Sachikonye notes that 'the emphasis now announced was on state powers to fix maximum wages'. Hence, he comments that 'by mid-1992, in the wake of the government's introduction of the Labour Relations Amendment Bill and the banning of ZCTU protest against it, tripartism appeared further away than ever' (*ibid.*).

The ZCTU expressed the following opinions regarding the design and implementation of the ESAP (ILO, 1992). Key points emerging from a trade union perspective were that:

(i)   the issue of *ownership* of capital was ignored. Hence, the political objective of moving towards a level playing field between 'emerging' indigenous entrepreneurs and industrialists and 'established' non-indigenous industrialists (both domestic and foreign) was not advanced;

(ii) the implementation of the ESAP was perceived as flawed and ill-planned in a number of respects, for example: (a) the trade liberalization measures, consisting of placing imported items on the list of the open general import licence (OGIL), were haphazard; and (b) the Social Development Fund was placed under a loans and grants allocation committee with no particular experience of the management of training and investment.

Another impact of adjustment is that the degree of unionization within sub-Saharan Africa has declined markedly under the SAPs. Comprehensive data are not available but the case of Uganda may constitute a typical example. The membership of the National Organization of Trade Unions (NOTU) decreased from an estimated 125,000 in 1987 to 52,647 by August 1995 – a decline of nearly 60 per cent with a concomitant weakening of their financial position (Egulu, 1995). This development in a context of declining real wages and falling employment renders views regarding the unionized 'labour aristocracy' out of date.

Regarding the role of trade unions, it is sometimes argued that the distributional outcome of unionization of the formal economy ... 'is likely to be regressive' (World Bank, 1995: 80). The role of labour market institutions is not evaluated in terms of efficiency, but in terms of a perceived negative distributional impact. It is pointed out that the percentage of workers which is organized or 'protected' is low – typically less than half the labour force in the formal sector. It is argued that these workers are usually not the lowest earning households within the economy. Hence, effective protection may increase the income inequality within the economy. A similar line of argument is advanced for the implementation of minimum wage legislation.

The income-distributional arguments against specific public regulations (such as the minimum wage) and the functioning of trade unions more generally, is based on at least two specific theoretical and empirical assumptions. The theoretical assumption may be called one of *segmentation* (or non-substitution) within the labour market: the effect of the improved conditions does not lead to an improvement in the conditions and terms, etc. of those people outside the organized segment. The empirical argument could be called one of *income selectivity*: the distributional argument assumes that the membership of a particular trade union is unevenly distributed across the income range, and only reflects an income category above the average. Within the sub-Saharan African context neither of these assumptions is likely to apply; we shall deal with each of them in turn.

The extent of organization in the labour markets in Africa is low and tends to cut across a wide range of different groups of employees; the highest degree of organized labour tends to be found in mining (both public and private), public utilities and services, including banks, the postal services, other non-privatized utilities and the civil service. These diverse groups of organized labour are not in the same labour market segment, nor is there necessarily much linkage between these diverse individual sectors. However, it is likely that agreements made between organized labour and the relevant employers will tend to affect the terms and conditions of employment throughout the sector, i.e. including non-organized workers. To the extent that this is the case, the theoretical assumption of non-substitution will not hold.

Furthermore, the diversity of organized workers (across sectors as well as within enterprises) implies that conditions of work and earnings will be diverse as well. Membership of trade unions includes earners below as well as above median earnings. The greater the spread of earning levels, the less likely it is that the underlying distribution of earnings will worsen because of trade union action or membership; indeed it may well improve.

The income-distributional changes in response to an effective implementation of the minimum wage cannot be predicted with certainty either. However, the nature of the regulation, which is focused on the lowest income category of wage earners, would tend to improve the existing income distribution. This is likely to remain the case even where there is a large category of low income non-wage earners, as is typical in subsistence agriculture. The two conditions are that: (i) the eligible wage earners are below the median income level and (ii) the number of people becoming unemployed and losing their wage earnings because of the introduction of an effective minimum wage is small relative to the number of earners who improve their income (but stay below the median income). These conditions appear quite plausible in the sub-Saharan African context.

Hence, the charge that trade union activities have negative income-distributional consequences may not be an accurate description of sub-Saharan Africa during adjustment policy reforms.

Impact of adjustment on employers' organizations
Owuor, representing the Pan-African Employers' Confederation, observed a range of economic and political effects of structural adjustment programmes which are likely to have a major influence on industrial relations (ILO, 1994). The economic effects which he observed have been confirmed by our survey. A reduction of formal wage employment levels and of the level of real wages is taking place through:

(i)   the loss of formal jobs through privatization and/or commercialization of state corporations, reductions in public expenditure and import liberalization;
(ii) subcontracting by larger firms to keep up with domestic and international competition which will tend to lower average wages;
(iii) repeal of minimum wage legislation in a bid, bound to be unsuccessful, to contain the expanding unemployment emerging from the restructuring process;
(iv) employers seeking to increase the flexibility of hiring and firing and remove rigid redundancy restrictions;
(v)   inflationary pressures forcing the removal of the wage guidelines.

Sachikonye analyses the relationship between state and enterprise in Zimbabwe in the context of the country's Economic and Social Action Plan (ESAP) adopted in 1990 (Government of Zimbabwe, 1991). He notes that two different diagnoses

of Zimbabwe's economic position run through the debates regarding the formulation, adoption and implementation of adjustment. The first explains the
country's sluggish GDP growth as the consequence of its insufficiently
favourable investment climate. Its policy prescription is to reduce: (i) the risks
associated with relatively high fiscal deficits; (ii) the costs as well as the uncer-
tainties surrounding the system of controlled foreign-exchange allocation; and
(iii) the cost of doing business in Zimbabwe more generally through price as well
as investment decontrols and amendment of the labour regulations. This diagnosis, espoused by the Bretton Woods institutions, became the main thrust of
ESAP's design.

The 'competing' alternative diagnosis is put forward by domestic industrialists
and independent economists. They point to the fact that GDP growth during
1985–90 stood at 4.2 per cent, notwithstanding the refusal by the government to
adopt a package proposed by the IMF with severe social expenditure reductions
in 1984. The relationship between private investment flows and adjustment
measures is questioned. Adjustment-related devaluations and the resulting
inflation hikes, which were not anticipated at the time of investment, were
among the reasons cited by investors for withholding further investment, especially in the manufacturing sector. The Director of the Confederation of
Zimbabwean Industries, representing large-scale manufacturing interests, went
on record in 1992 stating that the 'competing imports in their domestic markets
… could result in deindustrialization, not development' (*Financial Gazette*, 16
April, 1992).

In view of these changes, Owuor (ILO, 1994) suggests that income-maintaining
social safety nets will need to be introduced and the training of workers expanded.
He emphasizes that entrepreneurship training will also be needed to 'facilitate their
engagement in self-employment'.

Owuor noted a number of political trends, partly associated with structural
adjustment, which will reinforce the impact the far-reaching policy reforms may
have on industrial relations in Africa:

(i)   the move towards multi-party democracy may uncover and release pent-up
      pressures by trade unions which had previously been forced into 'political
      marriages of inconvenience' with dominant parties;[37]
(ii) political parties will seek to set up rival trade unions and splinter unions,
      thereby increasing the likelihood of industrial unrest;
(iii) the informalization of the African economies will adversely affect the quality of
      working conditions in the private sector and undermine the enforcement of
      labour laws and collective bargaining.

The process and pattern of moving towards multi-party democracy differs across
sub-Saharan African countries. A descriptive classification by Buijtenhuijs and
Thiriot (1995) distinguishes the 'old' democracies, such as Botswana, from countries
which held multi-party elections for the first time only in recent years. As a result of
these elections, governments changed in some countries, including Zambia, but in
many cases the governments did not change, for example in Kenya, Tanzania and
Zimbabwe from among our selected case-study countries. Finally, a few African-

---

[37]In sub-Saharan Africa this occurred in Benin, Burundi, Cape Verde, Chad, Congo, Gabon, Guinea-Bissau,
Rwanda, Togo, Tanzania and Zaire, according to the Secretary General of the Organization of African Trade Union
Unity (ILO, 1994).

style solutions to the pressures for democracy may be noted; the non-party-based elections of Uganda deserve special mention.[38]

Etukudo (1995) notes that, from the 1970s, it became increasingly difficult for employers' organizations to contribute to economic policy formulation. At independence, statutory tripartite bodies, covering subjects such as wages, prices and incomes and labour-management relations, existed only in name. African governments were hesitant to make use of them, in view of their domination by businesses identified with previous colonial regimes. It is only in the 1990s, with the advent of democratization, that a change of perception may be noted, though little of that has been put into practice to date.[39] A number of factors, political as well as structural, caused the weakness of tripartite consultations:

(i)   the weak or absent entrepreneurial middle class which, moreover, tends to be divided between the production enterprises (typically joining employers' organizations) and the distributive enterprises (represented through chambers of commerce), as well as other cleavages: small versus big business, multinational branches versus indigenous, etc.;

(ii) the preference of employers' organizations for bipartite consultations through separate exchanges with government and with trade unions;

(iii) meetings of the tripartite bodies were infrequent or not convened at all; moreover, governments were represented at a low level and placed greater weight on presidential advisory commissions.

Employers' organizations such as the Kenya Association of Manufacturers and the Federation of Kenya Employers (FKE) 'have offered no serious challenge to government', even in instances where adjustment measures may have worked against the interests of their members (as the FKE's survey on the impact of trade liberalization in Kenya showed (FKE, 1991)). This 'muted ally' stance is explained by Ngunyi and Gathakia (1993) as reflecting a context in which the membership of the FKE does not differ 'much from the composition of members of government'.[40] Using a similar line of argument, Ikiara and his colleagues, in the same volume, note that the major agricultural parastatal, the NCPB, was used by the government to achieve political goals, as licences for inter-district movements of maize 'became a source of new political clients during the decade [of the 1980s]', and that implementation of the agricultural sector's adjustment has been 'generally blocked by a political elite, who have a wide range of well entrenched state-protected interests' (Ikiara et al., in Gibbon, 1993: 99).

However, in the context of adjustment measures, in particular privatization and domestic market liberalization, the importance of the government as an employer has tended to diminish. Hence, the scope for bilateral consultations between employees and employers has improved. Moreover, the democratization process has tended to erode the extensive control which government traditionally had over the labour market, making more space for other civil society institutions, including

---

[38]In a number of countries the transition to democracy is at an impasse. Buijtenhuis and Thiriot present an eloquent overview of the progress of the recent research on the transition to democracy in sub-Saharan Africa as well as the debates regarding the obstacles encountered, the risks of derailment and theoretical debates about the style of democracy, issues of governance and the role of civil society institutions in general (Buijtenhuijs and Thiriot, 1995).

[39]President Chiluba of Zambia advocated a 'change in attitude towards the relationship between government, employers and workers' at the International Labour Conference in Geneva in June 1992.

[40]Moreover, the authors assert that organizations such as employers' federations and chambers of commerce may have a role to play in the patronage-ridden distribution of licences to local businessmen.

organized employers and employees. The next section presents some recommendatons about consultation at the national and the labour market levels, drawing from the case studies in this volume.[41]

Consultations about development and labour markets

National governments
Since development is about improving the standard of living, consultation with the people provides governments with the necessary mandate to carry through development programmes. National (social) ownership of development programmes is essential for their sustainability. In addition, social participation provides the necessary clarity in terms of policy direction and helps in providing a national vision with which diverse groups can identify. This, in turn, provides the consensus which is so essential for the success of development programmes. It also eases the process of reform by removing the element of surprise. Consultation also encourages responsible behaviour on the part of civil society groups. Consultation should be a means to an end and not an end in itself, therefore implying the importance of achieving binding decisions from the process itself.

Areas of consultation should cover both developmental issues and labour market and employment issues. At the least the consultation would include the following: economic policy reforms; employment policy; and the social dimensions of adjustment.

Moreover, on specific issues, such as labour market flexibility, effective tripartite consultation would be appropriate. For consultations to be effective, they must be accompanied by capacity-building, especially within the weaker organizations. The adoption of a comprehensive consultation policy by governments would imply an increased need for technical support to participants in the consultation process on legal and economic matters pertaining to the labour market and economic policy more generally. Capacity-building by the social partners for policy formulation becomes an important issue in its own right.

Although formal and informal modes of consultation may exist together, formal consultations are important as they involve public relations and accountability and enhance the sustainability of policies. A more formal structure also drives the informal process. Formal consultations should be institutionalized through Social and Economic Development Councils. Meetings should be held regularly – for example, quarterly – with an institutional link between the multipartite consultative body and the national parliament being developed. However, it is recommended that these two bodies maintain their separate identities.

For the consultative process to be representative and broad-based, all major national stakeholders should participate. Each country therefore has to identify the core national groups, which should include trade unions, employers' groups and NGOs. The process of creating the consultative body should be driven by the civic society groups, which should enlist the support of government and the international financial institutions.

A possible model for a Social and Economic Development Council may be South Africa's National Economic Development and Labour Advisory Council (NEDLAC).

---

[41]These recommendations were formulated at the 1996 Kampala seminar, which discussed different aspects of structural adjustment among government officials, workers, employers, NGO representatives, academics and officials from the ILO, IMF, World Bank and UNDP (see van der Geest and van der Hoeven, 1997).

However, the precise functioning of the councils has to be worked out at the national level, taking fully into account the existing institutions and the past experiences of each country separately.

National governments should also undertake specific measures for enhancing productivity in the economy. These are likely to involve the adoption of appropriate technologies and support for national productivity centres. In the dominant agricultural sector, issues relating to land tenure, credit and infrastructure should be included. The support of agriculture as the dominant sector should receive emphasis overall (alongside other sectors); the objective of employment promotion would be strengthened by the adoption of an explicit employment policy.

Employment and poverty reduction have not been explicit objectives of adjustment programmes in the past; these have concentrated on macroeconomic stabilization, and incentives for increased and regulatory reform. Employment and poverty reduction objectives should be included explicitly in the new 'fourth generation' of adjustment programmes, and regular review of the process in this regard is essential.

In order to operationalize these wider social objectives, *benchmarks* should be established with respect to target groups which may be bearing the brunt of poverty and unemployment; these would focus, in particular, on youth and on women. The benchmarks should be quantifiable in order to allow monitoring during the programmes. Safety nets should be provided for the vulnerable groups and these should involve employment promotion measures, including labour-intensive works. The implementation of such reviews will require the active participation of independent specialists and analysts, with the support of international development agencies (World Bank, ILO and others). The process would need to be initiated and followed by government ministries and agencies directly involved in the design and implementation of adjustment policies (finance, planning, central bank, trade and commerce, etc.). One implication is that direct collaborative efforts between the above-mentioned international agencies in the areas of trade policy review, civil and parastatal reform and public expenditure reviews, would be essential.

Ministries of Labour

Given the size of the shocks to formal labour markets under adjustment, in particular in view of the sharp reduction in public sector employment, Ministries of Labour may be required to broaden the scope of their activities beyond their traditional tasks of labour market regulation, inspection and monitoring as well as the exchange of labour market information. Amongst the new activities of Ministries of Labour may be an active role in the formulation of programmes to 'alleviate the social impact of structural adjustment' (ILO, 1994: 15). Such programmes will include, but cannot be limited to, two separate but related elements: (i) employment-oriented social funds programmes and (ii) skill retraining and self-employment training. We shall first discuss social funds programmes, drawing on a recent review by Stewart and van der Geest (1995), followed by a discussion of training initiatives.

Social Funds. Social funds (SFs) are a wholesale financing mechanism designed to accompany adjustment programmes. An early attempt was Ghana's Programme of Action to Mitigate the Social Costs of Adjustment (PAMSCAD). Social funds typically consist of a specified sum of money to be devoted to activities which will ease the pains of adjustment, including financing small-scale projects, training, and infrastructural projects. They are intended to be quick-disbursing and are often located outside the normal government machinery. Hence social funds programmes could be executed in consultation and collaboration with other social partners.

The objectives of SFs include poverty reduction; compensation of those directly adversely affected by adjustment programmes; gaining political support for adjustment programmes; and raising additional external finance. These objectives may conflict and often there is a mixture of motives; some schemes are more poverty-oriented and others more oriented towards political sustainability and direct compensation of those hurt by adjustment, for example in Zimbabwe.[42] Some SFs are multisectoral programmes which finance projects in economic infra-structure, social infrastructure, social assistance, as well as credit schemes. Ghana's PAMSCAD covered a variety of activities including urban public works, rural income-generating projects, school feeding and nutrition education. A major element of its funds (22 per cent) was allocated to the 'new poor' for compensation and training; two-thirds of the planned projects were urban. Zambia's Social Recovery Programme has financed labour-intensive projects in urban areas, designed to reach the poor. Zimbabwe's Social Development Fund (SDF) was to redeploy the retrenched as 'an immediate and urgent social imperative', but the government also recognized that 'there still remains the larger unemployment problem'. The SDF included an employment and training programme; provision of funds for projects initiated by ex-civil servants; targeted food subsidies; and refunding of the cost-recovery measures for vulnerable groups.

SF programmes have in general reached only a small fraction of the poor, partly because their total size is limited and partly because of poor targeting. Some countries have designed their own schemes without reference to external agencies and without external finance; these 'own-designed' schemes differ in significant respects from the externally supported SFs. Schemes designed, initiated and financed by the country itself in order to assist the poor during periods of crisis have been more effective in achieving that objective, being much more extensive and better targeted. Those schemes which tend to be supply-driven and utilize self-targeting, in particular through relatively low wage payments for work with low skill intensity, appear to have been more effective in targeting the poor, primarily as a result of self-selection mechanisms. Adopting administrative rules restricting access may also facilitate the coverage of deprived beneficiaries. Hence, the involvement of the social partners in the execution of social fund programmes is desirable from a political perspective as well as to achieve greater targeting efficiency in the design and implementation of the programmes. Nevertheless, in the sub-Saharan African context the financial constraints on the creation of employment-oriented social funds programmes will remain severe. Hence, their employment-creation impact can be expected to be quite limited. The social funds are primarily to be seen as a means of providing a safety net in the public sector retrenchment context and should not be seen as a substitute for the design and implementation of adjustment programmes which contribute to the creation of jobs and skills.

Training. Given the importance of training for improving productivity and building up technological capability (see above) and given the increased competition which local manufacturing and services will face under SAPs, a much greater effort to build up human capital is needed than is currently being under-

---

[42]This conclusion is derived from examining the stated objectives of the schemes and reviewing their main characteristics (Stewart and van der Geest, 1995: 8–12).

taken in sub-Saharan Africa. In view of the problems of labour retention within enterprises, training should be considered as a 'public good', as skills created are deployed elsewhere in the economy. Hence, training provision may merit government intervention. However the earning potential increases for individual workers in response to better training, it is high and may well be increasing further; in this sense training could be regarded as a 'private good'. Because of this dual character of skill formation, sectoral trade unions are well placed to be involved in the provision of training services as they represent the interests of potential beneficiaries.

The development of local institutions for industrial training is an area that requires urgent attention in Africa. In any given country, there are only one or two public institutions that seem to provide training support for local industry. The handful of institutions that train are characterized by a shortage of trained teachers, inadequate equipment, poor library facilities and limited contacts with overseas training institutions. Moreover, the bureaucratic operating procedures adopted by these institutions mean that there is little effective demand from industry for their services. Local firms rarely solicit public institutions to provide in-plant training for specialized technological needs. There is a need to create responsive, well-equipped training institutions in Africa; such institutions could adapt the experience of training and technology support for SMEs which is found in East Asia. (See Dahlman and Sananikoye, 1990, on the experience of Taiwan, China.)

Trade Unions
In view of the far-reaching impact which adjustment programmes have on the labour market and employment, it is desirable that trade unions improve their policy analysis and policy monitoring capacity. Given their limited capacity in this area at present, this could be achieved through a greater use of the existing networks of economic and legal analysts within the countries. This could be an input for a policy dialogue with the government which could focus on greater flex-ibility in the implementation of policy reforms, taking into account their direct and indirect employment consequences.

To participate in the design of public sector retrenchment programmes presents a strategic dilemma to trade unions: retrenchment involves a loss of employment and income opportunities for their members – indeed a loss of membership. However, the choice not to participate, which has been the common response in sub-Saharan Africa, may have led to results which were not the best possible. Where procedures and criteria for retrenchment are reviewed and negotiated with workers' represen-tatives and other associations, it is more likely that a greater degree of efficiency as well as fairness may be achieved.

Beyond policy advocacy trade unions will need to expand their welfare activities so 'as to cater for the social needs of the victims of structural adjustment' (ILO, 1994) through policy advice as well as direct service delivery to their membership. It appears important that the range of technical services which trade unions offer should be expanded. This would reinforce their established representative mandate which will remain focused on the negotiation of wages, the wider application of collective bargaining agreements and services related to the enforcement of workers' rights (legal services, court advice, etc.).

The specific problems of unmet training needs have to be addressed in a context of low investment by enterprises. The evidence indicates that the earnings premia on specialized technical training in sub-Saharan Africa are considerable (Horton *et al.*, 1994). The individual worker realizes this premium, either by changing enterprises or setting up a new one, except where set-up costs are prohibitively high. Though the acquisition of skills is a 'private good', the cost of organizing training is bound to be considerable and requires collective action. Hence, the provision of these services could benefit from inputs and management from larger organizations such as trade unions.

The informal sector appears to be the employer of last resort and is effectively the destination for the majority of school-leavers and retrenched formal sector workers across sub-Saharan Africa. It appears inevitable that trade unions will have to become actively involved in that sector too. Credit constraints are widely quoted as the binding constraint on small enterprise development and informal sector activities. Trade unions could take steps to develop mutual assurance savings and loans associations to help their members to start or expand small and medium-scale enterprises. This could be a component of SF programmes.

Employers' organizations

For employers' organizations, it appears equally imperative to improve their service delivery systems to private sector enterprises. This may take the form of the provision of management training, legal advice and counselling, etc. (see Bowland and Perera, 1985; Clemensson, 1993). Levels of employee training are extremely low in African industry compared with other developing regions that have successfully managed the transition to manufacturing for export. Few African enterprises, apart from multinational firms, invest in training their employees in modern technologies. As noted earlier, the traditional apprenticeship system does little to impart the requisite skills to absorb modern technologies. If Africa is to compete on international markets in a liberalized economic environment, levels of employee training need to be boosted. Firm-level training may be encouraged by tax breaks and grants, for a limited period, to permit the hiring of international trainers and to send employees abroad for in-plant training overseas. Multinational corporations should be encouraged to provide training to local subcontractors in order to upgrade industrial skills through time-bound incentive schemes.

Finally, employers' organizations should actively work closely with governments towards creating an enabling investment environment in sub-Saharan Africa.

Conclusion

This chapter has reviewed the available evidence on the dynamics of labour market behaviour under structural adjustment programmes in several sub-Saharan African economies. To the extent possible, it has tried to 'marry' empirical applications of the traditional labour economics literature in sub-Saharan Africa with recent work on the microeconomics of technical change and on the role of institutions. Such an eclectic approach sheds useful insights on a host of labour market issues not normally covered in surveys of this type – including industrial restructuring, employment change, real wage behaviour, the acquisition of technological capabilities, consultation and representative organization. The nature of the evidence and the unfinished adjustment agenda make it sometimes difficult to draw firm conclusions on the impact of adjustment programmes on employment and labour market institutions in sub-Saharan Africa. But the work surveyed indicates that the labour market is an influential determinant of the successful implementation of adjustment programmes and consequent economic performance and that further action is needed as suggested in the last section of the chapter.

On the basis of the issues raised above (in Chapters 1 and 2) and the literature review (in Chapter 3) the main propositions and questions on adjustment, employment and labour market institutions to be addressed through the country case studies may now be summarized as follows.

First, the stocks and flows of African employment will need to be charted in much greater detail. As for employment growth in a context of adjustment, to what extent has this taken place in the formal or the informal sector? Does the inflow of new job seekers into the labour market, reflecting the demographic situation, outstrip the increase in job opportunities? What is really known about the rural labour markets of sub-Saharan Africa? Did the expected favourable movements of agricultural income occur and have these translated into an expansion of agricultural work and jobs? What are the main data deficiencies for studying the stocks and flows in Africa's labour markets and how may these be addressed?

Secondly, an examination of real wage changes and productivity growth is called for and the implications for labour market policy need to be spelled out. To what extent have real wages fallen during adjustment, especially in view of the devaluation-inflation spirals which were found in adjusting Africa? Are there any countries where some form of indexation was practised successfully, even if only for segments of the labour market? Did the overall reduction in real wages result in an increase in the aggregate demand for labour? What are the main features of labour market policies for Africa's adjusted labour markets?

Thirdly, there is the overarching issue of human capital formation and technological capability acquisition. Have institutions for training and human capital formation emerged to deal with the mismatch between the skills required, especially in modern industry and services, and the skill profiles currently found? Are any of the institutions which facilitated East Asia's success in technology diffusion being replicated across Africa, either through private sector initiatives or through partnership with public support and development finance?

Fourthly, the organization and representation of labour and business in Africa's adjusted economies warrant close review. The 'rules of the game' are changing from

Table 3.6   *Summary of issues, indicators and emerging policy questions*

Issues to be examined	Indicators and impact analysis	Emerging policy questions
Adjustment-employment relationships	Formal/informal sector employment changes; average and marginal output; employment elasticities by sectors; public service employment and reforms	Does adjustment need to refocus on the informal sector? Is the formulation of a comprehensive public and private sector employment policy required?
Real wage developments, productivity and labour market practices	Changes in absolute and relative real wages; sectoral labour/value added profiles	Are core labour standards to be enforced? Is a minimum wage policy to be reinstated?
Training, skills and technology acquisition institutions	Institutional change and renewal; skill structures in production and trade	Are national productivity organizations focusing on the technology diffusion to be created?
Representative systems and effective articulation of interests	Emergence of consultative bodies and new coalitions; processes of democratization	How is analytical and policy advisory capability within and outside the public sector to be created?

protection-seeking public interventions, often characterized by low productivity, towards systems of regulation which enhance competitiveness. Has this also meant that old-style business and labour lobbying is being reformed? If so, what are the main dynamics of these processes? Are new representative organizations emerging and is new 'social capital' being created? What kind of new consultative arrangements are emerging? Do these imply that adjustment programmes are now home-grown and internalized?

Answers to all these questions may not be found for all the countries studied here: data deficiency remains a major problem. But more importantly, the examination undertaken may show that many of the important initiatives on the institutional side, relating to human capital formation, technology acquisition and the organization and representation of labour and business interests, may still need to be advanced a great deal in sub-Saharan Africa. But without institutional capability in these areas, positive responses to adjustment will be weak or missing.

References

Abdouli, A. (1989) 'Sources of Technical Efficiency in an African Context', *Public Enterprise*, Vol. 1, No. 9 (Ljubljana).

Bagachwa, M.S.D. and N.E. Lavanga (1993) *State and the Informal Sector in Tanzania: Report of a Study on the Development Policies and Institutional Environment for the Informal Sector in Tanzania*. Addis Ababa: ILO-JASPA.

Birks, S., F. Fluitman, X. Oudin and C. Sinclair (1994) *Skill Acquisition in Micro Enterprises: Evidence from West Africa*. Paris, OECD.

Bol, D. (1995) *Employment and Equity Issues in Tanzania*. Economic Research Bureau, University of Dar es Salaam.

Bourguignon, F. and C. Morrison (1992) *Adjustment and Equity in Developing Countries: A New Approach*. Paris: OECD.

Bowland, D. and J. Perera (1985) *Role of Employers' Organizations in Promoting Management Development*. Geneva: ILO.

Buijtenhuijs, R. and C. Thiriot (1995) *Democratization in sub-Saharan Africa, 1992–1995: An Overview of the Literature*. Leiden: Africa Studie Centrum.

Cassen, R. and G. Mavrotas (1997) 'Education and Training for Manufacturing Development' in M. Godfrey (ed.) *Skill Development for International Competitiveness*. Cheltenham, UK: Edward Elgar.

Clemensson, M. (1993) *Assistance to Employers' Organization (Project Report)*. Harare: ILO/SAMAT.

Cohen, J.M. (1993) 'Importance of Public Service Reform: The Case of Kenya', *Journal of Modern African Studies*, Vol. 31, No. 3.

Cooper, C. (1995) 'Technology, Manufactured Exports and Competitiveness', Maastricht: UNU INTECH (mimeo).

Cornia, G.A., R. van der Hoeven and T. Mkwandawire (1992) *Africa's Recovery in the 1990s: From Stagnation and Adjustment to Human Development*. London and Basingstoke: Macmillan.

Dahlman, C. and Sananikoye, O. (1990) 'Technology Strategy in the Economy of Taiwan: Exploiting Foreign Linkages and Investing in Local Capabilities'. Washington, DC: World Bank (mimeo).

Deraniyagala, S. and H. Semboja (forthcoming) 'Firm Performance under Trade Liberalisation in Tanzania' in S. Lall (ed.) *Opening Up or Shutting Down?* Basingstoke, UK: Macmillan.

Egulu, L. (1995) 'Structural Adjustment and Public Sector Employment Reduction in Uganda: A Trade Union Perspective'. Kampala: National Organization of Trade Unions (draft).

Etukudo, A. (1995) 'Reflections on the Role of African Employers' Organizations in Tripartism and Social Dialogue', *International Labour Review*, Vol. 134, No. 1.

Federation of Kenyan Employers (1991) 'Survey on the Impact of Trade Liberalization'. Nairobi: FKE (mimeo).

van der Geest, W. and R. van der Hoeven (1997) *Adjustment, Employment and Labour Market Institutions in Sub-Saharan Africa*. Employment and Training Paper No. 3. Geneva: ILO.

Gibbon, P. (ed.) (1993) *Social Change and Economic Reform in Africa*. Uppsala: Nordiska Afrikainstitutet.

Gunning, J.W. and C. Mbengegwi (eds) (1995) *The Manufacturing Sector in Zimbabwe: Industrial Change under Structural Adjustment*. University of Zimbabwe and University of Amsterdam.

Horton, S., R. Kambus and D. Mazumdar (eds) (1994) *Labor Markets in an Era of Adjustment*, Vols 1 and 2. Washington, DC: World Bank, EDI Development Studies.

ILO (1991) *Tanzania: National Informal Sector Survey 1991*. Dar es Salaam: ILO.

—— (1992) *Employment Prospects in Zimbabwe under the Economic Structural Adjustment Programme* (project report). Harare: ILO and UNDP.

—— (1993) *The State and the Informal Sector in Tanzania*. Addis Ababa: ILO/JASPA.

—— (1994) *Political Transformation, Structural Adjustment and Industrial Relations for English-speaking African Countries*. Geneva: ILO.

—— (1995a) *World Employment Report*. Geneva: ILO.

—— (1995b) *Employment Policy and Programme for Kenya*. Addis Ababa: ILO/EAMAT.

—— (1995c) *World Labour Report 1995*. Geneva: ILO.

Jamal, V. (1995) *Structural Adjustment and Rural Labour Markets in Africa*. The Macmillan Series of ILO Studies, London: Macmillan.

Jones, P. (1994) 'Are Manufacturing Workers Really Worth Their Pay?', Oxford: Centre for the Study of African Economies (mimeo).

Kiara, G.K. *et al.* (1993) in Gibbon.

Knight, J. (1981) 'Labour Markets in Developing Countries', *Oxford Bulletin of Economics and Statistics*, Vol. 43, No. 1.

Knight, J.B. and R.H. Sabot (1983) 'Role of the Firm in Wage Determination: An African Case Study', *Oxford Economic Papers*, Vol. 35, No.1.

Lachaud, J.P. (1994) *The African Labour Market*. Geneva: ILO.

Lall, S. (1996) 'Structural Adjustment and African Industry', *World Development*, Vol. 23.

—— and G. Wignaraja (1997) 'Skills and Capabilities: Ghana's Industrial Competitiveness' in M. Godfrey (ed.) *Skills Development for International Competitiveness*. Cheltenham, UK: Edward Elgar.

—— and G. Wignaraja (forthcoming) *Mauritius: Dynamizing Export Competitiveness*. London: Commonwealth Secretariat.

——, G. Wignaraja, P. Robinson and M. Sellek (1997) *Building Industrial Competitiveness in Zimbabwe*. London: Commonwealth Secretariat.

——, G. Barba-Navaretti, S. Teitel and G. Wignaraja (1994) *Technology and Enterprise Development: Ghana under Structural Adjustment*. London: Macmillan.

Latsch, W. and P. Robinson (forthcoming) 'Enterprise Growth and Technology under Adjustment in Zimbabwe' in S. Lall (ed.), *Opening Up or Shutting Down?* Basingstoke: Macmillan.

Mamuya, I. (1991) *Structural Adjustment and Retrenchment in the Civil Service: The Case of Tanzania*. WEP 2–43/WP.50. Geneva: ILO.

Mazumdar, D. (1994) 'Wages in Africa'. Washington, DC: World Bank (draft).

Meier, G. and W. Steel (eds) (1987) *Industrial Adjustment in Sub-Saharan Africa*. Washington, DC: World Bank.

Mhone, G. (1995) 'Can ESAP Sustainably Transform the Non-formal Sectors in Zimbabwe (Parts I and II)', *Southern Africa Political and Economic Monthly*, Vol. 7, Nos 7 and 8.

Moshi, H.P. and A. Maenda (1993) *Socio-economic Transformation in Tanzania: The Role of Employers*. Dar es Salaam: Association of Tanzanian Employers and Friedrich Naumann Stiftung.

Mosley, P. and J. Weeks (1994) 'Adjustment in Africa', *Development Policy Review*, Vol. 12, No. 3.

Nehru, V and A. Dhareshwar (1994) *New Estimates of Total Factor Productivity Growth for Developing and Industrial Countries*. Policy Research Working Paper 1313. Washington, DC: World Bank.

Nelson, J. (1994) 'Organized Labour, Politics and Labour Market Flexibility in Developing Countries', in Horton *et al.*

Ngunyi, G.M. and Gathiaka (1993) 'State-Civil Institutions Relations in Kenya in the 1980s' in Gibbon.

Organization of Tanzania Trade Unions (1992) *Structural Adjustment Programmes and the Tanzanian Economy*. Dar es Salaam: OTTU.

Pack, H. (1988) 'Industrialization and Trade' in H.B. Chenery and T.N. Srinivasan (eds) *The Handbook of Development Economics*. Amsterdam: North Holland.

—— (1993) 'Productivity and Industrial Development in Sub-Saharan Africa', *World Development*, Vol. 21, No. 1.

Page, J.M. (1980) 'Technical Efficiency and Economic Performance: Some Evidence from Ghana', *Oxford Economic Papers*, Vol. 32, No. 3.

Parker, R.L., R. Riopelle and W.F. Steel (1995) *Small Enterprises Adjusting to Liberalization in Five African Countries*. Africa Technical Department Series No. 271. Washington, DC: World Bank.

Peters-Berries, C. (1993) *Urban Informal Sector and Structural Adjustment in Zambia*. WEP 2–19/WP.62. Geneva: ILO.

Sachikonye, L.M. (1992) 'New Labour Regime under SAP in Zimbabwe', *Southern Africa Political and Economic Monthly*, Vol. 5, No. 7.

—— (1993) 'Compensation Measures in Structural Adjustment Programmes: The Case of Zimbabwe'. Harare: INTERDEP/ILO (mimeo).

Stein, H. (1992) 'Deindustrialization, Adjustment, the World Bank and the IMF in Africa', *World Development*, Vol. 20, No. 1.

—— (1994) 'The World Bank and the Application of Asian Industrial Policy to Africa', *Journal of International Development*, Vol. 6, No. 3.

Stewart, F. and W. van der Geest (1995) *Adjustment and Social Funds: Political Panacea or Effective Poverty Reduction?*, Employment Paper No. 2. Geneva: ILO.

Stoneman, C.J. (1988) *Zimbabwe's Prospects: Issues of Race, Class, State and Capital in Southern Africa*. London: Macmillan.

Syrquin, M. (1994) 'Growth and Industrialization since 1965: A Comparative Study of Fourteen Countries' in G.K. Helleiner (ed.) *Trade Policy and Industrialization in Turbulent Times*. London: Routledge.

Teitel, S. (1993) 'Technology Acquisition, Operation and Development in Selected Kenyan Manufacturing Establishments'. Washington, DC: World Bank (mimeo).

Trebilcock, A. (1994) *Towards Social Dialogue: Tripartite Cooperation in National Economic and Social Policy-making*. Geneva: ILO.

Wignaraja, G. and G. Ikiara (forthcoming) 'Adjustment, Enterprise Dynamics and Technology in Kenya' in S. Lall (ed.), *Opening Up or Shutting Down?* Basingstoke: Macmillan.

World Bank (1991) *World Development Report 1991*. New York: Oxford University Press.

—— (1995) *World Development Report 1995. Workers in an Integrating World*. New York: Oxford University Press.

Zimbabwe, Government of (1991) *Zimbabwe: A Framework for Economic Reform*. Harare: Government Printers.

II
Adjustment, Employment & Labour Market Institutions
COUNTRY EXAMPLES

4 Kenya

GERRISHON K. IKIARA & NJUGUNA S. NDUNG'U

Introduction

Structural adjustment policies in developing countries mainly involve changes in macroeconomic policies to make the economy adaptable to changing economic realities and basically more market-oriented. In a nutshell these policies aim at setting prices right by effecting changes in the relative macro price structure in order to give efficient signals to economic agents. Such macro prices include the rate of interest, the exchange rate, domestic goods prices and wages. These changes in the relative price structure are supposed to induce changes in both the level of real income and the productive structure through relative sectoral profitabilities and resource allocation (Jebuni et al., 1994). In this regard, effective changes in relative price structures will lead to resource flows into the profitable and expanding sectors of the economy. This, however, is the long-term goal; in the short term economic agents in developing countries are likely to get confused signals, due to the presence of policy lags and the likelihood of policy reversals as in the Kenyan policy-making process.

In Kenya, pervasive controls starting from the 1970s meant that the basic macro prices did not give the required signals to economic agents. Controls had been placed on foreign-exchange transactions, importation and licensing, export taxes and tedious paperwork, and domestic retail and producer prices, with wage guidelines, ceilings on domestic rates of interest and selective restrictions on bank borrowing. These controls had virtually been dismantled by the early 1990s, due to the structural adjustment programmes whose implementation had gathered momentum by that time.

The short-run consequences of structural adjustment policies have been a severe recession in many developing countries, rising unemployment, inflation and exchange-rate depreciations, with the accompanying short-run capital inflows. In many African countries the industrialization process relied on the easy phase of import substitution behind high protective tariff barriers. Such industries expanded, aided by a captive market, but with liberalization, many of them have found themselves incapable of competition and have been forced either to contract or to shut down altogether. A good example has been the textiles industry. While those firms that were export-oriented have stood their ground with liberalization and some are still expanding, those that were domestically oriented have been forced to shut down or move to commerce in line with consumer demand. The recent safety net scheme for retrenching civil servants, the so-called 'Golden Handshake', has also perhaps fuelled informal sector expansion. The expansion of the informal sector should thus be regarded as a consequence of rising unemployment during the adjustment period.

The outcome of events associated with SAPs in many African countries has thus been a reduction in employment growth and a reduction in real wages in the labour market. The expectation has been that labour could flow into the expanding sectors of the economy, but this has been slow in the formal sector. The growth of the informal sector has been dramatic; however, there are indications that this growth was not due to changes in the relative price structure signalling a flow of resources to the profitable and expanding sectors, but rather a response to rising unemployment. Furthermore, it has been seen to be related more to the rising number of establishments than to the expansion of existing units.

This chapter reviews the introduction and implementation of structural adjustment programmes in Kenya and how they have affected the country's labour market. It also examines the roles that the governmental and non-governmental labour market institutions and trade unions have played in the process of structural adjustment in Kenya and discusses how tripartite consultation between the government and employers' and workers' organizations could be used as a means of improving the design and implementation of adjustment programmes.

An overview of structural adjustment policies in Kenya: Objectives and targets

Historical background

Kenya was one of the first African countries to adopt SAPs in 1980 after the prolonged economic decline triggered by the two oil shocks of the 1970s, falling world commodity prices, fiscal and monetary instability and rising levels of unemployment had forced the country to seek IMF assistance in 1979. Kenya had already sought assistance from the IMF twice before: in 1974 for a loan under the Oil Facility and in 1975 for a loan from the Extended Fund Facility (Levin and Ndung'u, 1994: 2). Terms for a stand-by agreement were agreed by the Government of Kenya (GOK) and the IMF in 1979. However, failure by the government to reduce its borrowing from the Central Bank to the required level led to delays in disbursements by a year (Swamy, 1994: 200). This compelled the government to turn to the World Bank for quick-disbursing financial resources.

1980–84: Slow start and non-compliance

Kenya's 15 years' experience with structural adjustment can be divided into three phases: 1980–84, 1985–91, and 1992–5. The first phase was characterized by non-compliance with the agreed terms, due to timing and design shortcomings as well as limited commitment on the part of the Kenyan authorities (Swamy, 1994: 193).

The economic policies contained in Sessional Paper No. 4 of 1980 on how to deal with the prevailing economic crisis were largely in line with the recommendations of the World Bank and the IMF, and served as the basis on which Kenya's first Structural Adjustment Loan (SAL) was agreed and signed in March 1980 with the World Bank. A second stand-by agreement was signed in October 1980. These developments marked the beginning of the implementation of SAPs in Kenya. The failure to meet conditionalities, registered with the first stand-by agreement, continued in subsequent years and became a persistent source of friction between the government and the multilateral donor institutions. Poor implementation of recommended policy measures resulted in a delay in the disbursement of the second tranche of the second SAP signed by the government and the World Bank for the period July 1982 to January 1984 (Levin and Ndung'u, 1994: 3). Due to the government's general reluctance to implement the agreed terms of the programme, it had no major or noticeable impact on the country's labour market or other sectors.

The economic policy conditionalities attached to the 1979 stand-by agreement were improvement in tax revenues, reduction of government expenditure, establishment of ceilings on government borrowing from the domestic money market, wage restraint in the public sector and reduction of the public debt (Levin and Ndung'u, 1994: 2). The government's failure to meet these conditionalities led to the cancellation of the agreement in 1980 before any disbursement had been made. Thereafter, in March 1980, following a serious balance-of-payments crisis, the government and the World Bank signed Kenya's first SAL whose conditions were the adoption of a more outward-oriented industrial strategy, reform of the interest-rate regime and reduced deficit financing (*ibid.*; Gibbon, 1995: 11). A new stand-by agreement signed with the IMF in October 1980 was also accompanied by largely similar conditions such as the observance of ceilings on the Central Bank's net domestic assets and government borrowing from the Central Bank plus trade liberalization. This agreement was suspended when the government failed to meet the requirement for reduced government borrowing.

Between 1979 and 1982, the government made some attempt to implement some of the required macroeconomic reforms, like devaluation of the shilling by about 20 per cent, adoption of a crawling peg exchange-rate regime, tightening of monetary aggregates and introduction of real positive interest rates. This made possible release of the second tranche of the 1980 stand-by facility and the conclusion of a new stand-by agreement in January 1982. The new agreement had tougher conditions regarding ceilings on government borrowing, reduction of the fiscal deficit from 10.6 per cent of GDP to 7.5 per cent, import liberalization and a further devaluation of the shilling. This agreement was also suspended because the government failed to reduce government borrowing from the Central Bank. Furthermore, adoption of a crawling peg exchange-rate regime implied that the government accepted living with relatively high inflation. This meant that the policy of wage restraint was difficult to attain or that real wages were flexible downwards.

A World Bank study of the Kenyan economy carried out during 1981 and 1982 (World Bank, 1983) formed the basis for Kenya's second SAL, signed with the World Bank in July 1982. The conditionalities attached to the second SAL, which have formed the two major themes of the country's subsequent adjustment efforts, were trade liberalization and institutional and sectoral reforms, with a focus on agricultural sectoral reforms, especially the liberalization of maize marketing, plus interest-rate and energy sector reforms (Gibbon, 1995: 11; Swamy, 1994: 200). Liberalization of the maize and general cereals market has proved one of the most politically difficult reforms to implement. It was among the first reforms demanded by the lending institutions and among the last, with parastatal reforms, to be implemented.

In December 1982, a stand-by agreement was signed following the adoption of a crawling peg exchange rate in real terms. This became the first programme to be adhered to and led to some improvement in the external balance, a reduction of the internal budgetary deficit, a lower rate of inflation and a devaluation of the exchange rate (Levin and Ndung'u, 1994: 4). It also helped to improve relations with the IMF.

1985–91: Poor implementation of the agreed reforms
The period 1985–91 witnessed considerable official acceptance or ownership of the reform programme especially after the publication of Sessional Paper No. 1 of 1986 on 'Economic Management for Renewed Growth' (Republic of Kenya, 1986).

Although the pace of implementation remained poor, more efforts were made to introduce reforms in various sectors especially in agriculture, trade and industry, education, health, the parastatals and foreign-exchange markets, as well as the financial sector. In addition to the SAPs, which are basically medium to long-term economic policies directed at the supply side of the economy and aimed at the restructuring of the various economic sectors to enhance their efficiency and responsiveness to price and other market signals, the country undertook some macroeconomic stabilization programmes largely aimed at correcting short-term instabilities such as inflationary tendencies, and budgetary and balance-of-payments deficits.

The main objectives of the reform programme were seen to be the achievement of rapid and sustained economic growth, employment creation, improvement of the general standard of living through better access to basic needs and reduction of the rural-urban imbalance (Republic of Kenya, 1986: 5). In 1984, drought ravaged the economy and the resultant fiscal and external imbalances led the government to seek another stand-by facility which was signed in February 1985. The conditionalities attached to it included further reduction of government expenditures, improved price and marketing incentives, increased export promotion, import liberalization and maintenance of a competitive exchange rate. The first World Bank sectoral credit to Kenya was approved in June 1986. This was a quick-disbursing sectoral adjustment credit (ASAL-1), whose main condition was the restructuring of the National Cereals and Produce Board and a number of other parastatals (Swamy, 1994: 195), including implementation of reforms targeted at the reduction of the NCPB's claims on budgetary resources.

A new stand-by agreement with the IMF and a three-year Structural Adjustment Facility, together with credits from the IDA and other donors, were signed to support the country's stabilization and reform measures adopted in February 1988. The programme's main objectives were to strengthen macroeconomic policies designed to restore fiscal and monetary discipline, which had been eroded in the previous few years, especially during the mini coffee boom of 1986, and to facilitate the implementation of industrial and financial sector reforms.

The programme was replaced by a 3-year (1989–91) Enhanced Structural Adjustment Facility (ESAF) in May 1989. Its performance targets included rapid economic growth at a rate above that of population growth, deceleration of the inflation rate to the average rate of Kenya's trading partners, a reduction of the current account deficit and the build-up of the country's net official international resources (Levin and Ndung'u, 1994: 5; ROK/IMF/World Bank, 1991: 1). The ESAF programme was so poorly implemented, however, that donor frustration reached unprecedented levels. By 1991, the last year of the ESAF, three of the four quantitative performance criteria were not satisfied, namely, the ceilings on the net domestic assets of the domestic banking sector, reduction of government borrowing from the banking system and improvement in the net official international reserves (Levin and Ndung'u, 1994: 6).

Sectoral adjustment programmes designed for Kenya in the second half of the 1980s and the early 1990s included those for agriculture (1986 and 1990), industry (1988), the financial sector (1989), export development (1990) and education (1991). But most of them had limited results, due to lack of government commitment in terms of implementation.

Rapid implementation of SAPs: 1992–5
Donor frustration with the slow pace, and in some instances reversal, of the SAPs' implementation, reached a climax in 1991 when, during the donor Consultative

Group Meeting held in November that year, quick-disbursing aid to Kenya was suspended. The reasons given for this suspension were the poor implementation of the economic reforms, rising levels of corruption, failure to correct macroeconomic imbalances caused by fiscal indiscipline, slow reforms in the civil service and the privatization of public enterprises, lack of accountability of public enterprises, failure to establish a supportive environment for the growth of the private sector and the slow pace of political reform. These, in essence, served as the conditions that needed to be satisfied before aid could be resumed.

At the beginning of 1992, a shadow programme was negotiated with the IMF under which the government was required to stabilize the macroeconomic environment by reducing the budget deficit to 2 per cent of GDP in 1992–3 through improved efficiency in revenue collection, reduction of government expenditure, privatization and restructuring of parastatals and a tightening of monetary policy using open market operations and improved supervision by the Central Bank. In September 1992, the World Bank decided to postpone disbursement of the second tranche for the programmes that were in progress, again due to poor implementation of a number of the conditions attached to the sectoral programmes (Swamy, 1994: 195). In December of the same year the second tranche of the agricultural sector adjustment loan was cancelled because of the grain movement controls that had been reimposed two months earlier.

Although the monetary, financial and external sectors were the main areas of concern for the donors in 1992, there had been no significant improvement in them by the beginning of 1993. However, in an attempt to mend its fences with the donors, the government floated the shilling in February 1993 and quickly implemented a number of other reforms which had been required, such as reintroducing retention accounts for the traditional exports and service sectors, expanding the inter-bank market and undertaking some liberalization of the coffee and tea marketing systems.

Despite these efforts the IMF and the World Bank remained dissatisfied because the government had failed to implement the tight monetary policies required. It is important to note that, although in general the third phase of Kenya's reform programme (1992–5) witnessed much more dramatic implementation of the recommended reforms compared with the previous periods, considerable tension between donors and the government frequently emerged on specific issues. For instance, in March 1993 disagreement with the donors ran high, with some elements in the Kenyan political system threatening to reverse the reforms that had been introduced. This led to the abolition of retention accounts with a directive requiring the remittance of all export proceeds to the Central Bank at the official rate of exchange, the abandonment of flotation of the shilling and the collapse of the market for Foreign Exchange Bearer Certificates (Forex Cs). These frequent lapses in policy meant that liberalization of the financial system could not proceed until some basic stability had been achieved.

In April 1993 the government sought another agreement with the two multilateral donors. This meant a second mission to Kenya by an IMF/International Development Association team and the conclusion of a shadow programme with the IMF, under which the government adopted, in the period April-May 1993, the following measures in order to tighten monetary and financial sector policies: aggressive open market operations to mop up the excessive liquidity existing in the economy, raising of the cash ratio from 6 to 8 per cent with sanctions for non-compliance, abolition of the export pre-shipment discount facility, the placing of two of the weak banks under statutory management and eight non-bank financial institutions (NBFIs) under liquidators, and strengthening the Central Bank's supervisory role.

In November 1993, Kenya applied for a one-year arrangement under the ESAF, for a total of SDR 45.2 million. The IMF accepted the application, indicating that the loan would be disbursed in two equal instalments, so long as the following conditions were fulfilled: implementing more effective control of the fiscal deficit and of government borrowing from the Central Bank and setting and observing targets on its net international reserves, putting limits on new non-concessional external loans contracted or guaranteed by the government, and limiting increases in the government's short-term external debt. The second disbursement was to be released only if the government fully decontrolled the pricing and marketing of maize and petroleum products; increased the proportion of foreign exchange retained by exporters to 100 per cent of export earnings; and relaxed the restrictions on payments and transfers for current international transactions, imports, and for the balance of payments.

Except for 1994, the budget deficit to GDP ratio had not significantly changed when we compared the pre-adjustment and adjustment periods (Table 4.1); the period 1993–4 showed some attempt to cut back on the deficit and the financing of government activities. Equally unresponsive was the source for financing the deficit. Even though during the pre-adjustment period domestic financing was slightly higher than foreign financing, in 1984 and some years thereafter foreign financing was minimal. One aspect of the SAPs was the flow of funds to support the adjustment process, and this was perhaps responsible for the rising share of foreign financing of budget deficits.

By October 1995, the country was negotiating for a new three-year $200 million loan under the ESAF. The negotiations, started in January 1995, had stalled due to the country's poor implementation of both economic and political reforms. The stage was set for another consultative meeting with the donors in early 1996 in Paris to receive new aid commitments. However, there were strong hints from the IMF that this might not be possible because of unresolved differences, especially over massive corruption and scandals involving public resources. IMF officials were quoted in the local press as saying that fresh aid was unlikely to be committed by the IMF and other donors unless the 'Goldenberg Scandal' in which the government lost Kshs. 13 billion in fraudulent deals was brought to an end (*Sunday Nation*, 15 October, 1995). Stringent financial accountability, especially with regard to the avoidance of huge expenditures on unplanned and non-priority projects, in addition to good governance and human rights, were thus emerging as important conditionalities.

By the end of 1995, Kenya had implemented major political and economic reforms agreed upon with the multilateral and bilateral donors. The economic reforms implemented included the removal of virtually all price and foreign-exchange controls, the liberalization of domestic marketing trade, import liberal-

Table 4.1   *Fiscal deficit/GDP ratio, Kenya, 1972–94 (%)*

	1972	1975	1980	1984	1990	1991	1992	1993	1994
Deficit/GDP	7.7	8.9	10.9	6.6	7.3	1.9	3.6	5.6	3.6
Deficit financing									
Domestic resources	45.8	54.9	49.5	90.3	71.0	94.4	32.0	106.3	54.7
Foreign resources	48.2	45.1	50.5	9.7	29.0	5.6	68.0	−6.3	45.3

Source: *Economic Survey*, various issues.

ization, reduction of the budget deficit, financial reforms, privatization, removal of wage guidelines and other labour market reforms, and liberalization of the exchange rate.

Review of structural adjustment components in the period 1985–95
Kenya has adopted a wide range of policy reforms under the SAP since 1985, with seriousness in implementation accelerating after 1991. These reforms have included both those that enhance competitiveness and those that are largely oriented towards institutional change. These reforms and their effects on employment are discussed below.

Competition-enhancing policy reforms and their impact on employment
Some of the reform measures implemented were intended to enhance the competitiveness of Kenyan products in both domestic and external markets. Some examples of the reforms in this category include trade liberalization and exchange-rate reforms.

(a) **External trade liberalization** Liberalization of Kenya's external trade was one of the areas that received more attention in the three phases of the reform programme. Under the country's Fourth Development Plan (1979–84), a number of trade reform measures were implemented with the overall objective of making the industrial sector more efficient and more outward-oriented. These measures included the removal of quantitative restrictions (QRs), the reduction of tariff levels and export promotion, which was especially carried out in the third phase (i.e the 1992–5 period), and the establishment of a flexible exchange-rate regime. The first two trade reforms were adopted between 1980 and 1984.

Limited devaluation of the shilling and increased export compensation were also undertaken during the 1980–84 period. However, there was at that time a tendency to resort to selective import controls, especially during periods of deteriorating balance of payments. During 1982–4, for instance, as a result of a foreign-exchange crisis, tariffs were increased by 10 per cent across the board (Swamy, 1994: 209).

Import liberalization has made considerable progress since the early 1980s. Between 1980 and 1985 the share of items that could be imported without any restrictions rose from 24 to 48 per cent of the total value of imported items. The average tariff rate was also reduced by about 8 per cent over the same period (Swamy, 1994: 210). An improved import licensing system with restricted and unrestricted schedules was established. In 1988, import liberalization was taken a step further when the licensing system underwent significant improvements. The new system created five schedules I, II, IIIA, IIIB and IIIC in order to reinforce licensing requirements. Unrestricted licensing was gradually extended to schedules II, IIIA, and IIIB and several items moved from IIIC to IIIB over the years so that by July 1991 the only imported items that required licensing (those in schedule IIIC) were items largely restricted on health, security or environmental grounds. The system underwent further changes in the third phase when, between 1991 and 1993, the Foreign Exchange Allocation Committee, the Import Management Committee (IMC) and the requirement for a foreign-exchange allocation licence were abolished.

By November 1993, all administrative controls in international trade, including import licensing and foreign-exchange allocation together with their institutional set-up, had been abolished (Republic of Kenya, 1994a: 4). Tariff reform was also progressively implemented with tariff rates gradually lowered and tariff bands or categories reduced. For instance, between 1989–90 and 1991–2 the overall production-weighted tariffs had declined from 62 to 48.5 per cent (Swamy, 1994: 211).

The maximum tariff rate had been reduced from 135 per cent in the 1980s to 45 per cent by 1994, while the number of non-zero bands was reduced from 25 to 6 over the same period. Since 1987–8, tariff dispersion has been lowered as the number of tariff bands was reduced (Table 4.2). Harmonization of tariffs was another policy pursued, especially from the second phase. Average tariff rates declined significantly in the third phase. However, two factors disturbed the general downward trend: first, average tariffs reached their highest level in 1989–90 as a result of the replacement of quotas with equivalent tariffs; secondly crisis management in 1993–4 raised tariffs temporarily to cater for a shortfall in government revenue.

From Table 4.2 we observe a clustering of goods around the tariff level of 11–30 and a slightly smaller one at 31–50. On the other hand, average tariff rates have drastically fallen from 42.82 per cent in 1987–8 to around 27.3 per cent in 1994–95. Table 4.3 shows the average and weighted tariff rates:

Weighted average tariffs, on the other hand, declined from 31.8 per cent in 1990–91 to 22.2 per cent in 1994–5. The only element of protection in international trade remaining by the end of 1995 was the provision to impose countervailing duties, announced in the 1995–96 Budget Speech. This provision was aimed at curbing unfair competition from exports subsidized by other countries.

The other area of trade liberalization that received considerable attention was export promotion. Besides the export compensation scheme started in 1974, the Manufacturing Under Bond (MUB) Scheme was introduced in 1988. This scheme carried incentives such as waivers of import duty and tax on imports used for the production of export goods. A more general import duty and VAT exemption scheme was introduced following the shortcomings of the MUB. This was accompanied by regulatory reforms, and new improved and simplified investment procedures. Moreover, in 1990, export processing zones (EPZs) were started under which investors enjoyed 10 years of tax holiday, unrestricted foreign ownership and employment of foreigners and complete control over their forex earnings.

In addition to the above schemes, a number of other changes were made, especially in the third phase of the reform programme, to create a more conducive environment for export growth, including a substantial reduction and restructuring of tariffs, especially on raw materials and capital goods, abolition of export duties, improvement of capital allowances, improved provision of short-term export finance, and improved foreign-exchange and insurance regulations (Republic of

Table 4.2   *Percentage distribution of goods by tariff band, Kenya, 1987/8–1995/6*

Tariff band (%)	1987/88	1988/89	1989/90	1990/91	1991/92	1992/93	1993/94	1994/95	1995/96
0	6.9	7	5.8	6.1	3.7	2.9	3.1	3.2	3.3
1–10	0.3	6.9	1.6	1.6	4	4.6	5.2	4.9	1.8
11–30	30.7	29.6	37.6	37.4	47.6	47.6	56.5	67.8	71.8
31–50	45.4	43.7	23.8	21.6	17.6	20.8	35.2	24.1	23.1
51–60	3.9	5.6	6	6.3	3	24	–	–	–
61–70	3.8	4.1	–	–	24	–	–	–	–
71–	9	9.2	25.2	27.1	–	–	–	–	–
Total	100	100.1	100	100.1	100	99.9	100	100	100

Source: Ministry of Finance, Budget Speech 1995/96

Table 4.3 *Average and weighted tariff rates, Kenya, 1987/8–94/5*

	1987/88	1988/89	1989/90	1990/91	1991/92	1992/93	1993/94	1994/95
Average tariff rates	4.252	44.38	49.17	47.17	39.39	36.56	40.48	27.27
Weighted tariff rates	N/A	N/A	N/A	31.78	27.17	27.25	30.9	22.21

Source: ibid.

Kenya, 1995a: 18). The Export Promotion Council has worked closely with the donor-funded Kenya Export Development Support (KEDS) project to establish the private sector National Export Credit Guarantee Corporation. Institutional reforms have also been carried out to facilitate the growth of exports. These have included a clear definition of responsibilities among the institutions charged with export promotion, chiefly the EPC and the Export Promotion Programme Office (EPPO).

Trade liberalization is one of the components of structural adjustment that has had a significant employment effect in the country. Import liberalization was accompanied by massive imports of some products that led to the closing down of domestic firms, with considerable adverse effects on employment. While the loss of employment from firms closing down completely or scaling down their production levels has not been accurately assessed, it is estimated to be substantial. This has worried the government, manufacturers and the trade union movement considerably, prompting the Minister for Finance to recommend in his 1995 budget speech that the country should impose countervailing duties to 'prevent permanent damage being inflicted on some industries' (Republic of Kenya, 1995a: 21).

The growth in export firms expected from some of the trade liberalization measures could, however, mitigate some of these negative effects. The EPZs, for instance, had created 5,000 new jobs since their inception in 1990 (*Daily Nation*, 29 August 1995, p. 11).

(b) **Foreign-exchange and exchange-rate reforms** Kenya's third phase of reform programmes also witnessed far-reaching implementation of competitiveness-enhancing reforms with regard to the liberalization of foreign-exchange operations. These reforms included the removal of foreign-exchange controls and liberalization of the exchange rate, leading to a large devaluation of the shilling, especially in the 1992–3 period. Some of the other reforms related to foreign exchange in the early 1990s included the introduction of Foreign-Exchange Bearer Certificates in October 1991; the introduction of export earnings retention schemes for exporters in 1992; merging of the official rate of exchange with the interbank foreign-exchange rate; removal of exchange controls on current account transactions and on nearly all capital account transactions; and the scrapping of the 90-day foreign-exchange surrender limit (Republic of Kenya, 1994a: 5). These reforms had the overall effect of making the foreign-exchange market much more free than in the first and second phases of the reform programme. In the 1994 Budget Speech, all regulations pertaining to the Exchange Control Act were suspended, before parliament finally repealed the Foreign Exchange Act in December 1995. One of the latest reforms in the foreign-exchange market was the move to allow legalization of foreign-exchange bureaux in 1995.

The effect reforms in the exchange-rate regime had on employment was largely indirect, through their impact on international trade liberalization discussed above. The short-run effect of trade liberalization was an outflow of resources from production to commerce. Some of the production sectors of the economy have been contracting because of competition from imports. Thus, in the short run, it is realistic to expect rising unemployment associated with trade liberalization.

On the other hand, removal of foreign-exchange controls and liberalization of the exchange rate have considerably eased the constraints hitherto imposed on the country's productive sectors, especially manufacturing and agriculture, by the acute shortages of imported inputs due to the non-availability of foreign exchange when required. This had resulted not only in frequent interruptions in many firms' production schedules but also in chronic underutilization of installed capacity (Gotenborg University/University of Nairobi, 1995). One of the beliefs in Kenya was that industrial growth was hampered by foreign-exchange availability. This has been proved wrong, however (Ndung'u, 1995). So long as foreign-exchange controls persisted, imported inputs were a function of available foreign exchange allocations. But once this constraint is removed through liberalization of the foreign-exchange market, the determination of import demand reverts to its fundamentals with foreign-exchange availability no longer a significant determinant, although it may help to improve the transactions costs which were hitherto quite prohibitive. The improvement in the availability of foreign exchange following the reforms implemented can be generally said to have had a positive impact on the employment sector, especially for those competitive industries which were not adversely affected by import liberalization.

Results from the Regional Programme on Enterprise Development (RPED) show that foreign-exchange constraints for the majority of Kenyan firms had been dramatically reduced following the reforms undertaken in 1993 and 1994. About 72 per cent of the firms studied said that their access to foreign exchange had improved dramatically by 1994, while 89 per cent said that foreign-exchange availability was no longer a problem in their operations (Gotenborg University/University of Nairobi, 1995: 159). About 85 per cent of formal sector firms in the study indicated that foreign-exchange reforms had led to considerable improvement in their export opportunities.

Assessing the employment trends of the sample firms, the RPED study concluded that the economic reforms undertaken in the 1992–4 period had had a positive impact: 'The manufacturing sector as a whole has gradually improved its performance at least with regard to employment generation, and this seems to suggest that policy reforms are beginning to have a positive growth effect' (*ibid.*: 178).

(c) **Reducing barriers to foreign ownership and investment** A free exchange regime has facilitated repatriation of dividends by foreign investors. This, together with the removal of barriers to foreign commercial private borrowing, has provided a more enabling environment for foreign investors. Furthermore, the establishment of EPZs has allowed unrestricted foreign ownership and employment of expatriates as well as control over foreign-exchange earnings, in addition to extensive tax advantages.

Financial sector reforms, and in particular amendment of the Capital Markets Authority (CMA) Act, have further eased restraints on foreign ownership. The CMA, established in 1990, attempted to liberalize the country's financial and capital markets. As a result of these efforts, trading in the Nairobi Stock Exchange (NSE) market opened up, on a limited scale, to foreign investors in January 1995. In June 1995, the limit on portfolio investment by foreigners in Kenyan companies quoted on the NSE was raised from 20 to 40 per cent for the corporate group of investors and from 2.5 to 5 per cent for individual portfolio holdings (Republic of Kenya, 1995: 15). The investment environment has thus undergone significant changes aimed at encouraging local and foreign investment, including tariff and foreign-exchange reforms, rationalization of trade licensing and removal of discretionary clauses in the tax laws. Promotion of foreign ownership and investment was expected to create jobs and this constituted the main driving force for efforts in this direction. As noted elsewhere, it is already having positive effects on employment, especially in the export processing zones. However, although licensing requirements have been significantly reduced through amendments of the Trade Licensing Act, delays in initial investment approvals and the requirement of various licences by central and local government agencies still remain (Republic of Kenya, 1995b: 20). Improvement in the efficiency of infrastructural services, reduction of corruption in public administration, creation of a more efficient framework of licensing and other regulations are additional areas that need attention to improve further the investment climate. Because of the above constraints, in addition to the existing political tensions and the sour relationship with donors, measures taken to attract foreign investment have not had a noticeably significant impact in the EPZs.

(d) Domestic trade liberalization Price controls had been extended to most manufactured and agricultural products by the end of the 1970s. The origin of price controls in the Kenyan economy can be traced back as far as the Price Control Ordinance of 1956. Price controls on staple commodities were instituted to protect low-income earners, whereas those on manufactures sought to prevent monopolistic pricing practices (Swamy, 1994: 215).

Starting in 1983, domestic price controls on virtually all commodities had been dismantled by the beginning of 1995. Between 1983 and 1991, the number of commodities whose price was controlled under the general order dropped from 56 to 6 while those controlled under the specific order fell from 87 to 29 (*ibid.*). By September 1993, only petroleum products and some pharmaceutical products remained under price controls under the general order, while under the specific order only 3 items remained (Republic of Kenya, 1993: 7). By July 1995, the maize market, hitherto the most resisted reform and the central focus of donors, and the petroleum/oil sector, had been completely liberalized.

The move to dismantle price controls provoked sharply different reactions from the business community and the labour movement. While manufacturing and most other sections of the business community welcomed the move as a way of removing distortions in the economy, removal of price controls was strongly resisted by the labour movement, which argued that the process would lead to major increases in the cost of living and erode the workers' purchasing power. The trade unions argued for the removal of the existing wage guidelines, introduced in 1973, to enable the workers to negotiate freely with employers. The wage guidelines set the maximum wage increase awards below the prevailing cost of living index, a policy which over time led to a substantial decline in the workers' purchasing power throughout the 1980s and early 1990s.

The dismantling of price controls did not, however, lead to a dramatic increase in the cost of living, except in 1993 when inflation rates rose to over 100 per cent for the first time in the country's history. This was largely due to a reckless expansion of the money supply in the economy, associated, to some extent, with the financing of the multi-party general elections of December 1992. The fact that the removal of price controls did not immediately result in sharp price increases before 1993 was regarded as an indicator that the Kenyan domestic market was fairly developed with competitive structures for most goods and services. This was also in line with the World Bank's argument in 1983 that the supply response and demand restraint would stabilize prices. In the very short run, this has held true but not for the medium and long-term situations.

(e) **Financial sector reforms** Kenya's financial sector reform programme has focused on both market and institutional reforms in an attempt to remove distortions in the credit market. Positive real interest rates, the target of the market reforms, were aimed at enhancing efficient utilization of the available credit resources. Institutional reforms related to the financial sector focused on strengthening the Central Bank to enable it to undertake its inspection and regulatory roles more effectively.

The Banking Act was amended in 1989 to facilitate this. In addition to strengthening the Central Bank's regulatory and supervisory roles, other areas affected by the amendments included: the introduction of stricter licensing requirements on financial institutions, raising the minimum capital requirements, the establishment of the Deposit Insurance Fund, the issuance of new guidelines for the granting of loans and minimum disclosure requirements, and increasing penalties for non-compliance. Enforcement of the banking regulations even after the amendment of the Banking Act continued to be hampered by political forces, leading to a new banking crisis in 1986 when 11 banks and 20 non-bank financial institutions (NBFIs) got into liquidity difficulties. Financial sector reforms in the latter part of the 1980s and early 1990s emphasized tight credit control to suppress inflationary tendencies, especially through adjustments of the cash ratio requirements for the commercial banks and raising interest rates.

There have been complaints from the business community that the tight monetary policy had contractionary effects on their operations because of reduced lending by the commercial banks. For instance, the cash ratio was increased from 10 per cent in October 1993 to 20 per cent in March 1994 and subsequently reduced, following successful reduction of the money supply through limits on CBK credit and open market operations, to 18 per cent in September 1994. The problem was aggravated by the high interest rate Treasury bills that the government has been using to mop up excess liquidity. This has deprived the private sector of credit facilities, as investible resources were increasingly being put into government Treasury bills at a time when there was no secondary market for government securities. One of the disadvantages of the government floating commercial paper is that it hampers the development of the financial sector and the intermediation process. Commercial banks will opt for default-free commercial paper, sometimes with a higher interest rate, and relegate their financial screening role to the background. These factors had contractionary effects on production and employment creation.

Furthermore, strict enforcement of the financial sector reforms caused the closure of some banks, NBFIs and insurance companies, leading to considerable loss of employment opportunities. Some of the commercial banks, for example the Standard Chartered Bank, have restructured their operations, resulting in a significant number of retrenchments.

Institutional change-oriented policy reforms
(a) **Parastatal sector reforms** Very limited reform had been implemented in the parastatal sector by the end of the second phase of the reform programme. By 1990, the Kenya government owned equity in about 250 commercially oriented enterprises, 60 per cent of them in manufacturing and mining, 18 per cent in distribution, 15 per cent in finance and the rest in transport, electricity and other services. While the parastatal enterprises accounted for a large share of public sector employment, they also became a major source of budgetary deficits, as the majority of them depended on subsidization by the central government. Many of them were overstaffed and mismanaged.

These factors provided the rationale for the parastatal reform programme whose broad objectives were reduction of the financial burden on the Treasury, improvement in the efficiency of service delivery and enhancing opportunities for private sector investment (Republic of Kenya, 1995a: 12). The programme had two main components: restructuring of the strategic enterprises to raise their productivity and efficiency, and privatization of the non-strategic parastatals. While the reform programme has generally been slow, some considerable progress has been made since 1990.

Reforms in the parastatal sector began towards the end of the second phase, and intensified in the third period in 1990, when the State Corporation Act was amended to permit the expected reforms and to enhance the accountability of public enterprises. In the same year Kenya Airways (KA), the government-owned airline, started its restructuring programme. A total of 960 workers (30 per cent of KA's total workforce) were retrenched in that year, 96 per cent of them from the lower grades 1–8 (Ikiara, 1992: 31).

The National Cereals and Produce Board (NCPB) was also restructured in 1990. A performance contract was signed and marketing reforms and organizational restructuring were implemented. Some of its buying centres were closed and its role was reduced, with the objective of making it the buyer and seller of last resort.

In late 1991, the government identified 207 enterprises for divestiture, 10 of them listed for privatization by 1995, and 33 strategic enterprises whose ownership the government intended to retain. In 1991, the Kenya Wildlife Services (KWS) retrenched 1,600 of its workers, representing 32 per cent of its total workforce, although some were redeployed in various government ministries and departments. In September 1992, the Lake Basin Development Authority (LBDA) also announced its plan to lay off 1,545 workers (31 per cent of its 5,000 permanent employees) due to budgetary constraints. The Executive Secretariat and Technical Unit (ESTU) was established in May 1992 to implement the sale of parastatal enterprises.

Some of the other parastatal reforms carried out in 1991 included granting autonomy to the Kenya Railway Corporation to set its tariffs, and issuing a legal notice to establish the Audit and Exchequer (Exchange Risk Assumption) Fund to underwrite foreign-exchange risks on external borrowings by development financial institutions such as the Industrial and Commercial Development Corporation (ICDC), the Industrial Development Bank (IDC) and the Kenya Tourism Development Corporation (KTDC). The restructuring of the Kenya Posts and Telecommunications Corporation's management started. A number of measures were introduced to strengthen financial discipline and the accountability of parastatals, namely: discontinuation of budgetary support and forex allocation for capital expenditures except for approved development expenditures; application of market rates of interest to parastatal borrowing and clarification of the past financial support through Loan Agreements and financial restructuring; establishment of the Capital Budget Review Meetings to prevent unilateral actions by the Treasury on parastatal capital budgets; enforcement of parastatal reporting obligations and improvement of timeliness in audit preparation. In June 1991, the Parastatal Reform Policy Committee (PRPC) was created to take charge of decision-making, reform implementation, and review of the Parastatal Reform programme.

By January 1996, 76 of the 207 state enterprises listed for privatization had been sold off, generating a total of US$54 million for the Treasury. The sales included holding corporations such as the IDB, ICDC and the KTDC (*East African Weekly*, 8–14 January 1996, p. 14).

By early 1996 progress had been made in the restructuring of strategic parastatals. Thus, Kenya Airways and its subsidiary, the KAHL, were restructured to prepare them for privatization. Kenya Railways was undergoing restructuring, part of which was to make the passenger service an autonomous business and to contract to the private sector the maintenance of its locomotives. The Kenya Ports Authority (KPA) had contracted out the maintenance of its equipment and a study exploring the privatization of its container terminal and other activities had been completed. A decision was made to privatize the telecommunications business of the KPTC, while an action plan had been prepared to separate the generation, transmission and distribution of electrical power with the eventual aim of liberalizing power generation (Republic of Kenya, 1995: 13). Moreover, three cotton ginneries had been sold and four others brought to the point of sale by June 1995, while a study for the privatization of sugar factories had been completed and Mumias sugar company had been scheduled for sale. The Kenya Tea Development Authority (KTDA) had also transferred 43 factories to shareholders by that time. The government had targeted the privatization of one-third of the remaining state enterprises before the end of 1995.

The monopolistic hold of some of the large agricultural marketing agencies like the Kenya Planters Cooperative Union (KPCU), the Kenya National Trading Corporation (KNTC), the National Cereals and Produce Board (NCPB) and Kenya Cooperative Creameries (KCC) had been considerably weakened by the emergence of a growing number of competitors.

In spite of the progress mentioned, parastatal reform has been slow and is generally considered by many Kenyans and donors as a major area of concern (Republic of Kenya, 1995a: 12). Nonetheless, the parastatal reforms that have so far been implemented have had serious direct employment effects through their restructuring and privatization components. Some of the parastatals carrying out retrenchments during the period 1990–92 laid off an average 30 per cent of their total workforce (Ikiara, 1992: 34).

(b) Public expenditure control and reduction Control and reduction of public expenditures has been a major objective of most of the reform measures adopted under the SAPs, such as the budget rationalization programme, the civil service reform, the parastatal sector reforms, and the introduction of user charges.

From the first phase (1980–84), there have been attempts to reduce the budget deficit, principally through reduced public expenditures. Conditions attached to stand-by agreements with the IMF and the World Bank usually included control and reduction of government spending and observing ceilings on government borrowing from the banking sector. One of the components of the budget rationalization programme has been an increase in the share of non-wage operation and maintenance (O&M) in a bid to raise productivity in the public sector. Other measures carried out include improvements in expenditure control mechanisms, changing the composition of the expenditures and civil service reform.

By 1995, expenditure on most recurrent items had been reduced sharply and allocations for O&M expenditure had risen, while core projects received about 75 per cent of the development resources. Civil service reform was a crucial area for reducing government spending, especially in the third phase of the reform programme. The reform was instituted in April 1992 with the objectives of improving the quality of the public service, reducing government spending, raising the productivity of the workforce and rationalizing staffing levels. The programme had the target of reducing the 272,000 civil servants at an annual rate of 6 per cent for 5 years, with the emphasis on the unskilled and semi-skilled categories of civil servants. By October 1994 the number of civil servants had been reduced from 272,000 to 248,057, mainly through the Voluntary Early Retirement Scheme (VERS) (Republic of Kenya, 1994a: 11–12). Staff reductions constituted the first stage of the civil service reform programme, while the second stage was to lay emphasis on improvement of the performance of the service through increased training and incentives to the remaining workforce.

Reduction of public expenditure has had both direct and indirect negative effects on employment, especially with regard to the civil service where more than 20,000 employees had already been retrenched by the end of 1995. While civil servants have been apprehensive about this retrenchment, they have not been able to articulate their grievances because they have not had a union to represent their interests since the Kenya Union of Civil Servants was banned in the 1970s. Recent efforts to revive the union were a reflection of the need felt by civil servants to have their workers' union, especially at this historic juncture of economic adjustments. The government disallowed the move, however.

The retrenchment programme has increased the pressure in the country's already volatile unemployment situation. The public sector reforms, combined with the restructuring programmes of many large private sector employers, aimed at enabling the private sector to cope with the emerging competitive business environment. This has exacerbated the competition for the limited number of new jobs, estimated to be just over 100,000 a year in an economy where new entrants to the labour force number more than 400,000 annually. The situation has become highly challenging for virtually all graduates from the country's educational system, with a large number even of university students in both liberal arts and technical education programmes taking three or more years to find employment.

Apart from the direct adverse effect of public expenditure reductions on employment, the reform programme has been generally blamed for worsening the conditions of the vulnerable groups through reduced access to essential services such as education, health, housing, water and sanitation (Odada and Ayako, 1989). While the negative impact of some of the structural adjustment measures has tended to be exaggerated by some critics of the programme, it is widely acknowledged that some of the expenditure-reducing measures are likely to have negative effects on the socially vulnerable groups in the short term, especially in the absence of properly designed safety nets.

(c) Labour market reforms Until recently, Kenya's labour market was strictly regulated with wage guidelines, approval mechanisms for redundancies by the Ministry of Labour and Manpower Development, and the government involving itself in trade union elections.

There has been a widespread belief among the Kenyan authorities for most of the post-independence period that regulation of the labour market was indispensable for rapid economic development and improving the welfare of workers. For instance, it was argued that wage guidelines were essential to ensure that labour costs remained low, not only to attract foreign investment but also to encourage firms to use labour-intensive technologies to help create more employment opportunities. Government intervention in fixing minimum wages was regarded in the same way as an important way of protecting the interests of the workers. It was argued that high levels of unemployment created an environment for employers to exploit unskilled workers through underpayment.

One of the underlying motives for labour market control in Kenya was political. During the last decade of the colonial era, the trade union movement had played a major role in the struggle for the country's independence (Mboya, 1963). The labour movement thus had considerable political power at independence. The new government, led by Jomo Kenyatta, made subtle moves to curb this power and keep the movement under control through the government's control and close involvement in the trade unions' electoral machinery.

The labour market has undergone considerable liberalization, however, since the early 1990s. By July 1994, the Industrial Court had allowed trade unions to seek full compensation for price increases without hindrance through wage guidelines. As a result of this liberalization, various laws have been amended to allow firms to discharge redundant workers more easily when necessary. Thus, due to relaxation of the redundancy declaration procedures in 1994, enterprises can declare workers redundant without having to seek the approval of the Minister of Labour and Manpower Development. They are required simply to notify regional or district labour officers of their intention. The removal of wage guidelines makes it possible now for firms to negotiate and change the level of wages on the basis of productivity and performance rather than on the basis of cost of living indices, as was previously the case.

Impact of adjustment on the labour market

This section assesses the impact of structural adjustment on the labour market by providing quantitative descriptions of employment levels, wage levels and relative changes over time. It concentrates on the period 1972–94. This period is chosen so as to facilitate comparison between the period of controls prior to adjustment and liberalization and the period of structural adjustment. First, the general trends are described, followed by estimation of multiple regression equations to show the determinants of employment growth and nominal wages. The basic motive is to assess the influence over time of SAPs on the labour market.

The section is organized as follows. We first discuss trends in employment levels and growth in various sectors and try to relate them to the level of economic activity; we then discuss the trends and growth in earnings for various sub-sectors and try to show how real average consumption wages have declined in the adjustment period; finally, we summarize the observed trends in the labour market in the era of structural adjustment.

Employment growth trends

Formal sector employment growth has slackened over the years after a rapid expansion in the 1970s and 1980s. The share of employment between the formal and informal sectors has drastically changed, with the latter overtaking the former in employment absorption. These trends are shown in Table 4.4. Formal employment, which accounted for about 90 per cent of total employment in 1972, had its share fall to about 45 per cent by 1994. This spectacular decline occurred between 1990 and 1994 when the share of formal employment declined from 58.8 to 44.8 per cent. Equally dramatic was the decline in the shares of the public and private sectors, which declined to 20.5 and 24.3 per cent in 1994 from 35.7 and 53.9 per cent in 1972, respectively. The sub-sectors in the formal sector have also declined in their respective shares, with agriculture falling to 8.4 from 30.7 per cent, manufacturing to 5.9 from 10.5 per cent and commercial services to 11.8 from 20.7 per cent between 1972 and 1994.

Table 4.4   *Shares in total employment, Kenya, 1972–94 (%)*

	1972	1975	1980	1985	1990	1994
Public	35.7	36.0	39.6	40.4	29.2	20.5
Private	53.9	50.2	44.9	43.2	29.6	24.3
Total formal sector	89.6	86.2	84.5	83.6	58.8	44.8
Agriculture	30.7	25.3	19.4	17.0	11.3	8.4
Manufacturing	10.5	10.6	11.9	11.2	7.8	5.9
Commercial services	20.7	21.0	21.2	21.0	13.4	11.8
Government services	21.9	23.8	25.6	28.7	20.8	15.8
Building and construction	4.7	4.3	5.3	4.3	3.0	2.2
Informal sector	4.2	7.8	10.3	15.2	39.1[a]	53.4
Self-employed	6.2	6.0	5.2	2.3	2.0	1.7

Note: [a] New series, as revised by CBS. See *Economic Survey*, various.

Sources: 1) *Economic Survey*, various.
  2) *Historical Data for Kenya 1972–1990*, Technical Paper 91–12, Long-Range Planning Division, Ministry of Planning and National Development.

It is important to note the dramatic fall in the shares of formal employment between 1985 and 1990 and the spectacular rise in the share of informal sector employment in the same period. The rise in the share of informal sector employment only became noticeable with the revised series of employment data, which have a wider coverage of informal sector activities. Thus the data need to be interpreted with caution because the definition of the informal sector has been changed so that by 1990 it was a broader definition than in earlier years. By 1994, the informal sector was absorbing over half the total workforce, while the formal sector provided wage employment for only 44.8 per cent. Table 4.4 shows an increase in the labour force far higher than the expansion of formal sector employment, with the excess supply in the labour force finding its way into the informal sector.

The declining share of formal sector employment may perhaps help to explain the rising unemployment in the country with increasing labour supply, with the informal sector having to act as a cushion for those unemployed. This is reflected in the rapid rise in the informal sector share of the labour force, from a mere 4.2 per cent in 1972 to 53.4 per cent in 1994.[1]

Van der Hoeven and Vandemoortele (1987) argue that the average size of the informal sector units is 2.1 persons, but with a dominance of one-person enterprises. In addition, in Nairobi 45 per cent of informal sector workers earned less than the prevailing minimum wage. They further argue that the informal sector growth does not reflect an aspect of dynamism, but most probably acts as a residual recipient of labour. The informal sector also serves as a 'moonlighting' activity for formal sector employees. These are the consequences of liberalization and structural adjustment which we hope are short-run, but which may well persist in the medium to long term.

This may perhaps be true because the decline in employment shares in the formal sector does not in any way suggest a contraction of formal sector employment but rather an expansion of the labour force beyond what the formal sector can absorb. This fact comes out clearly from Figure 4.1 and Table 4.5. Figure 4.1 shows the trend in total formal employment. Employment has been steadily rising throughout, but towards the 1990s the rising trend slowed down somewhat. This slow-down was not, however, marked and thus does not necessarily imply a contraction of the sector.

---

[1] These data should be taken with some caution because the definition of the informal sector may be different in the data series.

Figure 4.1   *Formal wage employment, Kenya, 1972–96 (millions of persons engaged)*

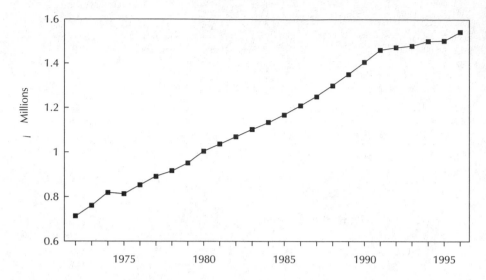

Table 4.5 shows the indices of formal sector employment. The formal sector is divided into public and private and we also show the major sub-sectors. There is an obvious slow growth in some sectors, but overall, except for the public sector, there was no decline in employment growth between 1972 and 1994. Public sector employment declined by 2 per cent between 1990 and 1994, largely due to the retrenchment of civil servants. These have accelerated since 1995.

Employment in the government services grew faster than in other sectors, which was generally consistent with the expansion of basic services like education, health, defence and the police force as the population increased. Employment in the agricultural sub-sector increased by 14 per cent over the period, and by about 17 per cent in building and construction. In other sub-sectors, like manufacturing and services, the growth was more rapid. The period 1990–94 saw an expansion of the agricultural sub-sector. The building and construction and mining and quarrying sub-sectors experienced periods of employment decline and periods of tremendous growth. In total, formal sector wage employment more than doubled, largely due to growth in public sector wage employment rather than in the private sector. The private sector employment index increased by 89 per cent over the 1972–94 period, compared with 140 per cent in the public sector.

Table 4.5   *Formal sector employment growth, Kenya, 1972–94 (1972=100)*

	1972	1975	1980	1985	1990	1994
Public	100	119	164	200	242	240
Private	100	110	123	142	155	189
Total	100	113	140	165	196	209
Agriculture	100	97	94	98	109	114
Manufacturing	100	119	167	188	221	233
Mining and quarrying	100	109	72	125	106	122
Building and construction	100	108	168	189	98	117
Commercial services	100	120	152	180	192	238
Government services	100	128	174	232	284	301

Source: *Economic Survey*, various; *Historical Data for Kenya* 1972–1990.

The number of persons recruited in the public sector between 1972 and 1994 rose by approximately 400,000, whereas the figure for the private sector was slightly lower, at 385,000. In terms of employment growth this implies a rather sharp shift because in 1972 the number employed in the public sector was far below that for the private sector (286,000 and 433,000 respectively). In the 1970s the private sector was absorbing a great deal of labour. This, however, changed in the 1980s when the relative importance of the private sector as a source of employment creation declined and the public sector took over. In the 1990s the share of the public sector in total wage employment declined again relative to the private sector.

Table 4.6 presents sectoral comparisons. We compare employment growth patterns in the private and public sectors. From this table, it seems that the services sector of the private sector is the only one that did not experience a major decline in employment growth. In contrast, there was a spectacular decline in the public sector. We compare the phenomena before adjustment with those of the adjustment period.

While agricultural sector employment in the public sector declined by –2.6 per cent annually during the 1980–84 period, there was a dramatic recovery in the adjustment period 1984–91, with employment in the sector growing at 5.7 per cent per annum, and a slow-down in the 1991–4 period, where the recorded growth declined by –1.2 per cent annually.

The public sector slowed down drastically in the adjustment period, except for the agriculture and services sectors. For a long time, public sector employment had been strongly determined by non-economic considerations, making it difficult to follow objective recruitment and staffing policies. It was not until the adjustment period that retrenchment through the popularly known 'Golden Handshake' started to help streamline public sector employment. The programme aims at creating a safety net attractive enough to induce workers in the public sector to opt for early retirement in order to reduce the public sector work force and the wage bill. The policy seems to be working, with employment growth between 1990 and 1994 declining by 2 per cent and labour costs in public sector recurrent expenditure falling by about 3.6 per cent between the 1993–4 and 1994–5 fiscal years. This form of safety net has become popular even in the private sector early retirement schemes.

Overall, in the adjustment period, growth in employment was recorded in the expanding sectors. The services industry of the private sector has been the most expanding sector, followed by the manufacturing sector. Most of the activities of the

Table 4.6 *Sectoral comparisons of employment growth, Kenya, 1972–80 to 1991–4 (%)*

Sector	1972–80	1980–84	1984–91	1991–94
Agriculture				
Public	3.8	–2.6	5.7	–1.2
Private	–0.85	0.02	1.2	1.4
Total	–0.18	0.88	2.4	0.8
Manufacturing				
Public	7.7	4.9	1.8	0.1
Private	7.3	1.4	2.5	1.3
Total	7.4	2.04	1.3	1.1
Services				
Public	20.1	5.5	3.6	–1.0
Private	4.8	4.2	3.4	4.1
Total	5.3	4.3	3.5	1.2

Source: Economic Survey, various; and Historical Data for Kenya 1972–1990.

public sector have been declining in terms of employment growth, perhaps due to government divestiture into private sector activities in the adjustment period. Furthermore, the growing labour force has to be absorbed in the informal sector which is characterized by heterogenous activities ranging from production and commerce to services.

Table 4.7 looks at employment in the formal sector over four time periods. It is clear that the growth of employment in the private sector is higher in the adjustment period compared with the period before adjustment, and vice versa for the public sector. Public sector employment rose markedly in the period 1972–80, but declined in the period 1980–84 and further in the 1984–94 period. In the private sector, however, average growth rates were almost the same in the 1972–80 and 1980–84 periods, and recorded some improvement in the 1984–94 period. Total employment declined continuously, but most markedly in the 1991–4 period. It may thus appear that, in the adjustment period, public sector employment growth suffered, which is consistent with the limits of fiscal spending and productive employment in the civil service pursued in the structural adjustment programmes.

Table 4.7   *Average annual employment growth, Kenya, 1972–80 to 1991–4*

	1972–80	1980–84	1984–91	1991–94
Public sector employment	7.1	3.2	3.0	−1.0
Private sector employment	2.6	1.9	2.5	2.7
Total formal employment	4.4	2.5	2.8	1.04

Source: *Economic Survey*, various.

Domestic output growth was not particularly impressive, especially in the 1980s. However, it started to improve after 1988 but slowed down again in 1991–2. By 1993–4 economic activity was showing signs of improvement. This coincided with an increase in informal sector growth and per capita growth. The informal sector growth can be regarded as a residual absorber of labour which the formal sector cannot absorb. Part of those working in the informal sector are also actively looking for jobs in the formal sector. Thus the informal sector could be considered as a sector that cushions the unemployed and those queueing for formal sector employment. This characteristic is based on the ease of entry into the sector. This, however, is the old interpretation of the role of the informal sector in employment. The informal sector in Kenya has grown tremendously and can no longer be regarded as a residual sector only absorbing the labour force. It is now an important source of employment. This new role has emerged as a result of the challenges from structural adjustment programmes, increasing population and contracting formal sector production activities due to the current wave of economic liberalization. The current view is that the informal sector promotes avenues of income-earning opportunities.

Table 4.8 investigates whether there has been any gender bias in employment growth by looking at the shares of women in the work force in various sub-sectors. The proportion of women in formal employment has been small but steadily increasing, from 12.2 per cent in 1964 to 17.8 per cent in 1983 and 23.1 per cent in 1994. In some of the specific sectors, the share of women in formal wage employment has been even more marked. In mining and quarrying, for instance, the proportion of women in employment rose to 26.1 in 1994 from a mere 2.9 per cent in 1983.

Equally spectacular change in the share of women was experienced in the provision of government services. However, changes in manufacturing and

Table 4.8 *Gender distribution of employment by major sector, Kenya, 1983–94 (%)*

Sector		1983	1985	1987	1989	1990	1992	1994
Agriculture	M	84.7	82.1	76.5	75.7	76.3	76.5	76.7
	F	15.3	17.9	23.5	24.3	23.7	23.5	23.3
Mining and quarrying	M	97.1	97.9	97.7	80.0	81.4	79.5	73.9
	F	2.9	2.1	2.3	20.0	18.6	20.5	26.1
Manufacturing	M	90.7	90.1	89.8	90.2	89.3	88.5	87.8
	F	9.3	9.9	10.2	9.8	10.7	11.5	12.2
Building and construction	M	95.5	97.4	94.5	93.7	94.3	94.4	95.0
	F	4.5	2.6	5.5	6.3	5.7	5.6	5.0
Commercial services	M	84.6	83.9	83.5	84.7	82.9	82.5	81.8
	F	15.4	16.1	16.5	15.3	17.1	17.5	18.2
Government services	M	74.8	72.8	72.4	72.9	72.4	69.3	69.2
	F	25.2	27.2	27.6	27.1	27.6	30.7	30.8
Total	M	82.2	80.3	78.8	79.2	78.7	77.1	76.9
	F	17.8	19.7	21.2	20.8	21.3	22.9	23.1

Source: *Economic Survey* and *Statistical Abstract*, various.

commercial services were slower. From the evidence in Table 4.8, it would seem that even though the share of women in formal sector employment has been low, it does not necessarily reflect an open gender bias in employment in general. Still, one expects the share of women to be higher in view of their higher share in the country's total population. This can be rationalized by the fact that the population in Kenya is predominantly rural. Women are mainly involved in smallholder farm activities, self-employed and as unpaid family workers.

Estimation results In this section, we are attempting to explain the growth of employment in the economy as a whole and in some specific sub-sectors. We estimate a multiple regression equation where employment growth is explained by growth in output, public sector expenditure, import surplus (or imports and exports) and investments (capital formation). This kind of analysis attempts to bring out salient indicators that contribute to employment growth. The main motivation is to assess whether we can associate any breaks in the regression equation with the structural adjustment period. This will be done by estimating the equations recursively and observing and testing the stability of the regression coefficients.

Employment growth is related to the level of economic activity, while other regressors relate to the objectives of adjustment policy reforms. Thus we include imports and exports or import surplus due to the fact that the industrial sector has been import-driven, that is, reliant on imported raw materials, while exports are income-generating for export-oriented industries and the agricultural sector.

In view of the statistical problems encountered in regressing non-stationary data, the time series properties of the data are first analysed. The problem with non-stationary data is that there is a danger of getting spurious regression results, and furthermore the standard test statistics for inference, like the F-statistic, are no longer valid. To avoid spurious results and to take into account the long-run information in the data[2] we estimate regression equations in rates of growth (that are stationary) and with an error correction term that allows our short-run model to hinge on the long-run relationship in the data (the results of these time series properties of the

---

[2]When time series data are differenced to make them stationary, the long-run information in the data would be lost. To incorporate this, it is necessary to estimate an error-correction model if the variables in the model are found to be cointegrated, that is, they form a long-run stationary relationship (see Engle and Granger, 1987).

data are not shown but can be obtained from the authors on request). In view of the simultaneity and likely collinearity of the variables, for instance gross domestic income and capital formation, a battery of tests will be performed to show whether this conditioning satisfies the basic assumptions of model residual behaviour.

In the first place we tried to estimate a total employment growth equation. Due to the smallness of the sample, this was a hazardous task. Total employment growth, ΔTEMP, was explained positively by import surplus, IMPSUP; positively by growth of capital formation, ΔCAPF; positively by domestic income growth, ΔGDP; positively by a long-run relationship between the variables in the model, GDECM (an error correction term), which shows that the long-run growth of GDP fuelled by other variables is to increase total employment, and two dummies, one for 1990 that spurs employment growth and the other for 1977 that dampens employment growth (all the variables are in logs, so that their first difference reflects growth rates). The dummies were introduced in the model after recursive estimation showed the presence of outliers that made the coefficients of the model unstable. The results are shown in Table 4.9.

Table 4.9 *Total employment growth, Kenya (estimation results)*

Variable	Coefficient	t-ratio
Constant	−.002	−.095
IMPSUP$_t$	.007	4.05*
ΔCAPF$_t$	.089	1.86**
ΔGDP$_t$	.319	2.38*
GDPECM$_{t-1}$	.334	2.86*
D77	−.064	−2.70*
D90	.168	6.97*

* indicates significant at 5% and ** indicates significant at 10%.
Statistical results: R^2 = 94, $F(7,13)$ = 27.60[.000], σ = 1.8%, DW = 2.02
Diagnostic tests: [3]AR $F(2,11)$ =1.70, ARCH $F(2,9)$ = 0.94, RESET $F(1,12)$ = 0.56, NORMALITY $\chi^2(2)$ = 1.14

From the model, we see that GDP growth makes an important contribution to total employment growth; a 1 per cent increase in GDP growth raises employment by 0.32 per cent. Also important are growth in capital formation (investment growth, a rise in capital formation by 1 per cent would increase employment by 0.09 per cent), import surplus and a general improvement in economic activity as reflected by positive shocks hitting the economy, but some of the shocks have a negative impact on total employment growth. The dummies should also be interpreted with caution. It is not always possible to motivate breaks in the data and in most cases the dummies should reflect our ignorance in terms of explaining the movements of the variable we have conditioned in the model.

In the second place an equation for formal employment growth (ΔTFEMPL) was estimated, where growth of GDP lagged one step and lagged growth of capital formation and lagged export growth (EXP) were found to spur formal sector employment growth. Shock dummies had a differential impact with 1983 and 1985 spurring growth and 1975 and 1993 dampening formal sector employment growth. The results are shown in Table 4.10.

---

[3]The diagnostic tests are to determine the appropriateness of the model through the behaviour of the residuals; AR, auto regressive test for serial correlation, ARCH, Auto regressive conditional heteroskedasticity for heteroskedasticity of the residuals, Normality test for the distribution of the residuals and the RESET test for regression specification to test for the linearity of the regression equation. These tests are not significant implying that the model tentatively reflects the data used.

Table 4.10 *Total formal sector employment, Kenya (estimation results)*

Variable	Coefficient	t-ratio
Constant	.008	1.75**
ΔGDP_{t-1}	.114	3.48*
$\Delta CAPF_{t-1}$	.151	5.43*
ΔEXP_{t-1}	.035	4.88*
D75	−.028	−3.65*
D83	.047	4.77*
D85	.036	4.91*
D93	−.034	−4.13*

* indicates significant at 5% and ** indicates significant at 10%.
Statistical results: R^2 = .91 F(7,12) = 16.83[.00], σ = .7%, DW = 2.07
Model tests: AR F(2,10) = 1.64, ARCH F(1,10) = .10, RESET F(1,11) = .14, NORMALITY $\chi^2(2)$ = .35

Here capital formation and GDP growth both lagged one year seem important in explaining formal employment growth. The presence of more dummies is a reflection of macro variables failing to account for fluctuations in formal employment growth in Kenya. The inability of the macroeconomic variables to explain the growth of formal employment growth may be puzzling, but when we consider the various controls on the labour market, stagnating income growth and tripartite agreements, economic factors may become less important. This is perhaps why dummies take over and have both positive and negative impacts.[4]

Next we estimated employment growth in the public ($\Delta PUBEMPL$) and private ($\Delta PREMPL$) sectors using the same variables as in the preceding two regression equations. The results are shown in Table 4.11.

The results for public sector employment growth show that economic variables have little to explain; employment is explained by shocks to the system which reflect ad hoc employment policies pursued in the public sector, not necessarily driven by economic fundamentals. In the private sector, growth in capital formation, employment lagged two years, imports and ΔGDP were important and positively contributed to employment growth. However, private employment lagged one year and growth in public expenditure dampened employment growth. A possible inter-

Table 4.11 *Private sector employment, Kenya (estimation results)*

Variable	Coefficient	t-ratio
Constant	−.012	−2.06
$\Delta CAPF_{t-1}$	.377	9.09
$\Delta PREMPL_{t-1}$	−.451	−6.02
$\Delta PREMPL_{t-2}$	.411	6.06
ΔIMP_t	.046	3.36
ΔIMP_{t-1}	.066	4.22
ΔGDP_{t-1}	.392	9.08
$\Delta PUBEXP_{t-1}$	−.542	−14.32
D83	.059	6.28
D85	.081	11.30
D89	.050	6.78

* indicates significant at 5% and ** indicates significant at 10%.
Statistical results: R^2 = 0.97, F(10,8) = 29.41[.000], σ = 0.6%, DW = 2.27, RESET F(1,7) = 0.04, NORMALITY $\chi^2(2)$ = 0.20

[4]It should not be lost sight of that dummies were included in all equations after recursive estimation showed the presence of outliers reflecting shocks to the system. Such shocks were then modelled using dummies. These outliers were a reflection of the regressors being unable to account for the fluctuations of formal sector employment growth.

Table 4.12 *Public sector employment, Kenya (estimation results)*

Variable	Coefficient	t-ratio
Constant	.015	2.94*
$\Delta PUBEMPL_{t-3}$	.404	4.69*
ΔEXP_t	−.042	−4.54*
D76	.024	2.73*
D79	.056	6.57*
D85	.028	3.33*
D86	−.019	−2.20*
D88	.026	3.04*
D92	.053	−6.22*
D94	−.014	−4.54*

* indicates significant at 5% and ** indicates significant at 10%.
$R^2 = 0.97$, $F(10,8) = 25.52[.000]$, $\sigma = 0.8\%$, DW = 2.08, RESET $F(1,7) = 0.17$, NORMALITY $\chi(2) = 0.228$.[5]

pretation is that an increase in public expenditure implies less resources for the private sector through domestic credit and may thus have a negative impact on private sector activities and employment.

Finally, an equation was estimated for informal sector employment growth using the same variables as in the other equations; the results are shown in Table 4.13.

There is a clear positive relationship between informal sector employment growth and growth of domestic output. Furthermore, the informal sector seems to thrive as formal sector employment grows rapidly; there are strong lagged effects. The interpretation of these results shows that an increase in the growth of national income (GDP) by 1 per cent would increase informal sector employment by 5 per cent and there would be an accelerating (lagged) effect of 3.32 per cent. Similarly, when total formal sector employment increases by 1 per cent, there is a trickle-down or reverberating effect on informal sector employment which increases with a lag at 5.54 per cent. Other variables are interpreted in the same way. Surprisingly, public expenditure growth dampens informal sector employment growth; this may perhaps imply that public expenditure falls on goods outside the informal market and as such does not spur its activities. Any shocks in employment growth in the short run adjust to the long-run trend through the error correction mechanism (ECM) coefficient, but at a very low speed, 7.1 per cent.

Table 4.13 *Informal sector employment growth, Kenya (estimation results)*

Variable	Coefficient	t-ratio
Constant	−.870	−5.57*
ΔGDP_t	5.00	7.49*
ΔGDP_{t-1}	3.32	3.82*
$\Delta TFEMPL_{t-1}$	5.54	2.44*
$IMSUP_t$	.921	4.35*
$IMSUP_{t-1}$	.391	2.45*
$\Delta PUBEXP_t$	−.674	−2.42*
$\Delta PUBEXP_{t-1}$	−1.59	−3.70*
ECM_{t-1}	−.071	−1.74**
D77	−.621	−4.22*
D81	.272	2.37*

* indicates significant at 5% and ** indicates significant at 10%.
Statistical results: $R^2 = .91$ $F(10,8) = 8.24[.0032]$, $\sigma = 0.82\%$, DW = 2.17;
Diagnostic tests AR $F(1, 9) = .16$, ARCH $F(1,9) = .43$, RESET $F(1,9) = .69$, NORMALITY $\chi(2) = 24$

[5]For Tables 4.11 and 4.12, AR and ARCH tests could not be estimated due to diminished degrees of freedom.

The models estimated in this section, though preliminary in many ways, have brought out the salient factors that contribute to employment growth in Kenya; these are domestic income growth, the level of economic activity, external trade and capital formation. Public expenditure looks an inefficient way of spurring economic activity and thus leads to a dampening of employment growth. Shocks to the economy have both positive and negative effects on employment growth.[6]

Earnings and real wage levels

Nominal average earnings growth in Kenya has risen in the adjustment period, as Table 4.14 shows. Earnings in the formal sector, on the other hand, have been relatively stable except for 1984–91 when they declined slightly. To show whether structural adjustment policies have had an impact on the labour market, we compare the growth rates of the previous period with the 1984–94 period. Whereas earnings fell in the 1980s compared with the 1970s, they increased in the adjustment period, and in the private sector this increase is far higher than that of 1972–80. In the 1980–84 period, growth in private sector earnings declined to 1.9 per cent compared with 2.1 per cent in the 1972–80 period. In the periods 1984–91 and 1991–4 the growth rates were rapid. If we compare the figures in real average earnings in the adjustment period, this increase in earnings is not reflected in real earnings. Real earnings have continued to fall in the 1990s.

Table 4.14 *Average annual earnings growth, Kenya, 1972–80 to 1991–4 (%)*

	1972–80	1980–84	1984–91	1991–94
Public sector wage earnings	7.8	10.1	7.2	7.2
Private sector wage earnings	2.1	1.9	7.6	11.0
Total formal wage earnings	7.6	9.4	7.4	9.2

Source: *Economic Survey*, various.

These are nominal earnings but when real earnings are considered (see Table 4.15) there is a rapid erosion of real earnings. These declines have been more drastic in the period 1991–4. In a nutshell, this shows that real wages or earnings are *not* inflexible downwards; perhaps the absence of full indexation aids this result.

Table 4.15 *Earnings growth, Kenya, 1990–1 to 1993–4*

	1990–1	1991–92	1992–93	1993–94
Formal/informal ratio	136	118	101	84
Average earnings, formal (%)	9.7	13.5	13.7	18.2
Real average earnings, formal (%)	–8.3	–10.9	–22.1	–8.3

Source: *Economic Survey*, 1995

One would expect to find some evidence of systematic changes in inter-sectoral relative wage rates over time, if structural adjustment is impacting on the labour market. Table 4.16 shows indices for the relative wages of the private and public

---

[6]It should be noted that the dummies were added to the analysis after the reduced model showed parameter instabilities due to the presence of shocks (outliers) in the system after recursive estimation was performed to test the validity of the models. In such situations we modelled these shocks. The danger is that even though we stabilize the parameters of the regression models we cannot always motivate these shocks. Some coincide with the structural adjustment period or other economic events. At the limit, even where we are able to motivate the shocks, the only valid and tentative conclusion is that the dummies reflect our ignorance in accounting for the movement of employment or earnings growth in the sectors we are analyzing during specific years.

sectors and for agriculture in relation to manufacturing (Agri/Manf), relative to building and construction, (Agri/B&C) and relative to the services sector, (Agri/ Services). Data used are average nominal annual wages and it is thus not possible to standardize for the changing skill composition of the different sectors (see Milne and Neitzert, 1994). Nevertheless, the data may show whether inter-sectoral wage differentials respond to market forces in a manner consistent with labour mobility between sectors (or immobility). The essential point to be investigated is whether structural adjustment policies that aim at reallocating labour between sectors should allow for a consequent rise in wages paid in expanding sectors (*ibid.*). In the extreme where labour markets are very segmented, this would act as a real obstacle to the success of structural adjustment policies. From Table 4.16, the private sector seems to be expanding faster than the public sector, at least in the structural adjustment period. The rest of the sectors do not show any substantial decline relative to agriculture, even though over time the agricultural sector is contracting gradually relative to the other sectors. This does not therefore show a significant movement of labour between sectors, although there is significant movement from private to public sector.

As such, there are no discernible trends that can be drawn; perhaps the period is not long enough to show the resource flows into the expanding sectors or perhaps the resources are not very mobile across sectors. But in general, there is movement to expanding sectors; agriculture in this case is the least expanding sector, as is the public sector in general.

Table 4.16   *Inter-sectoral relative wage rates, Kenya, 1972–94*

	1972	1975	1980	1985	1988	1990	1994
Private/public	89.5	70.9	85.5	83.8	87.6	. 93.5	102.5
Agri/Manf	24.9	23.6	28.9	28.3	30.0	30.1	39.2
Agri/B&C	28.9	28.1	32.0	35.4	38.9	40.3	46.5
Agri/Services	18.9	79.1	21.6	21.7	19.8	22.0	28.0

Source: *Economic Survey*, various

Table 4.17 shows indices of real consumption wages (average wages deflated by the Consumer Price Index) for staggered years between 1972 and 1994 for the formal sector. The decline in real consumption wages has been rapid. Real wages have fallen by more than 50 per cent between 1980 and 1984 in all sectors. The influence seems to have been tremendous increases in some macro-level prices, the domestic rate of inflation, the rate of interest and the depreciation of the currency (these macro-level prices are shown in Table 4.18).

The macro-level prices between 1988 and 1994 display a rapid increase. The exchange rate depreciated to Kshs 68.16 from Kshs 18.6 to the dollar between 1988 and 1993 – a nominal depreciation of 266 per cent. By 1994, the currency had slightly appreciated but still represented about 141 per cent depreciation compared with the 1988 level. Inflation, on the other hand, rose from 12.3 to 46 per cent in 1993 and then came down to 28.8 per cent in 1994. The interest rate, reflected by the Treasury bills discount rate (TDR) which is a benchmark for all interest rates, rose to 39.3 per cent in 1993 from 15 per cent in 1988 and then came down drastically to 17.9 per cent in 1994. These three macro-level prices have been shown to drive each other (see Ndung'u, 1995). The movements in these macro-level prices thus explain the downward slide of real consumption wages and real minimum wages in the adjustment period.

Table 4.17   *Real consumption wages, Kenya, 1972–94 (1980=100)*

	1972	1975	1980	1985	1990	1994
Public sector, total	121	109	100	84.1	81.7	41.1
Agriculture	n.a.	n.a.	100	73.4	74.4	37.5
Manufacturing	n.a.	n.a.	100	75.1	71.1	33.6
Mining and quarrying	n.a.	n.a.	100	66.5	51.2	21.5
Building and construction	n.a.	n.a.	100	107	91.7	53.8
Services	n.a.	n.a.	100	82.6	82.5	38.2
Private sector	126	92	100	82.5	89.3	49.4
Agriculture	109	90.9	100	81.1	89.7	59.7
Manufacturing	127	113	100	82.6	86.1	44.1
Mining and quarrying	183	195	100	74.2	109	59.6
Building and construction	113	98.9	100	69.2	67.9	38.7
Services	124	105	100	80.9	88.2	46.2
Grand total	108	98.8	100	82.8	85.6	45.2

n.a. = not available

Table 4.18   *Macro-level prices, Kenya, 1988–94*

	1988	1989	1990	1991	1992	1993	1994
Exchange rate (US$)	18.6	21.6	24.1	28.1	36.2	68.2	44.8
Inflation	12.3	13.3	15.8	19.6	27.3	46.0	28.8
Interest rate (TDR)	15.0	14.0	15.93	16.77	16.96	39.3	17.9

Source: Economic Survey, various.

In Table 4.19 we show the real minimum average wages for the urban and agri-cultural sectors. No doubt, the decline in real wages at the minimum level has been quite rapid, declining by almost 50 per cent between 1982 and 1994. The dramatic fall comes in the adjustment period, however.

As Milne and Neitzert (1994) argue, exogenous shocks hitting the economy are all expected to influence equilibrium employment levels in different sectors through changes in real product wages. Table 4.20 provides changes in real wages for sub-periods between 1972 and 1994 for the formal sector.

Table 4.19   *Real minimum wages, Kenya, 1982–94*

	1982	1985	1987	1989	1990	1991	1992	1993	1994
Urban (1982 = 100)									
Nairobi/Momba	100	88	85	78	85	74	64	59	55
Municipalities	100	87	85	83	87	75	65	59	55
Other	100	86	85	85	87	76	67	60	57
Agriculture (1985 = 100)									
Unskilled	n.a.	100	100	92	92	81	71	63	56
Skilled	n.a.	100	100	92	92	81	70	63	56

Source: Economic Survey, various, CBS Employment and Earnings in the Modern Sector, various.

Table 4.20   *Real product wages, Kenya, 1972–95 to 1991–4 (%)*

	1972–75	1975–80	1980–84	1984–91	1991–94
Public total	2.8	−1.2	−0.47	1.01	−1.5
Private sector	−7.9	3.0	−0.5	1.1	−1.2
Grand total	−2.6	0.09	1.12	0.93	−1.05

Source: Economic Survey, various; Kenya Historical Data 1972–1990.

In the 1991–4 period, real product wage growth was negative in all sectors, but had been positive in the 1984–91 period. This implies that employment levels have been more drastically affected in the 1990s than earlier and the decline in the product wage is more marked. This shows that shocks hitting the economy have reduced employment growth in the 1990s quite drastically and thus reduced the real earnings and the real wage cost has essentially declined.

Estimation results In this subsection, we attempt to explain movements in nominal wage earnings in terms of growth in income, inflation, per capita income, recurrent government expenditure and the exchange rate. This may help to account for movements in the nominal wage. In most studies, an earnings function is estimated to explain cross-section differences in earnings and between periods (see, for example, Milne and Neizert, 1994). This approach is of limited use for our purposes as we want to relate earnings to macroeconomic policies in the economy and over time. Furthermore, the basic aspect we wish to consider is that structural adjustment changes the relative price structure and rewards those sectors that set prices right through the supply-demand responses. Thus, a cross-section analysis makes an implicit assumption of homogeneity of labour across sectors, whereas we would like to differentiate the sectoral responses to adjustment policies. This becomes important in trying to understand the effects of economic crisis and adjustment on real and nominal wages. It may help, for example, in analyzing whether abolishing wage guidance councils had any effects on nominal or real earnings over time. Regression analysis would show this as instability of the coefficients implying a structural disturbance in the equation and thus calling for modelling of the shock periods by adding dummies. The results of regression equations are shown in Tables 4.21–23. In the first place we estimated an equation for an average wage for the formal sector and then proceeded to estimate separate equations for the public and private sectors. In each equation a battery of tests was performed to test the validity of the model.

Formal sector nominal wage growth (ΔAVE) is positively explained by inflation (ΔCPI) in the previous period and the total wage income growth (ΔTWINC), and negatively explained by its one-year lagged effects, public expenditure growth and shocks hitting the economy. For the private sector, nominal wage growth (ΔPRAVE) is spurred by public expenditure growth and growth in private sector wage income (ΔPRWINC) and by the exchange-rate movements (ΔEX), but is negatively related to the rate of inflation (though not highly significant), its own value one-year lagged effects and some shocks to the system. In the public sector, the most important

Table 4.21 *Formal sector nominal wage growth, Kenya (estimation results)*

Variable	Coefficient	t-ratio
constant	−.093	−5.92**
ΔAVE$_{t-1}$	−.158	−1.51
ΔCPI$_{t-1}$	.122	4.37**
ΔPCAPF$_{t-1}$	.20	3.99**
ΔTWINC$_t$	1.044	12.41*
ΔTWINC$_{t-1}$	.413	3.94*
ΔPUBEXP$_t$	−.036	−1.49
ΔPUBEXP$_{t-1}$	−.064	−2.79*
D77	−.051	−4.92*
D89	.040	−4.58*

* indicates significant at 5% and ** indicates significant at 1%.
Statistical results <: R^2 = 0.97 F(9,10) = 32.11[.00] σ = 0.77% DW = 1.96. Diagnostic tests: AR F(1,9) = 0.01, ARCH F (1,8) = 0.14, RESET F(1,9) = 0.05, NORMALITY χ^2(2) = 2.80

influence comes from the growth in the public sector wage bill (ΔPUWINC), public expenditure growth[7] and some shocks which relate in most cases to civil servants' salary reviews. Inflation has a negative and significant effect.

Table 4.22   *Private sector nominal wage growth, Kenya (estimation results)*

Variable	Coefficient	t-ratio
Constant	−.015	−.44
ΔPRAVE$_{t-1}$	−.20	−3.74*
ΔPUBEXP$_{t-1}$	.34	4.17*
ΔCPI$_{t-2}$	−.197	−1.62
ΔPRWINC$_t$	.995	2.99*
ΔEX$_t$	.06	1.69
D78	.321	10.36*
D82	−.198	−5.44*
D89	−.124	−2.86*

* indicates significant at 5% and ** indicates significant at 1%.
Statistical results: R^2 = .95 F(8,11) = 44.52[.00] σ = 2.5% DW = 2.03, AR F(1,10) = .07.
Diagnostic tests: ARCH F(1,9) = 1.90, RESET F(1,10) = 3.57[.0881], NORMALITY χ^2(2) = .99

Table 4.23   *Public sector nominal wage growth, Kenya (estimation results)*

Variable	Coefficient	t-ratio
Constant	−.04	−1.12
ΔPUAVE$_{t-2}$	−.272	−7.67*
ΔPUBEXP$_t$	.099	2.78*
ΔCPI$_{t-1}$	−.241	−5.93*
ΔPUWINC$_t$	.665	8.79*
D78	−.325	−22.94*
D82	.236	16.57*
D83	−.024	−1.78**
D84	.064	3.94*
D93	.024	1.62

Statistical results: R^2 = .99 F(9,10) = 145.92[.00] σ = 1.26% DW = 2.01, AR F(1,9) = .06.
Diagnostic tests: ARCH F(1,8) = .70, RESET F(1,9)=.43, NORMALITY χ^2(2) = .16.

Conclusion

This section has shown that the labour market has borne its own share of adjustment in the structural adjustment era. Employment growth in the formal sector has slackened and this has forced the ever increasing labour force to seek refuge in the informal sector, not necessarily for gainful employment but for an income-earning opportunity. Still more research is required to investigate whether the informal sector is beginning to be dynamic in terms of expansion rather than increases in atomistic units, and to make an assessment of earnings and wages paid.

Public sector employment has been under scrutiny in this era of adjustment because of the accommodative policies practised in the 1970s and 1980s. Economic factors were not important criteria for employment. The results from the regression equation show that the level of economic activity did not determine employment growth in the public sector. This reflects the use of non-economic factors in

---

[7]This does not in any way present any collinearity owing to the fact that the wage bill accounts for the major share in public expenditure since the regression is in growth rates, and is thus not even picked up by the diagnostic tests.

employment expansion in the sector. The current solution that seems to be working, at least for both parties, is the retrenchment of the redundant labour force through the 'Safety Net' package. This has come out somewhat in the analysis both in relative and in absolute decline.

Perhaps the most dramatic has been the fall of real wages in this period. Trends and indices come to the same conclusion, that real wages are not inflexible downwards. This implies that the long-term goals of structural adjustment may work, albeit slowly, in inducing labour to shift to more profitable sectors. This also implies that widespread indexation is not evident, and perhaps this may help redirect resources to the expanding and profitable sectors of the economy in line with the predictions of structural adjustment policies. The short-run consequences have been quite adverse for the labour force, since a fall in real earnings is transmitted to a fall in welfare. Moreover, the suffering of those who cannot get jobs and the open unemployment and underemployment in the informal sector have been immense.

Changes in employment policies and practices during adjustment

Employment, incomes and wages policies

The Kenyan Government's policy on employment has remained essentially the same in the post-independence period. The policy was centred on creating a conducive environment for the private sector to play the leading role in economic growth and employment generation. The country has also pursued a low wage policy throughout the last three decades aimed at attracting foreign and domestic investors and encouraging the use of labour-intensive technologies. The low wage policies were implemented through government intervention in wage determination in terms of minimum wage legislation and wage guidelines which have influenced collective bargaining since 1973.

Over time, the government has spelt out short, medium and long-term employment strategies. Short-run policies emphasized the need to stabilize the economy in order to create an enabling environment for investors. In broad terms the policies focused on fiscal and monetary discipline and the provision of price and other incentives such as setting appropriate agricultural prices to promote non-traditional and traditional exports and food crop production; intensification of farm production; diversification of economic activities, especially in rural areas, through public investments in infrastructure and other facilities and in regional urban centres to attract investments to the regional towns; industrialization and protection of industries; export promotion and elimination of anti-export bias; and continued support for the rural and urban informal sector through provision of water, power and other forms of infrastructure.

The medium to long-term employment policies included increased support to the private sector through infrastructural development; provision of agricultural research and extension services; increased efficiency and productivity of public investments; reduction in the fertility rate and in population growth achieved by education, health care and family planning services; undertaking reforms in the educational system in order to produce a well trained labour force with the right attitude and job expectations; and improved health care, housing, nutritional and water supplies that would lead to better standards of living and increased worker productivity.

The 1992 Sessional Paper on Employment and Development indicated that the government's employment policy had not radically changed as it continued to stress the need to increase private sector investments and savings, rural development and rural programmes, growth of small-scale industries and the informal sector, industrial growth, increased efficiency and restructuring of the education system (Republic of Kenya, 1994a: 204). However, some new dimensions had been introduced including the development of a strong data base on employment trends and labour market development, redressing the gender imbalance in public sector employment and encouraging early retirement from the public service. The civil service optional retirement age was lowered to 40. There was also increased focus on the reduction of child labour, and the use of higher wages to act as an incentive to raise labour productivity and create an innovative scientific and technology policy.

In the area of incomes and wages policy, commitment to achieving an equitable distribution of income and fair wages has been continued. However, following the decontrol of commodity prices it was no longer feasible to retain the policy of wage guidelines. In mid-1994, the labour market was substantially restructured when the wage guidelines were removed, giving employers and workers greater latitude in wage negotiations.

Legal framework of the labour market
Apart from a few changes, the legal framework of the labour market has not changed in any drastic manner during the structural adjustment programmes. The legal framework was largely guided by the government's desire to keep the labour movement under control without too much independence and power to destabilize the economy, and to keep wages as low as possible in order to encourage the utilization of labour-intensive technologies.

The key components of the legal framework were a decentralized collective bargaining system based on wage councils which negotiated minimum wages for various categories of workers for two-year periods; an industrial court for all industrial disputes; and a Minister of Labour who held tremendous powers in the tripartite arrangements and agreements between workers, employers and government representatives.

Wage guidelines For the period 1973–94, although wage determination was undertaken through collective bargaining between workers and employer representatives through wage councils in various sectors of the economy, wage levels were closely guided by wage awards below the cost of living index. The guidelines, published in 1973, were resented by the trade unions but were retained because the government did not want to create a high wage-cost economy.

After the abolition of virtually all price controls by 1994, it was found necessary to remove the restriction imposed on wage negotiations by the wage guidelines. This is, therefore, one of the changes in the legal framework of Kenya's labour market to take place due to the implementation of structural adjustment programmes (Republic of Kenya, 1995b: 59).

The guidelines were liberalized to allow for full compensation for increases in the cost of living. Another change in the guidelines is that labour productivity is to be given more weight in collective bargaining than was the case previously. A related change affects the period of collective agreements, which has now been left open, instead of the previously fixed period of two years.

Another wage-related change in the legal system was the move to allow employers to appeal against what they might regard as inappropriate or excessively high wage awards to workers by the Industrial Court judges.

Minimum wage laws The country's minimum wage laws have not been changed, in spite of the removal of all price controls in the product markets.

Virtually every year, usually during Labour Day celebrations, the government announces some increase in minimum wages, usually set separately for agricultural workers (in the Agricultural Wages Order) and for urban and other workers (in the General Wages Order). In the collective bargaining, various wage councils negotiate their own minimum wages, usually above the General Wages Order minimum wages.

Job security Job security has always been given high priority in Kenya's labour market. One of the legal provisions aimed at ensuring job security has been the redundancy laws, under which employers had to go through a well laid down procedure before the Minister of Labour and Manpower Development would grant them permission to declare workers redundant. Besides this, it was only through an Industrial Court award that an employer could declare a worker redundant. There were also considerable severance payments for workers declared redundant. To circumvent these constraints, a large number of employers used the unethical practice of maintaining casual employees for long periods, because laying off casual workers did not require observing the redundancy laws.

Through the Finance Act of 1994, the government has relaxed these redundancy procedures to make it much easier for employers to lay off their workers. Employers can now declare workers redundant without having to seek permission from the Minister of Labour. They are only required to notify the Ministry of Labour and the trade union movement of the reasons for and the extent of the intended redundancy. This measure was taken as a result of the argument that it was necessary to enable enterprises to restructure their operations in response to the economic adjustment taking place in the country.

While the practice of keeping workers as 'casual' for long periods had always brought a sense of insecurity to a large number of employees in the private sector, the relaxation of the redundancy laws is expected to aggravate the problem even more. Besides redundancy procedures, the private sector, like the public sector, has resorted to early retirement schemes in the retrenchment and restructuring of their organizations. In the cases where they have been tried, early retirement schemes have been over-subscribed.

Labour standards, health and safety regulations Kenya's labour standards have not changed so far due to adjustment. While legal provisions on labour standards and regulations on workers' health and safety at the place of work have existed for most of the post-independence period administered by the Labour Inspectorate of the Ministry of Labour, there have been complaints that they have not been adequately implemented by most employers, sometimes exposing the workers to a lot of health risks. Indeed, most sectors, 'either lack protective devices completely or use existing protective devices insufficiently or not at all' (Kasiynenko *et al.*, 1994: 58). A major constraint on the development of protective devices for the informal, Jua-Kali sector is the fact that the many different kinds of equipment in this sector make it difficult to design devices that can be used by all sectors.

Functioning of the Industrial Court The functioning of the Industrial Court has remained largely unchanged throughout the adjustment period. The Court's arbitration and settlement of disputes activities have contributed to the relative peace that has prevailed in the country's industrial relations. Its operations have remained fairly impartial, although both trade unions and employers have sometimes criticized some of its decisions. The employers, as already noted, have often been critical of the wage awards to workers and have recently lobbied to be allowed to appeal against such awards. Except for a few amendments of this nature, the structure and functions of the Court have not changed in response to the economic reforms taking place in the period 1985–95.

Rights of workers' association Kenya is a signatory to most of the international labour Conventions, and technically all Kenyan workers enjoy rights of association as long as they fulfil the required conditions. However, recent events have shown that the government can easily deny groups of workers their right of association. Some examples of this include the government's refusal to register trade unions formed by groups the government regards as sensitive or difficult to control. Between 1993 and 1994 lecturers from all the public universities in the country went on strike for almost one year protesting the government's refusal to register their proposed union, the University Academic Staff Union (UASU). During the same period, the government refused to register two other proposed trade unions: for medical doctors in public hospitals and for civil servants.

Disputes in industrial and service sectors
Table 4.24 shows trends in the number of strikes, the workers involved and the work-days lost in the period 1980–94. There is no strong evidence that implementation of the structural adjustment programme was directly related to the level of industrial strikes. The number of strikes varied considerably from year to year. The data show, however, that the average number of strikes per year was higher in the period 1985–91 compared with either 1980–84 or 1992–4. If there was a direct relationship between the strikes and the implementation of structural adjustment, one would have expected the average number of strikes to be highest during the third phase of the reform programme (1992–5) when the country implemented SAPs much more seriously than in the previous periods. In terms of average number of work-days lost due to strikes, the period 1985–91 was more heavily affected than the others, the most affected years being 1986–8. The number of workers involved has ranged between 17,000 and 21,000 for most of the period, except in 1983–4, 1986, 1987 and 1990 when the numbers were much higher or much lower.

Table 4.24   *Industrial strikes, Kenya, 1980–94*

Year	No. of strikes	No. of workers involved	Work-days lost
1980	81	18,980	32,479
1981	74	18,117	40,257
1982	100	22,372	26,659
1983	75	12,851	18,448
1984	69	7,663	39,396
1985	87	17,207	28,961
1986	110	33,588	168,014
1987	109	27,960	104,623
1988	92	18,631	70,094
1989	121	21,279	45,994
1990	92	7,839	23,821
1991	90	19,620	36,377
1992	97	19,684	49,436
1993	69	20,349	68,039
1994	55	20,749	41,827

Source: Republic of Kenya, *Statistical Abstract*, various issues.

It should be noted that the environment for staging a strike has not been conducive for Kenyan workers due to three main factors. First, the government adopted a negative approach to striking workers. It had virtually declared all strikes illegal. Secondly, because of the prevailing high levels of unemployment, it has been easy for employers to threaten to sack all striking workers. There have also been instances of government and employers intimidating trade union leaders or those regarded as the ring leaders in a strike. This environment has substantially discouraged workers from resorting to strikes. A large proportion of workers in the industrial and service sectors in the private sector are 'casuals', making it highly risky for them to participate in strikes. Thirdly, the trade unions are not financially capable of supporting their members when they are on strike and this renders the strike quite ineffective.

Responses of labour market institutions during adjustment

Public responses to SAPs by social partners and political interest groups
Public responses to structural adjustment measures and their outcomes have been mixed in Kenya. On the one side, there is a variety of groups comprising business people (Ikiara, 1994), opposition political parties and technocrats in the government who have generally supported economic reform. However, there are others including trade unions, some sections of the government and NGOs who have often expressed opposition to the reforms. Some groups have tended to blame SAPs for virtually all the economic and social problems facing the country.

Kenya's opposition political parties have been generally more pro-adjustment than the ruling party, KANU, while the trade unions have been clearly anti-adjustment (Gibbon, 1995: 17). Frequent reversals of adjustment measures already introduced have been one of the indicators that some sections of the Kenyan leadership have not been seriously committed to the structural adjustment programmes. Some politicians have viewed the conditionalities associated with SAPs as interference in the internal affairs of the country. This has been the case especially for reforms touching on governance. The opposition, on the other hand, has been pressing for stronger and more direct linkage of donor aid with the government's implementation of more economic and political reforms.

Employers' organizations
As noted above, the response to the SAPs received both support and opposition from the key employers' or manufacturers' organizations, the reactions varying with different components of the programmes. While they readily embraced some measures like the removal of foreign-exchange and price controls, there was strong lobbying against some aspects of trade liberalization. The two main employers' organizations, the Federation of Kenya Employers (FKE) and the Kenya Association of Manufacturers (KAM), complained that import liberalization had led to massive imports, and they called for protection of domestic producers through the imposition and effective collection of duties and other taxes on imported products and implementing measures against dumping and other forms of unfair competition. The FKE has also campaigned for the relaxation of the redundancy laws, to enable employers to declare workers redundant without too much bureaucracy. They argued that some of the components of structural adjustments were having adverse effects on their volume of operations and profits, which made it necessary to restructure their work forces. Largely as a result of lobbying by the FKE, KAM and the trade unions, the government formed a broadly representative committee to monitor the importation of products without duty and payment of taxes.

The employers' associations have further stepped up their monitoring of the impact of SAPs through surveys in order to establish the needs of their members. For instance, in April 1995, the FKE carried out a survey among its members to assess the impact of SAPs on their current and future employment levels, sales, costs of inputs, measures taken by enterprises to respond to challenges and opportunities arising from the economic reforms implemented, and areas that needed government intervention. The survey found that enterprises had used a wide range of strategies to respond to challenges and opportunities arising from SAPs. They included efforts to reduce costs of production through cutting down employment levels and other measures, retraining employees, greater attention to improved efficiency in the use of capital and labour resources, switching to cheaper sources of raw materials, improved marketing and export promotion, and wage and salary restraints.

The RPED study found that firms that were wholly dependent on an internal captive market had been forced to shrink and lay off workers. This thus portrays the structural adjustment and liberalization period as one associated with poor firm growth and declining employment growth. But the study also found that firms that were not outward-oriented were contracting with economic liberalization, while those that were exporting were restructuring and expanding with liberalization (Gotenborg University/University of Nairobi, 1995).

Other measures increasingly taken by these enterprises comprised efforts to improve product quality to increase their competitiveness in both domestic and export markets, increased market research, product diversification, aggressive debt collection, improved price competitiveness and customer services, increased waste material recycling and better maintenance of plant and equipment, smaller inventories of raw materials, higher implementation of finished products and increased sub-contracting of some services (FKE, 1995: 14–16). The survey results were used in the preparation of taxation and policy proposals by the FKE to the government for inclusion in the annual budget.

Trends in unionization
The Central Organization of Trade Unions (COTU), as the umbrella organization representing all Kenya's employees, was formed in 1966 when different trade unions were merged. Kenya's labour movement has changed from a fairly strong body in the 1960s and 1970s to an ineffective one, especially after 1985.

As the implementation of the SAPs gathered some momentum in the period 1985–91, raising the prospects of intensified tension in the country's industrial relations, the government tried to bring the affairs of the trade union movement under its control through wage guidelines, disallowing strikes and continued indirect control over the trade unions' electoral process. This culminated in the affiliation of COTU to the country's ruling party, KANU, in the second half of the 1980s, thus seriously emasculating the powers of the labour movement in the country at a time when workers felt they needed to assert themselves to project their interests as the adjustment process continued. The Trade Dispute Act of 1965, under which COTU was formed, empowers the Minister of Labour to declare strikes illegal if he feels that the union has not exhausted the voluntary machinery for settlement of disputes before calling the strike. The Act has enabled the government significantly to control the trade union movement in the country for most of the post-independence period.

Since 1992, when the political process was liberalized, allowing trade unions to exercise more freedom, COTU has emerged as a substantial source of opposition to some components of SAPs in Kenya. It has especially accused the IMF and the World Bank of forcing the government and the private sector to retrench many workers (Ngunyi and Gathiaka, 1993: 46). Nonetheless, there are some who argue that the trade union movement in Kenya has not been as aggressive in its opposition to SAPs as trade unions in some other African countries (Republic of Kenya/UNICEF, 1992: 21). Indeed, there are many workers who still regard COTU as largely benefiting the employers as a result of union leaders being compromised (*The Economic Review*, 13–19 June, 1994, pp. 4–6).

Nevertheless, given the many incidences of industrial protest that occurred in Kenya in the first half of 1994, following the serious stage of implementation of SAPs in the period 1992–5, COTU's opposition to SAPs cannot be ignored. COTU's opposition to certain reforms became more pronounced after the 1992 political liberalization, which led to the affiliation of the union to the ruling party, KANU. In April 1993 it organized a two-day work boycott to demand a 100 per cent increase in general wages to compensate for the decline that had taken place in workers' real wages due to the unprecedented high inflation rates in 1992–3. Some of the other industrial protests that took place at that time include the public university lecturers' strike to press for the registration of their union, the University Academic Staff Union (UASU); the doctors' strike demanding the implementation of an improved scheme of service and the registration of the Kenya Medical Practitioners and Dentists Union (KMPDU); and the threat by the Kenya National Union of Teachers (KNUT) to go on strike to demand the implementation of an improved scheme of service. The latter was resolved by the Industrial Court in May 1994. The following month, 140 locomotive drivers employed by the Kenya Railways went on a 5-day strike that paralysed two operations of the corporation, to push for a 10 per cent increase in wages, better housing, an improved medical scheme and better working tools.

External trade liberalization is one of the reform measures which has come under heavy criticism from trade union officials. In January 1995, nine trade union officials asked the government to establish an inter-ministerial task force to address the issue of cheap imports and dumping on the Kenyan market (*Daily Nation*, 17 January 1995).

COTU has campaigned for the halting and review of the civil service reforms because of the rapidly rising unemployment associated with retrenchment and for the local authorities to be exempted from SAPs (*Daily Nation*, 19 September, 1995, p.16). Moreover, the unionizable employees of the Kenya Reinsurance Corporation attempted to block the organization from implementing a proposed retrenchment scheme, while the Kenya Union of Commercial Food and Allied Workers tried to have the scheme suspended pending more consultation.

From the available literature and interviews with officials of Kenya's labour movement, it is clear that the trade union movement's opposition to SAPs is not total, but varies from component to component. Thus, the leading trade union movement broadly supports the stabilization and restructuring reforms the country is undertaking but accuses the government of having ignored it in the process of designing and implementing the reforms. The consequence of leaving the movement out of the reform process, COTU argues, has been inadequate attention to the social dimensions of adjustment; that is, little or no protection for the vulnerable groups that have been seriously affected by SAPs. In a background paper for a conference held by COTU in conjunction with the International Confederation of Free Trade Unions (ICFTU), COTU explains that it supports the fundamental need for stabilizing and restructuring the economy (ICFTU/COTU, 1995: 2). Its main complaint was based on the fact that workers felt that their organizations were not seriously involved in the process whereby policy measures to stabilize and restructure the economy were arrived at, in spite of the existence of tripartite consultative structures in the industrial relations system. COTU further identifies lack of serious attention to the social dimensions of adjustment as the fundamental deficiency of all the SAPs implemented in Kenya.

Overall, the feeling in the trade union movement is that SAPs have a positive impact in the long term but that the vulnerable groups, including low-income workers and the unemployed, need to be cushioned from the adverse impacts in the short term. Instead of targeting the social sectors for budgetary cuts, the movement would like the government to concentrate first on reducing wastage and unnecessary purchases by the government.

The labour movement in Kenya generally supports reduction of the government's role in the economy through privatization, but argues that the government should retain its role in such critical areas as regulation of the financial sector through the Capital Market Authority and the Central Bank (ICFTU/COTU, 1995: 10). COTU generally supports the privatization process but criticizes the manner in which it has been undertaken so far, without adequate transparency and without adequate participation by or representation of the workers. This has made it difficult for the unions to negotiate new collective agreements with the new employers. Parastatal firms get reasonable wages and general conditions of employment for those who are retained and redundancy packages for those workers who are declared redundant (ibid.: 12). The labour movement is of the opinion that the government should establish a trust fund to provide credit for employees of state enterprises being privatized to enable them to acquire shares in the new enterprises. These employees, moreover, should be accorded first priority in the sale of these shares.

Government policy on the industrial sector is supported by the labour movement. However, the movement cites the following as the bottlenecks that continue to stand in the way of attaining the policy's objectives: inappropriate land policy, poor infrastructure, lack or inadequacy of credit facilities; time-wasting and cumbersome licensing procedures; and urban bias in investment promotion (ICFTU/COTU, 1995: 15). Moreover, the trade union movement calls for selective protection of industries (such as the sugar and textile industries) instead of undertaking wholesale trade liberalization.

The trade union movement is also critical of the EPZs, arguing that they have not created significant employment opportunities and that they have relatively poor working conditions as a result of being exempted from labour regulations. The movement has asked the government to ensure that the ILO Tripartite Declaration of Principles concerning Multinational Enterprises and Social Policy applies to EPZs in Kenya.

The trade union movement supports the government's wages and incomes policy, and in particular maintaining minimum wages to protect low wage-earners, but argues that in a liberalized economy the government should not set any parameters for wage negotiations between workers' representatives and employers (ICFTU/COTU, 1995: 23).

Change in the redundancy laws giving employers greater autonomy in hiring and firing workers has also been criticized by the labour movement. It notes that, 'without regard for security of employment for workers, the Government of Kenya has seen the need to develop a system that allows firms autonomy in hiring and firing workers. This policy shift by the Government implicitly abets employers in their bid to declare redundant thousands of workers as they restructure their operations and are not effectively addressed by the collective bargaining process.' (ICFTU/COTU, 1995: 22).

The intensity of utilization of trade union services by workers in the formal sector seems to have increased as the effect of SAPs started to bite, especially in the third phase of the programme. Thus while in 1992 only 61,377 unionizable employees benefited from the 247 collective agreements registered with the Industrial Court, the number had risen to 78,014 employees and 337 agreements by 1993 and to 109,916 employees and 307 agreements by 1994 (Republic of Kenya, 1995b).

The push for trade unionism that was witnessed in 1994 when professionals like lecturers and doctors went on strike to demand registration of their unions reflected the growing demand for unionization in Kenya. It was also an indication that unions were increasingly regarded by more groups as essential vehicles for the protection and improvement of workers' welfare. These forces could be regarded as responses to SAPs as they gained momentum in the second half of 1993 and first half of 1994, soon after Kenya started more serious implementation of economic reform. It was also, to some extent, the result of liberalization of the political environment following the introduction of multi-party politics in 1992, which allowed workers' organizations to enjoy more freedom from government control.

The government's response to this demand for new unions was a refusal to register the unions. The attempts to revive the civil servants' trade union following intense pressure from the opposition and the ILO in 1994 were also opposed by the government. The government preferred the formation of welfare associations for professionals largely because welfare associations do not have the power to organize strikes and other forms of industrial protest like trade unions.

While the push for expanded unionization and greater freedom for trade union movements has been strong, a large proportion of workers and opposition leaders are not yet satisfied with the trade union situation in Kenya. There has been growing pressure from trade union organizations and opposition political leaders for the redrafting of the trade union constitution to make it more democratic.

As a result of the challenges to the workers arising from the implementation of SAPs, trade unions have increased their involvement in economic reforms and related discussions and issues. In recent years COTU has presented its views on SAPs more strongly and proposed ways of cushioning workers. It was involved in the design of the Social Dimensions of Development Programme presented by the Government of Kenya to the donor community in 1995.

Trade unions have also been more involved in negotiating terminal benefits with employers for employees declared redundant. In some cases, COTU has sued employers who have designed voluntary retirement packages without consulting the national trade union bodies. Some unions, such as the banking and sugar unions, contributed to the highly favourable terminal benefits negotiated for their members.

COTU, with the assistance of the International Confederation of Free Trade Unions (African Regional Organization) (ICFTU), has organized seminars to educate members about the effects of SAPs.

The trade union movement is planning to establish closer links with the informal sector which has hitherto been ignored by it. It is hoped that this will help initiate outreach programmes aimed at, among other things, developing skills in the informal sector (ICFTU/COTU, 1995: 25). This is in recognition of the informal sector's critical role in creating employment for those retrenched from the modern sector. Kenya's trade unions are also in the process of preparing proposals for employment-generating small-scale projects to submit to the European Union for funding under the Lomé IV Convention which has provision for funding social programmes to ameliorate the adverse effects of structural adjustment. The trade union movement, especially through COTU, is pressing more and more for consultation among social partners (employers, trade unions, government) on the need for special attention to social sectors such as health and education as well as a special focus on food security and population control, and economic empowerment of vulnerable groups especially women and youth, through financial and infrastructural support for the informal sector and the co-operative movement as key prerequisites for successful structural adjustment (*ibid.*: 26).

The Kenya Association of Manufacturers (KAM) KAM has also criticized some aspects of SAPs, especially import liberalization. It has often expressed its support for liberalization as long as a level playing-field is established, with appropriate taxes and duties collected on imports and ensuring that dumping does not take place. The textile industry has been identified by KAM as one of the sectors facing collapse because of cheap second-hand imports, illegal imports and dumping. Estimates by the textile manufacturers show that over 30 garment manufacturing enterprises may have closed down and many others were operating at very low capacities by mid-1995. Because of the same problem of cheap imports, some of which enter the country without payment of the necessary taxes and duties, KAM has been pressing for protection of manufactures, especially in the textile and motor industries.

It must be stressed here, however, that with the exception of import liberalization, KAM has generally been highly supportive of most of the other structural adjustment components. The reform process helped to remove some of the perennial headaches of the manufacturers over availability of foreign exchange, repatriation of dividends to foreign shareholders and price controls. Before the reforms, the association spent a lot of its time and resources lobbying with various government institutions about these problems.

Other civil institutions have also been very active in support of SAPs especially in the area of political reform. These include the Law Society of Kenya (LSK), the National Council of Churches of Kenya (NCCK), the Kenya Medical Association (KMA), the Kenya Business and Professional Women's Association, the Press Club and the International Commission of Jurists (ICJ), Kenya Chapter.

Effectiveness of lobbying with respect to SAP policies
One of the competition-enhancing policies that has led to intense lobbying with the overall objective of its removal is import liberalization. Employers' organizations such as the FKE and KAM, trade unions, manufacturing firms in the textile, motor, leather, sugar and other sectors as well as politicians have lobbied for some restrictions on imports. Many firms and trade unions persistently complained of loss of jobs due to uncontrolled importation. The result of the FKE Survey of 1995 already mentioned strengthened the arguments by the employers and trade unions that import liberalization was hurting domestic firms. It should be noted, however, that not all the available evidence shows a negative impact of the economic reforms. Recent research findings show that employment growth in the manufacturing sector accelerated during the adjustment period, indicating that policy reforms may have had a positive impact on parts of the economy (Gotenborg University/ University of Nairobi, 1995: 172).

More comprehensive research is necessary before the full impact of SAPs on employment and other macroeconomic indicators is properly established. The above lobbying has been successful, to some extent, in that the government committed itself, in the 1995/96 Budget, to impose countervailing duties to protect domestic industries from the dumping of subsidized products.

In the case of the liberalization of the food sector, serious lobbying has led to the reversal of some reform measures. As mentioned earlier, reform of the cereals sector, especially in the case of maize, has experienced at least a dozen failed attempts at policy reform. Senior government officials are known to have substantial interests in the farming sector and their strong lobby has ensured that the NCPB has remained unrestructured for most of the period since the 1980s, though its restructuring and liberalization of the cereals market were one of the earliest areas to be identified by donors for reform.

Another area of institutional reform that has been slow because of strong lobby interests has been the privatization of public enterprises. To date, only a few of the targeted enterprises have been privatized. The privatization process has lacked transparency and the indications are that most of these were sold at below the market value to buyers with political connections.

Impact of SAPs on the labour markets legal framework

Legal framework As part of the on-going reforms, the government has liberalized some aspects of the labour market. As indicated earlier, the mid-1994 liberalization of the wage guidelines established in the 1970s now makes it possible for workers and employers to negotiate wages freely to reflect productivity and compensate workers for the rising cost of living. Minimum wage legislation has not been repealed, however. Following representations by the FKE, the government also relaxed redundancy procedures, making employers free to declare workers redundant without seeking permission if economic conditions make it necessary.

Employment in the civil service Although the government stated its intention to reduce public sector employment as early as 1986, not much was actually done until 1992 when the first public sector employees were laid off by the Nyayo Tea Zones parastatal. However, earlier on, in 1991, the Ministry of Public Works had laid off its casual workers. Kenya's initial strategies to reduce public sector employment focused on the abolition of employment guarantee schemes to graduates from higher-level educational institutions and deceleration in the rate of public sector employment. The initial targets were to reduce the growth of central government employment to 2 per cent per annum or less, with effect from financial year 1990 (Ikiara, 1992: 15). Other measures announced in 1989 included redeployment of excess staff to deficient departments or sections of the same or other ministries, freezing of financial allocations for new posts or upgrading, freezing of new recruitment or promotions, deployment of existing staff to essential services, programmes and projects and abolition of additional hiring of temporary and piece-work staff. Moreover, in the mid-1980s the mandatory retirement age in Kenya was reduced from 60 to 55 and voluntary retirement, with full retirement benefits, to 50.

By 1992 the government was not only hiring the required university graduates but had also limited the annual admissions to 10,000 in the public universities, and with a further reduction in 1994. The reform programme was planned to be fully implemented in three phases. The first phase was to focus on reducing the number of civil servants to contain costs, the second on the improvement of performance and policy analysis capacity, and the third on the improvement of financial and management aspects (Republic of Kenya, 1995b: 11).

Progress and impact of civil service reform The implementation of the programme which had been planned to begin in July 1992 was delayed and rapidly fell behind schedule. By September 1995, only 24,000 civil servants had been retired instead of the planned 32,000. The delay has been attributed to initial reluctance, lack of commitment to the programme by the government, and opposition from some top government officials fearing political repercussions.

Between 1989 and 1994, employment in the civil service dropped by 7.7 per cent, while between 1993 and 1994 it fell by 3.1 per cent (Republic of Kenya, 1995b: 56). The voluntary retirement age has been further reduced to 40. The cost of retrenchment in terms of gratuities, training provisions and pensions by the end of the 1994/95 financial year, when 20,000 civil servants had been retrenched, was K£187 million (Republic of Kenya, 1995a: 11). Retirees are receiving training to enable them to engage in self-employment in the private sector.

In an effort to raise the efficiency and productivity of the remaining civil servants, the government started in September 1995 a training programme for all civil servants. It also restructured the Kenya Institute of Administration (KIA) to offer training, research and consultancy services on a commercial basis.

Parastatal reform programme
Rationale According to the policy paper on public enterprise reform and privatization published in 1992, the parastatal reform programme was meant to increase the role of the private sector, reduce the fiscal strains caused by the parastatals, reduce the role of the parastatal sector and help rationalize its operations. Another major objective of the programme was the improvement of service delivery by the public enterprises (Republic of Kenya, 1995a: 12).

The reform programme has two components: (i) the restructuring and retention of government ownership of the strategic parastatals; and (ii) the privatization of the non-strategic enterprises. Some of the parastatals earmarked for privatization also needed to be restructured financially and managerially to make it possible to dispose of them as going concerns in order to fetch better prices. The long period of time required for this restructuring before their sale has been given as the main reason for the slow pace of privatization (Republic of Kenya, 1995: 12).

The desire to have Kenyans participate more effectively in the privatization process through the purchase of enterprise shares has been hampered by the pre-emptive legal rights of investors in joint investments with the government (Republic of Kenya, 1995a: 13). At the start of the reform process, the 250 parastatals were categorized into two groups: 43 strategic and 207 non-strategic enterprises for sale.

Progress and impact of parastatal reform Both components of the reform programme have resulted in substantial retrenchment, averaging about 30 per cent of the workforce (Ikiara, 1992: 35). Only 61 of the 207 enterprises identified for sale had been sold by June 1995, earning the government and holding corporations a total of Kshs.120 million (Republic of Kenya, 1995a: 13). The privatization process has been criticized as lacking transparency and causing massive loss of funds as many of them were either not sold to the highest bidders or were sold below their market value.

One-third of the remaining state enterprises were targeted to be sold by the end of 1995, according to the Minister of Finance in his 1995/96 Budget Speech. Restructuring of the strategic parastatals has also been progressing fairly well. Kenya Airways, which retrenched about 1,000 of its lower cadre employees (30 per cent of its workforce) in 1990, was successfully restructured and partly sold off. Kenya Wildlife Services (KWS) is another parastatal that restructured early and laid off 32 per cent of its staff, targeting the lower cadre for retrenchment. The Lake Basin Development Authority (LBDA) also announced its intention to retrench about 31 per cent of its staff in September 1992 (Ikiara, 1992: 33). These parastatals have also been offering 'Golden Handshakes' to entice their workers out of employment. These were regarded by workers and their trade union representatives as unattractive, however. There have also been complaints that the management of these parastatals do not consult the workers or the trade unions when designing the benefit packages.

Other strategic parastatals whose restructuring had made progress by June 1995 include Kenya Railways, whose retrenchment was delayed, however, by financial constraints, the Kenya Ports Authority, the KP&TC and the Kenya Power and Lighting Company (Republic of Kenya, 1995a: 13). Restructuring and privatization of public enterprises have led to considerable retrenchment. Employment in parastatals fell by 0.9 per cent between 1989 and 1994 and by 0.7 per cent between 1993 and 1994 (Republic of Kenya, 1995b: 56).

Informal sector and SMEs support

The contraction of some industries in the modern sector as a result of the SAPs has caused the informal sector to emerge as a main source of new employment in the country. The informal sector had been recognized for some time as having the greatest potential for absorbing the workers that were becoming redundant since the early 1980s, and before. Between 1991 and 1994 employment in the sector increased by 68.6 per cent from 1,063,218 to 1,792,373 employees (Republic of Kenya, 1995b: 58). In 1994 alone, the sector provided 325,862 new jobs, a 22.2 per cent increase over the 1993 employment level, and accounted for 53.4 per cent of total employment in 1994.

In spite of the support extended to the informal sector and the small and medium-scale enterprises (SMEs), in the form of increased access to credit facilities and simplified licensing procedures, among others, the informal sector is still characterized by low productivity and a high rate of enterprise mortality (Republic of Kenya, 1995a: 17). The other problems besetting the sector are poor quality control, inadequate product and customer markets, limited access to credit, poor management skills, poor market organization as well as continued harassment by officials. These are the factors that are responsible, to a large extent, for the high enterprise mortality rate.

Conclusions and recommendations

Implementation of SAPs in Kenya so far has had both positive and negative effects on the country's industrialization process, employment and wages. Some manufacturing enterprises have benefited from the removal of price and foreign-exchange controls, which for more than two decades were major obstacles to their operations. For these types of enterprises the reforms have helped to stimulate their activities and improve their capacity utilization, efficiency and competitiveness.

On the other hand, import liberalization has had strongly adverse effects on some sectors, like garment manufacturing and the motor industry, because of excessive importation of cheap products. This is where some evidence of deindustrialization can be seen, as a substantial number of firms have closed down or reduced their levels of operations as a result of competition from imports.

The evidence presented shows that, because of the reform measures taken, public sector employment has fallen significantly while the growth of modern private sector employment has also, in some cases, declined. This has shifted the burden of job creation to the informal small-scale sector which currently accounts for about 70 per cent of new employment opportunities.

The evidence further shows that real wages have experienced a declining trend during the adjustment period. It is not clear, however, whether the decline has been a result of SAPs or of general poor performance in the economy. What is clear is that real wages are not downwardly inflexible, which would otherwise hinder the process of adjustment.

Most of the traded sectors, with the exception of the service sectors and some manufacturing, experienced stagnation or decline in the levels of employment during the adjustment period. The private service sector was the most expanding sector, followed by the manufacturing sector, in terms of employment. Employment in the public sector experienced some drastic decline, especially during the early 1990s.

In broad terms, the study finds the following, with regard to the impact of structural adjustment on labour markets:

- There has been a contractionary effect on the employment levels of the public sector and of a significant proportion of the private sector. On the other hand, employment levels of the informal sector have experienced a dramatic increase during the adjustment period.
- Real wage levels have declined significantly during the adjustment period, as the bargaining powers of trade unions were considerably constrained by government policies, the prevailing levels of unemployment and the overall macroeconomic environment.
- While comprehensive data on labour productivity were not available, it would seem that labour productivity may have declined during the adjustment period, partly because of the declining standard of living resulting from falling real wages. Labour/output ratios experienced a major decline during the period.
- Job security declined during the adjustment period as government inspection and other forms of involvement in the labour market declined at a time when trade unions were not strong enough to protect the interests of the workers.
- Training of workers to help them cope with the adjustment challenges was not taken up seriously in the public sector during most of the adjustment period. The government has started paying attention to the training of workers only since 1995. Training and reorganization of firms were more important in the private sector.
- Trends in Kenya's industrial strikes do not provide conclusive evidence that industrial relations have worsened due to SAPs. In spite of declining real wages, rising levels of unemployment and increasing insecurity of jobs, the data do not show that industrial tension increased directly with the more serious implementation of SAPs. This may be partly explained by the risks involved, and the government's heavy-handedness towards striking workers.
- Kenya's employers' and manufacturers' organizations have brought more pressure to bear in the last few years for more protection to those industrial sectors which have suffered worst from import liberalization, especially the garment manufacturing and motor vehicle assembling firms. They argue that some of the imported products have been dumped on the Kenyan market and that some have been imported without paying the official import duties.
- The SAPs have led to restructuring of some of the public sector corporations as well as private sector enterprises. In order to meet the challenges of a more competitive business environment, both manufacturing and service industries like banks have undertaken substantial restructuring of their operations including retrenchment of workers and organizational restructuring.

Table 4.25 summarizes the response to some of the reform measures by various institutions in the country. In some cases, some members of bodies like FKE and KAM supported certain reform measures while others opposed these measures, depending on the main activities of the members concerned.

While liberalization of the labour market was desired by both employers and trade unions, it has put the workers in a position where they could be exploited by employers because of the prevailing high level of unemployment and relatively weak trade unions. This impact is to some extent reflected in the declining real wages. It is in the interests of both trade unions and employers to avoid a drastic decline in real wages because it could adversely affect the overall productivity of labour, industrial relations and the performance of the whole economy.

Table 4.25   *Summary of responses to selected reform measures in Kenya by various institutions*

Policy reforms	Favourable about present implementation	Dissatisfied with present implementation
Import liberalization	• Kenya Consumers Organization • Kenya Association of Manufacturers (raw materials) • Federation of Kenya Employers (raw materials)	• Central Organization of Trade Unions • Federation of Kenya Employers (finished products) • Kenya Association of Manufacturers (finished products)
Removal of price controls	• Federation of Kenya Employers • Kenya Association of Manufacturers	• Kenya Consumers Organization • Politicians • Central Organization of Trade Unions
Political reforms	• Central Organization of Trade Unions • Opposition parties	• Ruling party
Retrenchment	• Federation of Kenya Employers • Kenya Association of Manufacturers	• Central Organization of Trade Unions • Politicians
Removal of foreign exchange controls	• Federation of Kenya Employers • Kenya Association of Manufacturers • Central Organization of Trade Unions	– – –
Devaluation	• Federation of Kenya Employers (exporters) • Kenya Association of Manufacturers (exporters)	• Central Organization of Trade Unions • Politicians • Federation of Kenya Employers (importers) • Kenya Association of Manufacturers (importers) • Kenya Consumers Organization
Privatization	• Federation of Kenya Employers • Kenya Association of Manufacturers	• Central Organization of Trade Unions • Politicians
Relaxation of redundancy procedures	• Federation of Kenya Employers • Kenya Association of Manufacturers	• Central Organization of Trade Unions • Politicians
Removal of wage guidelines	• Central Organization of Trade Unions • Federation of Kenya Employers • Kenya Association of Manufacturers	• Smaller unions

Recommendations

Consultation policy In the design and implementation of Kenya's structural adjustment programme, employers' organizations and trade unions were largely excluded. Thus, some of the criticisms that have been directed at the adjustment policies by these organizations reflect this problem. The policies that have been implemented are usually decided by the World Bank and the IMF, on the one hand, and the government, on the other. Private agents and stakeholders come to learn about them at the implementation stage. Equally puzzling is the confidentiality and secrecy that has surrounded the Policy Framework Papers (PFP) until recently. These policy papers have been confidential government documents, except for the 1996–8 PFP which was launched publicly by the President. If the country is to maximize the co-operation of employers' organizations and the trade union movement, it is essential to involve them in the various stages of formulating, implementing and reviewing reform programmes.

However, while this view is widely popular among the trade union movement, employers and researchers, there is considerable consensus that most of the trade unions do not have the necessary capacity to participate effectively in the high-level professional and technical discussions that may be necessary. Thus, for trade unions to be meaningfully involved in the design and implementation of reform packages it is necessary to raise the capacity of the workers' representatives.

Involving these interest groups would not only help to reduce opposition or resistance to the reform's implementation but would help to design programmes with less adverse effects in some of the sectors which are more directly affected in the short run. The scope of involvement could be large, ranging from the design and implementation of the reforms to the formulation of safety nets and other measures needed to ameliorate the adverse effects on sectors and workers.

For these interest groups to be effectively involved in the design and implementation of programmes, there will be a need to widen their understanding of the rationale, nature and likely impact of the reform programmes and also to help build their internal capacities in policy formulation through training, seminars, and other forms of exposure. The organizations would also need to upgrade their top-level personnel. These will require better run organizations with a wider coverage of membership, not only to raise more resources internally but also to help build up their bargaining power through this wider representation. For these efforts to succeed, concerted efforts by the interest groups, the government and the donor community will be needed.

Economic and social policy recommendations
Fiscal discipline is perceived as essential to prevent currency depreciation and accelerating inflation. Fiscal adjustment has been the most difficult and fragile part of structural adjustment. Part of the problem has been external (shocks, debt overhang and stress) and part internal (policy weaknesses/incompatibility and lack of political will). Improved administration of import taxes will be required to create a level playing field for all producers and those in commerce. A comprehensive employment policy should focus on informal sector productivity. Currently this seems to be lacking in a sector that seems to be rapidly expanding in terms of employment growth. The government should expand the retraining programme for the civil service in order to enhance their productivity, and progress more rapidly in the public service reforms. In addition, the management of Social Dimensions of Development programmes should be diversified by involving other ministries and NGOs instead of concentrating all management in the Office of the President.

There should be a concerted effort to encourage research on the informal sector. This should concentrate on the constraints inhibiting private sector growth and productivity, credit availability, the administrative environment, by-laws governing activities of the informal sector in major urban centres, and general environmental conditions and infrastructure in areas where the informal sector agents operate. In addition, there should be research focused on employment, growth, wage-setting behaviour and the welfare effects of import liberalization on the informal sector. The government should focus on management improvements in public sector enterprises, especially those that have been identified as strategic, e.g. the public utilities. This is because their inefficiency imposes heavy costs on firm operations with significant macroeconomic impact.

References

Engle, R. and C.W.J. Granger (1987) 'Cointegration and Error Correction: Representation, Estimating and Testing', *Econometrica*, Vol. 55, No. 2.

Federation of Kenya Employers (1995) *Federation of Kenya Employers Newsletter No. 200*. Nairobi: FKE.

Gibbon, P. (ed.) (1993) *Social Change and Economic Reform in Africa*. Uppsala: Nordiska Afrikainstitutet.

—— (ed.) (1995) *Markets, Civil Society and Democracy in Kenya*. Uppsala: Nordiska Afrikainstitutet.

Gotenborg University/University of Nairobi (1995) *Manufacturing in Kenya Under Adjustment*. May.

van der Hoeven, R. and J. Vandemoortele (1987) *Stabilization and Adjustment Policies and Programs*. Case Study No. 4, Kenya. Helsinki: WIDER, January.

Ikiara, G.K. (1992) *Public Sector Retrenchments and Redeployment: The Case of Kenya*. ILO/JASPA Working Paper. Addis Ababa: ILO.

—— (1994) 'Réformes Politico-économiques au Kenya: Les Perspectives de la Communauté des Entrepreneurs', *Politique Africaine*, Vol. 56, December.

International Confederation of Free Trade Unions, 'COTU (1995) 'COTU/ICFTU-AFRO Agenda For Social and Economic Development', Paper presented at conference on Building Equitable and Democratic Adjustment and Development in Kenya held in Nairobi, 25–27 April.

Jebuni, C.D., A.D. Oduro and K.A. Tutu (1994) *Structural Adjustment and the Labour Market in Ghana*. Legon: AERC Discussion Paper.

Kasiynenko, A.A., A.N. Mayaka and V.V. Popadeikin (1994) 'Protective Devices for the Workers at Kenyan Workshops', ILO: *African Newsletter on Occupational Health and Safety*, Vol. 4, No. 3, December.

Levin, J. and N.S. Ndung'u (1994) *Striving for Credibility: Kenya 1993–94*. Macroeconomic Studies No. 58/94. Stockholm: Swedish International Development Agency.

Mboya, T. (1963) *Freedom and After*. London: André Deutsch.

Milne, J. and M. Neitzert (1994) 'Kenya' in S. Horton *et al.* (eds.) *Labour Markets in an Era of Adjustment*, Vol. 2, *Case Studies*. Washington, DC: World Bank EDI Development Studies.

Ndung'u, N. (1995a) *The Dynamics of the Inflationary Process in Kenya*. Gotenborg University, Sweden.

—— (1995b) 'The Economic Situation in Kenya: Is the Floating Exchange Rate Regime Appropriate?', *Independent Review*, 95/02.

Ngunyi, G.M. and Kamau Gathiaka (1993) 'State-Civil Institutions Relations in Kenya in the 1980s' in Gibbon.

Odada, J.E.O. and A.B. Ayako (eds.) (1989) *The Impact of Structural Adjustment Policies on the Well-Being of the Vulnerable Groups in Kenya*. Nairobi: UNICEF.

—— (1985) *Sessional Paper No. 2 of 1985 on Unemployment*. Nairobi: Government Printer.

Republic of Kenya (1986) *Sessional Paper No. 1 of 1986 on Economic Management for Renewed Growth*. Nairobi: Government Printer.

—— (1991b) *Statistical Abstract* (various issues). Nairobi: Government Printer.

—— (1992) *Sessional Paper No. 1 of 1992 on Employment and Development*. Nairobi: Government Printer.

—— (1993) 'Kenya's Progress in Reforms: November, 1991 – September', memo.

—— (1994a) 'Kenya's Progress in Reforms: October 1994', memo.

—— (1994b) 'Country Position Paper: World Summit for Social Development', Discussion Draft.

—— (1995a) *Budget Speech: Fiscal Year 1995/96 (1st July–30th June)*. Nairobi: Government Printer.

—— (1995b) *Economic Survey 1995*. Nairobi: Government Printer.

—— *Economic Survey* (various issues). Nairobi: Government Printer.

——, IMF and World Bank (1991) *Policy Framework Paper for 1991/92–1993/94*. Nairobi: Ministry of Finance.

——, UNICEF (1992) *Children and Women in Kenya: A Situation Analysis 1992*. Nairobi: Reata Printers Ltd.

Swamy, G. (1994) 'Kenya: Patchy, Intermittent Commitment' in I. Husain and R. Faruqee (eds.) *Adjustment in Africa: Lessons from Country Case Studies*. World Bank Regional and Sectoral Studies. Washington, DC: World Bank.

World Bank (1983) *Kenya Growth and Structural Change*. Washington, DC: World Bank.

5 Uganda

GERMINA SSEMOGERERE

Introduction

Overview

This chapter gives a qualitative overview of the effects of the adjustment policies implemented in Uganda over the period 1987–95 on employment, the real returns to labour, and labour market institutions. In the first section, a general appreciation of Uganda's adjustment context is given. The next section outlines the adjustment policies pursued, highlighting *the implicit assumptions* made by the policy-makers on how adjustment would effect economic growth, employment, and poverty reduction.[1] It reviews the implementation process, laying emphasis on the major achievements at the macroeconomic level, using the available indicators.

The third section begins by defining the segmented labour markets in Uganda. The inclusion of agricultural smallholder self-employed labour in the rural labour market is justified at length, given that agriculture is the major employer. The other labour markets defined are: the public sector; the private modern sector and the informal sector. The meagre statistics available are then used to discuss qualitatively the effects of adjustment policies on employment, the returns to labour, and poverty reduction, in each labour market, identifying *serious gaps* both in the adjustment policy framework and in the illustrative data required to inform the policy process. The chapter finally gives the reactions of the concerned parties: the private sector; trade unions; the legislature and the political parties; NGOs; and women's groups.

The gaps between theory and reality in structural adjustment

One of the general thrusts of structural adjustment policies is to reduce the size of the public sector, which is regarded as inefficient (particularly in the provision of goods and services that can be undertaken by the private sector) and unsustainable, because of the huge public expenditure (well above tax revenue) required to finance this sector.

Several policy measures are used to downsize the public sector: retrenchment of excess labour from the civil service; privatization of loss-making parastatals; demobilization of excessive army personnel to free resources for economic and social infrastructure, etc. While the specific SAP measures differ, depending on the individual country's circumstances, the basic underlying assumption regarding the

---

[1] *The Way Forward I and II* (see p. 123) are the one-stop-shop documents which spell out Uganda's adjustment policies, both macro and sectoral, pursued either as specifically stated or implied by statements in these documents; the relationship between these and other policy documents is therefore emphasized. The playing down of the importance of employment creation, and the complete disregard of labour market institutions are made conspicuous.

employment response is the same, namely, that the workers laid off will be absorbed into the private sector, whose size will expand in response to a more stable macro-economic environment and to market-based incentives (Walton and Ghanem, 1995).

Yet the literature on employment growth in today's developing countries warns of the possible excessive pressure on the modern urban sector to create new jobs, to absorb the labour force from both normal growth *and* rural urban migration (Bhaduri, 1989); it is to this already serious problem that the unemployed resulting from the downsizing of the public sector are added. Analysts of the sub-Saharan African labour market indicate clearly that 'there is an urgent need for enhanced country-specific labour market research to improve the design and appropriateness of the new generation of structural adjustment programmes' (Vandemoortele, 1991). We flag five issues.

(a) **Which sectors are the potential sources of rapid employment expansion?** The SAP's policy framework must identify the job creation prospects of specific sectors, and data must be assembled to quantify the rate at which these sectors can absorb labour from normal growth, rural-urban migration, and displacement from adjustment. The same policy framework must identify which further price and non-price incentives, or/and supporting policies, are required to make this desired rapid growth in employment a reality. The potential of employment creation is the *first gap* between theory and reality in the context of adjustment in Africa.

(b) **Wage flexibility and employment in rural areas** Adjustment is intended to replace direct public intervention in the economy with a price mechanism that allocates resources more efficiently, to promote economic growth. In the case of labour, downward wage flexibility is another assumption which is expected to constitute a sufficient mechanism to clear the market (Nelson, 1991: Walton and Ghanem, 1995). However, wage labour is of limited importance in self-employed smallholder agriculture which absorbs the bulk of the labour force in many SSA economies (up to 80 per cent of the active labour force in Uganda). The existence of a large number of workers working in non-formal undertakings creates a *second gap* between theory and reality. The literature on what determines asset accumulation, and the returns to assets in self-employment for the smallholder in agriculture (Chenery et al., 1974), must form the basis of studying the response of self-employed labour to SAPs. The limited 'marketable surplus' makes it particularly difficult to study the change in returns to self-employed labour from the SAP's package in response to changes in the producer prices of marketed output, when production is largely for own-household subsistence.

(c) **Wage flexibility and employment in urban areas** Paul Collier's recent work has added a new dimension to the wage flexibility and employment response analysis: he argues that even when wage flexibility downward is pronounced in SSA economies, where real wages are eroded by inflation, there is no expansion of employment that is adequate to clear the labour market (Collier, 1994). He attributes this inadequacy to the risk in the private investment environment in SSA that is prone to policy and trade shocks. Collier's discordant note underlines the urgent need to analyze the constraints to the demand for labour in the modern private sector under adjustment. And the limited response to large real wage declines forms a *third gap* between the theory and reality of adjustment. Stein (1989) also reviews a substantial body of development literature which, as yet, has been unable to explain wage inflexibility downwards, despite rampant unemployment even in those situations where there are *no* labour unions or minimum wage legislation. Capacity-building efforts in Uganda assume that it is lack of appropriate skills that is causing unemployment. From Collier's study and Stein's work, however, there is a need to look more critically for obstacles to employment creation in all sectors of the under-developed economies today, apart from trade unions and minimum wages.

(d) The segmented labour market The labour market in SSA (including Uganda) is highly segmented. Locality is one dimension of segmentation: there are urban and rural labour markets. The second dimension of labour market segmentation is sectoral: there are public and private modern sectors; there is an informal sector in both rural and urban areas; and there is an agricultural smallholder segment, and estate sub-segments (Evans, 1992). The theory of adjustment assumes a smooth process of labour mobility between segments to eliminate unemployment and equalize the returns to labour, but in practice the mobility is far from smooth, indicating a *fourth gap* between theory and practice, raising the question whether we should pay more attention to non-price barriers to labour mobility between sectors.

(e) The role of labour market institutions during adjustment Small as the modern wage sector may be, it does employ organized labour. Adjustment affects the existing labour contracts, conditions of service, the willingness of employers to adhere to safety standards in a liberalized environment, and the ability of the unionized staff to demand such standards, the need to educate unions to adjust to a new policy environment, etc. Earlier efforts in adjustment policies to de-emphasize the role of trade unions (Nelson, 1991) points to a *fifth gap* between the theory and reality of adjustment policies.

Pre-adjustment actions over the period 1986–9
The main elements of the economic situation in 1986, just at the takeover of the current regime, are given in Table 5.1 (see p. 125) and some excellent reviews describe the distortions with which the economy was confronted.[2]

However, there are three aspects which are not sufficiently analyzed by the literature cited, the implications of which are important for our discussion of the adjustment experience, namely: the much greater destruction of rural productive assets, human capital and infrastructure in 1986, compared to 1981, because of the guerrilla war; the limitations of local councils to deliver public goods and services at the grass roots; and the very limited evolution of the participatory process in policy-making. We shall review these in turn.

The greater destruction due to the guerrilla war The military upheavals of the 1970s were restricted to the barracks and the destruction of factories, public installations and facilities in the modern sector, largely in the cities. Rural production shifted from the monetary to the subsistence economy (or into smuggling) because of the large price distortions and the high cost of monetary transactions under insecurity where theft, non-payment and the erosion of the value of money due to late payments were common. However, except in West Nile where populations were displaced because of reprisals after Amin and a spillover of insecurity from the Sudan, the rest of rural Uganda remained stagnant but cultivated, populated, and accessible.

In contrast, the war that brought the current government to power was waged deep in the villages, destroying schools, health facilities, public buildings, and private houses. A large number of people who survived became displaced. The fields went fallow, and productive animals like oxen in Teso were wiped out in the 1988–89 continuation of insecurity. The human capacity to carry out agriculture

---

[2]See Collier and Henstridge (1993); Loxley (1989); International Development Research Centre (1986); Republic of Uganda (1987); Tumusiime-Mutebire and Henstridge (1995); and the World Bank's Second Economic Recovery Credit 2087 – UG.

depreciated as well in the course of running for safety. The Relief and Rehabilitation Programme (1986) tried to resettle the displaced populations in the Luwero Triangle and West Nile, and give them emergency goods, blankets, hoes and simple tools. Many returnees found these amenities inadequate to *re-establish* their fields and to start a viable economic life. These people kept coming back to the government for assistance. Worse still, the continuation of insecurity after 1986 added new areas (Acholi, Lango, and Teso) to the rural destruction. By 1989, it was clear that a large programme was needed to address the aftermath of rural destruction, paying attention to war widows without productive assets, war orphans and the urban poor unable to settle back in rural areas.

The Programme for the Alleviation of Poverty and the Social Costs of Adjustment PAPSCA (1989), which referred also to potentially retrenched civil servants, was trying to address these problems since the Relief and Rehabilitation Plan (1986) had been unable to solve them. However, the key assumption that the people whose fields, productive assets, human capital and infrastructure had been destroyed, would respond to the market-based structural adjustment incentives without more intensively applied measures to restore a productive base was a grave conceptual error which explains the lack of funding for this programme. The extensive but underestimated rural destruction, in our view, is responsible for the widened rural-urban gap and the large unequal income distribution.[3] The weakness of the rural self-employment labour market to respond to adjustment in some parts of the country is evaluated against this background, and the newly instituted Anti-Poverty Strategy (1996) has its roots in the problems outlined here.

The local councils In historical perspective, local administration in Uganda has been destroyed systematically since 1969 by harassment from the local militia, the ruling party chairpersons, the parallel security agencies, and other appointed supporters of the oppressive regimes imposed on the people.

Whereas the PAPSCA document highlighted the absence of public goods and services in the poor communities it covered, it did not grasp the equal importance of the absence of regularly paid and motivated civil servants to assist the local councils in daily administration. Until the seriousness of this gap is acknowledged and acted upon systematically in the decentralization process, the lack of public inputs will limit the success of NGOs and private sector initiatives in responding to adjustment, be it in labour markets or in other activities related to poverty reduction.

Participation in decision-making When the current administration took office in 1986 it distanced itself from the Obote II structural adjustment policies of 1981–4 which had tried to liberalize and decontrol markets. The initial controls were imposed on 'essential consumer goods': paraffin, sugar, salt, soap, corrugated iron sheets, etc., which were in short supply. Economizing on scarce foreign exchange was done by importing a variety of goods through barter trade, while the nominal exchange rate was kept fixed. The failure of the control regime is well documented (in Loxley, 1989). Inflation worsened from an annual rate of 130 to 365 per cent; the exchange rate depreciated from 1,400 U. Shs. per US$ to 6,000 by May 1987; and price controls worsened the shortage of essential commodities. An informal donor conference to address these issues at an early stage failed to materialize. The regime, having run out of foreign exchange, turned to the IMF and World Bank, which it had previously resisted.

---

[3] The 1995 Country Economic Memorandum entitled *The Challenge of Growth and Poverty Reduction* notes the widened rural-urban gap, and ILO/UNDP (1995) reports the unequal income distribution.

To save the deteriorating economic situation, a macroeconomic adjustment programme was adopted, outlined in the government's Rehabilitation and Development Plan 1987/88–1989/90. The objectives of this programme were: to achieve a growth rate of real GDP of 5 per cent per annum; to bring down inflation to 10 per cent per annum; and to achieve a sustainable balance-of-payments position by 1990/91. At the sectoral level, the programme was to restore productive capacity in agriculture and import-substitution industries producing essential consumer goods, and to rehabilitate the social and economic infrastructure. Whereas the adoption of the Rehabilitation and Development Plan brought much needed donor support, implementation was far from consistent. There was continued uneasiness with adjustment policies within the government.

To get out of the inconsistency dilemma, a small circle, the Presidential Economic Council (PEC), consisting of the Ministers in charge of economic Ministries and senior personnel led by the Ministry of Economic Planning and Development, took charge and argued for macroeconomic stabilization and broad market-based liberalization. The narrowing of the circle was advantageous to government; it enabled the administration to sort out a consistent policy and to organize an 'inner movement circle' committed to implementing the policy. The small circle was equally advantageous to the donors: it constituted 'a one-stop-shop' to argue out and implement policy.

At the end of 1989, a 'broad-based' seminar entitled 'A Critical Look at Uganda's Economy Under the National Resistance Movement Government' was held for politicians, academics and technocrats to debate economic policy. From the inner circle's point of view, however, the seminar was only intended for sensitization about the policy to come, which had already been crystallized. In retrospect, the inner circle may have been necessary to draw up a coherent economic policy framework. However, this continued narrowness seems a disservice to the policy process for the country as a whole. Now that liberalization is under way, a positive response to policies has to come from a wide range of stakeholders, from whom inputs at the policy formulation stage are a necessary step to 'own' policy and lead to a smoother implementation.

The objectives, strategy and conditionality of the SAP

The adjustment programme reflecting the philosophy of the Bretton Woods institutions is best described in two documents: *The Way Forward I*, approved by the Presidential Economic Council (PEC) in June 1990, and *The Way Forward II* that accompanied it in August 1991. *The Way Forward I* is the most comprehensive policy document to which practically all the other adjustment policies can be logically linked. The adjustment programme was implemented in a series of 3-Year Rolling Rehabilitation and Development Plans, each of which consisted of macroeconomic and sectoral policy documents and a set of project profiles.

Given the poor performance of the past control regime, the government fully embraced the Bretton Woods institutions' overall philosophy whereby 'the role of government policy has to be to "facilitate" or "enable", change in the economy,' and to operate under market-based incentives.

A summary of the adjustment programme was given in *The Way Forward I* as follows:

(i)   An underlying precondition for dealing with current economic problems is to tackle the macroeconomic roots of such problems. A strategy with two main components was proposed:

   (a) stabilizing the currency by controlling inflation; and
   (b) promoting exports.

(ii) The central policy measures to be pursued were:
   (a) prudent, non-inflationary budgeting, allied to measures designed to increase taxable economic activity;
   (b) devaluation to a competitive exchange rate for exporters, allied to measures to liberalize the marketing of crops; and
   (c) a sectoral investment strategy focused on enabling the efficient and equitable operation of the market.

The adjustment of the government consisted of three elements: (i) the mobilization of resources; (ii) maintaining macroeconomic stability; (iii) the promotion of exports.

Mobilization of resources
Since the objective was to build 'an independent economy', the strategy was to mobilize 'own resources' to minimize external debt and donor conditionalities. Domestic resources were to be mobilized by attaining and maintaining liberalized and positive real interest rates to attract domestic savings into the banking system. The *Financial Sector Review of 1991*, conducted by the World Bank, outlined the weaknesses of the entire financial sector that stood in the way of achieving this objective. The IDA-funded Financial Sector Reform Programme 1993 therefore addressed systematically the problems of the financial sector including: strengthening the regulatory role of the Central Bank; restructuring the parastatal banks (Uganda Commercial Bank, Co-operative Bank, and Uganda Development Bank) to make them solvent and efficient; preparing for the privatization of the two commercial banks; and maintaining a liberalized positive interest-rate regime.

   Foreign resources were to be mobilized through export promotion. Foreign-exchange inflows were also attracted by putting in place an Investment Code in 1991; by creating the Uganda Investment Authority as the one-stop-shop to promote investment, especially foreign investment; and by streamlining payments procedures. Inflation was to be controlled to put in place an environment to attract private remittances from abroad that do not create a debt burden.

Macroeconomic stability
Macroeconomic stability was to be achieved by reforming both the revenue and the expenditure sides of fiscal policy.

   On the revenue side, the emphasis was on generating non-inflationary revenue to finance the budget, and to put a halt to printing money. The tax rates were revised to fewer codes; value added tax was started in July 1996 to widen the tax base; exemption from import taxes was narrowed in fiscal year 1995/6; the exchange rate was liberalized partly to enable government to raise budgetary revenue from import-support sales of foreign exchange at the higher market-based rate; and overall market liberalization was undertaken partly to bring economic activities into regular channels which can be taxed and away from parallel markets and smuggling. The Uganda Revenue Authority was set up to administer the tax system more efficiently; the previous Income Tax Department had neither the autonomy nor the incentives to collect taxes aggressively.

   On the expenditure side, the strategy consisted of identifying *cuts* in public spending, and *streamlining* the *composition* of public expenditure to support essential social and economic infrastructure. The needed reforms were identified in *The Public Choice for Private Initiatives: Prioritizing Public Expenditure for Sustainable and*

Equitable Growth in Uganda by the World Bank in 1991. Measures for cost-sharing in the White Paper on Education (1992) and the Three Year Health Plan (1993/4–1995/6) were put in place to shift the emphasis in spending towards primary and preventive health care and primary education, to reach more people in pursuit of equity without sending the budget sky-high since the better-off would share part of the costs. Reform of the civil service was meant to increase the pay of a small remaining public service to achieve efficiency without exploding the budget; demobilization of the army was meant to cut public spending on defence and reorient it to the economic and social sectors – agriculture, health and education. The Public Enterprise Reform and Divesture Statute 1993 was also part of streamlining public spending away from loss-making parastatals producing private goods and services. Overall, the budget conditionalities were to keep public spending low, to emphasize spending on infrastructure and social services rather than private goods and services, and to finance the budget by non-inflationary revenue, on a cash basis.

Export promotion
The most important policy measure was exchange-rate unification to eliminate the parallel market in foreign exchange by legalizing bureaux in 1990, and to remove the implicit tax on exports by gradually adjusting the official exchange rate through a series of auctions. Exchange-rate unification was achieved in November 1993. Maintaining a market-based exchange rate is a conditionality which has since been adhered to. This exchange-rate policy is underlined in *The Way Forward I* as 'a key component in both the government's anti-inflation strategy and export promotion

Table 5.1 *Stabilization and structural adjustment performance indicators, Uganda, 1970–94*

	1970	1986	1994
Overall growth of GDP:			
1. GDP index	100.0	93.9	153.9
2. Growth rate of real GDP in 1991 constant prices	1.1	9.4	7.0
Income distribution:			
3. GDP per capita index	100.0	57.5	74.3
4. Growth rate of real GDP per capita in 1991 constant prices	0.0	−1.6	6.1
Internal balance:			
5. Overall fiscal deficit as % of total domestic revenue		17.0	18.0
Financing as % of total deficit:			
6. Foreign		10.0	100.0
7. Domestic		90.0	0.0
8. Banking system		91.0	0.0
9. Non-bank		9.0	0.0
10. Total recurrent revenue as % of GDP	14.6	4.2	9.7
11. Inflation: Annual % change in CPI (1988 = 100)		356.0	12.0
12. Exchange-rate premium (% of parallel over official rate)		306.0	0.0
13. Real effective exchange rate (1990 = 100)			72.7[a]
14. Current account balance (excluding grants, US$m.)		−140.8	−317.4
15. Gross reserves (US$ m.)		86.0	219.0
16. Current private transfers (inflows, US$ m.)		100.2	303.5
17. External debts (total including arrears, US$ m.)		1401.0	3170.0
18. Debt service ratio (%)			52.0
19. Trade balance (US$ m.)		−194.0	−463.7
20. National income distribution by quartile in 1992 (%)	I	II	III	IV
	8.84	15.56	23.36	52.25

[a]1993 data.
Sources: Republic of Uganda, *Background to the Budget 1995–1996;* ILO/UNDP Report (1995a); World Bank (1995a); Tumusiime-Mutebire and Henstridge (1995).

strategy' (Republic of Uganda, 1991). The process of exchange-rate unification involved: legalizing the parallel market by introducing Foreign Exchange Bureaux in 1990; devaluations to reduce the premium between the official and parallel market exchange rates 1987–90; and auctioning official holdings of foreign exchange to arrive at a market-based exchange rate. Table 5.1, row 12 shows that the exchange-rate premium was reduced from 306 per cent in 1986 to zero by 1993 and the exchange rate has since remained unified. Another aspect of exchange-rate reform was the control of inflation; this has enabled the policy-makers to depreciate the real effective exchange rate from a base index of 100 per cent in 1990 to 72.7 per cent by 1993 (Table 5.1, row 13).

The Agricultural Policy Committee, financed by the World Bank's Agricultural Sector Adjustment Credit (ASAC), set up nine Task Forces whose recommendations led to complete liberalization of the export regime by: dismantling the monopolies of the state marketing parastatals, the Coffee Marketing Board (CMB), the Produce Marketing Board (PMB), and the Lint Marketing Board (LMB); simplifying export-import procedures, including the elimination of barter trade; decontrolling producer prices of export crops which used to be set annually on budget day; and streamlining crop finance so that export producers can be paid cash on delivering the produce.

Competition-enhancing reforms

The reforms under this heading fall into two categories: those directed at improving international competitiveness and those directed at the local market.

The liberalization of international trade has been followed most systematically in the export sector. Not only have all export receipts been cashed at the market exchange rate since 1991 (including coffee), thus removing the 'implicit tax' on exports, but the export marketing parastatals, the Coffee Marketing Board for coffee and the Lint Marketing Board for cotton, have also been dismantled. In addition, one licence, renewable every 6 months, is issued for exports, replacing restrictions on licensing and barter trade. The producer prices of export crops have been liberalized and connected to world prices through a market-based exchange rate. The explicit export duty on coffee was removed in 1990.

The liberalization of the import regime has been less systematic. Tariffs have been rationalized to fewer categories; exemptions from duty on raw materials and capital goods under the Investment Code of 1991 and other exemptions sought by industrialists to keep down the cost of imported inputs as exchange-rate liberalization proceeded, are also in place. The necessity to raise non-inflationary revenue from a narrow tax base, however, has led to instituting high tariffs on a few items: beer, cigarettes and petroleum. It is not clear, therefore, whether the overall effective tariff rate has gone down during the liberalization period. Frequent reviews of the tariff rates in order to enhance revenue collection have marred observation of any trends.

The complaint from exporters, substantiated by studies by the Uganda Investment Authority, is that existing incentives discriminate against exporters while providing import-substitution producers with high effective rates of protection. The result is a less competitive trade regime, taxing exporters and subsidizing import-substitution activities (Uganda Investment Authority, 1993).

Regarding the reduction of barriers to foreign ownership and investment, two policy measures were adopted: the return of Custodian Board properties previously confiscated from the Asians under the Amin regime, rule and the adoption of the Investment Code 1991 with incentives to attract foreign investment.

Practically all *domestic price controls have been removed*, the last one being the decontrol of petroleum prices. The Produce Marketing Board parastatal (PMB) was dismantled and other restrictions on trading in food crops across districts removed.

Interest rates have been fully liberalized, and the Treasury Bill rate plays only an indicative role. The financial sector has been under reform since 1993. This includes: strengthening the capital base and regulatory powers of the Central Bank; restructuring the parastatal banks – the Uganda Commercial Bank (UCB), the Co-operative Bank, and the Uganda Development Bank; and preparations to privatize the Uganda Commercial Bank, as well as downsize it, in order to make the commercial banking sector competitive.

Institutional change-oriented policy reforms

This section briefly describes the roles of three new institutions which have been set up under adjustment: the Public Enterprise Reform and Divestiture (PERD), the Uganda Investment Authority (UIA), and the Uganda Revenue Authority (URA).

(a) PERD The institutional framework for the reform and divesture of public enterprises was provided by the PERD Statute No. 9 of 1993. The framework consisted of: the Divesture and Reform Implementation Committee, to implement the divestiture policy; the Policy Review Working Group, to review policy issues; and the PERD Secretariat. Because of the slow progress in privatization and the numerous complaints about lack of clear-cut procedures, a Presidential Directive was issued in January 1995 to restructure the PERD framework. The Secretariat and the Policy Review Working Group were dismantled and replaced by a Parastatal Monitoring Unit under the Secretary to the Treasury to monitor the financial flows to parastatals, and a Privatization Unit to handle the divestment.

The privatization period was restricted to the end of 1997 but progress has been modest. The whole issue of privatization is under lively debate, however, and the reactions of the legislature to the manner in which the policy is being implemented is covered in a later section of this chapter.

(b) UIA The Uganda Investment Authority was created in 1991 to provide a one-stop-shop for disseminating information to promote private investment, and to administer the 1991 Investment Code whose objectives were to encourage efficient import-substituting and export-oriented activities which would enhance foreign-exchange earnings and savings, create employment opportunities for human resources, provide value-added (processing or manufacturing) to natural resources, and encourage efficient production using indigenous resources.

In particular, the UIA was to assist investors in circumventing the administrative bottlenecks they would have faced in regular government ministries; in gaining faster access to infrastructure and utilities; in gaining access to the investment incentives; and to correct unintended policy biases against investment.

The implementation of the investment code is hotly debated, however. The major incentives are exemptions from duties on plant, machinery and construction materials, exemptions from duties on industrial inputs, tariff protection and corporate tax holidays. Opponents contend that the tax holidays deny government revenue it badly needs and that duty exemptions encourage import-intensive import substitution and discourage backward linkages as well as the creation of employment. These issues are revisited in a later section which examines the impact of investment policy on employment in the modern private sector.

(c) URA A major conditionality in the adjustment programme was switching the source of financing the fiscal deficit from printing money to non-inflationary revenue. The Uganda Revenue Authority is a semi-autonomous institution that was created in 1991 to collect taxes aggressively, improve tax administration and enlarge the tax base. Row 10 of Table 5.1 shows that this objective is being attained, with an increase in total recurrent revenue as a percentage of real GDP from 4.2 to 9.7 per cent between 1986 and 1994.

Performance indicators of the adjustment programme
Row 1 of Table 5.1 shows that the growth objective is being attained, with the GDP index having risen from 94 to 154 per cent, a figure well above the base value in 1970. The average annual growth rate of real GDP in 1991 constant prices is about 5.6 per cent; growth in 1995 and 1996 has been estimated at approximately 10 per cent.

Improvements in internal balance are being achieved, not only by increasing non-inflationary revenue (row 10) but also by switching the financing of the fiscal deficit from bank to non-bank sources (rows 7–10). Despite the fact that the fiscal deficit as a percentage of total domestic revenue has changed little between 1986 and 1994 (row 5), the annual rate of inflation has fallen drastically from 356 to 12 per cent (row 11). The average annualized rate was 10 per cent in 1995/6. This tremendous improvement is largely attributed to financing the budget on a cash basis.

The changes in external balance indicators are given in rows 13–20: a unified nominal exchange rate has reduced the 306 premium in 1986 to zero and a depreciated real effective exchange-rate index has come down from 100 in 1990 to 72.7 per cent in 1994. The trade balance and the current account balance were both still negative in 1994 (they improved in 1995 due to the coffee boom). Gross reserves have grown from US$86m to US$219m (row 15), and current private transfers (row 16, taken as a sign of confidence in the economy) have tripled.

On the macroeconomic front, therefore, most indicators show good performance, with the exception of large inequalities in income distribution (row 20) which are discussed in the next two sections.

Given that labour market issues were not part of the adjustment package, there was no assessment or anticipation of the effects of the package on employment. One can only infer from the policy statements from the Ministry of Finance and Economic Planning that the removal of market distortions and the resulting improvement in efficient resource allocation were expected to bring about growth and employment, and to redistribute income equitably. The validity of these *'implicit'* assumptions is examined in the following section.

The impact of adjustment on the labour market

This section: (i) describes the major characteristics of Uganda's labour market that are relevant to the assessment of the impact of adjustment;(ii) outlines the effects of adjustment on employment, and the real returns to labour; (iii) weighs the capacity of each component of the labour market to absorb labour in order to increase productive employment; and (iv) draws overall conclusions regarding the effects of adjustment on economic growth, employment and poverty reduction.

Characteristics of Uganda's labour market
Characteristics by employer Table 5.2 lists employment by type of employer and by sex in 1992. Although the exact proportions may have changed because of the

Table 5.2 *Level of employment by employment status and sex, Uganda, 1992*

Employment status	Male No.	% by sex	Female No.	% by sex	Total No.	% of total emp't
Self-employed	2,183,271	52.77	1,954,372	47.23	4,137,643	56.6
Household enterprise employees	599,873	22.29	1,448,453	70.71	2,048,326	28.02
Private sector employees	550,377	80.01	137,462	19.99	687,839	9.41
Government and public sector employees	271,217	73.56	97,537	26.44	368,854	5.05
Unemployed	42,972	63.64	24,557	36.35	67,529	0.92
Total	3,647,810	49.90	3,662,471	50.10	7,310,191	100.0

Source: Ministry of Planning and Economic Development, IHS Reports, 1993

policies pursued since the Integrated Household Survey (IHS), it remains the case that the predominant form of employment in Uganda is *self-employment*, both within and outside households. Rows 1 and 2 of Table 5.2 accounted for 84.62 per cent of total employment of the entire labour force in 1992. Within the self-employed category, women predominate in household enterprises.

The second source of employment is the modern private sector, taking on a total of 9.41 per cent of the labour force in 1992; men constitute 80 per cent of this labour market. The remainder, 5.05 per cent of the labour force, mostly men, were employed in the public sector, both government and parastatal, at the time of the IHS.

Two key features which emerge from Table 5.2 are especially important for our analysis. The predominance of self-employment makes it difficult to recognize the impact of adjustment on the labour market using the conventional measures of changes in real wages and labour mobility: moreover, data on these measures are not available, in most cases. This chapter devotes the bulk of the analysis to tracing the return to own labour, on the assumption that an increase in the returns to own labour raises productive self-employment.

Secondly, the figures for unemployment create the impression that there is full employment in the labour market; since most people are obliged to earn a living on their own, they are, by definition, employed. The hidden problems of underemployment grossed over by this definition must be addressed, however. These problems are examined by sector, particularly the informal sector.

Characteristics by sector Table 5.3 gives the broad share of each sector in total employment. Agriculture has the largest share, with declining relative importance, however, between 1963 and 1992, from 88 to 80 per cent of total employment. The share of industry is not only minute but is even less in 1992, compared with 1963. The share of services is the one that is growing steadily from 8 to 17 per cent between 1963 and 1992.

Table 5.3 *Employment by sector, Uganda, 1963–92 (%)*

Sector	1963	1972	1982	1992
Agriculture	88	85	83	80
Industry	4	5	6	3
Services	8	10	11	17

Source: ILO/UNDP, 1995b: 67.

However, for the purposes of analysing the effects of adjustment it is better to sub-divide the sectoral characteristics as follows:

(i) *The rural labour market*, consisting of three sub-divisions: smallholder agri-culture; estate agriculture; and hired labour.
(ii) *The modern public sector labour market*, consisting of government ministries, both central and local, parastatals, and semi-autonomous institutions such as Makerere University or the Uganda Revenue Authority, and Uganda Airlines.
(iii) *The modern private sector labour market*, consisting of employment in manufac-turing, mining, construction and services.
(iv) *The informal sector urban labour market* in manufacturing, handicrafts, services and petty trade.

The response to adjustment is discussed by sector by examining changes in the number of jobs and changes in the real returns to labour, whether from the surplus from self-employment or real wages from paid labour. Ideally, the changes examined should be compared with counterfactuals established from econometric projections, using time series, in order to net out what is due to adjustment from the normal trend and from other factors unrelated to adjustment. Unfortunately, the meagre data in Uganda do not allow this methodology to be applied. The changes described reflect how the labour market was impacted upon both by adjustment policies and other factors over the period 1987–95.

The segmented rural labour market under adjustment
The rural labour market is highly segmented. The *first* and largest segment consists of self-employment on own smallholder plots of land with an average size of 0.5 to 12 hectares per family, engaged in crop and animal husbandry as well as off-farm supplementary activities.

The *second* segment consists of hired labour on permanent contract, or casual terms during peak seasons, hired by smallholders and small estates.

The *third* segment consists of labour on large estates above 12 hectares. The tradi-tional estates grow tea and sugar; estate coffee is less important but is grown in some parts of the country. Recently, modern estates are cropping up to grow flowers, pineapples and other horticultural crops for export.

The size of land holdings in Table 5.4, category 3, gives a rough idea of the relative importance of each farm-size category. Category 1, row f, of Table 5.4 gives the percentage of hired labour on the farm by region, with a national average of around 32 per cent: in other words, family labour on own smallholdings constitutes the bulk of Uganda's rural labour market, i.e. close to 70 per cent by deductions, as well as of the overall national labour market since smallholder agriculture is the single largest employer.

The self-employed smallholder The first feature of this labour market is that the smallholder derives his/her income from a variety of sources, of which agriculture yields an average of 60 per cent, as illustrated in Table 5.5, row 1, columns 1 and 2. Adjustment policies only concentrated on the agricultural component. The design of future adjustment packages should also take into account the effects of these packages on other income sources to widen the opportunities for self-employed labour. The multiplicity of sources of income applies to the urban sector and cuts across income classes: Table 5.5 is therefore referred to in discussing other labour markets as well.

A second feature of the smallholder agricultural labour market is that cash crops constitute only 4.5–6.1 per cent of household agricultural incomes across income

Table 5.4   *Socioeconomic characteristics of Ugandan farms*

	Western	Central	Eastern	Northern	Total/Average
1. Socio/demographic					
(a) Mean age of farm owner	44.0	40.0	45.0	42.0	42.0
(b) Family size	10.0	9.0	13.0	12.0	11.0
(c) Full-time farmers (%)	84.5	78.6	79.0	80.7	80.2
(d) Consumption as % of production	35.4	45.2	0.0	32.4	39.4
(e) Self-financing (%)	93.0	81.7	81.5	93.2	88.6
(f) Hired labour (%)	28.2	37.0	28.4	28.4	31.7
2. Land tenure					
(a) 'Owned' (%)	75.0	79.9	85.4	81.0	80.4
(b) Borrowed	12.6	10.6	13.0	3.3	9.8
(c) Rented	5.0	6.5	1.6	3.3	4.8
(d) Communal	7.4	2.9	0.0	12.2	5.1
3. Farm Size (ha)					
(a) 0–2 (%)	28.2	25.5	42.4	10.2	26.6
Mean	1.3	1.3	1.2	1.9	1.4
(b) 2.01–12 (%)	56.3	56.9	48.1	6.8	54.5
Mean	5.3	5.4	6.3	6.2	5.8
(c) 12.01–40 (%)	11.3	12.4	16.0	22.7	22.4
Mean	18.7	24.4	24.5	22.0	6.5
(d) 40.01 + (%)	4.2	5.2	6.2	10.2	10.2
Mean	163.0	176.9	114.7	142.4	144.3
4. Distribution of costs (%)					
(a) Land preparation	38.7	40.8	30.2	36.6	37.3
(b) Planting	14.7	16.0	21.4	12.8	16.1
(c) Weeding	25.6	21.4	28.6	31.8	26.0
(d) Harvest	20.8	21.8	20.0	18.7	20.6

Sources: Evans, (1992); Bank of Uganda, Agricultural Secretariat.

Table 5.5   *Income sources in Uganda (%)*

Source	Rural		Urban	
	Poor	Non-poor	Poor	Non-poor
1. Agriculture	59.31	60.40	18.03	6.98
2. Business	6.75	13.71	19.47	39.82
3. Employment, *of which:*	3.86	8.15	33.31	35.37
(a) Government employment	*1.69*	*4.38*	*11.65*	*15.08*
(b) Private employment	*2.17*	*3.77*	*21.66*	*20.29*
4. Residual earned income	1.36	1.47	2.67	1.50
5. Total earned income	71.28	83.73	73.47	83.67
6. Miscellaneous, *of which:*	28.72	16.27	26.52	16.32
(a) Rent	*2.18*	*1.01*	*3.97*	*3.88*
(b) Remittance	*19.85*	*12.30*	*19.24*	*11.25*
(c) Transfer	*0.59*	*0.13*	*0.20*	*0.14*
(d) Dowry	*4.18*	*1.72*	*1.83*	*0.35*
(e) Inheritance	*1.92*	*1.12*	*1.29*	*0.72*

Source: Balihuta and Appleton (1994)

groups, as illustrated in Table 5.6, row 2a. Because cash crop earnings are important for the balance of payments, they were the focus of adjustment policies within the agricultural sector.

The package to improve the returns to the producer from earnings from cash crops (i.e. coffee, cotton, tea, and tobacco), consisted of decontrolling producer prices and reforming crop finance to pay the producers promptly on delivering the

Table 5.6 *Major sources of household agricultural income in Uganda (by % contributions to total income)*

Source of income	Income group			
	Poorest	Middle	Well-off	Rich
1. Total agriculture	54.3	56.08	53.36	n.a.
2. Crops as % of total agriculture, *of which:*	95.0	94.94	89.22	92.38
a. Cash crops	5.93	6.15	5.84	4.45
b. Food crops	89.07	88.79	89.88	87.93
c. Livestock	5.0	5.06	4.78	7.62

Source: Balihuta (1994)

Table 5.7 *Share of producer in world price for traditional export crops, Uganda (%, at market exchange rate)*

Year	Robusta coffee (clean)	Arabica coffee	Cotton (lint equivalent)
1987	12	12	22
1988	18	16	47
1989	14	12	38
1990	18	22	56
1991	40	81	62
1992	38	39	43
1993	35	47	63
1994	46*	49*	51

*These figures refer to one month. The rest of the data are annual averages.

Source: Agricultural Secretariat, Bank of Uganda, 1994.

crop; these reforms eliminated the inflation tax on producers. A second policy was to liberalize the nominal exchange rate; this eliminated the implicit tax on exports. As the international prices of export crops slumped in the late 1980s, especially for coffee, the explicit export tax was eliminated as well. Without the export tax, the need for the parastatal marketing monopolies dwindled and these were also eliminated, namely, the Coffee Marketing Board (CMB), and the Lint Marketing Board (LMB) for cotton.

The combined effect of the favourable adjustment policies can reasonably be taken as responsible for increasing the share of the producer in the world market price up to about 46–51 per cent in the cases of cotton and coffee, as illustrated in Table 5.7. Assuming other things remain equal, the rising share of cash crop producers in the world market price implies an increase in the real return to own labour, and an increase in the demand for labour and employment in cash crop production. The overall impact on employment, however, is extremely small since cash crops contribute only about 5 per cent of rural agricultural income. The policies, therefore, were more important in raising foreign exchange to improve the balance of payments, rather than to increase employment in agriculture.

A third feature of the smallholder agricultural labour market is that food crops production constitutes the major source of agricultural household income across income groups, as illustrated in row 2b of Table 5.6. From the policy point of view, however, the dismantling of the Produce Marketing Board (PMB) parastatal, freeing inter-district trade, and abolishing barter trade were the only components of the adjustment package that were directly addressed to food crops.

In order to weigh the effects of this limited package, unlike in the case of cash crops, time series are unfortunately not available to show a change in the share of the producer in the market price. Tables 5.8 and 5.9 show the situation only in 1993 and for only a very limited range of food crops.

Table 5.8 *Final market price of each local market participant, Uganda (% share)*

Crop	Farmer	Buyer	Transport	Wholesaler	Retailer	Total
Groundnuts	57.4	2.1	6.4	31.9	2.1	100
Bananas	56.0	11.0	8.0	7.0	18.0	100
Beans	33.0	3.0	15.0	29.0	20.0	100
Rice	29.2	29.0	12.4	13.9	14.6	100
Irish potatoes	24.0	4.0	17.0	35.0	20.0	100
Field peas	22.0	2.0	10.0	55.0	11.0	100

Source: Msemakweli (1993). The data are based on a survey of 12 districts.

Table 5.9 *Farmer's share in world price of non-traditional exports, Uganda (at market exchange rate)*

Commodity	% share
Chillies	50
Pyrethrum	42
Vanilla	40
Mulberry silk	39
Cashew nuts	26
Ginger	21
Okra	7
Mixed vegetables	7

Note: The farmer's share is based on the processed product equivalent, by taking into consideration the out turn.

Source: Agricultural Secretariat, Bank of Uganda 1993.

A careful look at the farmer's share in the market price suggests that policy should address improvements in the market chain. In the cases of groundnuts, beans, Irish potatoes, and field peas in Table 5.8, for example, the wholesalers in the marketing chain need to be more competitive through policies that lower the costs of procurement and storage. The non-traditional food crops in Table 5.9 are emerging as new exports, along with beans, maize, fish, groundnuts and simsim. There are several problems confronting farmers and other participants in this sector, such as low and substandard production at the farm level due to lack of improved inputs and extension advice; high collection and transport costs due to poor feeder roads; lack of a cold store to preserve quality; lack of information on international prices; very large swings in demand, especially for maize and beans sold through the World Food Programme to war-ridden areas such as Sudan, Rwanda and Burundi; and overall lack of financial services especially for production and marketing credit (National Forum, 1995a). Non-traditional crops represent a very attractive opportunity to increase the returns to own labour for the self-employed smallholder, by keeping the farm-gate price attractive. However, to raise the share of the farm-gate price in the market price, the government must put in place policy packages which address the above multiplicity of problems in this sub-sector. A fourth additional feature of the smallholder agricultural labour market is that the 'marketable surplus' of food crops is extremely small. Most food crops are grown for own subsistence consumption.

Table 5.10 shows that the marketable surplus of the most important food crops is extremely small, ranging between 5 and 30 per cent of total output.[4] Yet it is these food crops that are grown by the largest percentage of households as

---

[4] Table 5.4 showed similar information in row 1(d).

Table 5.10   *Marketable surplus of food crops, Uganda (%)*

Food crop	% of production marketed surplus	% of households growing the crop
Sorghum	5	20
Simsim	10	40
Finger millet	10	55
Sweet potatoes	10	90
Irish potatoes	15	25
Peas	20	15
Bananas	20	65
Groundnuts	20	70
Cassava	25	85
Beans	25	90
Maize	30	85
Wheat	50	2
Pineapples	80	<1
Passion fruit	90	<2
Rice	90	<1
Soya beans	95	3
Sunflowers	100	<1

Source: Uganda Development Bank, 1993.

indicated in Table 5.6. It follows that the bulk of households in Uganda are simply by-passed or outside the adjustment policy framework, which leaves mass poverty intact.

A fifth feature of smallholder agriculture which is become increasingly debated is the gender dimension in the division of labour and the producer's access to market cash-based incentives. Table 5.11 illustrates the gender division of labour in post-harvest activities, and access to cash from the 'marketable surplus'. The women who do the bulk of the work are left outside the cash incentive since 70 per cent of the marketing is done by men, in the 12 districts that constitute the sample from which the data are summarized.

In summary, if food crop agriculture is to become an employer it must be able to pass on a larger share of the market price for many of the food crops to the producer *directly*, especially in the case of women producers. At the same time it must be possible to increase the quantity of output, not only for own home consumption for household food security, but also for a larger 'marketable surplus'. There is no direct connection as yet between adjustment and these desirable changes; any existing connections are largely indirect.

A sixth feature of the smallholder labour market is the unemployed who are unable to respond to adjustment. The smallholders in the 12 districts enumerated in the PAPSCA document are unable to respond to the cash crops incentive, or to the overall improved policy environment which might have an indirect beneficial effect on employment in the foods sub-sector. This category of labour needs to be restocked and endowed with productive assets, and the destroyed infrastructure in the war-ravaged areas needs to be reconstituted. This should feature prominently in the Anti-Poverty Strategy (1996) and any subsequent pacification plan for war-torn areas.

The poor performance of the now discontinued PAPSCA project failed to achieve the restocking of assets and the reconstitution of infrastructure to enable this group to start remunerative employment. In our assessment, the higher incidence of poverty in the North, North-East, and Luwero Triangle, identified in the Household Surveys in 1989, 1992–3, and the Country Economic Memorandum (World Bank,

Table 5.11   *Gender roles in decision-making, Uganda (by district and %)*

	Day-to-day outflow of grain from store			Marketing of grain		
District	Husband	Wife	Both	Husband	Wife	Both
Kabale	36	74	11	68	11	10
Kapchorwa	33	62	5	90	0	10
Nebbi	38	42	20	35	17	48
Luwero	5	95	0	70	24	6
Rakai	0	95	5	80	7	13
Tororo/Pallisa	15	85	0	74	18	8
Lira/Apac	10	90	0	62	23	15
Arua	13	67	20	88	8	4
Mukono	20	80	0	70	10	20
Mpigi	0	95	5	70	25	5
Masindi	5	67	28	75	16	9
Kabarole	17	83	0	87	23	20
Mean (rounded)	16	78	7	72	15	14

Source: Sillim *et al.,* 1993.

1995a), is due to the fact that adjustment policies have not brought these ravaged areas back into remunerative employment. These areas must therefore be counted as representing a large subsection of the labour market which is having a high unemployment rate, and as being by-passed by adjustment. The problem is compounded by the historical breakdown of local administration: the NGOs cannot therefore adequately address this problem.

Workers hired by smallholders and small estates This market for wage labour is segmented by region, by crop season, and by lack of information flows. Smallholders with family farms above 5 hectares, and small estates of 12 hectares and above, hire labour for peak seasons to plough in time for planting, to weed, and to harvest. The most densely populated districts like Kigezi donate rural labour to less populated areas like Kibaale District. Although labour mobility should move by crop season, poor rural feeder roads prevent movements of both agricultural produce and labour, and depress rural wages, especially in rainy seasons.

Lack of information to standardize contracts also prevents unification of the rural wage labour market. Farmers prefer to hire labour from within the vicinity where they can collect information on reliability and performance. They also prefer to extend flexible short-term piece-work contracts where the wage rate can be more easily estimated. Table 5.12 shows that real rural wages have doubled for permanent labour and almost doubled for contract labour, but have remained practically stagnant for casual labour. These data suggest that there is an excess supply of casual labour from within the vicinity at a constant real wage rate. However, because of communication difficulties and lack of information, permanent and contract labour markets experience rising real wages since adjustment has improved the macro-economic and sectoral environment for agriculture.

Additional policies to enhance labour mobility and improve the process of making labour contracts are required to unify the rural wage labour market and raise the demand for labour and rural employment, as adjustment improves the profitability of agriculture. Data on the seasonal behaviour of rural labour markets in different localities are absolutely required to guide the additional policies. Evans (1992) reports, for example, that besides the profitability of agriculture, the availability of alternative non-agricultural employment opportunities fishing, border

Table 5.12   *Real rural wage rate, Uganda, December 1987 to May 1993 (various categories of labour)*

Year/period	Casual labour Shs./6-hour work-day	Permanent labour Shs./month	Contract labour Shs./ha
December 1987	4.85	36.40	169.90
December 1988	3.47	42.11	109.47
December 1989	4.32	57.88	180.90
December 1990	4.65	52.25	203.25
December 1991	4.10	57.33	245.70
December 1992	4.55	65.02	368.55
May 1993	4.72	88.4	294.82

Source: Agricultural Secretariat, Bank of Uganda (1993): *Economics of Crop Production* (the data are deflated).

trade, etc. also bids up rural wages. The influence of these activities should be incorporated in the data collection.[5]

The estate rural labour market   Large estates which employ permanent labour occupy on average 6.5 per cent of the agricultural area under production, as illustrated in Table 5.4, row 3 (c) and (d). There is hardly any published information on the estate labour market. The brief account given here is based on a rapid rural appraisal by Evans (1992) undertaken jointly with the Agricultural Policy Secretariat.

As of 1992, adjustment had not altered the adverse features in the estate labour market. According to Evans (1992):

> ... Estate wage rates are significantly below open market levels. One day's work on a tea estate provides a worker with less than one-quarter of the wage he/she could earn in the open market as a casual agricultural worker. It is also well below returns to labour in fishing, petty trade, pit sawing and on-farm production.

The low wages are part of a history of low returns to estate agriculture in the 1970s, depressed by large price distortions from controlled producer prices, high inflation, and a fixed nominal exchange rate. The estates dealt with these problems by hiring long-term contract labour from distant markets, so as to avoid paying the competitive wages required to draw nearby labour from its next-best use, namely smallholder production of the more profitable food crops in the vicinity of the estate whose prices were not controlled. For example, workers on Kakira and Lugazi Sugar estates in Mukono District were hired from Nebbi, Arua, Rwanda and Kigezi, for one-year contracts at a time.

As agricultural activities recover in the smallholder cash crop and food crop subsectors, the tea and sugar estates are experiencing labour shortages; workers are unwilling to keep long-term fixed contracts which deprive them of opportunities to earn money income from cash crops or/and the 'marketable surplus' of food crops. Faced with labour shortage, the estates are contracting outgrowers to grow sugarcane and tea. The outgrowers compete for labour on the open rural market by offering additional payments in kind, such as food rations or paying graduated tax for their farm workers.

It is also reported that estates, as local monopsonists for rural wage labour, have tried to collude in depressing rural wages in those areas where outgrowers are not strong: this uncompetitive market behaviour is not solving the labour shortage problem on estates, however. In order to increase the returns to estate labour and expand employment on estates, apart from adjustment, additional policies are

[5]Table 5.5 shows that agriculture contributes only 60 per cent, on average, to household income.

required to improve working conditions on estates and promote competition in the labour market to raise estate wages. To guide the additional policies, research is needed to generate data on the demand for estate labour, the working conditions on estates, and the market conduct of estate employers. Research is needed particularly because adjustment policies appear to have stimulated *new* types of estates that were not there before. Horticulture, the growing of roses, and the rearing of fish and crocodiles represent welcome new investments for export to increase agricultural output and foreign-exchange earnings. However, in order to overcome the risk of crop failure due to variation in weather or pests, and to ensure a reliable supply to overseas customers, these new investments are highly skill-intensive; they are managed by expatriates. The likely influence of these new estates on the estate demand for labour and employment, especially for the semi-skilled categories, needs to be investigated so that the current estate labour shortage does not become a constraint on these desirable growth prospects.

The rural labour market: Conclusions The predominance of *self-employment* in smallholder agriculture is key in analyzing the changes in employment and returns to labour. Self-employment in smallholder agriculture constitutes 80 per cent of total rural employment; rural wage employment is only around 10 per cent, as is estate agricultural employment. Adjustment was directed at agriculture, which contributes 60 per cent of income in rural areas. The effect of adjustment on the other 40 per cent of non-agricultural sources of rural household income is unknown, and must have been *indirect* in any case.

Within agriculture, the bulk of adjustment policies were directed at cash crops, which contribute less than 10 per cent of total agricultural income. The available evidence shows that the policies improved the share of the producer in the world price for traditional cash crops. This must have had a favourable effect on the returns to own labour in self-employment in smallholder cash-crop production. However, the overall increase in the demand for rural labour from this source must be extremely limited, given the small share of cash crops in smallholder income. The overall policy objective appears to have been to improve the balance of payments, rather than employment. The smallholder foods sub-sector must have benefited *indirectly*, as witnessed by the emergence of non-traditional food exports: maize, beans, horticulture, vegetables and fish. The extent of the indirect benefits is not known, however: data on the determinants of these benefits are not available. The limited one-year data in Tables 5.8 and 5.9 indicate that the benefits must still be limited: the share of the farm-gate price in the market price is below 50 per cent for most food crops; the marketable surplus is only 5–30 per cent for the most widely grown foods; and the gender division of labour limits women's access to cash despite the fact that they are the ones who undertake the bulk of food production.

Real rural wages for permanent and contract labour rose appreciably during adjustment, benefiting the labour force that secured employment. However, the rural wage labour market is very small and highly segmented: the limited mobility and lack of information flow constrain the effect of adjustment on raising the demand for labour.

The changes in employment and real wages on the traditional estates under adjustment appear to be very limited, given the monopsonistic hiring practices. Labour market data on the new emerging estates in horticulture, flowers, fish and crocodiles are not available: this makes it impossible to pass judgement on the changes in employment and returns to labour on these estates. The farmers in the war-ravaged areas whose production assets were destroyed and who face destroyed infrastructure, were not in a position to respond; they were by-passed by adjustment.

The overall impression is that the increase in employment and returns to rural labour under adjustment is limited: the greatest contributor to self-employment rural income is the food sector on which the effects of adjustment were indirect. The past effects of war in several districts further limited the response of employment and returns to labour from adjustment policies. There is serious lack of data to back these impressions, however: they must be taken as tentative, pending further research and documentation.

The future analysis of rural labour markets in SSA needs to centre around the concept of self-employment, which is the dominant form of employment for the smallholder in these markets.

According to Chenery *et al.* (1974), increasing self-employment and the real returns to labour requires two policy measures:

(i)   policies to increase the rate of accumulation of production assets, to raise the marginal product of labour;
(ii) policies to increase the returns to assets already being utilized, by raising the price of the output.

The combined effect of (i) and (ii) is to raise the value of the marginal product of labour or the real return to labour, and therefore, the demand for labour.

In the SSA context, and for Uganda, in particular, policy measures under (i) should cover *ensuring access to land*, the most important production asset in agriculture. Fortunately, as illustrated in Table 5.4, row 2(a), 'owned' land constitutes over 80 per cent of the total land area under cultivation. The policy in Uganda, therefore, is not land redistribution but enhancing security of tenure by proper administration of land title to those already possessing land and by administration of the Land Fund to enable those without land to purchase title. A further important policy is to ensure access to rural credit: to capitalize the farm by purchasing productive animals, building farm houses, planting permanent crops, protecting the land from soil erosion and degradation, and to purchase variable inputs like improved seeds, fertilizers, hiring farm labour, etc. These policies need to be complemented by ensuring human capital formation in agriculture by spreading functional literacy, combined with extension services, as well as improving rural health and sanitation.

The policy measures under (ii) should cover: improving feeder roads to lower transportation costs and raise farm-gate prices; improving information flow about commodity and factor markets to reduce local monopolies; improving labour mobility and labour contracts to ease labour shortages during peak seasons; improving financial services to monetize exchange, in order to transform the rural economy from subsistence; putting in place mechanisms to manage food storage, to enable farmers to reap better off-season prices, manage continuous on-farm cash flow and reduce exposure to risk from large price fluctuations, etc. However, there is also a need for ensuring access to the cash incentive by women farmers through policies of promoting legal reforms, cultural change, and education programmes that reduce gender barriers.

The policy measures suggested here have been debated in response to the Anti-Poverty Strategy (1996); they were not part of the adjustment packages of 1990–95. These measures are so important in raising agricultural employment and the returns to rural labour that they should be systematically incorporated into future SAP packages.

The prevalence of *underemployment* in Uganda raises many problems which this chapter cannot adequately address, such as the adequacy of existing economic incentives for various activities, barriers to entry, inadequate resource endowments, etc. Helleiner *et al.* (1995), in their report of an independent working group, advanced the view that agricultural sector-led growth is the most feasible option for the structural transformation of the Ugandan economy. This proposition cannot materialize, however, under the current widespread underemployment in agriculture. One way to combat underemployment and promote structural change is to encourage the transition of smallholder semi-subsistence farms into family farms. A family farm, in the Ugandan context, should consist of 5 hectares and above with the capacity to grow enough food for home consumption, to generate a 'marketable surplus' to earn cash income, and to hire labour and pay for other farm inputs. Our estimations (Ssemogerere *et al.*, 1995) suggested a figure of 300,000 U.Shs. cash income per household of 6 members per month as a rural living wage for full-time employment in agriculture. This income of 3,600,000 U.Shs. per annum would cover household needs, home maintenance, health and education expenditure, repayment of a rural small loan to purchase inputs, and rural saving.

A farm-management framework should be developed to teach farmers to organize the combination of crops, animal husbandry, and off-farm activities from which to raise a cash income of at least 5 million U.Shs. per annum. Land administration should seek to allow a critical number of farm families to acquire control over farms of optimal size on which to raise the 5 million U.Shs. cash income, such as the Land Fund suggested in the Constitution (1995).

These policies need to be complemented by: developing technologies for on-farm storage so that the household can market its output all the year round, taking advantage of off-season prices, for continuous cash flow; creating infrastructure to develop rural markets for inputs, outputs and hired labour; and strengthening an extension service to teach farm management and budgeting, as used to be offered at the District Farm Institutes.

The public sector labour market under adjustment

Prior to adjustment the public sector was the largest formal sector employer. The share of public sector employment as part of total formal sector employment had grown during the years of civil strife and economic mismanagement from the low of 36 per cent shortly after independence in 1967 to 56 per cent by 1977, due to haphazard public sector hiring, particularly of employees without contract, the springing up of parastatals, especially after the expulsion of the Asians and the takeover their properties by the Custodian Board in 1972, and the general decline of private sector formal activities due to insecurity, high inflation, parallel markets and smuggling to evade price and exchange-rate controls.

The objectives of public sector reform under adjustment were:

(i)   to reduce the sector to a size that is affordable by means of retrenchment of the civil service, demobilization of the army, privatizing most parastatals making private goods and services, and restructuring those which were to be retained to increase efficiency;

(ii) to raise wage levels, eroded by past inflation and devaluation, to a living wage, and to improve the welfare of the workers and their efficiency at work by reducing absenteeism;

(iii) to improve performance by a wide variety of measures including: capacity-building through on-the-job or further training; enforcing work discipline through Results-Oriented Management (ROM); equipping the workplace with the necessary tools and logistics; and restructuring the pay structure as well as job descriptions to provide incentives for promotion.

Public sector employees, whose downsizing is examined, are defined as including: the traditional civil servants on the established pay-roll of the Public Service Commission and/or relevant employing ministries; the group employees placed on the public payroll by block budget appropriations to government departments, without permanent contracts; the teaching service professionals; the central police and prison departments; and employees of public enterprises.

Employment-level changes in the public sector The figures in Table 5.13 should give the orders of magnitude in public sector employment during adjustment. They are to be interpreted with great care, however. The ILO/UNDP Report (1995b) argues that 'ghost workers' should not be counted as retrenched since they did not exist. This indicates the difficulties of making estimates, because the official data are incomplete.

Over the period 1991–5 the reduction in total public sector employment amounted to 104,000 persons. However, many semi-autonomous bodies were concurrently created, such as the Uganda Revenue Authority, the Uganda Investment Authority and the Statistics Department (see above). These bodies hired highly skilled personnel; this may not only have cushioned the overall reduction in public sector employment, but may also have changed the composition towards a higher quality labour force. This was in line with the intention of policy reform: '... a tendency to replace junior, unskilled staff with more highly paid professionals, as the service delivery targets of the service are raised.' (Budget Framework Paper FY 1966/67).

The statistics in Table 5.13 reveal various qualitative aspects which are frequently discussed in the Ugandan press. For example, many personnel in the police force appear to be leaving in protest against the meagre pay which stood at only U.Shs. 50,000 per month in 1996 and which is routinely paid late. The ad hoc adjustments in numbers by adding persons with contracts of limited duration is not an answer since they are not a properly trained force: quite a few of them are frequently caught in arbitrary shooting and other crimes. The reform programme had in fact planned to *increase* the size of the police force by 3 per cent. A serious look at changes in number and quality in this category is required to ensure that the force is adequately staffed with qualified personnel to maintain internal law and order, the

Table 5.13   *Public sector employment under adjustment, Uganda, 1982–95*

Employment category	1982	1991	1993	1995
1. CGE ('000s)	191	269	215	148
2. TPSE ('000s)	271	406	369	302
3. TPSE/FWE (%)	–	37	35	31
4. TPSE/LF (%)	–	6	5	4
5. FWE/LF (%)	–	17	15	13
6. PFWE/LF	–	11	10	9

Row 3 is estimated (for comparison) from Republic of Uganda, 1996a: 11 (Graph)

Key:
CGE = Traditional civil servants on the established payroll of the Public Service Commission or relevant Ministry employing them, plus members of the police and prisons administration
TPSE = CGE plus employees of public enterprises
FWE = Formal wage employees in both the public and private sectors (i.e. TPSE plus formal wage employees in the private sector)
LF = Total labour force
PFWE = Private formal sector wage employment

Note: Figures are rounded off to the nearest whole number.

Source: Chapters 2 and 3 of this volume.

lack of which jeopardizes economic development. Teachers are also frequently paid late, especially up-country. Recently they were subjected to transfers to effect an equitable distribution of qualified teachers throughout the country: unfortunately the transfers were arbitrarily executed and led to a lot of resistance. Apart from ghost teachers and overdue leavers, the members of the teaching service were not to be reduced under adjustment.

Also, the seemingly endless character of the entire retrenchment exercise is undermining the confidence of those who are still at work, and is forcing the better qualified and more able to opt for voluntary retirement. Furthermore, some personnel are being arbitrarily rehired; this has raised the question of whether retrenchment is 'cleansing', an issue which cannot assist in improving work performance.

In summary, the data in Table 5.13, in order to reflect accurately the objectives of retrenchment, should be updated by category, preferably on a quarterly basis. The purpose should be to ensure that the changes in magnitude, by category, are moving towards the stated policy objectives, and the composition of the service is improving in quality. The policy-intended rate of growth is 9.5 per cent per annum, which just covers replacement from natural wastage. Indeed, the change in employment is a key economic indicator that signals the ability of the public sector to deliver public goods and services to the entire economy and should appear in the quarterly *Key Economic Indicators*.

Wage levels in the public sector One of the objectives of adjustment was to trim the civil service wage bill to a size that is 'affordable' in terms of a living wage. The semi-autonomous institutions were to apply a 'cash limit' to hiring only that number of personnel who could be paid a living wage within the budget allocated to them and other monies they were allowed to raise on their own. The traditional public sector was to apply the 'number' limit by increasing hiring at a rate no higher than 9.5 per cent per annum.

There are no data available that are assembled in a form suitable to trace changes in real wages paid to the civil service.

(i)   Monetization of the benefits makes it impossible to extrapolate the deflated annual wage bill. It is tempting to conclude that monetization increased real wages for the lower cadre of employees who previously were unable to claim the benefits in kind because of red tape or favouritism. However, for this to have been the case, the monetized component must exceed the rate of inflation; it must also *not* move the employee into a higher taxable income bracket.

(ii) Late payment is frequently reported within the teaching and police services; postponed wages are eroded by inflation.

(iii) There have been annual increments, but the government is the first to admit that these increments have yet to produce a living wage, the realization of which was earmarked for the 1996 Budget. This commitment has been quite late in forthcoming.

What is needed is to publish a quarterly public sector wage index, adjusted for inflation, monetization of benefits, and annual increments. Until these data are available, it remains difficult to evaluate the effect of adjustment on public sector real wages.

Changes in efficiency The third objective of public sector reform was to create a small, efficient civil service which would deliver high quality public goods and services. There is *no* evidence available as to whether a system to monitor improvements in performance is in place, and what the results have been so far. Instead, observation of the reform process reveals elements that might be running counter to work motivation and improvement in efficiency, such as: unending retrenchment which has created job insecurity; delayed payment of a living wage which makes it difficult for workers to be full-time on the job; shortfalls in recurrent expenditure for office logistics such as paper, light bulbs, etc.; narrow bands between salary scales which do not inspire harder work to get promoted (Muyingo, 1996). The reform process was also intended to remove large distortions in the wage structure so that equal pay by rank, by qualification, and by performance, becomes possible. Unfortunately wages structures are being reformed by ministry: teachers, judges, legislators, etc. This is exaggerating wage distortions and leading to strikes to which the government response is very poor. The government has a Capacity Building Plan (1994) in place (Republic of Uganda, 1994b). This is a welcome effort in the right direction; however, in addition to training, some of the demotivating factors noted also need to be removed, if efficiency is to be improved.

   Demobilization under adjustment The policy objectives were to reduce the size of the army as the country was returning to peace, pay the remaining force a living wage to improve performance, and reorient the budgetary savings to civilian expenditure, particularly education and health. Demobilization of the 500,000 target number did occur as planned. However, the achievement of the other objectives does not seem to be materializing. Some key senior officers indicate that donors did not disburse sufficient re-deployment funds as planned. The result was insufficient skills training and funding of many demobilized soldiers to enter civilian employment. Newspaper reports cite large-scale unemployment of ex-soldiers who are periodically called upon for odd jobs – to clear the water weed in Lake Victoria, beef up security at election time, and return to the armed forces to fight insurgency in the nomadic parts of the country. This matter requires careful evaluation since it has serious adverse implications for the maintenance of security: a tracer study should be conducted to document which ex-soldiers have successfully settled into civilian productive employment, and which are still failing to do so, identifying the constraints causing this failure. The objective of budgetary reallocation from military to civilian spending, especially on education and health, requires a public debate in many fora by Ugandans and donors. Is Uganda investing sufficiently in the peace-making process? Neither the constitution-making process nor the general elections, as conducted, appear to have provided satisfactory answers to this question.

The private formal sector labour market
The adjustment policies provided a macroeconomic environment conducive to the private sector flourishing: a market-based exchange rate; a decontrolled, and more stable, price-incentive structure under lower inflation; a liberalized trade regime, including simplified export and import procedures. It was assumed that the private sector would respond to this improved environment by faster growth of output and employment, without further need to put in place a specific employment policy.

   Additional sector-specific policy reforms covered: the privatization of loss-making parastatals; the return of custodian properties to their former owners; financial sector restructuring; and an Investment Code (1991) to attract private foreign investment. These reforms were assumed to be compatible with the macro reforms, and were therefore expected to enforce output growth and employment. By 1994, a survey of 265 Uganda enterprises, designed and supervised by the World Bank and carried out by the Uganda Manufacturers Association (UMA), had this to say:

... investment and supply response from firms has been weaker than would be expected on the basis of macroeconomic policy reforms. The strongest response has been in the area of non-traditional agriculture commodities and primary goods, and in import-substituting manufacturing, especially in areas of food, beverages and tobacco (UMACIS, 1994:1).

This section makes a qualitative assessment of whether, on the basis of the rudimentary information available, there is any substantial increase in employment, real wages and welfare.

The information is woven together from the following ongoing studies: the UMA survey referred to above; the UIA study (1993) on the structure of incentives, including the Investment Code 1991; Muyingo's report (1996); Ssemogerere's on-going 'Survey of the Effect of Trade Liberalization and Regional Integration on 100 Manufacturing Enterprises' (1995); Kashugyera's research (1995); UNIDO's report of the ongoing study of the Indicative Industrial Plan (IIP) for the Government of Uganda (1994); and the *Background to the Budget*. These sources do not address labour market issues, except the ILO/UNDP Report (1995b), referred to extensively above, but they do contain rudimentary information that is used to question the assumption that the current macroeconomic and sectoral policies are leading to an increase in employment and real wages in the formal private sector that are sufficient to justify the absence of a specific employment policy within the current SAP package.

Changes in employment and real wages Approximately 9.5 per cent of wage earners are employed in the private formal sector. The relative importance of this labour sector in total employment has remained unchanged between 1992 and 1995, despite adjustment.[6] This figure is extremely small, given the demand for formal wage employment arising from the normal growth of the labour force, rural-urban migration, retrenchment and demobilization. The formal private sector labour market would have to grow extremely fast to absorb the labour that the designers of the adjustment package assumed it would.

Ideally one should decompose the formal private sector to search for both the sources of output growth and the elasticity of output with respect to employment. Unfortunately, on this issue, we have only fragments of evidence pieced together from diverse sources. The ILO/UNDP Report argues that private formal sector employment in manufacturing declined by 23 per cent between 1988 and 1992, despite growth in output; and that real wages in the formal sector as a whole (both public and private) have risen by 90 per cent over the same period (1995b, chapter I, section 1.2). This again suggests that the growth taking place is not labour-intensive.

The overall index of industrial production published annually in the *Background to the Budget* shows that, taking 1987 as the base = 100, the index grew by 56 per cent between 1987 and 1990, and decelerated to a growth rate of 38 per cent between 1990 and 1993.

This suggests that the growth in the industrial component of the private formal sector is decelerating. The largest components of the index are food processing, beverages and tobacco (46 per cent of the weight in the index) according to the UMACIS Survey (UMACIS, 1994);[7] but these sub-sectors are reported to have the lowest value-added, relative to total output, by the census of Business

---

[6]It should be noted that the self-employed in the private sector are classified under the informal sector or household enterprises. This is a grey area which future statistical definitions need to clarify.

[7]UMACIS stands for Ugandan Manufacturing Association Consultancy and Information Services.

Table 5.14   *Number of establishments, average number of employees per establishment and real annual wage bill, Uganda, 1985–94*

Year	No. of establishments	Average no. of employees per establishment	Price deflator	Real annual wage bill (Shs.m.)
1985	80	22,314	2	22
1986	70	15,681	8	81
1987	89	17,351	21	693
1988	108	19,286	46	3,337
1989	104	18,008	69	4,108
1990	113	18,469	86	5,086
1991	130	16,373	122	4,704
1992	135	15,945	154	5,609
1993	132	15,309	170	7,394
1994	148	13,609	182	9,154

Source: Republic of Uganda, *Background to the Budget*, various issues.

Establishments (1988). This offers little hope of creating productive employment for labour.

Perhaps worse still, some of the incentives under the Investment Code (1991) contradict the stated policy objectives and may be partly responsible for the growth process which is anti-employment. The stated objectives of the incentive regime are:

(i)   to enhance foreign-exchange earnings or savings;
(ii) create employment opportunities for human resources:
(iii) provide value-added (processing or manufacturing) opportunities for natural resources;
(iv) encourage efficient production activities based on indigenous resources, including climate conditions and fertile soil;
(v)   develop human skills and the technological base (VIA, 1993: 24–5).

The fiscal incentives in place under the Investment Code 1991 are:

(i)   duty exemptions on plant, machinery and construction materials;
(ii) duty exemptions on industrial inputs.

These incentives implicitly subsidize imported capital and inputs, encouraging capital-intensive investment and discouraging the use of local labour and locally made inputs. The latter would spread employment through backward linkages and raise aggregate demand through wage payments, which would in turn stimulate another round of output and employment. Hence, this incentive regime contradicts some of the policy objectives, in particular (i), (ii) and (iv) above.

Those reforming the Investment Code must look not only at whether it puts Ugandan and Kenyan investors on an equal footing within the Preferential Trade Area (a key debate), but also at whether the code is fair to the users of local versus imported inputs, particularly as this input usage pattern affects job creation, and the fact that most *new* investment is by local firms and partnerships as documented by the UMACIS Survey (1994). This shows that entry of new firms has accelerated in recent years, with 45 per cent of the firms surveyed having entered since the initiation of the SAPs (after 1987) (UMACIS Survey, 1994: 2). Table 5.14 (column 2) confirms the survey data: indeed, the number of establishments surveyed for the *Background to the Budget* is increasing annually – it has risen from 89 to 148 since 1987. Column 5 of the table shows that the real annual wage bill is also increasing rapidly during adjustment. However, column 3 shows that the average number of employees per establishment is shrinking. This raises a disturbing note as to the type of growth that may be taking place.

Another aspect of the investment incentive regime is that it is encouraging import substitution with a limited market where 69 per cent of the sales of output go to the government (UMACIS Survey, 1994), with 51 per cent of the new investments oriented towards import substitution, while only 4 per cent are oriented towards export markets, which, after overcoming the high costs of entry and competition, would provide a larger market and stimulate employment. The other 45 per cent of enterprises appear to be oriented towards non-tradeables (UIA, 1993: 35).

The tentative results of ongoing analysis on privatization, repossession, financial sector restructuring, and employment creation revealed that of the 84 enterprises in existence, listed in the Census of Business Establishments (1988), 42 were closed down by 1994 due to: very rapid change of ownership from public to private or due to repossession, where the new owners could not as yet run the enterprises; bankruptcy, particularly because of the higher working capital requirements for imported inputs at the market-based exchange rate; unresolved ownership disputes; and stiff competition from imports following trade liberalization. Whether some of the closed enterprises could be reconsidered in a government programme designed to preserve employment is a question which is still being looked at; sheer inefficiency should not be tolerated, but closure of promising firms because of improper sequencing of policies, beyond their control, requires re-examination. Privatization creates temporary unemployment as the new owners restructure the enterprises. The long-term change in employment depends on demand conditions, the incentive structure, the choice of technology and the efficiency of the enterprise. Muyingo (1996) and Kashugyera (1995) provide the tentative results that only small increases in employment took place between the starting period of privatization and 1995. A frequently cited argument for privatization is to save the Treasury payments to loss-making parastatals. Tentative data (Kashugyera, 1995) show privatized enterprises which have not yet paid the purchase price, and small inflows of tax revenue. The ILO/UNDP Report (1995b) questions the outright closure of enterprises which are awaiting buyers but which could be run profitably by the private sector if restructured and therefore cease to be a drain on public revenue. The trade-off between the revenue and employment objectives, in our view, needs closer scrutiny. If public enterprises can be restructured and run efficiently, then public revenue can be saved without loss of employment. Kashugyera cites promises by the new owners to expand employment, which are never followed up by the privatization unit. The government is engaged in a comprehensive public campaign to popularize privatization. This campaign, to be convincing, must provide concrete data on savings in revenue due to privatization, employment creation and growth, and payment of the purchase price by the new owners. Otherwise, privatization is still interpreted by a wide public as 'hidden' income redistribution of cheap handouts of public assets to a few, as partly predicted by Loxley (1989).

Financial sector restructuring is also affecting employment creation. Whereas the long-term objective to create a sound financial sector is not in dispute, its implementation is associated with temporary liquidity shortage: high lending interest rates are maintained as banks struggle to stay solvent on the basis of a few performing assets; higher collateral requirements are making loans inaccessible; slow loan disbursements from the Uganda Development Bank (UDB) and the Development Finance Corporation Uganda (DFCU) are making enterprises bankrupt and pushing them to be closed, with their assets to be sold under the auspices of a trust set up to liquidate non-viable enterprises; the slow pace of creating the stock exchange is depriving the private sector of this source of financing. The UMACIS Survey (1994) reports that over the period 1987–94 only 39 per cent of the enterprises surveyed had access to credit from the banking sector. Tighter monitoring of the effects of sectoral reforms on overall economic objectives, including employment creation, is desirable.

The survey further notes other constraints facing the private sector: poor infra-structure and irregular power supply; limited availability of serviced industrial sites; improper assessment of taxation and lack of an appeals procedure; critical shortages of certain categories of labour. The UNIDO Report (1994) also gives another list of constraints, in particular the very low levels of capacity utilization due to obsolete machinery and equipment with spare parts no longer available from the original suppliers and a lack of information on standards of locally made spares, etc. Some of the constraints are being addressed. For example, the Private Sector Foundation has been set up to assist the private sector. The participatory study process spearheaded by the UNDP and conducted by the UIA is also addressing some problems identified in the UNIDO Report (1994). However, closer monitoring is required to ensure that the constraints are lifted in a manner consistent with job creation and improved real wages and working conditions in the private formal sector labour market.

The informal sector labour market
Figures in various publications put the size of employment in the informal sector at 40 per cent of the total labour force (Ochieng, 1995).

The supply of labour to the informal sector currently goes beyond the normal ongoing rural/urban migration. It also includes women and children as male household heads are retrenched; school-leavers who can no longer automatically count on the public sector to absorb them; as well as retrenchees from the army, parastatals, and the public sector. It is in this sense that the informal sector is a residual, absorbing the excess labour ejected by other markets. Undocumented evidence of the excess supply of labour in this sector is seen in towns swelling with half-idle shoe shiners, cross-border transporters, standing car washers, and the ugly scenes of street children, a new phenomenon on Ugandan streets.

Improvements in real wages and welfare have to come from an increase in the demand for labour. Within the adjustment package, there is no provision for increasing the demand for labour in the informal sector. The higher prices for commodities, made possible by price decontrol, liberalization of trade and exchange-rate reform, cannot have influenced the returns to informal sector oper-ators appreciably since they were already operating on the parallel market. A careful study of price changes is required to address this further.

Profit rates are reported to give entrepreneurial informal sector operators incomes 7.5 times more than those of their employees, and 6.4 times more than formal sector wages, for comparable skills grades. However, these data are based on a survey of 1989 which is outdated, particularly because of the many changes during adjustment that squeeze profits: the many indirect taxes, for example the high cost of transport due to the petroleum tax; the higher rents due to changing business premises that have followed the return of Custodian Board properties to their former owners, etc. The presumably lower returns to self-employment in the informal sector after the introduction of adjustment packages could have been increased if entrepreneurs had more capital and tools to work with. This is some-thing which needs further investigation. What is documented is that many retrenchees from the civil service were not properly equipped with sufficient packages and advice (ILO/UNDP, 1995a). The project on 'Counselling, Training and Credit Support for the Retrenched', costed at US$3.8 million, including the establishment of the Credit Support Fund, was never implemented as planned by the Ministry of Labour and Social Welfare and the Ministry of Public Service (Republic of Uganda, 1994a). The extent to which the army retrenchees were given adequate assistance to take on civilian employment was discussed above. The administration of adjustment put the emphasis on retrenchment, not on where the retrenchees were to go. The demand for informal credit for micro-enterprise finance being closely examined by the Bank of Uganda and the Vocational Training for Employment Modernization Project (1996) being examined by the Ministry of Labour and Social Welfare, are testimonies to this felt lack of supporting institutions for increasing productive employment in the informal sector. The assessment here is that the informal sector in Uganda is the dumping ground of ill-equipped retrenchees, as found in many other countries in SSA (see, for example, Vandemoortele, 1991).

The public response by social partners and political interest groups

In Uganda, five major interest groups can be identified: the Private Sector Forum; the trade unions, especially NOTU; the NRC Committee on the Economy and the Political Parties; the various NGOs; and the women's networks. Government institutions involved in dialogue are mainly the Ministry of Economic Planning and the ministries most closely concerned with labour issues, namely, Public Service, Labour and Social Welfare.

The Private Sector Forum
The government's policy of private sector-led development gave the modern private sector a special opportunity to react by defining its role and by seeking partnership with the government. The private sector, led by the Uganda Manufacturers Association, formed the National Forum for Strategic Management for Private Investment and Export Growth. It invited senior civil servants and independent academics to interact closely with it to study government policy on privatization, which it regards as questionable; identify problem areas of implementation; define the roles of those in the private sector and in government – who should act, and how they should act in a liberalized environment; and recommend specific actions to be taken, within a specific time-table. The Forum meets annually since 1992 and is a recognized, prestigious body. Between meetings it has 4 working groups through which it interacts with the government in identifying issues and monitoring the implementation of policies. The working groups present their reports to the Annual Meeting.

Forum members have had to learn some hard lessons, however; for example, that the exchange rate is market-based and will not be fixed as exporters and importers prefer; that protection, especially import bans, is not the best way to promote the private sector in every case; that taxes have to be paid; and that complaints to government must be backed by reliable data. Policy advocacy required that data be collected and this provided the impetus to a 'Survey of Post-Liberalization Constraints Facing the Private Sector', which was financed by the World Bank and carried out by UMACIS (1994, see above). The government has also had to learn some hard lessons: for example, that frequent and unpredictable tax changes are resented by the private sector and prevent it from planning; that politically motivated selective protection, within the private sector, will not go unnoticed; and that the private sector is a partner to be consulted and is entitled to make specific inputs into the policy process, such as tax proposals into the annual budget.

The Forum has benefited from funding by USAID during its formative years. It has set up a Private Sector Foundation to raise its own donor support. Unfortunately, the Forum does not address employment and labour market issues, perhaps because a policy in this area is not on the books. The Annual Meeting in 1995 was asked to contribute to the formulation of employment policy, by the Minister of Finance. The Capacity Building and Human Resources Working Group is addressing the issue of critical shortages of certain skills in the private sector, but the Forum has not yet come up with an overall formulation of employment policies.

The National Organization of Trade Unions (NOTU)

The NOTU has reacted to government statements on labour disputes; but this has been confrontational, to deal with problems which had already escalated into a crisis, such as the medical workers' strike. The NOTU was represented in the Constitutional Assembly, as one of the special interest groups, by two members, one of whom supported the NRM and the other the multi-parties. This left the image of NOTU as a possible partner in policy-making ambiguous in the eyes of the National Resistance Movement (NRM) policy-making circles. Meanwhile, organized labour supports adjustment but has genuine complaints about its implementation which cut across existing employer/labour contracts and demoralize the NOTU membership, who perceive the organization as unable to articulate their interests. A policy on employment must be put in place immediately so that NOTU has a policy framework through which to relate to the government. The privatization policy, for example, was of great advantage to the private sector in claiming its role as a partner with government on privatization. The employment policy must articulate the role of labour institutions in a liberalized economic environment, particularly because as, Nelson (1991: 37) puts it, 'Organized labour is usually viewed as an obstacle to labour market adjustment.'

NOTU has to rethink what its appropriate role should be in a liberalized environment. Suggestions which come to mind are: negotiating for a moderate increase in wages which is consistent with a rise in employment in a monopoly-monopsony situation where the interests of both employer and employee are met; working for safety standards which protect labour and at the same time reduce business costs by avoiding accidents at work – but which the private sector is likely to ignore without a union watchdog; defining and formalizing working hours to ensure a regular and reliable supply of labour as skill requirements and productivity demands go up; such formalizing promotes higher productivity for the employer, while protecting job security for the employee. The identification of common interests between labour and employers is needed to enlist the private sector as co-partner to strengthen NOTU's negotiations with the government. If this co-partnership is not built, NOTU's efforts to get a better hearing from government will be undermined by the employers. The NOTU also has to rethink its appropriate role in dealing with government in order to show that organized and disciplined labour is essential to ensure successful adjustment and that massive unemployment and poverty are neither good for political stability nor for adjustment, and laid-off workers therefore need assistance to get re-employed elsewhere, and the adjustment package should explicitly include measures to create employment.

The NOTU has to mobilize donor support to carry out research to substantiate its causes in order to be listened to. Whether the World Bank and USAID will be as willing to assist NOTU as they have been to assist the private sector remains to be seen, since these institutions may regard organized labour as an obstacle to wage flexibility and labour mobility during adjustment. The ILO is a possible partner whose links with NOTU should be strengthened for the purpose of improving consultation on labour market development.

The NRC Committee on the Economy

The NRC Committee on the Economy was created in November 1989 and began to operate in February 1990. The objectives of the Committee are:

(i)   to examine and monitor the state of the national economy;
(ii) to explore new ways and means of improving the performance of the economy, making it national, independent, integrated and self-sustaining;
(iii) to examine any other areas which improve the performance of the economy;
(iv) to make appropriate recommendations to the NRC and the government at regular intervals.

The Committee breaks up into sectoral sub-committees to study the budget of every Ministry and make appropriate recommendations. For example, in its 1993/94 Report, the Committee noted the anomaly of underfunding of the Ministry of Gender and Community Development, which had gone without public releases for two full months, February and June 1993. The Committee has also noted the under-funding of the essential services supposed to be rendered by the Ministry of Labour and Social Welfare, such as the Industrial Court, a factor which leads to delays in settlements between unions and employers, and escalations of wage demands that are outdated in changing economic conditions.

In general, the Committee's recommendations are well argued and responsible; if followed, they would greatly improve the policy process. It is not clear, however, whether they are heeded by the government. The Committee has one weapon, to confront the relevant Minister by presenting a tough report to the NRC when the budget for the Ministry is due to be debated. Whereas this can lead to a delay in funding for a few weeks, it does not lead to cuts in the budget: it simply exposes arguments to the public. This confrontational channel is not the best way to contribute to the policy process.

More fundamentally, the NRC itself is supposed to be made up of 'individuals elected on personal merit'. Although it is well known that these individuals are affil-iated to political parties, the activities of the parties have been suspended since 1986 informally; the suspension was formalized in the New Constitution (1995) for another three years. The NRC members cannot therefore use their parties to organize a forum to contribute to the policy process in an effective way that can be heeded by decision-makers in government. This echoes the narrow inner NRM circle within which policies are made, which has persisted since 1989 despite the claims of a broad-based Movement Government. A new legislature took office in July 1996. It remains to be seen whether it will be more effective in making its voice heard on economic policy.

Non-governmental organizations

NGOs have been called upon to participate in the implementation of the anti-poverty-focused components of adjustment because they are regarded by government as the most cost-effective channel through which to reach the poor at the grassroots and to mobilize community-based actions and resources. This view is well argued in the 1989 PAPSCA document (Republic of Uganda, 1989).

In 1994 NGOs were again called upon to implement the 'Entandikwa' poverty-focused credit scheme. Complaints were voiced under PAPSCA by some NGOs that they were called upon to implement a project following guidelines to whose formulation they had not been a party, in particular, strict procurement and audit procedures which were extremely time-consuming and whose costs were out of proportion to the small goods and services delivered. NGOs operating at the district level appear to be better incorporated into the planning process. What some Districts like Mukono do is:

(i)   identify the NGOs which have special competence to implement project X;
(ii) cost the project, identifying resource requirements and contributions from NGOs and local government;
iii) put in place agreed mechanisms to implement and monitor the projects.

The poor in rural communities can be regarded as unemployed or underemployed and unable to respond gainfully to the market-based adjustment incentives. To make the intervention of the NGOs effective, it appears that two conditions must be met: that the NGOs have a forum at the national level to address issues (i)–(iii) as is done in some districts; and secondly that full-time government officials are put in place with whom the NGOs can interact.

The World Bank Office in Kampala is facilitating data collection on NGOs' capabilities and a new forum has been set up. Whether these initiatives will lead to a meaningful role for the NGOs and constructive interaction with government to improve the policy process, is to be awaited. The NGOs have been invited to participate in the formulation of the Anti-Poverty Strategy, published in the *Background to the Budget 1996/97*.

The women's groups

There are informal reactions that women suffer more from retrenchment than men because they are in the lower skills grades that are retrenched first, and their lack of skills makes finding alternative employment difficult. Our study of Arua District showed that women in the food sector are growing food for domestic consumption, but have no access to the price incentive from adjustment since they do not control the 'marketable surplus'. The importance of this point for the agricultural sector was illuminated earlier in this chapter. Women are further disadvantaged in cost-sharing because they lack the cash to pay. They therefore have less access to education and health services (Ssemogerere *et al.*, 1995). This limits the amount of human capital formation they can access in order to improve the value of their marginal product.

The Ministry of Gender and Community Development, which could organize an effective women's lobby to participate in the policy process, is grossly underfunded. The women's NGO networks suffer from the same shortcomings as other NGOs. Measures to strengthen the lobbying capacity of the Ministry of Gender and Community Development in the policy process are urgently needed and should be assisted by donors and backed by research to substantiate the complaints about the more severe impact of the adverse effects of adjustment, such as retrenchment, on women.

A new initiative on the Gender Dimensions of Agricultural Policy in Uganda is being spearheaded by the UNRISD/UNDP Project – Phase III, to collect hard data on gender-related obstacles affecting the returns to women farmers under adjustment and then use these data to lobby to incorporate gender systematically in agricultural sector policy. The logistics for this initiative are being handled by the

Centre for Basic Research and the Agricultural Policy Secretariat; it should be watched with interest.

Conclusions: Governance and economic liberalization
According to Boeninger (1991), the rise of a market economy and the advance of pluralistic political systems go together. A business-labour coalition is needed to support liberalization policies. In the Ugandan context, the Forum and NOTU should develop together.

A committed political consensus on adjustment is needed to reduce the uncertainty that results from an abrupt change of direction of economic policy at elections or military takeover. Political groups outside government must be taken as partners with a real possibility of gaining power: their views on the economy should converge with those of the ruling authorities into a consensus to avoid accumulating grievances and misunderstandings that are the breeding ground for radical economic changes at each successive change of government. Unless radical swings in policy are avoided, the long-term benefits of adjustment cannot materialize. If Boeninger's analysis is taken seriously, then the five groups identified in this chapter should be further encouraged to participate in the formulation, implementation and monitoring of the effects of adjustment on employment, labour market institutions, and poverty reduction.

The hostility towards labour market institutions, the underfunding of women's lobbies and the Ministry of Gender, the disregard for the NRC Committee's contributions, and the silencing of political parties should all be revisited to open up pluralistic systems for participation in the policy process as the only method consistent with the rise of a liberalized market economy, particularly on such key issues as changes in employment, real wages, and workers' welfare. This change should also contribute positively to an improvement in the peace-making process and make it possible to achieve the objectives of demobilization.

References

Balihuta, A.M. and S. Appleton (1994) *A Note on Income Sources of the Poor in Uganda: New Evidence from the Integrated Household Survey 1992.* Makerere University, Department of Economics, and University of Oxford, Centre for the Study of African Economies.

Balihuta, A.M. (1994) 'Major Sources of Income in Uganda', Background paper to ILO/UNDP Employment Advisory Mission. Addis Ababa: ILO.

Bhaduri, A. (1989) 'Employment and Livelihood: The Rural Labour Process and the Formulation of Development Policy', *International Labour Review,* Vol. 128, No. 6.

Boeninger, E. (1991) *Governance and Development: Issues and Constraints.* Proceedings of the World Bank Annual Conference on Development Economics. Washington, DC: World Bank.

Chenery, H.B. *et al.* (1974) *Redistribution with Growth: Policies to Improve Income Distribution in Developing Countries in the context of Economic Growth.* New York: Oxford University Press.

Collier, P. (1994) *African Labour Markets.* University of Oxford: Centre for the Study of African Economies.

Collier, P. and M. Henstridge (1993) 'Uganda's Structural Adjustment Programme 1992/93' (draft).

Evans, A. (1992) *A Review of Rural Labour Markets in Uganda.* University of Sussex, UK, School of African and Asian Studies.

Helleiner, G. *et al.* (1995) *Report of an Independent Working Group on the Ugandan Economy.* Kampala: Makerere University.

International Development Research Centre (1986) *Economic Adjustment and Long-Term Development in Uganda.* Report of Uganda Economic Study Team.

ILO/UNDP (1995a) *Employment Generation and Poverty Reduction in Uganda: Towards Sustainable Human Development.* Report of the Tripartite Seminar between the Government of Uganda, ILO and UNDP. Addis Ababa: Eastern African Multidisciplinary Advisory Team.

—— (1995b) *Employment Generation and Poverty Reduction in Uganda: Towards a National Programme of Action.* ILO/UNDP Advisory Mission, Addis Ababa: Eastern African Multidisciplinary Advisory Team.

Kashugyera, L. (1995) 'The Likely Effects of the Ugandan Privatization Process'. Draft dissertation, MA in Economic Policy and Planning, Makerere University, Department of Economics.

Loxley, J. (1989) 'The IMF, The World Bank and Reconstruction in Uganda' in B. Campbell and J. Loxley (eds): *Structural Adjustment in Africa.* Kampala: Madhalla.

Msemakweli, I. (1993) *Internal Food Marketing in Uganda. Proceedings of a Workshop on Export Diversification and its Impact on Food Security in the PTA Region.* Kampala: World Food Programme.

Muyingo, S.C. (1996) 'Structural Adjustment and the Role of Labour Market Institutions: Case Study of Selected Enterprises'. Kampala: Ministry of Public Service (mimeo).

National Forum on Strategic Management for Private Investment and Export Growth (1995a) *Financial Sector Development.* Position Paper by Working Group No. III. Kampala: National Forum.

—— (1995b). *Tax Policy and Administration Working Group Report.* Kampala: National Forum.

Nelson, J.M. (1991) 'Organized Labour, Politics, and Labour Market Flexibility in Developing Countries', *World Bank Research Observer*, Vol. 1, No. 1.

Ochieng, E.O. (1995) 'Macroeconomic Policy Framework for National Development and Employment Promotion' in ILO/UNDP, 1995a.

Republic of Uganda (1987) *Rehabilitation and Development Plan 1987/88–1989/90.* Kampala: Ministry of Finance and Economic Planning.

—— (1989) *Programme for the Alleviation of Poverty and Social Cost of Adjustment (PAPSCA).* Kampala: Ministry of Finance and Economic Planning.

—— (1990) *Report of the Public Service Review and Reorganization Commission (1989–1990) Vol. 1 Main Report.* Kampala: Ministry of Public Service.

—— (1991) *The Way Forward I: Macroeconomic Strategy 1990–1995 and The Way Forward II Sectoral Strategies.* Kampala: Ministry of Finance and Economic Planning.

—— (1994a) *Management of Change: Context, Vision, Objectives and Plan/Civil Service Reform.* Kampala: Ministry of Public Service.

—— (1994b) *Capacity Building Plan.* Kampala: Capacity Building Secretariat, Economic Planning Department, Ministry of Finance and Economic Planning.

—— (1995a) *Policy on the Budget for the Financial Year 1995/96* by Hon. Dr. Stephen Chebrot. Kampala: Ministry of Labour and Social Welfare.

—— (1995b) *Statutory Report on Implementation of Provisions of PERD Statute No. 9 1993 for the period ending June 30th 1995.* Kampala: Privatization Unit, Ministry of Finance and Economic Planning.

—— (1996a) *Uganda Civil Service Reform Programme: Status Report.* Kampala: Ministry of Public Service.

—— (1996b) *Employment Creation as a Measure Towards Poverty Eradication.* Kampala: Ministry of Labour and Social Welfare (draft).

—— (1996c) *Policies Towards Vocational Education and Training in Uganda*, German Technical Cooperation. Kampala: Ministry of Labour and Social Welfare.

—— *Background to the Budget* (Annual). Kampala: Ministry of Finance and Economic Planning.

—— *Budget Speech* (Annual). Kampala: Ministry of Finance and Economic Planning.

Sillim, M., N. Odongo and A. Agona (1993) *Food Storage and Post-Harvest Losses.* Procedures of a Workshop on Exports Diversification and its Impact on Food Self-sufficiency in the PTA Region. Kampala: World Food Programme.

Ssemogerere, G. *et al.* (1995) *Women and Structural Adjustment: A Case Study of Arua District.* Kampala: Uganda Women's Network, Tricolour Printers.

Stein, H. (1989) 'Development Economics: A Survey', *Economic Journal*, Vol. 99, No. 397.

Tumusiime-Mutebire, E. and M. Henstridge (1995) *Africa, Markets and Development.* Kampala: Ministry of Finance and Economic Planning: Oxford: Centre for the Study of African Economies.

Uganda Development Bank (1993) *The Financing of Agricultural Enterprises with Emphasis on the Food Sub-sector.* Kampala: World Food Programme.

Uganda Investment Authority (1993) *Study of the Effectiveness of Policies, Facilities and Incentives for Investment Promotion.* Kampala: Maxwell Stamp plc.

UMACIS (1994) *Enterprise Survey 1994.* Kampala: Uganda Manufacturing Association Consultancy and Information Services.

UNIDO (1994) *The Indicative Industrial Plan (IIP) for the Government of Uganda: Part 1,* unedited draft. Kampala: Uganda Investment Authority.

Vandemoortele, J. (1991) *Employment Issues in Sub-Saharan Africa.* Special Paper 14. Nairobi: African Economic Research Consortium.

Walton, M. and H. Ghanem (1995) 'Workers in the Global Economy: Workers Need Open Markets and Active Governments', *Finance and Development*, Vol. 32, No. 3.

World Bank (1993) *Uganda: Growing Out of Poverty*, World Bank Country Study. Washington, DC: World Bank.

—— (1995a) *Uganda: The Challenge of Growth and Poverty Reduction*. Country Economic Memorandum, Report No. 14313–49. Washington, DC: World Bank.

—— (1995b) *World Development Report 1995: Workers in an Integrated World*. Washington, DC: Oxford University Press.

6 Zambia

VENKATESH SESHAMANI & EPHRAIM KAUNGA[1]

Introduction

Zambia today is undoubtedly one of the countries with the most liberalized economic regimes of the African continent. The present phase of liberalization, however, was not attained through a smooth, gradual, logical and consistent pattern of economic policy changes. The catastrophic impacts of the well-known oil and copper price shocks in the mid-1970s sowed the seeds of a protracted economic crisis in Zambia. Economic management was by means of rather ad hoc approaches which only served to deepen the crisis over the years. This is evidenced by the alternating phases of controls and liberalization and the 'love-hate' relationship which the country had with the IMF. The past two decades has been characterized by a series of economic regimes that can be summarized as shown in Table 6.1.

This study will cover the period from 1989 and focus in particular on the developments since 1992 when a rapid and consistent phase of policy reforms was initiated.

Table 6.1 *Zambia's policy regimes, 1982–96*

Period	Policy regime
Before December 1982	Controlled regime
December 1982–October 1985	Process of decontrol and deregulation
October 1985–April 1987	Highly liberalized regime
May 1987–November 1988	Controlled regime
November 1988–June 1989	Controlled flexibility and partial decontrol
July 1989–April 1991	Highly flexible regime with intended moves towards full-scale liberalization
May–October 1991	Economic liberalization influenced by political transitional developments
October 1991 to date	Full-fledged structural adjustment programme and stabilization policies

Objectives and targets of the structural adjustment programmes

The Government of the Republic of Zambia launched the Fourth National Development Plan (FNDP) in January 1989.[2] It was ushered in against a backdrop

---

[1]The views and interpretations expressed in this study are those of the authors and do not necessarily represent the views of the ILO. Comments from participants at seminars in Lusaka and Kampala as well as from the editors of the volume are gratefully acknowledged.

[2]This was a medium-term programme (termed the New Economic Recovery Programme – NERP) for the period 1989–93.

of deteriorating economic conditions in the country notwithstanding the series of attempts to implement IMF/World Bank-supported structural adjustment programmes. This Development Plan, to a large extent, highlighted the main objectives and targets of macroeconomic policy as perceived by the government of the day.

Amongst the major stated objectives of the FNDP were:

- to create a self-reliant and self-sustaining economy;
- to achieve an overall annual economic growth rate of 3 per cent in real terms over the plan period;
- to reduce inflation to below 20 per cent by the end of the plan period;
- to reduce the rural/urban socio-economic disparities;
- to expand and diversify the country's export base;
- to restructure production and consumption patterns to conserve foreign exchange;
- to strengthen the parastatal and private sectors by promoting their operational efficiency and productive capacities;
- to increase the contribution of the private sector to 45 per cent of GDP;
- to periodically review the exchange rate and the rate of interest;
- to improve the efficiency of the civil service; and
- to reduce the overall government budget deficit to below 2 per cent of GDP.

This list of objectives did not specifically highlight any hierarchy or priority. The objectives would have called for the marshalling of considerable resources. One would have expected a more deliberate attempt to strategize and prioritize, according specific weighting to priority areas/objectives. For example, if the agricultural sector was seen as a priority, the allocation of resources in the FNDP should have reflected this. The Plan should have addressed the issues of what the sources of growth might be and how these growth sectors could be accorded priority in resource allocation and the plan's implementation framework. The strategies of the FNDP seemed more like 'survival' or 'holding' measures. The list was fairly extensive but the required focus was lost and very little linkage was established between the strategies articulated and specific action programmes.

The issues addressed by the FNDP are in many respects similar to those of earlier SAPs. The one major difference in approach was the government's deliberate emphasis on 'growth from own resources' and the recourse to a more administratively managed set-up as against a market-oriented and liberalized system. Unfortunately the government's statements on domestic resources mobilization were not very specific as to the expectations in respect of the amount of financial resources. From the government's point of view, there was merely a reference to the need to expand the revenue base and improve revenue collection.

The plan document also envisaged a critical role for the financial sector in enhancing the development process. This was to be achieved by way of: (i) mobilization of domestic financial resources; (ii) ensuring that mobilized savings were channelled to priority sectors such as agriculture and small-scale and export-oriented industries; (iii) maintaining the stability of the financial institutions.

Over the plan period, there was to be increased provision of banking facilities, especially in the rural areas. The undertaking by the government to encourage the mobilization of medium- and long-term savings by the introduction of financial instruments of varying yields and maturity was of special significance. Under a tightly regulated financial regime, the efficacy of these proposed instruments was perhaps doubtful. However, a few years later under a liberalized financial regime, the new government was to make a lot of mileage from this scheme via Treasury bills and government bonds.

In the Budget address of November 1990, the Minister of Finance of the United National Independence Party (UNIP) government outlined the main focus of government policy as follows:

- to remove restrictions hindering the establishment of business ventures, i.e. to improve the investment climate and streamline administrative procedures and legal regimes to facilitate new investment;
- to attract foreign investment;
- to encourage the non-traditional export sectors (tourism, gemstone industry, etc.);
- to reduce government involvement in commercial undertakings and enhance private sector participation; and
- to implement other measures to enhance restructuring of the economy.

Earlier in 1990, President Kaunda had made a fundamental pronouncement giving way to possible disposal of the government's share-holding in parastatal companies.[3] This was the basis of what later emerged as the privatization programme.

The Movement for Multiparty Democracy (MMD) government, after multi-party elections in October 1991, ushered in a more robust phase of economic reforms. The main thrust of the government's reform programme was to improve efficiency in both the public and private sectors through the creation of appropriate market conditions and the implementation of competition-enhancing policies. The liberalization of the economy was to be the cornerstone of the new government's economic policy. Accordingly, the MMD Government laid stress on:

- good governance and accountability;
- a minimal role for government in commercial activity reflected through privatization, private sector development and market-directed economic activity;
- encouragement of new investors, both local and foreign, on a non-discriminatory basis;
- reduced government budget deficits through fiscal discipline, a leaner government and reduced inflation rate;
- reduced external debt burden and therewith an improved credit rating for Zambia.

While expecting very significant benefits from the austere SAP regime, the government also acknowledged the costs and sacrifices that the reform measures would entail. Hence, a deliberate component of SAP strategy, aimed at cushioning the most vulnerable groups through social safety net measures, was foreseen. The Ministry of Community Development and Social Services was entrusted with the task of supervising and co-ordinating various safety net programmes. A National Safety Net Council was also established. Non-governmental organizations were also expected to support the objectives of the safety net. It was presumed that careful co-ordination of NGO activities would go a long way in cushioning the vulnerable groups from the adverse impacts of SAPs.

---

[3]This was reinforced by the Budget address which suggested the government's willingness to sell off some parastatals.

SAPs during 1989–95

Structural adjustment under the UNIP government
Towards the end of 1988, some dialogue between the Zambian Government and the World Bank and the IMF had resumed. This was to signal a new phase of Bank/IMF-supported economic reforms.

In January 1989, the government took a bold step towards making a fresh beginning with the Bank and the Fund by entering into a 'shadow' agreement with the IMF. A formal agreement was not possible at that stage in view of the substantial arrears owed to the Fund that had rapidly accumulated due to non-payment since June 1987 when the government adopted a go-it-alone policy. An Economic and Financial Policy Framework Paper (PFP) covering the period 1989–93, prepared in collaboration with the Bank and the Fund, was to form the basis of a fairly comprehensive reform programme that was announced in July 1989. This programme marked the 'reconciliation' between the government and the Bretton Woods institutions and was quite far-reaching, especially when viewed against a backdrop of nearly a decade of wide policy swings between controls and liberalization.

The main objectives of the PFP were:

- rapid diversification of the economy with improved efficiency;
- restoration of economic stability;
- attainment of a GDP growth rate of 3.5 per cent per annum;
- reduction of inflation.

The basic strategy for the attainment of the above goals was to bring about a diminution of the state sector which currently controlled 80 per cent of the economy and a progressive enhancement of the role of the private sector. In other words, the underlying philosophy of the reforms was to effect a shift from a commandist, state-controlled economy to a market-driven, private sector-dominated economic set-up. The government took a set of actions which bear testimony to the seriousness of its intentions. As regards *government budget expenditure/deficits*, the issue of subsidies received priority attention. In August 1989, the maize meal price was increased by 60 per cent. Parallel to this, the value of the meal coupon which had been introduced earlier was raised by the same margin. The issuing of coupons was restricted to people earning less than K20,000 per annum and for a maximum of six dependants per family only (see Pearce, 1994). In addition, the government introduced user fees for higher education. It was anticipated that these, together with other austerity measures, would assist in containing the budget deficit to a maximum of 7 per cent per annum. In order to contain inflation, the government adopted the standard tight *monetary measures* to complement fiscal measures. Also an active *exchange-rate system* was embarked upon. An initial devaluation of the kwacha by 49 per cent against the SDR was followed by a crawling peg resulting in a cumulative depreciation of 100 per cent. A dual exchange-rate system was later introduced with a market rate of K40 per US dollar, while the official rate fluctuated between K24 and K40 per US dollar. The higher market rate was intended in particular to provide an incentive to non-traditional exporters.

The government eliminated *price controls* on all commodities except maize. Road haulage rates were likewise liberalized. These measures were designed to remove the accumulated distortions in the operations of companies, both in the private and the parastatal sectors. With market-determined prices it was expected that the efficiency of companies would be improved, with consequent benefits to the consumer in terms of higher production and better quality.

The PFP of August 1989 made reference to the promotion of *privatization* in order to 'facilitate a phase-out of non-viable parastatal operations and encourage joint ventures with the private sector'. Most significantly, President Kaunda, in an address to the 5th Extraordinary National Council of UNIP on 28 May 1990, made a landmark announcement that the government would devolve part of its share-holdings in parastatals to the general public. It was further announced that the government would set up a stock exchange. In the Budget Address of 1990 the Minister of Finance also announced that the government would consider the outright sale of some parastatals.[4]

It is important to note that alongside these 'macro' concerns regarding efficiency, the government and its co-operating partners also actively addressed issues of microeconomic operations. To this effect, a series of company-specific restructuring studies were carried out, specifically focused on the utility companies (Post and Telecommunications Corporation, Zambia Railways, Zambia Electricity Supply Company).

The zeal and commitment with which the 1989 agreed programme was launched could not, however, be sustained as the pain of adjustment made its mark within a short time. In June 1990, food riots erupted following a further attempt to cut the maize meal subsidy which caused a doubling of the meal price, and the attempted military coup of 30 June 1990 sent telling signals to the author-ities. Subsequently, adherence to the reforms began to slacken. A series of momentous changes on the political front occurred. The Constitution was amended in December 1990 to allow for multi-partyism and this ushered in the Third Republic. Multi-party elections were announced for 1991. As a result of these developments, political expediency took the helm. Informal price controls were reintroduced. Public expenditure got out of control in the wake of the partial restoration of subsidies, revaluation of meal coupons and an 89 per cent increase in civil service salaries. The government defaulted on the economic and financial benchmarks of the IMF as well as payments to the Bank, the Fund and the Paris Club of donors. As could therefore be expected, donors withheld aid flows and the Bank suspended disbursements.

Structural adjustment under the MMD government
The presidential and general elections of 31 October 1991 saw the exit of UNIP and the coming to office of the MMD with an overwhelming mandate. The advent of the MMD government saw a more robust phase of economic reforms.

The new President, Frederick Chiluba, wasted no time in spelling out the direction his government wished to take. In an address to the representatives of the donor community on 5 December 1991, he stated that the government was to diminish its role in the running of the economy through privatization. Liberalization of the economy was to be the cornerstone of the new government's economic policy. And further, he clearly stated that in the programme of privati-zation there would be no 'sacred cows'. The new government adopted a vigorous

---

[4]Between 1986 and 1988, the Industrial Development Corporation (INDECO), which was almost synonymous with the industrial sector, benefited from a World Bank-funded diagnostic study done on 12 companies. As a follow-up to this study, the government commissioned another study on the restructuring of the apex holding company, ZIMCO (Zambia Industrial and Mining Company), and its subsidiary holding companies. The final report presented in May 1992 led to a fundamental transformation of ZIMCO and the scrapping of its three holding companies by end March 1993. The MMD Government later announced its decision to dissolve ZIMCO (Budget Address, January 1994), which decision came into effect in March 1995.

reform agenda encompassing virtually all aspects and sectors of the economy. The major areas of focus were:[5]

- reduction of the government's fiscal deficit; the PFP document for 1992–4 set the target for the deficit at no more than 2 per cent of GDP in 1992, the budget was to be balanced in 1993 and there was to be a surplus of 0.5 per cent in 1994;
- reduction of monetary expansion to contain inflation;
- elimination of distortions and controls on key prices such as exchange rates, interest rates, public utility tariffs and prices of agricultural commodities and inputs;
- reduction in the size of the government;
- parastatal reform and privatization;
- creation of a conducive business environment to entice local and foreign investors.

The new mood of reform led to an outpouring of goodwill from donors. Bank arrears were again cleared in January 1992 and disbursements resumed. A new adjustment credit – the Privatization and Industrial Reform Adjustment Credit (PIRC I) – was made to Zambia. Among some of the major actions and monitorable conditionalities under PIRC I were the following:

- Privatization
  - (i)   enactment of Privatization Act;
  - (ii) offering of the first tranche of 19 companies for open bids;
  - (iii) review and update of privatization timeframe (tranching programme);
  - (iv) launching of the Investment Centre.
- Parastatal reform
  - (i)   preparation of terms of reference for the consultancy study on ZIMCO restructuring;
  - (ii) execution of ZIMCO restructuring study and adoption of report for implementation;
  - (iii) adoption of a plan for non-ZIMCO parastatals.
- Fiscal reform
  - (i)   removal of subsidies on fertilizer and maize;
  - (ii) civil service reduction (initial retrenchments).
- Monetary/financial sector reform
  - (i)   monetary policy;
  - (ii) banking deregulation;
  - (iii) exchange-rate adjustment.
- Trade liberalization
  - (i)   deregulation of maize and crop trade;
  - (ii) study on external tariffs and reduction of tariffs.

We shall discuss their implementation in turn.

The institutional basis for the *privatization programme* was immediately strengthened with the appointment of the Ministry of Commerce, Trade and Industry as the supervising ministry to work towards the creation of a legal basis for the programme. The Technical Committee on Privatization was transferred to this ministry to operate on a semi-autonomous basis. In July 1992, the Privatization Act

---

[5]These measures and more were contained in the MMD's own PFP document for the period 1992–4, which replaced the PFP of the previous government.

was enacted by Parliament and the Zambia Privatization Agency came into being. According to the 1996 Budget address of the Finance Minister (26 January 1996), 102 companies had been privatized, the assets of 10 non-performing parastatals had been sold and 100 companies had been restructured to facilitate their privatization. A number of big companies joined the list of privatized firms, such as Chilanga Cement, Zambia Breweries, Refined Oil Products (ROP), Zambia Engineering and Contracting Company (ZECCO) and Zambia Sugar Company. There have been ongoing efforts to review the privatization process with a view to increasing the pace. Most importantly, the government has been studying the options for privatizing the mining company, the Zambia Consolidated Copper Mines (ZCCM).

At the beginning of 1993, the government established the Lusaka Stock Exchange (LuSE).This was designed to facilitate the growth of the stock market, which should help the growth of private enterprise. In the 1996 budget, the government proposed reducing company income tax from 35 to 30 per cent for those companies listed on the LuSE. This aimed at inducing more companies to trade their shares on the exchange and thereby raise more capital domestically and consequently ease the external debt situation. The government also set up the Zambia Privatization Trust Fund (ZPTF) to hold shares in trust from some of the privatized companies for ultimate flotation to the public – Zambian nationals. Of the K27.5 billion that had been realized from the privatization exercise by 1996, K12.5 billion has been used to pay retrenchees and to meet the operational expenses of the ZPTF. There has been a tight programme of reviewing various pieces of legislation relating to the business sector in order to create an easier legislative regime for new and existing investments.[6] The Companies Act was amended and there is ongoing dialogue between government and interested stakeholders on further refinement. The Investment Act was similarly revised and the Investment Centre was established. The Centre (under generous donor funding) is meant to be a one-stop clearing organ to facilitate the processing of new investment ventures. The repeal of the Insurance and the Building Societies Acts was designed to remove the monopoly previously vested in the sole state companies in these industries. The opening up of these industries has led to the emergence of many new firms in insurance and at least one more building society.

The government also made headway with *parastatal reform*. ZIMCO Limited, the apex holding company for parastatals, was transformed into an Investment Holding Company with effect from 1 April 1993. It was thereafter dissolved as of 31 March 1995. Efforts continued to restructure the operations of major utilities such as ZESCO and Zambia Railways. ZAMTEL was split from the Postal Division in the restructuring of the Postal and Telecommunications Corporation (PTC). Two companies have now been set up – Zambia Telecommunications (ZAMTEL) and the Postal Services Corporation (ZAMPOST). Under PIRC, there was provision for carrying out a utilities regulation study, with the objective of establishing the appropriate regulatory structures to oversee the operations of utilities in order to ensure that the public interest is protected both in terms of the tariffs levied and the quality of services provided. The regulatory authorities would also control entry of new investors in these industries.[7] In response to the consultants' report, the government set up a regulatory authority for the communications industry. Although the consultants had proposed the establishment of a unified regulatory

---

[6]Some of the major laws listed for review have been: the Companies Act; the Trade Licensing Act; the Land Act; the Insurance Act; the Building Societies Act; the Banking Act; and the Investment Act.

[7]The consultants Boot, Allen and Hamilton undertook the study.

commission to cater for all utilities, the government opted for separate industry-specific regulatory bodies. The government is also looking at the modalities of setting up a Competition Commission to monitor the operations of private sector companies to ensure that fair competition practices are adhered to.

In order to speed up *fiscal reforms*, the MMD government eliminated subsidies on all commodities, including maize and maize meal almost overnight. The Public Sector Reform Programme (PSRP) was launched. This entails a rationalization of the civil service which, over the years, had become bloated, inflating the personnel remuneration component of the government budget to the detriment of operational expenditure. The main objective of the civil service reform exercise is to have a leaner but more effective public sector. The oversized public service made it difficult for government to pay staff realistic salaries that reflected their market worth. The net result was a low level of retention of highly skilled manpower and low morale in the service. Another aspect of the fiscal reform is the review of the pattern of public expenditure. The government wishes to see more resources channelled to the operations and maintenance of infrastructure – social (health, education) and economic (roads, bridges, etc). The level of the deficit has been a matter of concern. The government is now committed to reducing the deficits and adopted a cash budget to heighten the level of fiscal discipline and accountability. The concept of the cash budget was first enunciated in the 1993 Budget address. It was designed to break the persistent pattern of budget deficits that had contributed in large measure to the dislocation of the economy over the period 1975–91. The main objective of the cash budget was to bring about fiscal discipline in the budgetary process as a way of combating inflation. The experience of the first two years of the cash budget points to some notable successes, particularly in the area of inflation control and fiscal discipline. The average annual inflation rate, which stood at 191.2 per cent at the end of 1992, was reduced to 35.1 per cent by the end of 1994. Most of the gains in inflation control were registered in 1994.

Progress was made in reducing the budget deficit. A primary surplus of K17,752 billion was recorded at the end of 1993. This should be viewed together with the already noted declining trend in budget deficits as a percentage of GDP. It is important to point out that, while the 1993 budget showed a surplus, part of this must be attributed to some huge legitimate expenditures being deferred by the government, notably through the payment of promissory notes to farmers totalling K17 billion. The subsequent decline in agricultural output in 1994 could be attributed to this default by the government.

But while there was some gain in deficit control in 1993, the inflationary spiral continued to cause concern. This was largely due to the continued growth in money supply from the already high 99 per cent in 1992 to 107.2 per cent in 1993. Money supply was brought under control in 1994 with its growth rate coming down to 58.3 per cent. This was a welcome sign, indicating that perhaps the austere monetary policies and fiscal restraints would soon be vindicated. However, the statistics for 1995 show the complicated nature of the relationship between macro-economic variables. The growth rate of money supply came down further in 1995 to 39.6 per cent (although this was higher than the target of 35 per cent) and yet inflation went up to 45.5 per cent at the end of 1995. The 1996 Budget address attributes this to 'the financial difficulties of the banking sector early in the year' which 'led to stress in the financial system which showed up through abrupt rises in both the exchange rates and interest rates. These changes, in turn, put pressure on prices.' The experience of the cash budget to date also seems to suggest that strict enforcement of fiscal discipline tends to have a bias against capital expenditure. The out-turns for 1994 show declines in the real outputs of three key sectors: agriculture declined by 19.8 per cent, mining by 10.9 per cent and manufacturing by 6.7 per cent. These declining trends continued in 1995, especially in agriculture and mining. While it is acknowledged that the impact of the cash budget on the economy has been largely deflationary, this should not detract from the positive gains in terms of infusing fiscal discipline. To sustain the cash budget method, some genuine cost cutting (i.e. implementing the much delayed Public Sector Reform Programme) is inevitable. At the time of writing (early 1997) this had not yet been done. Without this reform, the cash budget has meant that needed capital expenditure (and growth) have been jeopardized.

The *liberalization of the financial sector* can be traced back to the deregulation of interest rates and greater recourse to market instruments towards the end of 1992. There was significant growth in the trading of Treasury bills and government bonds, leading to a sharp rise in interest rates. The very high interest rates resulting from Treasury bill operations severely constrained the ability of the commercial banks to lend funds for working capital. The Treasury bill transactions have had, among other things, the effect of increasing the government's obligations. Early in 1994, the government instituted a 10 per cent income tax on interest earned from Treasury bills. In 1995, it undertook to convert the majority of the statutory reserves of the commercial banks into government bonds, with the net effect of reducing the actual reserve ratio by about 3 per cent. In terms of the legislative regime guiding the operations of the financial sector, several pieces of legislation have been enacted, such as the Bank of Zambia Act and the Banking and Financial Services Act, to address, among other things, the following: licensing and prudential supervision of financial institutions by the Bank of Zambia; licensing and regulation of a stock exchange and related entities by a competent body; enhancing the autonomy of the Bank of Zambia; the central bank has itself been undergoing a restructuring process. The opening up of the financial sector resulted in the entry of several new institutions. As at the close of 1994, there were 32 commercial banks in addition to various non-bank financial institutions such as insurance companies and pension funds.

The government progressively liberalized the *exchange rates*. Foreign-exchange bureaux were introduced in September 1992. The two-tier rate was unified by the end of 1992. The 1994 budget made further fundamental reforms by suspending the Exchange Control Act and allowing the opening of foreign currency accounts in Zambia by both foreigners and nationals – the purpose being to create full convertibility of the Zambian kwacha and thereby allow free flow of funds into and out of Zambia. This would create a higher degree of confidence on the part of foreign investors.

The government had committed itself to *trade liberalization* as a conditionality under the Privatization and Industrial Reform Credit (PIRC 1) from the World Bank (IDA window). It would be useful to elaborate on the progress made by the government in the area of trade liberalization and to try and assess the impact of the opening up on local industry. Looking at the period since 1989, Zambia has implemented fairly extensive reform of its customs and external trade regime. In 1991, for example, the number of tariff rates was reduced to 6 and the new minimum and maximum tariffs were set at 15 and 50 per cent respectively, with only a few exceptions in the form of a small number of luxury goods with a 100 per cent duty imposed on them. The objective of these measures was to simplify the tariff structure to allow for freer trade and better revenue collection. Further simplifications of the system were to follow a year later. As of 1995, there were three tariff rates, with 40 per cent applied on finished imported products and 30 per cent or 20 per cent on intermediate products and raw materials respectively. It is important to note that many goods are classified as duty-free or zero-rated, including government imports and some health and education products. Goods sourced from the COMESA (Common Market for East and Southern Africa) countries were levied duty at 60 per cent of the tariff rates applicable to non-COMESA countries.

The 1996 Budget introduced further tariff relief, especially for local industry. Table 6.2 highlights the changes announced in the budget as seen against the previous status.

Table 6.2 *Budget tariff adjustment by category, Zambia, 1996 (%)*

Category	Existing rates	New rates
Exempt raw materials	0	0
Non-exempt raw materials	20	5
Agriculture and mining machinery	20	0
Other production machinery	20	5
Intermediate goods	30	15
Finished products	40	25

The existing rates for COMESA countries were in general below 10 per cent; the new rates for COMESA countries are in general 40 per cent of those applicable to other countries.

Source: Ministry of Finance, Budget 1996.

It is clear from the foregoing that Zambia has come a long way on the road of trade liberalization as seen against the highly protective tariff structure prevalent in the 1970s and 1980s with multiple tariff lines. Moreover, the process has been implemented quite swiftly. As of 1990, the level and dispersion of customs duty rates were in the range from zero to 100 per cent with 11 tariff bands. In 1991, the number of bands was reduced to 6 with a minimum tariff set at zero and a maximum at 50 per cent. In 1993, tariff rates were set between zero and 40 per cent. The 1996 Budget set the bands at 0, 5, 15 and 25 per cent with effective tariffs reducing significantly since then.

Maize marketing and all crop trade was liberalized in 1993. Since then maize and other crop producers are free to sell to any buyer locally and abroad at market-determined prices. In the industrial sector, the protection of local firms no longer exists. Local manufacturers now have to compete with imported products. The objective in opening up the economy is to remove the inefficiencies and distortions promoted by the old protective regime. Local producers are induced to attain higher efficiency as they face the full brunt of international competition.

The government's tariff reform programme should also be viewed in the context of the multilateral agreements and regional commitments it has entered into over the years. Apart from the structural adjustment programmes pursued with the Bretton Woods institutions, the country has entered into agreements with the following organizations: World Trade Organization (WTO), the European Union Lomé Convention, COMESA and the Southern Africa Development Conference (SADC). Zambia has been a long-standing member of the General Agreement on Tariffs and Trade (GATT), the forerunner to the WTO, and enjoys Most Favoured Nation (MFN) status with other member states. Under the Lomé Convention its non-traditional exports enter the European Union free of customs duties, plus other benefits such as concessional financing from the European Development Fund. Zambia is the host country and an active member of the regional grouping – previously known as the PTA (Preferential Trade Area). The COMESA Treaty came into force in December 1994 upon ratification by 11 countries. Article A of the treaty states:

Member states agree to the gradual establishment of a common external tariff in respect of goods imported from other countries within a period of ten years from entry into force of this treaty and in accordance with schedules to be adopted by the Council.

Zambia is also an original member of the SADC which was first established as the Southern African Development Co-ordination Conference. Proposals for a merger of COMESA and SADC have come to nothing. Recently the SADC trade protocol was signed in Maseru. Zambia has been examining a number of issues contained in the protocol before committing itself fully to the agreement.

The pattern that emerges is one indicating a growing negative balance of trade with South Africa and Zimbabwe within the regional groupings of SADC and COMESA. The removal of tariff barriers has had a significant effect on the growth of imports from the region. Zambia's compliance with COMESA requirements on tariff reductions definitely made imports from COMESA countries more competitive compared with those from non-COMESA sources. It could be argued, however, that the earlier growth in imports was to some extent a result of the over-valuation of the local currency. The progressive liberalization of the foreign-exchange regime in Zambia in later years should contribute to a gradual normalization of the balance of trade trends. The indications are that the change in the balance of trade between 1995 and 1994 was lower than that between 1994 and 1993 in the cases of both South Africa and Zimbabwe.

Concerns have been expressed regarding the speed of the trade liberalization. Local industrialists have bemoaned the rapid pace of the opening up of the Zambia market to foreign imports and claimed that this resulted in an 'uneven' playing field. It was also claimed that the major trading partners, South Africa and Zimbabwe, have not reciprocated in opening up their own markets. In particular, it has been noted that South Africa was offering export subsidies of up to 20 per cent, and that Zimbabwe put in place a number of bureaucratic non-trade barriers to imports (slow approval of import licences, etc.) thus making it difficult for goods from Zambia to compete effectively. The response by the Zambian Government has been to introduce the possibility of the countervailing duty in the Budget Address of 1995 – a measure designed to counter any protective measures in place in other regional countries, e.g. Zimbabwe and South Africa. However, the processing of claims has been made so cumbersome that at the time of writing it had not been implemented to the benefit of any local industry.

Some anomalies in the Zambian tariff structure were identified, especially in respect to the COMESA tariff rates. Of special concern to domestic industry was the fact that Zambia used to levy duty on raw materials, whereas finished products from COMESA could come in duty-free while other COMESA countries allowed only raw materials imports duty-free. This anomaly arose because COMESA does not have a common external tariff. To some extent some of these anomalies have been addressed by Zambia. It is expected that the proposed Common External Tariff (CET) system will address the problem at regional level. However, the CET proposal is complex and will require detailed review and comprehensive country-to-country negotiations before it can be successfully implemented. The main issues are: (i) the initial imbalances between countries and the need to level the playing field; (ii) the exchange rates – the need for eventual harmonization of currencies; (iii) the rivalry between the two regional organizations, SADC and COMESA (there is a case for rationalization); and (iv) political commitment to make a success of these regional arrangements.

Government commitment to reform
In July 1992, the IMF endorsed a Rights Accumulation Programme (RAP) for Zambia and decided to monitor it through to the end of March 1995.[8] Zambia could accumulate rights for up to a maximum equivalent to SDR 836.9 million. The RAP is a special arrangement designed for countries which are serious about economic adjustment but are ineligible to use the IMF's financial resources because of outstanding debt-service arrears. Zambia completed the programme in December 1995 (it failed to complete it by the original target date of March 1995). By doing so, it was able to encash these rights in order to clear its arrears to the IMF and thereby become eligible for financial support from the IMF through its concessional Enhanced Structural Adjustment Facility (ESAF). In response to the new government's commitment to reform, other donors also provided substantial balance-of-payments support as well as debt relief through the Paris Club.

In May 1993, the government negotiated a further adjustment credit, PIRC II. There was, as might be expected, considerable overlap in the conditionalities/monitorable actions. In addition to the monitorable actions listed already, under PIRC II the government committed itself to address the following:

- action plans based on reviews of industrial licensing and a regulatory framework for small-scale enterprises;
- review of the future roles of specialized financial institutions, such as the Development Bank of Zambia (DBZ), Lima Bank and EXIM Bank;
- restructuring of Zambia Airways; subsequently the company has been liquidated;
- adoption of automatic price/tariff adjustment mechanisms for major utilities, Zambia Railways, PTC, ZESCO and ZIMOIL; this has already been achieved for ZESCO, ZIMOIL and PTC;
- safety net measures to mitigate the adverse impact on affected groups (the retrenched and vulnerable groups). The main components of the safety net are: the Welfare Assistance Fund; the Programme to Prevent Malnutrition; and entrepreneurial development and training for retrenched employees.

The MMD government has shown remarkable resolve in the implementation of the SAP measures. The intensity of the reform can be gauged from the huge changes that have been witnessed in the quantitative magnitudes of some indicators within a fairly short period of time. For instance, an average budget deficit of 13.8 per cent for the period 1985–91 was changed to a surplus of 1.4 per cent in 1993. Nominal interest rates which had been fixed at 15 per cent in the pre-SAP era crossed into three-digit figures by 1993. The exchange rate of the kwacha to the dollar was K8 to a dollar in 1987; by the end of 1995, it had risen to over K1000 to a dollar. The index of the nominal effective exchange rate was 7.6 in 1994 compared to a base index of 100 in 1990. As part of the tight monetary policy, the statutory reserve ratio had moved up from 30 in 1987 to an average of 71 during 1994. And in terms of economic restructuring, over 100 companies were privatized within a period of two years.

Indeed, some argued that the government was proceeding with too much haste in some areas such as privatization. The sacrifice and pain associated with the transition continue unabated. The government has been urged to take a more serious look at the safety net arrangements so that the SAP can be seen to have a human

---

[8]Zambia was the first country to be put under a RAP.

face. The next section will address these concerns in the context of the improved interface between the government and the labour market institutions.

Public responses to the SAP

In order to gauge the general public response to the on-going SAP, views were solicited during September and October 1995 from a number of organizations representing social partners and political interest groups, such as employers' organizations, trade unions, and other groups such as the churches. This was done by engaging important officials in these organizations in discussions that revolved around a specific set of questions.

The churches
A number of SAP measures have had adverse effects on the people: for example, cuts in government spending on social services and the introduction of user fees in the education and health sectors have meant rising costs of medical care, and the inability of poor parents to pay school fees; the removal of subsidies on food has meant rising food prices. Poverty alleviation measures are not an integral part of the adjustment programme and are, therefore, insufficient to cushion the poor and vulnerable. Hence there is no doubt that the SAP continues to hurt the poor. Church organizations experience higher demands for charity and assistance. Anecdotal evidence shows that some parishioners have even become insane as a result of job losses due to retrenchments and closures. There is a general feeling of deception about the notion of job creation as a result of liberalization. In the view of the churches, this is tantamount to increasing numbers of people having to do piece work to compensate for inadequate earnings.

The challenging voice of the churches on various crucial issues relating to SAPs, such as land reform for instance, has been allowed to be heard. However, very few suggestions made by the bishops and other church leaders have been implemented so far. One important suggestion, for example, is to have a more co-ordinated Social Safety Net (SSN) programme through tripartite consultations; but little has been achieved in this regard. The SSNs are in disarray. There is no proper reporting on the use of SSN funds.

The churches recognize the need for the SAP, but feel that it should have a development content which is lacking at present. The government seems to lack a compassionate face. 'Hear the cry of the poor', the title of a 1993 Pastoral Letter issued by members of the Zambia Episcopal Conference, has become the theme song of the church. But the poor do not seem to be heard, because leaders apparently do not feel politically threatened by ignoring them. The 1993 Pastoral Letter bluntly states: Appeals to Zambians to 'make sacrifices' and 'tighten belts' can only be perceived as cynical at best, abusive at worst, when they come from officials who receive disproportionately high salaries and benefits.

Church leaders argue that there should be no doctrinaire approach to the implementation of the SAP. It should be implemented in a form that is more sensitive to its social consequences.

Trade union perspectives
The Zambia Congress of Trade Unions (ZCTU) The ZCTU is the national body that co-ordinates over 80 different types of trade unions and worker associations throughout the country.

The ZCTU laments the drastic decline in formal employment levels and in real wages that has occurred since the start of full-fledged adjustment in 1991. Though the Minister of Finance claimed in his 1995 Budget Address that 8,000 new establishments had come into existence in 1994 as a result of liberalization policies, the ZCTU argues that most of them were briefcase companies and family enterprises that have had little impact on employment. Even if some jobs have been created, they have been overwhelmed by the much larger number of jobs lost. For example, in Livingstone alone, between 1992 and 1994, over 60 companies closed down leading to a loss over 3,000 jobs.

Real wages have gone down because during the period 1990–94, when the economy experienced 3-digit inflation, nominal wages went up by only 30 per cent per annum. This, alongside the imposition of payments for services such as health and education, has greatly eroded the general living conditions of workers' families.

The ZCTU had insisted on a wage policy in order to eliminate wage differences within industry as well as suggesting a living wage for workers based on data from the Food and Nutrition Commission. A Task Force on the Poverty Datum Line and Minimum Wages has been announced, but nothing has been done so far.

The ZCTU feels strongly that it has had very little involvement in the formulation and implementation of the SAP, which has been the province of the government from the beginning. The government consults the ZCTU as a fire-fighting organization only when it is faced with problems. For instance, when individual companies within a holding company were being privatized, it became necessary for workers from the privatized companies to be transferred to the other companies. But a service clause requires that such transfers can be effected only with the permission of the employees. The government sought ZCTU's assistance to allow the privatization agency to effect such transfers.

The ZCTU is of the view that the government's argument that there would be insufficient funds to meet the much higher wage bills should a Poverty Datum Line (PDL) be accepted is not valid. It argues there may be scope for the government to save a considerable amount of money elsewhere.

The ZCTU challenges the government's spirit of dialogue. According to the ZCTU, it appears mainly concerned with meeting its international obligations and benchmarks, and has been paying very little attention to the social dimensions of the SAP which are mostly addressed by the NGOs and donors. The government itself has put very little money in the budget for this purpose.

Although adjustment is seen as inevitable, the ZCTU considers that the speed of implementation has been too fast to allow enough time for a smooth transition. There is too much emphasis on stabilization which is a prerequisite for growth but not an automatic guarantee of growth. There is a lack of sequencing of policy measures. Everything is being implemented at the same time. How can one, for instance, practise divestiture of companies and expect indigenous Zambian participation in the purchase of those companies when the money market is being crowded out at the same time?

The ZCTU would like to have a fuller involvement in the SAP. Though structures such as the tripartite council exist, they have not been effectively used. The government should bring to the agenda of such fora key issues and proposals, such as those relating to the Paris Club. The ZCTU could provide valuable inputs relating to the experiences of the people under the SAP and suggest ways to strengthen the government's negotiating capacity at such meetings.

Mineworkers Union of Zambia (MUZ) The views of the MUZ regarding the impact of the SAP on employment, real wages and general living conditions are similar to those of the ZCTU. In 1990, wages became equal to those prevailing in 1982 in real terms; but thereafter, they have gone down severely, owing to inflation and the companies' reduced ability to pay.

The MUZ says that the government has been pursuing the SAP under its party manifesto, which did not reflect what its social partners would like to see. It has been mainly donor-driven and aimed at fulfilling the benchmarks of the IMF. The government has therefore, among other things, committed itself to a silent wage limit that has no bearing at all on the PDL. As a result, the MUZ has had to contend with this government policy, even in cases where companies had the ability to pay higher wages. For instance, the MUZ had agreed with the ZCCM in 1996 for a 46 per cent increase in wages. But this was frustrated because of IMF conditionalities.

The MUZ feels that the process of dismantling ZIMCO was not properly handled and that the liquidations of companies could have been avoided. The government proposed a mandatory payment of K 20 million as a dividend for all companies, even if they were loss-making. Mamba Collieries is a case in point. But though this money was now paid to the Ministry of Finance, the responsibility of superintending the companies continued to remain with ZIMCO. But the latter now had no financial capacity to bail out companies with problems and they consequently went into liquidation.

The government has only occasionally paid heed to suggestions from the MUZ. For example, the MUZ succeeded in preventing the implementation of the recommendations of an advisory study undertaken by the Kienbaum group on the privatization of the mines which, in the MUZ's view, could have created a social upheaval by leading to the collapse of subsidiary manufacturing companies. The MUZ is in favour of a green-field investment policy for the mining sector.

The MUZ has fundamental differences with the government over the pace of privatization, the need for strong safety nets, and the need for promoting productive investment rather than trading. At present, there is a parasitic dependence on the manufacturing firms for tax revenue and this has caused these firms to shift to trading which affords higher mark-ups. Furthermore, tax bands and tax credits are not sufficiently adjusted for inflation.

In general, however, the MUZ seems insignificant in the eyes of the government as far as policy formulation is concerned. In its intellectual arrogance of pursuing macroeconomic policies on its own, the government has created intractable problems, according to the MUZ.

The National Union of Commercial and Industrial Workers (NUCIW) The views of the NUCIW on the SAP effects also coincide with those of the ZCTU and the MUZ.

In 1993, the NUCIW had 28,000 members; by 1996, it had 25,000. The axe of retrenchment has fallen equally on both sexes. The minimum living wage suggested is K 30,000 per month. At least 5 per cent of the workers, mostly employed in shops, are earning below this figure. Many retrenched workers have turned into destitutes because of poor retrenchment packages. The government's programme for the rehabilitation of retrenched workers has so far remained on paper. No workers had benefited from it by the end of 1996. The tripartite Labour Council is not working according to advice. The NUCIW feels that the government should take a more medium- to long-term perspective in the implementation of the SAP.

The Civil Servants Union of Zambia (CSUZ) The CSUZ is the trade union representing the interests of unionized workers in the civil service category who are not covered by specific professional unions, such as the one for teachers.

In principle, the CSUZ appreciates the rationale for the SAP as the only visible option for sustained resolution of the country's economic problems. It has serious reservations, however, regarding the way the SAP is being executed.

First, there is no proper consultation with the relevant stakeholders, such as the CSUZ. Secondly, there is lack of clarity in the direction and goals of the SAP. This perhaps is the result of inadequate consultation with relevant partners. The net result is that a lot of uncertainty is generated, especially among the workers. The prospect of impending retrenchment often associated with the SAP serves to heighten despondency and general collapse in workers' morale. Thirdly, there is need for safety net measures to be put in place *before* implementation of the SAP. The government has failed to make adequate arrangements to mitigate the adverse social impact of SAP measures. Retrenched workers, for instance ex-Customs Department workers who were retrenched at the creation of the Zambia Revenue Authority, were left in limbo over long periods. Issues of level of terminal benefits, timely payment of the same, possible redeployment or assistance to relocate into alternative self-employment, etc. call for the government's serious attention as an integral component of the SAP. These are precisely the issues which have not been carefully considered in the implementation of the Public Sector Reform Programme (PSRP) which the CSUZ otherwise supports. Fourthly, there has been poor co-ordi-nation in the execution of the SAP. There is an apparent inability on the part of senior government officers, even at the Permanent Secretary level, to articulate the essence of the SAP measures.

The government did start to consult the CSUZ on some of these issues. The CSUZ held a series of meetings on the PSRP to which senior government officials were invited. This helped to disseminate information on various aspects of the reform programme more widely. The information gap that has persisted over the imple-mentation of the SAP may gradually be removed.

But though there is now greater dialogue over aspects of the SAP, some outstanding issues still remain. The CSUZ and the unions in general are not yet happy with trade union legislation relating to strikes. The issue of the PDL which President Chiluba championed so vigorously before coming to power remains ignored, despite repeated reminders by the unions.

Implementation of the PSRP has been stalling. One related factor was the apparent lack of feedback or information on the results of the management audit exercise which preceded the manpower rationalization.[9]

On the whole, the CSUZ is in full support of the continuation of the adjustment programme. It would like, however, to see greater consultation by the government of all relevant players and a moderation in the 'hasty' approach hitherto followed in implementing the measures.

A serious bone of contention between the CSUZ and the government has concerned the process of resolving disputes on collective agreements. Towards the end of January 1996, the Industrial Relations Court pronounced a verdict over a dispute between the two parties, awarding the civil servants and public service workers a 45 per cent salary increment for 1995, independent of the 30 per cent increase which the government had already effected. While the CSUZ urged the government to effect the necessary payment expeditiously, the Minister of Finance refused to do so, saying that it was impossible for the government to find the money

---

[9]The audit exercise commenced in 1996; it has to be completed before a comprehensive retrenchment scheme can be effected.

for this purpose without derailing the budget for 1996 and consequently describing the court's decision as 'irresponsible'.

Employers' perspectives
The Zambia Federation of Employers (ZFE) The ZFE is the umbrella organization which brings together the major non-government employers in the country. The organization acts as a forum through which employers can exchange views on matters of mutual interest and for channelling views and concerns to the government and the labour movement.

The ZFE lends full support to the SAP. However, like the CSUZ, it too has serious reservations on some aspects of the SAP and its implementation process.

One major area of concern is the social impact of the SAP and the very little that has been done to cushion the poor and the vulnerable groups against these negative effects. Fear of retrenchment, inadequate termination packages and their delayed payment cause insecurity in many quarters.

In tackling the parastatal sector, the MMD government did not fully appreciate the size and significance of the sector. Otherwise it would have taken greater care in dissolving the parastatals to ensure that minimal damage and disruption were occasioned by the restructuring.

The opening up of the economy without adequate measures to protect local industry will exact a high cost on the economy. Of special concern is the fact that Zambia is now an open market for imported goods from South Africa and other countries, while these same countries still maintain protectionist measures against Zambian exports. For example, Zambia's Chilanga Cement produces a surplus of 150,000 tonnes, but cannot export it to Zimbabwe because of that country's market access restrictions. Textiles similarly cannot enter the South African market; yet milk from South Africa is sold in Zambia. Colgate Palmolive's soap-making plant in Zambia has been lying idle for a year since, according to its management, it is cheaper to import soap from Zimbabwe.

The Zambia Privatization Agency (ZPA) displays inadequate understanding of the operations of some companies on the privatization list. Little effort is made to restructure and strengthen some companies prior to privatization. On the contrary, they are apparently allowed to collapse and, as a result, one sees increasing recourse to liquidation, and hence the ZPA realizes only a minimal return on them.

As a result of the rapid opening up of the economy, Zambia has been flooded with investors in commerce and trade but not manufacturing. The local manufacturing sector is virtually dead. The very high interest-rate regime driven by the Treasury bill market has affected industry badly. There has been a diversion of funds to Treasury bills away from industrial ventures.

Real wages for the workers have declined and general living conditions are poor. The general investment climate is also quite poor.

The government pays only lip service to the consultative process. The ZFE has made several representations to the government with no response. Amongst its major proposals were: (i) companies due for privatization should be restructured; (ii) there should be a social security scheme (reactions on this have been pending since 1991); and (iii) amendments to the Employment Act. The ZFE is concerned that the time lag between consultations and government reaction could render the whole exercise meaningless.

In the ZFE's view, privatization should not be wholesale. The government should ensure that Zambia remains internationally competitive. Adequate safety net measures should be put in place. The formulation of the SAP should be seen to be local. Last but not least, the government itself should set a good example by exercising fiscal discipline. At present, government expenditure is too high and the government owes a lot of money to many key companies.

Zambia Association of Chambers of Commerce and Industry (ZACCI) ZACCI is generally supportive of the SAP. The organization acknowledges that the government's intentions are well-founded and that the country needs to pursue this arduous but necessary path if the economic malaise that has set in over the years is to be overcome. But ZACCI has reservations on the management of the SAP and the government's own commitment to implementing aspects of the programme, especially those relating to the size of the government.

The level of morale in the civil service is so low that effective implementation of programmes is not possible. It is regrettable in this context that the much talked about civil service reform programme is not progressing at a desirable pace, due to apparent inertia in some quarters.

The government is not sticking to its own principles in implementing the SAP. Government 'downsizing' is not being adhered to. The PSRP is proceeding at a snail's pace. For example, under the MMD government, ministerial positions have increased instead of being reduced. Government overexpenditure persists despite the pronouncement of a cash budget. The Treasury bill system has been abused by the government instead of being used to mop up liquidity. Defence expenditure has gone out of control. The recent bailing out of the Meridian Bank is yet another instance of government inconsistency.

The business community has experienced severe hardships as a result of the SAP. The general investment climate is poor. Profitability is down. Very little expansion is occurring in industry, and employment levels have fallen. The liberalized economic environment has led to a flood of imports into Zambia. Zambian manufactures, however, are not able to penetrate external markets because of protectionism in the form of both tariff and non-tariff barriers.

ZACCI acknowledges the useful consultative arrangements that have been put in place over the past few years prior to the presentation of the government budget. ZACCI has taken advantage of this to make several useful proposals relating to the business environment. The government has taken favourable consideration of some of these proposals, such as those relating to the duty on public transport vehicles and on imported raw materials, especially for the pharmaceutical industry. (As a more recent development, it may be added that ZACCI expressed tremendous satisfaction over the 1996 budget.)[10]

However, it is the considered view of ZACCI that the economy would stand to benefit immensely if the process of consultation and mutual trust associated with annual budgets were replicated for SAPs. The acceptability and ease of implementation of the SAP would be better assured if all the relevant players were part of building the SAP programmes rather than being relegated to the role of proposing improvements after the programmes are 'imposed'.

The government
Since practically all the relevant socio-economic groups have been highly critical of the ongoing SAP as well as of the government's attitudes and actions, it was also felt

---

[10]A full-page advertisement was taken in the *Times of Zambia* on 31 January 1996 in which the organization congratulated and saluted the Minister of Finance and the government for a 'progressive and extremely positive' budget.

necessary to obtain the government's reactions in order to have a balanced presentation of views.[11]

The government does not deny that the SAP has hurt all sections of the society so far, and especially the poor. But it asserts that, contrary to what its critics say, it has a long-term and not a short-term perspective. And while the effects of the SAP on industry, employment and general living conditions may be adverse for the time being, in the longer run SAP policies will prove beneficial by stimulating investment and growth.

Having inherited a regime of hyperinflation and highly deteriorated social infrastructure and services, the first task of the MMD government was to deal with the stabilization and overhaul of the institutional framework to facilitate the delivery systems. This task took about four years (from 1991 to 1995) and it is only now that a modicum of stabilization has been achieved. The government therefore plans to devote the years 1996 to 2000 to focusing on issues relating to the supply side. It intends focusing on extending the notion of the ASIP (Agricultural Sector Investment Programme) that is already in place for agriculture to other sectors, such as MASIP for the manufacturing sector, WASIP for water, and so on.

In the manufacturing sector, the government will be providing concessionary finance to firms engaged in non-traditional exports, assistance to firms using local raw materials to help them re-equip and create potential export capacity, grant finance for technical assistance and incentives for small-scale industries through the transformation of SIDO (Small Industries Development Organization) into a more effective Small Enterprise Development Authority. It has also done the legal work for the provision of support to the Export Board of Zambia and the Zambia Bureau of Standards in order to upgrade them.

The government is aware of the unlevel playing field that currently exists for Zambian firms in the international trade sector and attributes it to the anomalies that prevail in the SADC/COMESA trade regimes. For example, South Africa is not as open to goods from Zambia as the latter is to South African goods, and South Africa pleads excuses for this on the basis of the previous trade agreements that it has inherited and which will require time for adaptation. Again, Zambia levies tariffs on raw material imports while Zimbabwe does not and this makes Zimbabwe's exports cheaper than Zambia's. But Zambia is unable to eliminate the tariffs on raw materials quickly since these tariffs provide a significant source of revenue to the government, and eliminating them would therefore cause a serious problem for the government budget. This issue has for some time been a source of some disagreement between the Ministries of Commerce, Trade and Industry and Finance. However, in the 1996 Budget, the government announced the elimination of duty on productive machinery for agriculture and mining, reduced the duty on other machinery and raw materials from 20 to 5 per cent, reduced the duty on intermediate goods from 30 to 15 per cent, and on final products from 40 to 25 per cent. Furthermore COMESA rates are to be set at 40 per cent of the general tariff rates. These measures are expected to improve the competitiveness of Zambia's producers relative to others in the sub-region.

The Minister of Finance announced at the time of the 1996 budget that the government was unable to implement the PSRP since the financial costs were beyond its capacity, even with donor support. The government therefore

---

[11]The government's point of view was summarized on the basis of an interview with the Minister of Commerce, Trade and Industry and reports of statements of the Minister of Finance.

intended to create a Ministry of Transition which would absorb the redundant employees from all other ministries and departments where they would remain until they were retrained and redeployed. This latter statement of the Finance Minister created controversy, however. A spokesman from the Cabinet Office announced that, in making this statement, the Minister was only expressing his personal views and not the decision of the government. No such Ministry has been created.

Summary of views

Although the different organizations interviewed have expressed their views from their own respective perspectives, a number of common strands of thought are readily visible. First, all of them are agreed that there is no visible viable alternative to the SAP. Second, there is general agreement that the SAP has adversely affected all interest groups through its negative impact on employment and real incomes. Third, although the government's intentions may be well-meaning, it has pushed the SAP at a pace that has been beyond the capacity of most socio-economic groups to bear. Fourth, among the various liberalization measures, trade liberalization seems to have created an uneven playing field for the local manufacturing industry. Fifth, social safety nets have been given very low priority. Sixth, the government has failed to implement some of its promises, such as the formulation of an effective minimum wage policy based on a PDL and the implementation of the PSRP. Finally, the government can do a lot better in regard to consultation with its social partners on matters relating to the formulation and implementation of the SAP. The main concerns and recommendations of the different social groups are summarized in Table 6.3.

Table 6.3   *Main concerns and recommendations of social groups, Zambia*

Social groups	Main concerns	Recommendations
I. Trade unions (ZCTU, MUZ, MUCIW, CSUZ)	(a) Marked decline in formal employment and real wages (b) Lack of a policy on wages (c) Lack of consultation by government in formulation and implementation of SAP (d) Speed of implementation of SAP measures, especially privatization (e) Inadequate safety net measures	(a) Announce a Poverty Datum Line and reactivate the Minimum Wages Act (b) Enhance government by consultations with all social groups on all major policy changes and negotiations (c) Adopt a more medium- to long-term perspective on implementation of SAP (d) Effectively implement programmes that already exist on paper for rehabilitation of retrenched workers
II. Employers' organizations (ZFE, ZACCI)	(a) Lack of a level playing field in regard to competition from imports (b) Inadequate restructuring of parastatal companies before privatization (c) Policies geared to the promotion of commerce rather than manufacturing (d) Slow pace of implementation of the PSRP (e) Lack of consultation by government on SAP	(a) Restructure tariffs and duties to ensure international competitiveness of Zambian manufactures (b) Restructure and cut down on government expenditure (c) Replicate for SAP the consultation process associated with annual budgets
III. The churches (ZCTR, CCZ)	(a) Alarming social dimensions of SAP (b) Lack of development content in SAP (c) Neglect by government of suggestions from church leaders	(a) Put in place an effective and co-ordinated Social Safety Net Programme; (b) Ensure effective consultation with social partners, including the churches

The impact of adjustment on the labour market

Statistics on employment in Zambia are far from accurate. For instance, publications from different sources such as the Central Statistical Office (CSO), the National Commission for Development Planning (NCDP) and the Ministry of Labour and Social Security (MOLSS) provide different figures on formal employment.

Nevertheless, all sources are indicative of a common trend in formal employment, namely, one of noticeable decline. The CSO being the apex statistical organization in the country, our analysis will be based largely on CSO statistics.

Size and gender distribution of the labour force

In 1994, the size of the labour force was estimated to be 3.6 million. This is based on an extrapolation of the Labour Force Survey figure of 3.2 million in 1991. This shows an 18.5 per cent increase over the figure of 2.7 million obtained from the 1986 Labour Force Survey. Part of this increase, however, is due to change in the definition of the labour force. In 1986, the labour force was defined as all persons over the age of 12. In 1991, the lower age limit was reduced to as low as 7. It is noteworthy that the CSO rationalizes this change in definition on the basis of the harsh effects of the SAP which had caused an increase in child labour. Based on the information recorded regarding the economic status of children aged between 7 and 12, an additional 200,000 children were included in the labour force. Thus 40 per cent of the increase in the labour force during the five-year period from 1986 to 1991 was due to the increased incidence of child labour. The fact that this occurred despite the existence of a law prohibiting child labour is proof enough of the significant increase in economic vulnerability of the Zambian population.

The increase in the labour force has been unevenly distributed between the sexes. The male labour force over the period 1986–91 increased by 22 per cent; the female labour force by only 14 per cent. The rise in employed persons among males was 8.3 per cent, whereas it was 4.4 per cent among females. But the rise in unemployed persons was more dramatic. Male unemployment rose by 164.5 per cent while female unemployment rose by 60 per cent. The overall change in employed labour is 6.7 per cent, while the change in unemployed persons is 96.6 per cent.

The employed labour force as a percentage of the total labour force changed from 87 per cent in 1986 to 78.4 per cent in 1991. This ratio for the male and female labour force changed from 91.3 to 81.1 per cent and from 82.2 to 75.1 per cent respectively. Thus, although the ratio had declined for both sexes, the decline was greater in the case of males (11.2 per cent) than of females (8.6 per cent).

Changes in formal sector employment: Production and service sectors

If there is one area where development planning in Zambia has failed spectacularly, it is in promoting employment. During the period of the First National Development Plan, employment increased from 233,000 in 1966 to 310,000 in 1970. This is the only period when some notable increase in employment was recorded. Although the Second National Development Plan had a target of creating 20,000 additional jobs every year, employment increased by only 2,820 during the entire plan period (1972–6). In 1988, total formal employment stood at 351,395.[12] This

---

[12]The employment series, which was revised later by the CSO for the years 1985 onwards, gives the formal employment figure for 1988 as 533,400. But for consistent comparison with the earlier periods, we have to use the original estimate for 1988.

means an addition of merely 41,000 formal jobs in nearly two decades. A major task of the Fourth National Development Plan was therefore to tackle the problem of growing unemployment. It had set itself the modest task of arriving at 400,000 formal jobs by the end of 1993. The 1993 figure, according to the revised series, was 520,000. Given that the revised figure for each year is at least 100,000 higher than the figure in the old series, the FNDP target was barely realized. But given the increase in the labour force to nearly 3.5 million by 1993, this target achievement has done little to alleviate the unemployment problem.

Table 6.4 gives statistics on formal employment for the years 1989 to 1994 in the various production and service sectors. In all the non-agricultural production sectors (mining and quarrying, manufacturing, electricity, gas and water, and construction) employment declined over the period, whereas in agriculture, forestry and fishing employment grew slightly. But in the service sectors employment either increased (finance and social services) or remained stable (wholesale and transport). As a consequence, the ratio of service sector employment to total employment increased from 51.2 per cent in 1989 to 57.7 per cent in 1994. The most pronounced increase in employment was in community, social and personal services, which predominantly depends on government administration. It is a reflection of the fact that the much touted Public Sector Reform Programme (PSRP) remained very much in the embryonic stage during the period to 1996. Finance, insurance, real estate and business services also grew noticeably and this is attributable primarily to the rapidly expanding banking sector. From fewer than 10 commercial banks in 1989, there were over 30 banks in 1994. The one service sector that had pronouncedly declined in employment since 1991 is transport and communications, due to the restructuring of the transport industries.

However, despite the increase in employment in the service sectors from 276,500 in 1989 to 289,900 in 1994, total employment drastically declined during the same period by 37,600. This implies that the cut in employment in the economic sectors was overwhelming. From 264,000 in 1989, the employment level in these sectors fell to 213,000 in 1994, a decline of 41,000. The bulk of the decline took place after 1992 when retrenchment, closure and liquidation of companies began to assume serious dimensions, and the brunt of the decline was borne by the mining and manufac-

Table 6.4 *Formal sector employment by sector of economic activity, Zambia, 1989–94 (mid-year estimates in thousands)*

Sector of economic activity	1989	1990	1991	1992	1993	1994
Agriculture, forestry and fishing	81.9	79.8	77.8	82.0	82.8	83.5
Mining and quarrying	64.6	64.7	64.8	62.1	52.2	49.5
Manufacturing	75.2	77.1	75.4	73.6	67.6	56.0
Electricity, gas and water	7.1	7.1	7.6	8.4	5.7	5.1
Construction	35.2	33.4	33.1	27.8	22.1	18.5
Wholesale, retail trade, restaurants and hotels	54.3	55.1	53.2	51.3	49.3	49.2
Transport, storage and communications	33.3	33.8	34.3	31.0	29.0	27.5
Finance, insurance, real estate and business services	32.2	32.9	35.8	39.0	37.0	36.9
Community, social and personal services	156.7	159.4	162.2	170.7	168.3	176.3
Total	540.5	543.3	544.2	545.9	520.0	502.9

Source: CSO.

turing sectors. Employment in the mining sector fell by nearly 15,000 between 1991 and 1994, while that in manufacturing fell by over 19,000 during this period.

The decline in formal employment recorded in construction is, to some extent, due to the sector having tended to become more informal over recent years, with more workers being employed on a temporary or contractual basis. As such persons are not readily recorded in surveys, the decline in the construction industry is perhaps somewhat overestimated. However, it must also be noted that construction has been undergoing technological changes whereby it has continued to become less labour-intensive, despite experiencing real growth in investment, and this also accounts for the employment reduction.

Changes in formal employment: Government, parastatal and private sectors
Consistent and comparable statistics are not available on formal employment breakdown by legal status for the period under review. Table 6.5 reflects a number of features and has been assembled from different sources.

There has been a significant increase in the absolute employment level in the central government. Ironically, the most rapid increase of 9,600 occurred between December 1993 and June 1994, after the PSRP had been officially launched. However, there has been a persistent decline in local government employment, but this is less than the increase in employment at the central government level.

The parastatals recorded a decline of 17,600 between December 1992 and June 1994, bringing the parastatal share in total formal employment down from 32 to about 30 per cent. As a consequence, the private sector remains the largest employer in absolute terms as well as in terms of its relative share in total employment, which has been stable at around 40 per cent (39.6 per cent in December 1992 and 40.2 per cent in June 1994).[13]

One should note, however, that the parastatal figures for the years 1989 to 1991 are for ZIMCO companies only; hence this excludes statutory bodies and other organizations in which the government has a controlling share. As such, the ZIMCO figures are lower than the parastatal figures. It is noteworthy, however, that employment in ZIMCO went up from 130,500 in 1987 to 146,200 in 1990. During the period 1989–91, ZIMCO employment grew by 9,200 while total employment grew by only 3,700. There was thus a net decline in non-ZIMCO employment of 5,500. Since employment in the central government also grew by 6,278 during this period, it must imply that 11,778 jobs were lost in the remaining sectors. Since the proportion of employment in local government is quite small, it can therefore be surmised that this job loss must have occurred mostly in the non-ZIMCO

Table 6.5 *Formal sector employment, Zambia: Government, parastatal and private, 1989–94*

	1989	1990	1991	1992	1993	1994[a]
Central government	110,634	115,214	116,912	123,000	123,900	133,600
Local government	n.a.	n.a.	n.a.	23,700	18,900	17,600
Parastatal[b]	136,800	146,200	146,000	166,900	159,700	149,600
Private	n.a.	n.a.	n.a.	205,400	200,100	202,000
Total	n.a.	n.a.	n.a.	519,000	502,600	502,800

[a]Figures are for June 1994; all other data are for December.
[b]Figures for years 1989–91 are for ZIMCO only.

Sources: Republic of Zambia, 1995a; CSO publications: rest of data.

---

[13]The co-operatives are included in the private sector.

parastatals and/or the private sector.[14] It may be reasonable to assume this percentage for the earlier period as well. It can be inferred that much of the job loss must have occurred in the non-ZIMCO parastatal sector which comprises a fairly large number of companies, such as the Dairy Produce Board, Mulungushi Textiles, TAZARA, the Development Bank of Zambia, the Export-Import Bank, etc. It has not been possible, however, to secure data on employment from all the non-ZIMCO companies.

Job loss and job creation in the formal sector
Some idea of the amount of job loss and job creation can be gained by comparing formal employment levels with the number of registered redundancies. Table 6.6 gives the relevant figures. The data in the table can be divided into two sub-periods, namely 1989–92 when there was a growth in employment and 1992–4 when there was a decline. Between 1989 and 1992, employment grew by 9,400, while the number of registered redundancies was 13,962. This means that at least 23,362 formal jobs were created in the economy during this period. The figure of 9,400, in other words, is a net increase in which job creation, job loss, job changing and natural wastage all played their part.

Between 1992 and 1994, employment declined by a massive figure of 47,900 while the number of registered redundancies, although higher than for the preceding sub-period (1989–92), was only 18,712. It is unlikely in such a context that any new formal jobs could have been created during this period.

For the period of our review as a whole, 1989–94, the total job loss was 38,500 and the total number of registered redundancies was 26,448.

Table 6.6   *Formal sector employment and registered redundancies, Zambia 1989–94*

	1989	1990	1991	1992	1993	1994
Employment	540,500	543,300	544,200	549,900	520,000	502,000
Registered redundancies	1,474	2,765	3,503	6,220	4,873	7,613

Source: CSO.

The above statistics provide, in our view, sufficient testimony to the damaging impact that SAP policies have had on the overall formal employment situation in the economy, especially given that the decline in employment occurred pronouncedly during the rapid phase of policy reform implementation under the MMD government. In this regard, the government's arguments regarding the establishment of new companies and the appearance of numerous daily advertisements for jobs in the press constitute an ineffectual attempt to underplay the seriousness of the growing unemployment situation in Zambia.

Employment in the informal sector
Having seen the severe contraction in formal sector employment, it is only logical to examine the corresponding changes in the informal sector. However, no detailed informal sector survey has been conducted so far and it is difficult to know what precisely has been going on in this sector. It is, of course, clear even from casual observation that the informal sector has expanded significantly. But it seems plau-

---

[14]But furthermore, since the private sector seems to have retained its share in total employment at 40 per cent even during the most active period of company closures and retrenchment, namely, 1992–4, it may be reasonable to assume this percentage for the earlier period as well. Extrapolating this percentage to 1989 and 1991 yields employment estimates for the formal sector as a whole of 216,200 and 217,680 respectively for the private sector.

sible that the sector may have expanded more in terms of *jobs* than of *persons*. This is because it is not only those who have lost jobs in the formal sector who are having recourse to this sector, but even those employed in the formal sector, because of the increasing inadequacy of their formal wages, are seeking secondary employment in this sector. The results of the 1991 Priority Survey indicate that this has been happening, as the data in Tables 6.7 and 6.8 reveal.

Table 6.7 shows that 9 per cent of workers had secondary jobs in 1991. It is interesting that a significant percentage of even professional, technical and managerial workers are engaged in secondary employment. In absolute terms, the 1991 Priority Survey found that approximately 230,000 people had secondary jobs. Table 6.8 provides data on secondary employment of workers by employment status and sex.

The self-employed, being the most numerous of the workforce by employment status category, obviously predominate as secondary job holders.

As has been stated, it is difficult to know how much of the informal sector expansion has been caused by SAP policies through their adverse effects on formal employment and on real wages leading to increasing numbers of workers resorting to secondary jobs, or through more direct incentive effects stimulating informal sector expansion. Part of the informal sector expansion would also have occurred as a result of the labour force growing much faster than the formal sector can absorb.

The CSO has used a methodology that would enable a consistent comparison of the informal sector between the 1986 Labour Force Survey and the 1991 Priority Survey. The employed are divided into two categories: the 'mainly formal' sector which includes paid employees and employers and the 'mainly informal' sector

Table 6.7 *Percentage of workers with secondary jobs by occupation in main job and by sex, Zambia, 1991*

Occupation	Total	Male	Female
Professional, technical and related workers	10	10	9
Administrative and managerial workers	7	7	10
Clerical and related workers	2	3	1
Sales workers	7	7	7
Services workers	10	11	1
Agriculture: forestry, fisheries workers	10	12	8
Production and related workers	9	9	14
Not stated	8	4	13
Total	9	10	8

Source: 1991 Priority Survey.

Table 6.8 *Percentage of workers with secondary jobs by employment status in main job and by sex, Zambia, 1991*

Employment status	Total	Male	Female
Self-employed	14	10	9
Government	9	9	7
Parastatal	8	8	4
Private	6	7	4
Employer	7	11	4
Unpaid family worker	5	4	5
Other	2	2	0
Not stated	6	4	8
Total	9	10	8

Source: 1991 Priority Survey.

which includes those who are self-employed as own account workers and unpaid family workers. A small number of workers in each category could fall into the other category.

Table 6.9 reveals that, over the period 1986–91, there was a decrease in employment in both the mainly formal and mainly informal sectors. The decline in employment in the non-agricultural mainly informal sector must be interpreted with care since many persons engaged in agriculture are also engaged in other informal sector jobs. Depending on the agricultural season, people move from informal jobs in agriculture to informal jobs in other industries. In addition, many informal sector activities are temporary or of short duration.

Table 6.10 provides data on employment by sector and sex for three years in the 1990s. Unfortunately, the central government payroll, which is the main source for central government employment, does not provide data disaggregated on the basis of sex.

Table 6.9 *Composition of the labour force, Zambia, 1986 and 1991*

	1986		1991	
Category	No.	%	No.	%
	Mainly formal sector			
Employers	14,000	0.5	10,000	0.3
Paid employees	597,000	22.0	607,000	18.9
	Mainly informal sector			
Agriculture	1,309,000	48.2	1,545,000	48.0
Non-agriculture	444,000	16.3	357,000	11.1
	All sectors			
Total working	2,364,000	87.0	2,519,000	78.4
Unemployed	354,000	13.0	695,000	21.6
Total labour force	2,718,000	100.0	3,215,000	100.0

Source: CSO estimates based on *Employment and Earnings Surveys*, 1986 and 1991.

Table 6.10 *Employment distribution by sector and sex, Zambia, 1992–4 (% share)*

Sector	March 1992		March 1993		June 1994	
	Male	Female	Male	Female	Male	Female
Central government	–	–	–	–	–	–
Local government	83	17	85	15	83.6	16.4
Parastatal	89	11	87	13	81.3	18.7
Private	82	18	85	15	83.8	16.2
Total	85	15	86	14	87.1	12.9

Source: CSO.

It can be seen from the table that there was a 2 per cent decline in female employment between March 1992 and June 1994. Given that total employment fell from 548,000 in March 1992 to 502,900 in June 1994, the absolute employment levels fell for both males and females. In the case of the males, despite a 2 per cent rise in their share, their employment fell from 466,140 in March 1992 to 438,026 in June 1994 – a 6 per cent decline. In the case of the females, the employment figure fell from 82,260 to 64,874 over the period – a sharp decline of slightly over 21 per cent. It is, therefore, clear that female workers have borne the main brunt of employment contraction during the SAP period so far.

GDP and employment
Comparing the trends and growth rates of GDP with the trends in employment reveals an unconventional relationship between the movements in GDP and the movements in employment levels.

Between 1990 and 1991 there was virtually no growth in real GDP but there was a marginal improvement in the employment situation. Between 1991 and 1992, real GDP declined by 3.4 per cent but employment expanded by 1,700. Between 1992 and 1993, real GDP grew by a striking 7.5 per cent and employment fell by 25,900 – nearly 5 per cent. Thus, contrary to the well-known Keynesian convention whereby employment and real incomes are treated coterminously, Zambia has been witnessing a situation of growthless job creation followed by jobless growth. Perhaps one important inference that can be read from this peculiar income-employment configuration is that policies aimed at generating economic growth need not automatically lead to a concomitant growth in productive employment and that it is necessary to design policies aimed directly at creating the latter. Weeks and Mosley (1997) explain the erratic employment creation by the fact that adjustment took place through contraction of the non-tradeable sector rather than through expansion (via price adjustment and investment) of the tradeable sector.

Looking at the relation between sectoral growth rates and total GDP, the one sector that has a close correlation with GDP is agriculture. In 1992, agriculture fell drastically owing to an unprecedented drought, bringing down its contribution to GDP from 18.4 to 12.7 per cent and thereby bringing down overall GDP as well. In 1993, agriculture grew by a staggering 79.6 per cent owing to good rains and a bumper harvest, increasing its contribution to 21.3 per cent and thereby boosting the growth rate of GDP as well. However, the correlation between agricultural GDP growth and growth in agricultural employment remains weak.

Changes in real wages
Consistent, comparable and fairly comprehensive data on earnings are available only from 1991, after the start of the CSO's publication *Quarterly Employment and Earnings Survey*. Prior to 1991, data are available on average earnings in the mining, manufacturing and electricity sectors. But the data even for these sectors may not be comparable for years before and after 1991 owing to differences in methodologies.

Specific studies, however, confirm that there has been a tremendous erosion of real earnings of all categories of workers. The government's public expenditure review, for instance, states that the minimum basic pay for a general worker in the public service in 1994 was only 56 per cent of the 1984 value, and those of the nurse and the teacher only 37 and 38 per cent respectively. Even for the entry point of a graduate professional, the real pay in 1994 had fallen sharply to a mere 24 per cent of the 1984 pay. For all categories of workers in the public sector, real wages in 1994 were about 42 per cent of their 1984 values. Much of the erosion of the real value of wages must have occurred after 1989 with the onset of three-digit inflation, which was somewhat contained only by the end of 1994.

Since the macroeconomic impacts of SAP measures have been most seriously felt only since 1991, we use CSO data from the *Quarterly Employment and Earnings Survey* to analyse the changes. Table 6.11 provides the statistics on total nominal and real earnings and the index of consumer prices reflecting inflation. A few observations can be made on the earnings trends.

First, while average nominal earnings went up by K84,296 (1,057 per cent), real earnings went up by only K2,896 (about 36 per cent). Second, much of the

Table 6.11   *Nominal and real average monthly earnings, Zambia, December 1991 to June 1994*

Date	Nominal earnings (Kwacha)	Index of consumer prices (Dec. 1991 = 100)	Real earnings (Kwacha)
December 1991	7,978	100.0	7,978
March 1992	9,293	150.3	6,181
June 1992	15,480	181.5	8,530
September 1992	17,635	221.5	7,978
December 1992	21,081	291.2	7,240
March 1993	30,331	394.4	7,691
June 1993	40,397	565.3	7,146
September 1993	47,997	676.9	7,091
December 1993	58,342	693.4	8,414
June 1994	92,274	848.6	10,874

Source: CSO.

improvement in real earnings occurred only in 1994 when inflation came down substantially – a 'catch-up' effect. Third, the deflators used were based on aggregate price indices instead of low-income group indices. The latter would have been more applicable to a large majority of the employees in the public and even the private sectors whose average nominal earnings are much below those of other sectors.

For instance, as shown in Table 6.12, the average nominal earnings of K92,274 in June 1994 are on account of the high earnings in the parastatal sector, amounting to K142,994. The average nominal earnings of a central government employee, for instance, rose from K8,165 in December 1991 to K49,349 in June 1994. Using the index of consumer prices (1991 = 100), the 1994 nominal earnings would have amounted in real terms to only K5,826. In a similar vein, average real earnings declined from K5,077 in December 1991 to K4,874 in June 1994 for the private sector. These declines would have been even greater had we used a deflator based on the low-income group price index which would have been more relevant to these groups. It is only the parastatal employees whose average earnings in real terms went up from K12,246 in December 1991 to K16,902 in June 1994.

Table 6.12   *Quarterly earnings by sector, Zambia, December 1991 to June 1994*

Date	Central government	Local government	Parastatal	Private
December 1991	8,165	4,320	12,246	5,071
March 1992	8,921	5,963	13,062	6,915
June 1992	15,043	12,764	21,102	11,284
September 1992	16,803	17,658	20,939	15,737
December 1992	16,803	17,146	28,616	17,964
March 1993	21,136	23,216	50,342	21,596
June 1993	22,243	22,320	75,149	26,792
September 1993	32,921	26,901	78,178	35,449
December 1993	29,446	50,438	99,043	45,116
June 1994	49,349	48,630	142,994	41,232

Source: CSO.

Earnings and gender

Only very limited data are available on earnings by sex, partly because the central government payroll does not yield this information. Some comparative pictures can be drawn only for the parastatal and private sectors combined. The CSO publication

Table 6.13   *Earnings by sex in the parastatal and private sectors, Zambia, June 1991 to March 1993 (in Kwacha)*

Date	Males	Females
June 1991	5,862	4,217
September 1991	6,633	4,257
December 1991	8,213	5,799
March 1992	9,087	6,144
March 1993	34,682	28,397

Source: CSO; our estimates based on CSO data for March 1993.

gives data on male and female earnings for the quarters between June 1991 and March 1992. The next available data are for March 1993 but the male and female earnings for this quarter are given separately for the parastatal and private sectors. Using the information on the proportions of parastatal and private sector employment in total employment (36.6 and 40 per cent respectively) and the proportions of male and female employment in parastatals (88.6 and 11.4 per cent respectively) and the private sector (74.1 and 25.9 per cent respectively) in March 1993, we have calculated the male and female employment in the parastatal and private sectors combined. The data are shown in Table 6.13.

The CSO explains the differences in male and female earnings by the fact that high proportions of females are employed in the agricultural service industries where salaries are lower. However, between June 1991 and March 1993 male salaries went up 5.9 times, while female salaries went up 6.7 times, resulting in a reduction in disparities. In June 1991, average female earnings were 72 per cent of average male earnings, while in March 1993 the relevant ratio was 82 per cent.

Earnings in the informal sector

Little is known about earnings in the informal sector during the period of our study. A World Bank study relating to the informal sector (Seshamani and Mwikisa, 1994) conducted a survey of 222 persons engaged in informal sector activities in Lusaka and the Copperbelt. Data were obtained from the individuals on their household expenditures. The mean household expenditure was found to be K82,647 per month. Assuming that these households save virtually nothing, so that this figure can be taken to represent their income, and given that there were found to be two adults on average per household (which also has an average of 2.6 children), if both of them are assumed to be working informally, we arrive at a monthly average income of nearly K42,000 per person. This figure compares favourably with average formal sector earnings, especially in the government and the private sector.

The study also sheds some light on the effect of the SAP on the general living conditions of informal sector households. Prior to 1992, 72 per cent of household expenditure went on six necessary items (mealie meal, other food items, rent, clothing, fuel and lighting and transport), while in 1994 this percentage was 92.

The most notable change in the expenditure pattern was that, whereas 40 per cent of the expenditure had been devoted to mealie meal and other food items previously, this percentage was 59 in 1994. The percentage allocation to the staple food, mealie meal, more than doubled and, within the food sub-category, the allocation to mealie meal increased from 17.5 to 28 per cent. All this amply demonstrates the pressures that SAP policies, particularly with the withdrawal of food subsidies, have brought to bear on the living standards of informal sector households.

Changes in employment policies and practices during adjustment

Legal framework of the labour market

In Zambia there is a wide variety of labour laws that seek to regulate the operations at the workplace, impose statutory obligations on employers and afford protection and security to workers in a number of ways. Appendix 6.2 lists some of the major laws that are in force.

Despite the existence of a large number of laws, there are still numerous operational problems, either because some laws are not effectively enforced or because they are not adequately comprehensive in coverage. The law relating to minimum wages is a case in point. In the absence of a PDL, there is no definitive concept of a minimum wage and, as has already been indicated, a significant section of the workforce is working for very low wages. The NUCIW had suggested a minimum wage of K30,000 per month. The ZCTU also had a minimum wage figure based on minimum nutritional criteria worked out with the Food and Nutrition Commission, which would enable a worker to meet the nutritional requirements of a family of six.[15] Perhaps the fear of the government in this regard is that the minimum wage figures may be so much higher than the prevailing levels that enforcing them could counteract the goal of stabilization. This is perhaps also illustrated by the reaction of the ZCTU to the 1996 Budget in which the government proposed raising the exemption limit for personal income tax to K50,000 per month. The ZCTU has argued that this is not enough since, according to its estimates, the basic wage required to sustain a family was K132,000 per month in 1996. This statement has in turn caused a reaction from employers' organizations who have said that it would not be feasible for them to implement such a minimum wage in the prevailing circumstances.

The absence of a minimum wage level may be one of the important factors contributing to the pronounced wage differentials that exist in industry. According to a ZCTU/LO-Norway survey of 52 firms in Lusaka and the Copperbelt conducted in 1994, wages tended to differ greatly from enterprise to enterprise even where performances were at more or less the same level. There were also wide wage differentials between management and non-management employees, a situation which tended to militate against the lower workers, as Table 6.14 reveals. Such disparities are bound to result in increasing cases of corruption, pilferage, low morale, job dissatisfaction and low productivity. It is pertinent to record here that productivity levels have drastically declined in Zambia, according to estimates of the National Commission for Development Planning (*Economic Reports*, 1990, 1991).

There has been some improvement of late in the functioning of the industrial courts, especially with the opening of an additional court in Ndola. But this still

Table 6.14 *Monthly remuneration, Zambia: Management and non-management (%)*

Income levels in Kwacha	Management	Non-management
Below 50,000	0.00	21.16
50,000 to 100,000	1.92	71.15
100,000 to 150,000	63.71	7.69
150,000 and above	30.77	0.00

Source: ZCTU/LO–Norway (1994).

---

[15]It would not cover other basic needs such as clothing, rent, medical fees, school fees, etc. The details of the calculations are shown in ZCTU (1994a). At the time of writing (early 1997), the government had not made any announcements on PDL or minimum wage.

means that there are only two courts (the other being in Lusaka) for the whole country. This is inadequate and causes significant delays in the settlement of disputes, even though the average duration of a dispute has come down from one year to six months. One reason for this is that the judges are part-time. The government's feeling has been that one can always go to the normal law courts to fight one's case. But the ordinary courts deal with a variety of disputes and cannot give industrial disputes the priority they may require. Since industrial relations courts in this context will be handling cases in one line, they are bound to function more expeditiously. Employees and unions also feel it would be much more convenient if the judges themselves were mobile instead of the workers having to travel all the way to Lusaka or Ndola.

Laws relating to the health and safety of workers are also quite ineffective. According to the ZCTU, several polluting companies, especially under the former INDECO, have damaged the health of the local populations, but virtually no action has been taken by the government. Only a trivial fine exists on paper and, what is more, such a fine can be paid in advance by a firm anticipating legal action against it. Furthermore, the compensation paid to workers who have contracted occupational diseases is trivial. For example, workers found with diseases like silicosis, pneumoconiosis and tuberculosis while on duty are paid K1,500 (a dollar and a half at the prevailing exchange rates) and K50 to K60 pension per month to those who have retired.

As a result of non-compliance with safety regulations by supervisors, fatal accidents continue to occur in the mines. During the first nine months of 1995 alone, there were 15 fatal accidents in ZCCM's mines. A Safety Task Force comprising the Mines Safety Department, the Government Safety Department and the MUZ Safety Department was created in 1996. The Task Force, mandated to monitor safety standards, can inspect any department and, if any official is found negligent, take the necessary corrective measures.

While the number of social security schemes, such as the Civil Service Pension Fund, the Local Authorities Superannuation Fund, the Zambia Provident Fund and the Workmen's Compensation Fund, are very important in that they provide the basis for meeting the social protection needs of the workers through self-financing, they suffer from several weaknesses. First, they are limited in coverage to formal sector workers and provide no support to workers in the informal sector, to the self-employed, or to those working on their own account or as casual labourers in agriculture. Furthermore, schemes such as the Mukuba Pension Scheme and the Pneumonoconiosis Compensation Fund are restricted to miners.

Secondly, even with their restricted coverage, these schemes have generally proved ineffective in providing adequate protection. While this can be attributed to a great extent to the various aspects of the economic crisis and the SAP reforms adopted, other factors have also played a significant part. There are deficiencies in the benefit structure of the schemes, in their management and in their financial systems, which need to be addressed. None of the public schemes is able to meet the expectations of their members either in the level of the benefits provided or in their service. The schemes are also facing financial difficulties caused by falling income from contributions and investment and rising costs. The pension provisions for the public sector workers have also suffered from a lack of autonomy and from increased benefit obligations in respect of workers encouraged to take early retirement.

It is therefore being proposed to reform the social security system along the following lines:

- a national policy for social protection and social security will be formulated which recognizes the respective roles and responsibilities of the state, the individual workers, their employers and their families;
- the Zambia National Provident Fund will be replaced with a new pension scheme based on social insurance principles administered by an autonomous organization fully accountable to its contributors and beneficiaries. With this, an estimated additional 1.7 million people will become eligible to receive social security;
- the pension provisions for public servants will be reviewed in the context of the implications of retrenchment and the PSRP, with a view to establishing both an appropriate pension programme for public servants and a sound and autonomous institution responsible for its administration;
- the role and operation of private pension funds and saving schemes will be defined and regulated;
- the institutional arrangements for the administration of social security schemes, including the integration of the Workmen's Compensation Fund and the Pneumonoconiosis Fund, will be rationalized and strengthened;
- the range of benefits will be extended to other contingencies, such as medical care sickness, maternity and unemployment;
- suitable forms of social security will be devised to meet the social protection needs of groups currently excluded from coverage.

It has been agreed through discussions of the World Bank and the ILO with the government that, under the aegis of the Bank's Financial Sector Review Project, a review of the social security system with particular reference to social security provisions should be carried out. This would provide for a programme of reform and development to be presented to a National Social Security Reform Committee (Republic of Zambia, 1995b).

Incidence of disputes in the industrial and service sectors
There has been a remarkable reduction in the number of strikes during the period under review. This is evident from Table 6.15 which provides a breakdown by industry for the years 1990 to 1994 of the number of strikes, number of workers involved and the number of work-days lost. These three variables, whose respective values stood at 103 strikes, 51,606 workers and 219,375 lost work-days in 1990, came down to 15 strikes, 3,363 workers and 6,467 lost work-days during the period January to April 1994. In particular, there were no further strikes in the non-government service sectors during 1993–4.

On the face of it, these statistics may be indicative of a significant improvement in industrial relations. Indeed, it has been suggested in some quarters (e.g. the NUCIW) that, during the Third Republic, there have been improved communications between the management and the workforce, which have promoted cordial relations and understanding of issues. During the Second Republic, in the event of a dispute between workers and management, it is alleged that the government would intervene and side with the management. In the present liberalized environment, such intervention does not exist and there is scope for freer bargaining between employers and workers, which may have resulted in a relative improvement in conditions in some firms. Furthermore, workers have also been urged by their union leaders to exercise patience and restraint in order to give a chance to the government to implement its SAP policies.

While there is some truth in the above argument, there are also other explanations for the relative absence of industrial disputes in the last few years. First, a number of

Table 6.15 *Strikes by sector of economic activity, Zambia, 1990–94*

Sector of economic activity	1990			1991			1992			1993			1994[a]		
	No. of strikes	No. of workers involved	No. of work-days lost	No. of strikes	No. of workers involved	No. of work-days lost	No. of strikes	No. of workers involved	No. of work-days lost	No. of strikes	No. of workers involved	No. of work-days lost	No. of strikes	No. of workers involved	No. of work-days lost
Agriculture, forestry and fishing	14	4,845	10,677	11	6,208	58,926	9	4,130	n.a.	5	1,093	1,650	1	200	800
Mining and quarrying	4	6,955	24,547	3	175	165	–	–	n.a.	–	–	–	1	1,050	1,050
Manufacturing	38	13,385	27,061	33	4,911	30,621	29	6,309	n.a.	13	3,512	7,069	5	730	2,929
Electricity, gas and water	–	–	–	–	–	–	–	–	n.a.	–	–	–	–	–	–
Construction	3	314	438	7	554	1,114	7	2,034	n.a.	5	1,876	9,847	2	345	327
Wholesale, retail trade restaurants and hotels	9	1,483	2,718	3	220	219	5	663	n.a.	3	255	273	–	232	263
Transport, storage, communication	8	3,429	4,146	8	4,841	62,718	4	2,054	n.a.	3	2,171	2,127	–	–	–
Finance, insurance, real estate and business services	10	8,331	21,271	11	3,792	12,876	7	1,858	n.a.	1	79	158	–	–	–
Non-government service	7	544	627	14	2,793	12,876	17	4,080	n.a.	–	–	–	–	–	–
Government service	10	12,320	127,845	12	8,294	82,118	13	4,580	n.a.	18	24,372	678,496	5	806	1,088
Total	103	51,606	219,375	102	31,788	258,061	91	25,658	n.a.	48	33,358	699,620	15	3,363	6,457

[a]Only strikes up to April 1994 are registered.
n.a. = not available

firms have folded up, resulting in fewer formal workers. Secondly, it is not easy for workers today to prosecute a strike action effectively. In the pre-SAP era, many strikes were illegal, but workers were seldom penalized. Today, only legal strikes are permitted and illegally striking workers face more real prospects of dismissal. And the procedures to be followed for calling a legal strike are quite cumbersome. Thirdly, with the possibility of job loss owing to retrenchment hanging over their heads like the proverbial sword of Damocles, employees hesitate to strike and incur the displeasure of their employers, thereby enhancing their job insecurity. Fourthly, in the present capitalistic environment, many workers believe in improving their own lot through tacit individual negotiations with their employers rather than through collective bargaining. Fifthly, as a result of reduced membership and the consequent smaller money reserves at their disposal, unions do not have the capacity to sustain their workers during the strike period. For example, in 1993 when workers in Kafue Textiles went on a legal strike, it only brought hunger to them and their families. Finally, the law does not allow essential workers to go on strike. This prevents most of the miners, for example, from going on strike. The Industrial Relations Act of 1993 characterizes 'any service for the safe and sound condition in a mine' as a strategic service and workers engaged in such service are not allowed to strike.

In view of the above restrictive clause in the Industrial Relations Act, miners have at times resorted to indirect ways of expressing their discontent. For example, while discontented miners cannot strike, their wives and families can demonstrate. And when they are arrested, the miners use that as an excuse for not going to work. But the fundamental problem still remains, namely, neither the MUZ nor any other union can come up with a meaningful strike fund.

In summary, it can be acknowledged that problems relating to the occupational health and safety of workers, inadequate recourse to legal redress, weak social security, and so on, existed even before the SAP era. The social dimensions of the SAP and the reorientation towards a more capitalistic economic framework have, however, as we have indicated in the foregoing discussion, accentuated some of these problems. Several initiatives have nevertheless been mooted to address these issues. It is imperative that the measures initiated are implemented with the alacrity they warrant.

Responses by labour market institutions during adjustment

Formation and strengthening of employers' organizations
According to the ZFE and ZACCI, while there may have been no noticeable growth in the number of employers' organizations during the period under review, it is generally acknowledged that the role and importance of the existing organizations, such as ZFE, ZACCI, Zambia Bankers' Association and others, are well appreciated by the government. The common observation is that the government could have done more in terms of seeking the views and inputs of employers' organizations to assist in shaping the adjustment programmes. It is generally expected that the consultation forum, as enshrined in the revised Industrial Relations Act, will go a long way to entrench the position of employers' organizations. Complaints persist from the organizations about the long time lag between consultations and feedbacks.

Changes in unionization of the labour force in the formal sector
During the period under review, two important changes have occurred in the unionization of the labour force in the formal sector. First, there has been a signif-

icant drop in the membership of all the unions collectively from 357,967 in 1990 to 312,389 in 1994. The overall decline is, in the main, a reflection of the deindustrialization that has occurred as a short-run result of the SAP. There is evidence that membership went down further in 1995. For example, in 1995, the NUCIW membership was 25,000 and the MUZ 41,000 members.

This decline in membership has tellingly impaired the financial strength of the unions. The MUZ, for instance, collects 1 per cent of the wages as a membership fee. A decline in membership by over 17,000, therefore, is bound to bring down its receipts substantially. As has been stated in the previous section, the reduced resource base of the unions adversely affects their capacity to sustain a strike. An organization like the MUZ is therefore trying to widen its resource base by undertaking other activities. It has set up an Investment Committee and initiated new commercial activities, such as running a farm, renting out houses, and so on.

While the decline in trade union membership as a result of closure or scaling down of firms is readily understandable, it is interesting to note that even where industries are growing, unions are shrinking. This paradoxical situation is perhaps a reflection of the loss of confidence of employees in the power of collective bargaining. Reportedly, several employers do not want unions or to recognize them; and many employees, living in the shadow of retrenchment, do not wish to rub their employers the wrong way and hence prefer not to join the unions.

The second important development with regard to trade unions occurred in 1995. Several major unions, such as the MUZ, NUCIW, NUBEGW (National Union of Building and Engineering Workers) and others, broke away from the parent body, the ZCTU. These breakaway unions have advanced their own reasons for detaching themselves from the ZCTU. In their view, the ZCTU has not been effective in promoting the workers' cause. There has been growing frustration at the ineffectual way in which it has interacted with the government on the SAP. It has failed to pay due regard to the views put forward by the member unions and to settle disputes lodged with it. For example, ZUFIAW (Zambia Union of Financial and Allied Workers) could not reach an agreement with the Bankers' Association of Zambia and 500 bank employees were dismissed in the process. The ZCTU had done nothing about this at the time of writing. It has also not shown sufficient sensitivity to the problem of worker productivity and this has not been consistent with the wishes of its affiliates.

The ZCTU, on the other side, has its own story to tell. In its opinion, the real reason for the breakaway was political. It was people who failed to get elected to the ZCTU executive in the 1995 elections who mooted the idea of a rival national centre. Again, when the ZCTU was invited to attend the MMD national convention in 1994, it did so as an observer rather than as an affiliate of the MMD, since it wished to remain non-partisan. But some of the breakaway unions have argued that this was contrary to an earlier resolution. According to them, the ZCTU, since the late 1960s, had agreed to support a progressive party. It supported UNIP at that time. But a 1990 resolution stated that the labour movement would support the MMD under the new multi-party set-up but that individual members were free to support the political party of their choice. It is this resolution that the unions feel the ZCTU has violated.

Whatever the reasons, the partial disintegration of the ZCTU is bound to provide yet another source of emasculating labour power vis-à-vis employers and the government.

Changes in effectiveness of lobbying with respect to competition-enhancing policies
ZACCI was asked to review the effectiveness of its lobbying on trade liberalization, import access, foreign investment and related policy areas. The organization

acknowledges that it has been an uphill struggle to get the government to listen to its representations. Nevertheless, it argues that the government has to some extent taken into account some of its views on trade liberalization. Nonetheless, in terms of implementation and practicality, some of the measures, such as the 'counter-vailing duty', still leave a lot to be desired. It is the feeling of ZACCI that there is an apparent bias in favour of foreign investors as opposed to local ones. The tax rebate to new investors was mentioned as an example in point. ZACCI thinks the government needs to take the views of local investors more seriously.

On the positive side, there is appreciation of the government's receptive attitude to inputs from ZACCI to the annual budget preparation process since 1993. The organization was also able to make substantive inputs to the tax regime following a general appeal for comments by the government. The government has also made the positive gesture of inviting ZACCI to join discussions with the IMF and the World Bank missions visiting Zambia.

Among other fora, ZACCI has also taken advantage of public fora organized by the Zambia Privatization Agency to express its viewpoint on issues relating to priva-tization. Occasionally, it has also linked up with the Economics Association of Zambia to address some burning economic issues. All in all, the effectiveness of lobbying by ZACCI is definitely on the rise.

Civil service reform
Although reform of the civil service under the aegis of the PSRP is seen as an integral part of the SAP, the need for overhauling the civil service had long been recognized as far back as the 1970s. The civil service was seen as too large, costly, inefficient and unproductive and it was recognized that its size had to be greatly reduced in order to reduce public expenditures, improve capacity utilization and deliver public services efficiently. Yet, by early 1996 the reform remained only on paper. The only attempt worth mentioning was the retrenchment of 15,000 casual daily employees (CDEs) during 1991 and 1992. But the size of the civil service in 1994 was larger than in 1989. The total number of civil servants in the central government rose by 19 per cent from 110,634 in 1989 to 131,712 in 1994. During the same five-year period, the number of established posts increased by 37.2 per cent (see Table 6.16).

Most of the difference between the established posts and the actual payroll is due to the inclusion of 30,000 CDEs on the payroll who are not included in the Establishment Register. What is more, despite all the talk of retrenchment that had been vociferously going on since full-fledged adjustment started in 1991, not a single established civil servant had been retrenched by 1996.

There are no accurate statistics of the level of employment in local government. In July 1994, the combined employment in the central and local government was estimated to be about 150,000 (World Bank, 1995: 92).

According to CSO statistics, the public service employed 161,000 people in 1992, which was 30 per cent of formal sector employment. In 1993, both formal and public

Table 6.16   *Size of public sector employment, Zambia, 1989–94*

	1989	1990	1991	1992	1993	1994
Central government payroll	110,634	115,214	116,912	140,980	132,589	131,712
Established posts	71,669	73,119	74,740	100,704	98,331	100,420
Local government (new definition)	n.a.	n.a.	n.a.	24,087	21,253	. .
					18,900	17,600

Source: Republic of Zambia, 1995a: 92.

sector employment decreased but the fall in the latter was greater and hence the percentage came down to 27 per cent.

The government's *Public Expenditure Review* (PER) document (1995a) provides four main reasons for the differences between established posts and payroll numbers:

(i)   the open-door policy whereby graduates from certain public educational institutions in the fields of agriculture, health and education are automatically offered employment by the respective sectoral ministries, regardless of the existence of vacancies;

(ii) ministries can recruit staff without related posts being on the establishment;

(iii) ministries can obtain funding from the Budget Office for personal emoluments in respect of posts which are not on the establishment; and

(iv) the relatively low rates of natural attrition from the public service since it is viewed as a lifetime employer, given the unavailability of alternative employment opportunities.

The PER document brings out four important issues that need to be taken into account in determining a reasonable and affordable size of the public service:

(i)   Zambia cannot afford to spend more than 4 per cent of GDP on personal emoluments in the short to medium term. Given this benchmark and the need to enhance the salaries of the remaining public servants, it has been estimated that a retrenchment of 20 per cent will allow only a 25 per cent increase in salaries across the board; 33 per cent retrenchment will raise salaries by 50 per cent. Hence the numbers to be retrenched will depend on the desired percentage by which salaries are to be raised and that the relationship between retrenchment and possible wage increases has a high positive elasticity;

(ii) since the composition of the wage bill is heavily biased in favour of the highly skilled and professional categories, sufficient saving cannot occur unless there is significant retrenchment in these categories;

(iii) there has to be a clear and determined objective of linking the size of retrenchment to the required level of salary enhancement. A firm commitment is required to carry out retrenchment. During the formation of the ZPA and the restructuring of the Cabinet Office, for instance, the redundant workers were retained in the civil service. Such actions will compromise the aims of the PSRP;

(iv) a meaningful severance package has to be negotiated with the unions in such a way as not to overcommit the government in terms of its financial burden.

It is in respect of this last issue that the greatest impediment to the implementation of the PSRP seems to lie. The cost of retrenchment is potentially so large in relation to the available resources that the government cannot afford to meet the high outlay required for a large-scale retrenchment. For instance, in 1994, it was estimated that in order to retrench only 3,000 civil servants and 3,000 CDEs (less than 5 per cent of the employees), about 26 billion kwacha would be required, or one-third of the total budgeted personal emoluments for 1994.

The Minister of Finance admitted in November 1995 that the government did not have the necessary financial resources, even with donor funding, to implement the PSRP. His suggestion that this could be done only by creating a Ministry of Transition to accommodate staff not absorbed in the restructured public service aroused instant controversy. The proposal met with strong disapproval from the CSUZ and the Cabinet Office dissociated itself from the proposal saying that the Minister was only expressing his personal views.

Conclusions and recommendations

Improved labour market data base

There is a dire need to improve information on the labour market. Currently information is scanty and lacking in accuracy. In such a situation, it is not possible to evolve a sound labour market policy capable of handling issues such as unemployment and impending redundancies. It is recommended that the relevant government authorities, i.e. the Central Statistical Office and the Ministry of Labour, streamline the timely compilation of data on the labour force (broken down by sex and age groups), retrenchment/layoffs of workers, school leaver levels coming on stream, and a poverty datum line.

The proposed strengthening of the data base would greatly enhance the capability of monitoring the movements in critical areas. For example, an employment area which is not well documented is that of secondary employment in the informal sector. It is generally known that a substantial segment of the labour force is engaged in low-level income activities in the informal sector. While various efforts have been made to estimate the size of the informal sector, there is not much authoritative data on this or breakdowns on the various activity levels and corresponding income generations. For policy purposes it would be useful to distinguish between the viable informal activities which enable participants to earn reasonable incomes (above the poverty level) and the 'marginal' activities which are merely last-resort occupations taken up only because participants are unable to secure more lucrative economic employment. It is also proposed that the data base be such as to facilitate monitoring of the status of particular vulnerable groups such as young people and women.

Experience of privatization and liquidation-related retrenchments calls for more co-ordinated compilation of information. While the Zambia Privatization Agency (ZPA) has made efforts to portray a positive picture with respect to the employment impact at the time of divestiture, very little follow-up has been done to ascertain the eventual retrenchments when new owners settle in. It may be desirable for the Ministry of Labour, in liaison with the ZPA, to enforce existing requirements for companies/employers to make regular returns on employment movements.

Internal reform of trade unions and employers' organizations

Appreciation was expressed by organizations such as the Zambia Confederation of Chambers of Commerce and Industry (ZACCI) of the government's endeavours in recent years to take note of industrialists' representations, especially in formulating the Budget. Nevertheless, some emphasized that the government had not consulted enough prior to implementation of the structural adjustment programme.

While accepting that the government as the 'senior partner' in this relationship should play the key role of providing a congenial environment to foster a greater exchange of views, the other stakeholders need to take a more proactive stance. The employers' organizations and the unions should come of age and develop a more aggressive stance, if their input to policy formulation is to gain importance. It would appear that these organizations have been content with merely adopting a reactive posture. To adjust to the new challenges will require that these organizations undergo some internal reforms.

As for the employers' side (ZFE and ZACCI) perhaps one could build upon what appear to be the sound institutional foundations already in place. Both organizations could benefit immensely from some infusion of specialized professional support, even on a part-time basis, to create capacity for policy analysis. This would enhance their lobbying power and credibility with local authorities as well as with multilateral agencies as the need may be.

The proposed institutional improvements would require a stronger resource base. The employers' organizations are commercial concerns and, given good management, the membership would marshal the funding needed to maintain an effective secretariat. Donor assistance could be sourced for a few specialized positions as is already the case (for ZACCI). If the institutional and technical capacity of the organizations can be strengthened there could be special desks focusing on a regular basis on aspects such as the government budget, taxation, structural adjustment, and so on. This would greatly enhance the dialogue with the respective line ministries.

The trade union side perhaps calls for a little more in terms of internal reforms. In the first place, the unions need to consolidate their positions vis-à-vis the government and other employers. As noted above, the integrity of the unions appears to have been under great strain since 1991 – starting from the apex body, the ZCTU itself. The emergence of splinter unions and the disaffiliation of some leading unions from the ZCTU have sent serious warning signals about the legitimacy of the unions. The urgency of a serious introspective look by the ZCTU and its membership need not be doubted.

As is the case for the employers' organizations, the unions will need to address the issue of institutional capacity-building if they are to meet the challenges of the new liberalized economic environment. While not all industry unions can afford secretariats with research wings, at least the umbrella organization, with support from its member unions, should provide a pool of expertise which member unions could call on as they lobby and negotiate.

Perhaps the unions may need to review their mission and roles to keep in touch with present realities. For example, the issues of retrenchment and terminal payments have been subjects of great interest in the wake of privatization and the many company liquidations. It may be time for the unions to widen their mandate to look at the ultimate fate of the worker after employment is over. The unions should indeed take an interest in the structure of the existing pension schemes to ensure that workers' future welfare is better provided for.

Economic adjustment policy

The influx of imports following the rapid liberalization of the trade regime has been the focus of many representations from the Zambian business community. The main concern is that many items imported into Zambia are subsidized from source (especially South Africa). On the other hand, Zambian manufacturers and business people have great difficulty penetrating the markets of some of their regional partners, notably South Africa and Zimbabwe, due to various barriers. There has been a call for a levelling of the playing field. The countervailing duty system does not seem to be working in practice. Government needs to address these matters vigorously.

On the subject of privatization, a number of organizations expressed concern at the state of some of the companies awaiting divestiture. The feeling is that a number of these companies have been literally orphaned since the closure of ZIMCO and very little is being done to restructure and revamp their operations. It is recommended that the ZPA pays more attention to the health of the companies *prior* to privatization and that every effort be made to ensure that, where possible, companies are restructured and revamped in preparation for sale. It is argued that this would be a good investment in that many of these are going concerns which must continue to make a contribution to the economy, apart, of course, from guaranteeing a higher transfer price. It is recommended that, in future, the government, in liaison with the relevant organizations, prepares adequately to mitigate the social impact of liquidations and/or retrenchment from privatization.

One cannot overstress the importance of the above argument.[16] The great fear now is that the privatization process is being associated with running down companies and inevitable retrenchment. This image needs to be shaken off through vigorous publication of statistics, especially since reports on privatization reveal that not much retrenchment did in fact take place since the privatization exercise began.

Employment and wages

Aggregate, sectoral and firm-level statistics all unambiguously show that there has been a decline in employment and real wages during the period of our study (1989–95). According to the National Commission for Development Planning, formal employment as a percentage of the labour force was 23.9 per cent in 1980. Our calculations, using CSO data, show that this percentage declined to 17 per cent in 1991 and went down further to 14 per cent in 1994.

Responses from industry indicate that the SAP has led to a general decline in industrial activity. Local manufacturers are operating far below capacity and many have closed down. The very high cost of borrowing and the influx of cheaper (subsidized) imports are mentioned as major factors. Industry company case studies reviewed in Appendix 6.1 show that their employment levels declined as a result of either planned retrenchment to streamline operations or redundancies to respond to the depressed business climate.

There is little evidence to support the hypothesis of expansion of employment opportunities in traded sectors. Of the case studies undertaken, two were from construction and real estate and the data there show declining opportunities. It is possible that the expansion in private sector involvement in passenger transport following the liquidation of the United Bus Company of Zambia may have translated into the creation of more jobs than were lost. However, specific data on this would need to be collected to confirm the recent pronouncements by the Minister of Finance that indeed more employment opportunities have been generated in this sector. If so, the employment growth and the consequent tangible improvement in the transport situation are the direct result of the government's decision to suspend excise duty on imports of buses and mini-buses.

Unions and employers' organizations have made strong representations regarding the impact of the SAP on employment. The general feeling was that the government had not fully taken into account the impact of liquidations. The protracted wrangles over terminal benefits for ex-employees of Zambia Airways and UBZ were quoted as cases in point. It has been reported that 10 months after the liquidation of UBZ and the death of 50 workers, who were among those who lost their jobs, the remaining workers had yet to receive their terminal benefits from the official receiver.

---

[16]A leader in one of the main newspapers makes the following comment on the parastatal company, Supaloaf, which is in the bakery business: 'With regard to Supaloaf's attractiveness, we are aware that many new private bakeries have been set up in the last few months. These investors have calculated that they could enter the bakery business more cost effectively by setting up from scratch than by acquiring Supaloaf. Many of the other companies lined up for privatization will face the same problem, thereby remaining on the shelf indefinitely' (*The Post*, 17 November 1995).

Consultation policy

Many organizations feel that the government tended to marginalize them in terms of consultations leading to formulation of economic policy. The government needs to strengthen the consultation fora with these organizations. It is also necessary to ensure that there is a formal system of government feedback to these and other organizations. At the moment the feeling is that the government often opts for ad hoc consultations and after that very little happens in the way of follow-up.

The government needs to design standing arrangements for obtaining inputs on a non-committal basis in the proposal stages of SAP measures. At the implementation level committees of officials could perhaps co-opt representation from the relevant interest groups to assist in monitoring and evaluating the execution of SAP activities.

In implementing the enhanced involvement of interest groups, it is important not to fall into the trap of merely providing institutional representation. These organizations must be required to supply *effective* representation on a regular basis. As much as possible, the organizations could be invited to make written submissions on specific areas of interest. In this way, the government could receive categoric positions which the respective groups would have thought through thoroughly.

References

Central Statistical Office (various issues). *Quarterly Employment and Earnings Survey*. Lusaka: CSO.
—— (1994) *Employment Trends, 1985–1993*. Lusaka: CSO.
—— (1995) *Consumer Price Statistics*. Lusaka: CSO.
Department of Economics, University of Zambia (1994) *An Analysis of the 1994 Budget*. Lusaka: UNZA, March.
—— (1995) *An Analysis of the 1995 Budget*. Lusaka: UNZA, May.
Mineworkers Union of Zambia (1993) *Organising Secretaries Manual*. Kitwe: MUZ.
National Commission for Development Planning (various issues) *Economic Report*. Lusaka: NCDP.
Pearce, R. (1994) 'Food Consumption and Adjustment in Zambia' in W. van der Geest (ed.) *Negotiating Structural Adjustment in Africa*. London: James Currey.
Republic of Zambia (1989–95) various issues, *Budget Address, Minister of Finance*. Lusaka: Ministry of Finance.
—— (1994) *Economic and Financial Policy Framework, 1994–1996*. Lusaka: Ministry of Finance.
—— (1995a) *Public Expenditure Review*. Lusaka; World Bank.
—— (1995b) *Social Sector Rehabilitation and Development Programme*. Lusaka: NCDP.
—— (1995c) *Zambia's Country Strategy (CSN) (1997–2002)*. Lusaka: Office of the President NCDP, May.
Seshamani, V. and C.N. Mwikisa (1994) *Cost Structure of Informal Sector Enterprises in Zambia*. Lusaka: World Bank.
Weeks, J. and P. Mosley (1997) 'Structural Adjustment and Tradables: A Comparative Study of Zambia and Zimbabwe', in L. Pettersson, (ed.). *Post-Apartheid Southern Africa, Economic Challenges and Policies for the Future*. London: Routledge.
World Bank (1993) *Zambia: Prospects for Sustainable and Equitable Growth*. Washington, DC: Country Operations, World Bank, August.
—— (1994) *Zambia Poverty Assessment* (several volumes) Washington, DC: Population and Human Resources-Southern African Africa Regional Office, World Bank, August.
Zambia Congress of Trade Unions (1994a) *The Proposed Living Wage in Kwacha Amount*. Kitwe: ZCTU.
—— (1994b) *Productivity Constraints*. Kitwe: ZCTU.
—— (1995a) *Economic Indicators and Employment Trends*. Kitwe: ZCTU.
—— (1995b) *Employment Policies and Labour Market Measures*. Kitwe: ZCTU.
—— /LO-Norway (1994) *Wage Survey*. Lusaka: International Labour Organization.
The Zambian RPED Study, Regional Programme on Enterprise Development in Zambia. SNF Foundation for Research in Economics and Business Administration, University of Oslo/University of Zambia.

Appendix 6.1: Industry case studies of labour market impact

Introduction

Some case studies were conducted on companies in the industry and service sectors. The companies selected fell into the following categories:

(i)   Labour-intensive manufacturing industrial (sub)sector
        Speciality Foods (Z) Ltd – Food processing
        National Milling Company Ltd – Food Processing
(ii) Capital-intensive manufacturing industrial (sub)sector
        Monarch (Z) Ltd – Steel fabrication and building products
        National Breweries Ltd – Opaque beer production
(iii) Non-traded service sector (construction and real estate):
        Zambia Engineering and Contracting Co. Ltd. – Construction, furniture, steel
        fabrication
        ZIMCO Properties Ltd – Real estate and construction

A questionnaire was sent and interviews were held with the respective company managements to extract information on various aspects of company operations, to enable us to get an idea of the extent and nature of adjustments made over the SAP period 1989–94. The questionnaire focused on the following areas: (a) staffing levels by gender in top, middle and other categories; (b) turnover/sales; (c) price per unit of major product/service; (d) quantity produced of major commodity/service; (e) total wage bill; (f) financial performance indicators; return on capital employed (ROCE), gross profit, net profit; (g) qualitative assessment of training efforts.

   The results are based on answers to the questionnaire and interviews with top management. The data obtained are summarized in Appendix Table 6.1.

   The objective of these case studies is to provide a clearer picture of the patterns of employment and wages and the overall performance changes under the adjustment process.

Case 1: Zambia Engineering and Contracting Company Ltd (ZECCO), Lusaka

ZECCO was created in 1965 following a decision by Zambia National Holdings and Energoprojekt of Belgrade, Yugoslavia to form a joint company. Since its inception, the company has been associated with a number of major construction and civil engineering projects. Amongst the long list of projects ZECCO can take credit for are the following: ZAMEFA, Luanshya; University of Zambia phase 1; Kafue Gorge (subcontract); Kariba North (subcontract); Zambia National Building Society Head Office Block, Lusaka; TAZAMA Office Block, Ndola; Mulungushi Conference Centre, Lusaka; Mulungushi Village, Lusaka; FINDECO House, Lusaka; Cobalt Plant for ZCCM, Kitwe; and Nitrogen Chemicals of Zambia, Kafue.

   The fortunes of ZECCO over the adjustment period (1989–94) have taken a generally downward trend. The financial performance for the period shows a largely depressed pattern. The net profit was negative except in 1990, 1992 and 1994. In terms of operational profit, the position was getting worse from 1991 through 1993 with a slight improvement (in relative terms only) in 1994. But even then the company posted an operational loss for the fourth year in succession. The declining trend in the company's financial performance is attributed largely to the generally

Table A6.1   *Employment and profitability, Zambia, 1989–94*

Turnover in K'000	1989	1990	1991	1992	1993	1994
Zecco Ltd.	54,282	97,314	204,471	333,557	623,484	1,477,747
Monarch Zambia Ltd.	34,053	91,987	204,127	330,430	778,823	1,547,670
Nat. Breweries Ltd.[a]	369,471	657,638	1,438,507	4,143,755	8,965,168	15,522,469
Speciality Foods Ltd.	59,700	75,200	142,400	289,400	550,400	557,100
ZIMCO Ltd.	8,304	18,699	47,043	83,607	157,272	488,835
Nat. Milling Comp. Ltd.	604,729	1,150,233	2,189,052	5,137,300	14,722,856	26,694,716

Net profit in K'000	1989	1990	1991	1992	1993	1994
Zecco Ltd.	(5,873)	868	(8,095)	14,470	(32,963)	24,908
Monarch Zambia Ltd.	1,835	11,172	20,150	56,175	204,802	410,524
Nat. Breweries Ltd.[a]	58,661	58,288	114,031	538,426	1,706,929	2,502,966
Speciality Foods Ltd.	900	900	3,700	4,800	11,600	(27,700)
ZIMCO Ltd.	709	3,956	9,758	6,653	10,121	109,716
Nat. Milling Comp. Ltd.	53,076	117,980	66,638	701,601	713,721	963,180

Employment in persons	1989	1990	1991	1992	1993	1994
Zecco Ltd.	1,403	1,397	1,158	787	879	429
Monarch Zambia Ltd.	321	313	316	296	246	185
Nat. Breweries Ltd.[a]	634	668	691	652	625	591
Speciality Foods Ltd.	131	164	142	123	107	97
ZIMCO Ltd.	119	119	117	110	113	92
Nat. Milling Comp. Ltd.	1,364	1,340	1,316	1,821	1,774	1,611

Total wages in K'000	1989	1990	1991	1992	1993	1994
Zecco Ltd.	1,838	4,340	11,210	12,404	38,224	30,069
Monarch Zambia Ltd.	4,549	15,756	32,617	83,793	193,571	337,085
Nat. Breweries Ltd.[a]	28,867	70,844	179,065	462,927	935,424	1,218,786
Speciality Foods Ltd.	–	4,600	12,200	45,800	57,900	67,300
ZIMCO Ltd.	3,364	3,653	3,922	25,699	47,008	69,506
Nat. Milling Comp. Ltd.	17,192	30,564	69,177	189,814	1,131,664	2,119,813

Average nominal wage	1989	1990	1991	1992	1993	1994
Zecco Ltd.	1,310	3,107	9,680	15,761	43,486	70,091
Monarch Zambia Ltd.	14,171	50,339	103,218	283,084	786,874	1,822,081
Nat. Breweries Ltd.[a]	45,532	106,054	259,139	710,011	1,496,678	2,062,244
Speciality Foods Ltd.	–	28,049	85,915	372,358	541,121	693,814
ZIMCO Ltd.	28,629	30,697	33,521	233,627	416,000	755,500
Nat. Milling Comp. Ltd.	12,604	22,809	52,566	104,236	637,917	1,315,837

Real average wage	1989	1990	1991	1992	1993	1994
Zecco Ltd.	1,310	1,552	2,437	1,574	1,593	1,586
Monarch Zambia Ltd.	14,171	25,154	25,981	28,275	28,818	41,217
Nat. Breweries Ltd.[a]	45,532	52,996	65,228	70,917	54,814	46,650
Speciality Foods Ltd.	–	14,016	21,626	37,192	19,818	15,695
ZIMCO Ltd.	28,629	15,340	8,438	23,335	15,236	17,090
Nat. Milling Comp. Ltd.	12,604	11,398	13,231	10,411	23,363	29,766

[a]National Breweries uses fiscal years instead of calendar years.

poor state of the economy over the period, resulting in a slump in the construction industry.

To some extent, ZECCO's competitiveness has been adversely affected by its poor capitalization structure, rendering the company unable to execute jobs at high efficiency levels and to keep to time schedules. However, the major factor has been the tight economic environment in which a good number of projects tendered for have not proceeded beyond the tender stage for lack of financing on the part of clients.

The tight monetary policies under the SAP invariably impacted adversely on the construction and real estate sector.

Manning levels in the company registered a very significant fall between 1989 and 1994. The company's total employment fell from 1,403 in 1989 to 429 in 1994. A further breakdown reveals that the decline was sharper for the categories of artisans, clerical and casual/temporary workers compared with top and middle management. While the total labour force fell by 69 per cent, the relative fall for the top and middle management levels was of the order of 25 per cent. However, the artisans and clerical level fell by 85.8 per cent, while the temporary/casual cadre fell by 47.7 per cent.

With the changed economic environment, the company seems to have restructured its manning levels significantly. There has been a marked shift to the use of more temporary/casual labour. In 1989, the proportion of temporary/casual labour was 38 per cent. The artisan and clerical level, at whose expense the temporary category rose, saw a fall from 59 per cent in 1989 to 27 per cent in 1994.

The total amount spent on wages and salaries in 1989 was K1.8 million. Of this, the lower categories accounted for 82 per cent, while the top and middle management had a share of 18 per cent. By 1994, the total wage bill had soared to K30.1 million, with the lower category workers accounting for 72 per cent and the top and middle management taking 28 per cent. The shift in the shares reflects the restructuring of the workforce which led to a massive reduction in overall numbers and a greater bias towards employment of temporary and casual workers whose proportion went up from 38 per cent in 1989 to 66 per cent in 1994.

The prognosis, according to management, still looks gloomy. There has been increasing competition in the construction industry from a few foreign entrants who have come in specifically through some major projects (often foreign-funded) such as the Holiday Inn rehabilitation, and United Nations Office and flat complexes. It is admitted by ZECCO management that the greatest advantage the foreign firms have is their higher skills base among the artisan cadres. It is a matter of regret, therefore, to note that the efforts ZECCO has put into human resource development over the 1989–94 period do not in any way reflect the critical deficiency in the level of skills. Perhaps this has to be seen in the context of the depressed financial outturns over the same period.

Only 5 employees benefited from specific formal training programmes. It is worth noting that of these, 2 undertook training on their own initiative and only received reimbursement from the employer. There seems to be no systematic structured on-the-job training, although management claims that this is an ongoing process.

From the foregoing it is clear that very little effort has gone into skills upgrading during this period. It is not therefore surprising that ZECCO, as the management freely conceded, has turned out to be less competitive in terms of quality of workmanship and speed of execution of projects. This is likely to have contributed to the company's declining performance over the past few years.

The uncertainty surrounding the future of ZECCO prior to privatization also affected the business standing of the company according to the management. It would appear that the ZECCO management had great difficulty in winning the confidence of potential clients because of doubts as to the future status of the company. To some extent this also seemed to affect the company's standing with its bankers in terms of ability to access financing. In this respect the experience of ZECCO was not perhaps unique, as other state-owned enterprises and parastatals experienced similar difficulties. The trading sector companies (NIEC Group), Kapiri Glass Products Ltd and Mansa Batteries Ltd are but a few examples in this category.

Case 2: Monarch Zambia Ltd., Kitwe

Monarch Zambia Ltd is a state-owned enterprise. It is engaged in metal fabrication and production of items such as geysers, wheelbarrows, window and door frames. The company has recently signed an agreement with the Zambia Privatization Agency (ZPA) for a management buy-out of 75 per cent of the shares, with the remaining 25 per cent reserved for purchase by the workers.

Over the period 1989–94, Monarch Zambia's market share shrank from 60 to 40 per cent. The company nevertheless retains its number one position since many of its competitors have gone under. Big rival firms such as LENCO and BMS Engineering have significantly cut down their activities, and have reportedly not been responding to tenders. Monarch's only competitor worth mentioning is Amalgamated Engineering. It is a small company, however, and hence is a competitor only for small products like geysers. The shrinkage in the market share for Monarch came in the wake of trade liberalization when imported products came in without payment of duties. However, the management says that with the introduction of VAT in 1994, the company's products are becoming competitive again.

The total output of geysers rose by 28 per cent from 907 in 1989 to a peak of 1,165 in 1991. Thereafter production went down by 27 per cent compared to 1991 to 849 in 1994. The total production figure for 1994 was in fact 6 per cent below the 1989 level. The slump in production can be attributed to the general slowdown in the Zambian economy over the period. Exchange-rate depreciation of the Kwacha and the general foreign-exchange shortages resulted in severe operational difficulties for companies such as Monarch which were dependent on imported inputs. There was enormous pressure on the company's liquidity and operational capital, generally emanating from the exchange-rate fluctuations. The pricing of the major product shot up from K3,438 per unit in 1989 to K196,288 per unit in 1994, largely reflecting the exchange-rate depreciation factor.

The financial performance record for the period shows a consistent upward trend, notwithstanding the decline in production of the major product. The net turnover went up 45-fold from K34.1 million in 1989 to K1,547.1 million in 1994. Profit before tax also registered very impressive growth from K1.8 million in 1989 to K410.5 million in 1994. The return on capital employed (ROCE) rose from 0.33 in 1989 to 0.96 as at March 1994.

The total labour force fell from 321 in 1989 to 185 as at December 1994, a drop of 41 per cent. The decline in labour force by category is shown in Appendix Table 6.2.

It is significant that the technician category was depleted to zero, suggesting that the company was unable to retain these critical workers. The clerical and general worker categories suffered the next highest losses respectively. In terms of gender, female workers did not experience any loss, in fact a marginal increase was registered. However, very few changes occurred at the top and middle management levels.

Total wages in 1989 stood at K4.55 million, which was 13 per cent of the net turnover. By 1994, the total wage bill had risen to K337.1 million, which was 22 per

Table A6.2   *Percentage labour force decline: Monarch Zambia Ltd., 1989–94*

Category	% decline
Supervisory	20
Technicians	100
Clerical	52
General	35

cent of turnover. As already noted earlier, the rate of inflation had risen sharply over the period and so the wage bill escalation can be seen as a reflection of the galloping inflation experienced across the economy. The price of the company's major product had also increased by just over 57 times during this period.

The schedule on training programmes outlines the full range of training activities sponsored for the staff between 1989 and 1994. The training ranges from technical, production-related courses to accounting and management programmes. Apart from the welding course, which ran for one month in 1994, most of the technical, production-related courses were short, one to five-day stints. The more substantive training tended to be in the management and accounting fields. This gives the impression that not much emphasis was placed on technical training and this may be a factor in the high attrition rate of the technician category.

Case 3: National Breweries Ltd. (NBL), Kitwe

National Breweries Ltd. is the sole commercial level producer of opaque beer, Chibuku, in the country. The company is a state-owned enterprise with some minority shareholding. Recently, a privately owned brewery has been established in Lusaka, thus offering some competition at least in the Lusaka region initially. NBL has a number of plants spread across the country. At the time of writing, the company was due for imminent privatization through takeover by its minority shareholder LONRHO, which was due to acquire a 70 per cent shareholding.

Between 1989 and 1994, the production of Chibuku fell by 44 per cent. The production cost, however, rose from K230 per hectolitre in 1989/90 to K13,500 in 1994/5, reflecting the massive escalation in inflation in the Zambian economy over the period. It is worth noting that during this period Zambia experienced two serious droughts (in 1991/2 and in 1994/5). This invariably affects production of NBL which uses maize as a major input (although sorghum is a good substitute).

The reintroduction of the pre-packed product 'Shake Shake' seems to have been well received on the market and should improve the competitive position of NBL. Gross turnover rose from K369.4 million in 1989/90 to K15.5 billion in 1994/95. The gross profit figures also show impressive growth from K104 million in 1989/90 to K4.6 billion in 1994/95, a growth of over 4000 per cent. The return on capital (ROC) moved from 75 per cent in 1989/90 to 110.24 per cent in 1994/5. These impressive financial performance indicators have to be viewed against the rather severe depreciation in the exchange rate of the Kwacha against the US dollar and other major currencies and the high inflation rate.

Employment levels at NBL have remained relatively stable over the period. The total labour force dropped marginally from 634 in 1988/9 to 591 in 1994/5 – a fall of 7 per cent. The largest reduction was in the category of middle management, with a fall of 24 per cent, while the 'others' category suffered a drop of only 3 per cent.

The total wage bill in nominal terms rose by 4,122 per cent over the period 1989–94. The price of the main product had risen even more – by 5769 per cent. The ratio of the wage bill to turnover was 8 per cent in 1989 as well as in 1994, reflecting a stable relationship between the two variables.

During the period under review, two people were sent abroad for training in accounting and in marketing management. It is reported that the ACCA graduate remained in the UK upon completion of the programme, and the marketing management graduate left the company soon after returning from his studies, illustrating the problem of retention.

The company provides in-house training for brewers since there are no training institutes for this, in view of the peculiar nature of the production process. Industrial science graduates provide this training. At the supervisory level, government factory inspectors provide training.

Case 4: Speciality Foods Ltd., Kitwe

Speciality Foods (Z) Ltd. is a leading manufacturer of confectionery and other allied products. The company was incorporated in 1966 as one of the two subsidiary companies of Denton and Kennedy, a Zimbabwe-based holding company. In 1983, it was taken over by Chibote Ltd. and operated under them until January 1987 when it had to close down following a fire which gutted the factory and offices. The company reopened in April 1987 under new management. The company product range can be categorized into two: (i) sweets – six labels under various flavours; and (ii) foods – sixteen labels (including corn puffs, peanut butter, crisps, baking powder, etc.).

Overall production for the three major products increased consistently over the 1989–94 period, except for Huberts Rolls, which registered a sharp drop (57 per cent) in production between 1993 and 1994. This contrasts with the pattern over the 1989–93 period when the quantity produced was in the range of 15.4 to 18.4 thousand units per annum, an increase of 20 per cent.

In respect of the other two major product lines (baking powder and peanut butter), the increases in production between 1989 and 1994 were 206 per cent (for baking powder, taking into account a change in unit packaging) and 86 per cent respectively.

The steady position maintained by the company in terms of production performance should be seen against the fact that their inputs are agro-based; about 60 to 70 per cent are locally sourced. This means that it was not subjected to the foreign-exchange crises to the extent that import-oriented manufacturers were. It also enjoyed a fairly secure market position in respect of most of its range of products. However, with the liberalization of the import regime, the company has experienced a severe impact on its market share for sweets which has come down from 90 per cent to as low as 10 per cent. It is unable to withstand competition from the sweets imported from the Asian countries which enjoy economies of scale in production which a Zambian company cannot match.

The company's turnover went up from K59.7 million in 1989 to K557.1 million in 1992. However, this rate of growth began to decline after 1992, and between 1993 and 1994 it was only 1.27 per cent. The gross profit level showed an increase up to 1993 but registered a drop of about 15 per cent between 1993 and 1994. In 1994, the company suffered a loss of K27.7 million.

In 1989, the total labour force was 131, 10 of whom were in top and middle management. In respect of gender, female workers were in the majority (72). By 1994, the company had trimmed down the workforce to 97. The female workers suffered the brunt of the reduction as their number fell by 54 per cent to 33 in 1994. The female workers were mostly unskilled and doing routine operations and were thus more vulnerable in any rationalization exercise.

The total wage bill rose from K4.6 million in 1990 to K67.3 million in 1994 – an increase of 1,363 per cent. In 1990, top management accounted for 22 per cent of the total wages. By 1994, this share had risen to 43 per cent. Considering that management's share in employment had risen from 8 to 12 per cent, the proportional rise in their share of total wages must reflect relative improvements in the remuneration package to attract and retain skilled manpower.

In respect of training, there is a heavy weighting towards technical and production-oriented courses. This reflects a commitment by management to upgrade the skills of workers in the core activity.

Case 5: ZIMCO Properties Ltd. (ZPL), Lusaka

ZIMCO Properties Ltd. is a wholly state-owned enterprise engaging in real estate and construction. It was one of the two real estate companies under the now dissolved ZIMCO, the other being INDECO Estate Development Company. This company was established to manage the many real estate properties that were previously under state companies that have since been dissolved and wound up. Some of the properties under ZPL were assets of such companies as Rural Development Corporation, Lakes Fisheries of Zambia, State Finance Development Corporation and National Transport Corporation. ZIMCO, the holding company, and the group as a whole underwent a series of transformations by way of restructuring and rationalization of the parastatal sector. It became necessary to have a depository company to take over the real estate of dissolved entities.

The bulk of ZPL's revenue is from its management of real estate properties, both residential and commercial. The company does undertake some jobbing and construction contracts but these contribute only a small proportion to its total revenue.

Properties available for rental remained more or less static during the period under review. The few additions registered in the later years were the result of new transfers from the ZIMCO group to ZPL. This could be attributed to two factors, namely the lack of an aggressive policy on expansion of company operations and the poor revenue position of the company due to low rental rates in the early part of the period.

The Board and management had defined quite a passive policy for the company as managing the existing real estate directly under the company and any other properties under the apex holding company, ZIMCO Ltd., on a commission basis. The revenue base and profitability of the company also inhibited any ambitious investment ventures. The company had inherited a legacy of rather depressed rental charges. This was partly because ZPL did a lot of business with the ZIMCO group of companies and hence there was an inbuilt inertia in adjusting rents. The other factor that kept rentals depressed was the cumbersome statutory procedure for getting rental increases approved. Landlords were required to carry out a revaluation of properties for rent adjustments and thereafter seek the written consent of the Commissioner of Lands before effecting adjustments in rent. Experience was that by the time these channels were exhausted, the adjustments were invariably overtaken by market developments.

The financial performance of ZIMCO Properties Ltd. for the period 1989–94 shows a phenomenal nominal growth in turnover. The profit figures also show a consistent improvement over the period, except for a loss situation in 1992. The liberalized economic environment that was ushered in with the advent of the MMD government led to a relaxation of some of the controls on pricing. The regulation on rent adjustment was relaxed. At parastatal level, ZPL was mandated to deal on purely commercial lines with companies. The combined effect of the above was that ZPL was able to make timely adjustments to rental charges and deal firmly with defaulting clients in accordance with the terms of lease agreements. The sharp increase in the ROCE ratio in 1994 sums up the impact of the various positive factors.

Total employment stood at 119 in 1984. The top and middle-management categories had a total of 10 or 8 per cent and the others accounted for 92 per cent of total labour force. The female workers had a share of 22 per cent in 1989. The total labour force had shrunk to 92 in 1994 with top and middle management accounting for 7 (8 per cent, as in 1989) and the other category keeping their share of 92 per cent. The female workers' share dropped only marginally to 21 per cent. The downward adjustment in workforce was necessary on account of the tight economic environment and the static level of company operations.

The total wage bill for the company was K3.4 million in 1989. The breakdown by employee category shows that top management accounted for 39 per cent of total wages with middle management and the lower category of workers taking up 25 and 36 per cent respectively. The total wage bill had risen to K69.5 million, with top management accounting for 19 per cent and the middle management and the lower category 14 and 67 per cent respectively. It would appear that the lower category of workers benefited from some substantial increases in emoluments – ostensibly to cushion the effects of inflation, as this is the category with very few fringe benefits. The middle and top categories suffered a reduction in their share in total wages.

The ratio of total wages to turnover was 41 per cent in 1989 and 14 per cent in 1994. The sharp reduction in the ratio reflects the rationalization in the labour force.

Training programmes were undertaken by some staff in the accounting and finance field. It is interesting that not a single programme was in the real estate and/or construction-related fields even though these are the core activities of the company. Perhaps the advent of competition with opening up of the real estate industry and mushrooming of real estate agents will compel the ZPL management to pay more attention to the need for specialized training.

Case 6: National Milling Company Ltd. (NMC), Lusaka

National Milling Company is the largest and perhaps the oldest miller in Zambia. The company has a network of mills spread across the country. It has one maize milling plant in Lusaka, two in Livingstone and two in Kabwe; it has a stockfeed plant in Lusaka; and it has one wheat flour mill in Lusaka and two in Kabwe. As indicated from the spread of operations, the range of products covers maize meal, wheat flour and stockfeeds. The company also deals extensively in trading of iodized salt (course and fine) and rice.

NMC's production figures over the period 1989–94 for maize meal and wheat flour show a declining trend in recent years. The production of maize meal rose from 115,736 mt in 1989 to 148,238 mt in 1993, but thereafter output declined, reaching a level of 77,813 mt in 1995 – a fall of 32 per cent over the 1989 level. For wheat flour the story is more or less the same, except that the decline is smaller. By 1995, the flour output was down to 50,015 mt, a fall of 13 per cent over the level for 1989. The stockfeed production was 44,643 mt in 1989 but the level went down to 17,724 mt in 1995, a fall of 60 per cent over the 1989 level.

The company's production trends were influenced by two main factors: the droughts of 1991, 1992 and 1994/5, and the liberalization of imports leading to an influx of imported maize and wheat products at lower cost. The drought factor was to some extent mitigated by inflows of imported maize and wheat. The significant upturn in production in 1993 reflects the bumper crop harvests in that year. Perhaps the most significant factor also linked to the SAP was the influx of imported products. There was quite a reaction from the farming community over the flooding of the local shops with cheap imported wheat flour. Of special concern was the fact that most of the flour was coming in duty-free or subsidized at source.

The representations on wheat flour had led to some corrective measures, resulting in levelling of the playing field for a while. However, it would appear that the problem has resurfaced according to industry sources. It is said that massive quantities of flour have been allowed in under COMESA preferential terms, although the content of some is over 80 per cent foreign, contrary to the local content requirements under COMESA rules.

Maize meal imports flooded the local market early in 1995 when the maize shortage was acute. In this case, the local millers made representation to the government to protect them since they added value to the imported maize, which was in due course subjected to duty. The same story was repeated for stockfeeds. Perhaps the impact of imported products has been even more severe for the stockfeed line where the output level for 1995 was 60 per cent below the 1989 level.

In terms of financial indicators, the company registered impressive gains in net turnover/sales and profit over the period 1989–94. The turnover/sales ratio went up about 44 times. Profit before tax rose from K53.1 million in 1989 to K963.2 million in 1994. The return on capital, however, shows a persistent decline over the period (from 37 to 12 per cent) perhaps reflecting the increased competition in the market and also the higher cost structures as a result of upward wage adjustments.

The data on labour force levels show that total employment went up from 1,364 in 1989 to 1,821 in 1992. But from 1992 to 1994 the total labour force dropped to 1,611. This must be related to the reduction in production levels referred to above. The percentage of female employees has remained more or less constant at around 5 per cent.

The increase in the cost structure is shown by the rise in the total wage bill from K17.2 million in 1989 to K2.119 billion in 1994. The average wage per annum rose from K12,604 to K1,315,837; if expressed in real terms per employee, this would mean an increase from K12,600 to K29,800. This increase also reflects the changed composition of the company's workforce.

The company made some efforts at human resource development over the period under review; a range of courses were pursued. The skills levels in the company are reasonable and the company has acquired some reputation for providing consultancy and extension service to customers (especially bakers and livestock farmers).

Appendix Table 6.1 above summarizes the changes in employment and wage indicators for the period 1989–94.

Appendix 6.2: Overview of major laws relevant to employment and economic restructuring

(i)   *Employment Act Cap 512 No 57–1965*. Among other things, this stipulates the form and enforcement of contracts, specifies the number of advances and deductions to be made from an employee, covers housing and welfare of employees, rights to wages on dismissal, appointments, duties and powers of labour officers and, under Section 54 subsection 2, the controversial provision of one day's leave of absence for working women.

(ii)   *Factories Act Cap 514.* This Act provides regulations for the 'safe' operation of factories and industries. The Act tries to foster the occupational safety and health of employees through such requirements as factory inspection of plant and machinery by factory inspectors who are empowered to prosecute the offenders. The Act covers a wide range of topics.

(iii) *Employment (Special Provisions) Cap 515.* This is a very short Act. Its main element is prohibiting employers from dismissing any worker 'except with the approval of an officer or authority specified by or appointed under the regulations'.

(iv)   *Industrial Relations Act No.36 of 1971 Cap 517.* This Act incorporates the provisions of a number of legislations into one and came into effect on 1 April 1974 except for part VII (Works Councils) which came into effect on 1 May 1976 through Statutory Instrument No.76. It must be noted that some parts of the 1971 Act were repealed in the 1990 Act currently undergoing repeals.

(v)   *Minimum Wages and Conditions of Employment Act.* As the title suggests, this Act sets out minimum wages and conditions of employment.

(vi)   *The Zambia National Provident Fund Act Cap 513.* This Act was enacted shortly after independence. All employees including domestic servants are covered under this Act, which provides for social security.
Benefits to members: a) Maternity grants
                     b) Housing loans
                     c) Funeral grants
                     d) Pensions

(vii) *The Workmens' Compensation Act Cap 509.* This Act provides for the compensation of workers who are disabled by occupational accidents and diseases or provides for their relatives in case of death. It also provides for a scheme aimed at the prevention of occupational accidents and diseases, through the promotion of health and safety at places of work throughout the country.

(viii) *Mukuba Pension Scheme.* The scheme was jointly established by ZCCM and MUZ in 1982 specifically to cater for miners as a means of providing pensions to them after retirement from the mining industry.

(ix)   *The Civil Service Pension Fund.* This provides pensions or gratuities on retirement to established civil servants, based on payment of monthly contributions. The scheme is administered by a board under the chairmanship of the Permanent Secretary of the Cabinet Office and has also assumed responsibility for the administration of similar schemes in respect of members of the armed forces and teachers.

(x)   *The Local Authorities Superannuation Fund.* This is a similar scheme covering employees of local authorities and some parastatal organizations. It is also supervised by a Board appointed by the Minister of Local Government and Housing.

(xi)   *Employment of Women and Young Persons and Children Act Cap 505.* This law was enacted primarily to protect women and children. Its application is under Mining Regulations part XXI Section sub regulation (1).

(xii) *Public Holidays Act.* This Act not only fixes the number of days to be observed as public holidays but also empowers the Minister of Labour to declare any other day(s) a public holiday.

(xiii) *Income Tax Act Cap 668.* This Act is deemed to have come into operation on 1 April 1966, and is responsible for the collection of revenue for the government.

(xiv) *Pneumoconiosis Act 326.* An Act to provide for medical examination and standards of physical fitness to be required by workers. Also to make new provision for the assessment and payment of compensation.

7 Zimbabwe

GODFREY KAYENZE

Introduction

The adoption of an orthodox structural adjustment programme in Zimbabwe in 1991 entailed a fundamental shift from a comprehensive intervention system to one largely driven by market forces. The expectation was that the Economic Structural Adjustment Programme (ESAP) would raise investment levels, thereby facilitating higher growth rates and employment creation and lifting the standard of living of the majority of the people (Government of Zimbabwe, 1991a).

To achieve this, it had as its main components competition-enhancing measures including trade and exchange-rate liberalization, domestic (including labour market) deregulation and financial sector reform, and institutional reforms. These institutional reforms encompassed reduction of fiscal and parastatal deficits and the privatization and commercialization of public enterprises. The ESAP also included measures to mitigate the social costs of adjustment through the Social Dimension of Adjustment Programme. These reforms were supported by a World Bank Structural Adjustment Loan (SAL) of US$125 million and an IDA Structural Adjustment Credit (SAC) of US$50.81 million, and an Enhanced Structural Adjustment Facility (ESAF) from the IMF.

Review of the Economic Structural Adjustment Programme, 1991–5

Competition-enhancing policy reforms
Competition-enhancing policy reforms, which can be further divided according to whether they affect the external or domestic regimes, were a key component of Zimbabwe's Economic Structural Adjustment Programme (ESAP). Those policies that focus primarily on the external trade regime include trade liberalization, exchange-rate adjustment and full convertibility, reducing barriers to foreign ownership and investment. The range of policies focusing on the domestic regime encompass the removal of investment sanctions, commercializing marketing boards, financial sector reforms, labour market reforms and deregulation of controls (including price controls).

On the trade and exchange regime, much progress has been achieved in liberalizing trade and foreign-exchange markets.[1] The Export Retention Scheme (ERS), which was introduced in October 1990, was expanded by raising the original

---

[1] Following the devaluation of December 1982, the government adopted a managed exchange-rate policy whereby the Z$ was allowed to depreciate against a basket of undisclosed currencies.

retention rate from 5 per cent for mining and agriculture and 7.5 per cent for the other sectors, such that, from 1 April 1993, the retention rate was 50 per cent for all sectors.[2] Originally, the retained earnings were to be utilized to import raw materials and capital goods for the exporter's operations. However, this was modified to enable exporters to use ERS entitlements to import almost any goods and key services. In addition, these entitlements could be freely traded through local commercial banks and authorized dealers.

At the early stage of the reform process in October 1990, a restricted Open General Import List (OGIL) system was introduced to enable the cement, packaging, textiles, and mining industries to import inputs. In February 1991, the list was expanded and in July 1991 an unrestricted OGIL system was introduced. This was further expanded in December 1992 to cover close on 20 per cent of imports. This unrestricted OGIL system implied that no import licence was required to import goods on the list.

Furthermore, the Export Revolving Fund (ERF), which had been established in 1983 to assist exporters with procuring imported inputs in order to enable them to meet verified orders, was replaced by the Export Support Facility (ESF). This ESF was established to provide foreign exchange for importing raw materials required by exporters who did not have enough ERS resources. Additional measures included the introduction of foreign currency-denominated accounts (FCDAs) in June 1993 allowing the individual to participate freely in the market for foreign exchange at market-determined rates. In effect, the current account transactions for individuals had now been liberalized.

The FCDA facility was extended to the corporate sector in January 1994. This was accompanied by the introduction of a transitional two-tier exchange-rate system involving an official rate quoted by the Reserve Bank as well as one determined through the inter-bank market (the market rate). Private sector transactions were conducted at the market rate, while fuel, government and PTA imports were done at the official rate. The performance of the foreign-exchange market was indeed satisfactory, as reflected by the existence of an excess supply of foreign exchange. With the subsequent appreciation of the nominal market exchange rate the gap between the official and market rates narrowed from the initial 5 per cent in January 1994 to less than 1 per cent by the end of June of that year. This allowed for the unification of the two rates, which was effected in July 1994, with exporters being allowed to retain 100 per cent of export earnings.

In view of the liberalized current accounts, Zimbabwe agreed on 2 January 1995 to abide by the obligations under Article VIII, sections 2, 3 and 4 of the IMF's Article of Agreement. Through this acceptance, Zimbabwe committed itself to maintaining a liberalized current account. By so doing, it joined a select group of 98 other members of the IMF that have fully committed themselves to these obligations.

Exchange-control regulations were substantially modified to allow for large increases in business and holiday travel allowances, for education and health care among others. The establishment of foreign-exchange bureaux was allowed and the private sector was permitted to borrow up to US$5 million from abroad without having to seek the approval of the External Loans Co-ordinating Committee. Restrictions on remittance of new dividends by foreign companies were abolished in January 1995 with past dividends to be unblocked over a period of 3 years. To facilitate investment projects, domestic borrowing limits for foreign investors were also removed.

---

[2]The ERS was designed to allow exporters to retain a percentage of their export earnings.

It is important to note that, at the donors' conference held in Paris in March 1995, the donors were happy with the progress made with respect to the exchange and trade regimes. The World Bank (1995c) pointed out, however, that anomalies remained in the tariff/tax structure, observing that the effective protection for many exports remained substantially negative.[3]

Much progress has also been experienced with respect to the domestic sector. A one-stop window, the Zimbabwe Investment Centre (ZIC), was created in 1993 to facilitate and promote investment. Investment projects are registered with the Centre so that they can be checked for compliance with normal environmental, health and safety considerations. Otherwise, the ZIC only evaluates and approves large projects; the threshold was raised in March 1994 from US$10 million to US$40 million.

Regulations governing foreign investment have been liberalized. Since 1 May 1993, all after-tax dividends arising from new investments can be remitted in full, as long as these are paid in foreign exchange injected as capital into the project and as long as that foreign currency has been obtained through the normal banking channels, at the market rate. Foreign investors are now allowed to buy shares on the Zimbabwe Stock Exchange. Whenever these shares are sold, the proceeds are remittable in full, after deducting a 10 per cent withholding tax. However, foreign investors were limited to buying up to 25 per cent of the total equity in a company, with single foreign investors limited to 5 per cent.

The domestic marketing of agricultural products has been liberalized. The three main agricultural parastatals, Dairy Marketing Board (DMB), Cotton Marketing Board (CMB) and Grain Marketing Board (GMB), were, as at the end of 1994, converted into companies wholly owned by the government. In January 1995, the government took the decision to take over the accumulated debts of these marketing boards to enable them to start with a clean slate and to facilitate their own borrowing from banks.

Since April 1995, the GMB has been given autonomy to set producer and selling prices of white maize on the basis of supply and demand. The GMB acts as a residual buyer and seller, defending a floor price while retaining its monopoly over the export of maize. The government finances the maintenance of the Strategic Grain Reserve, which draws its seed money from the drought levy (5 per cent of income tax) effective since 1 April 1995 for individuals and companies. As for cotton, producer prices have been market-based since 1993–4, with the CMB negotiating prices with producers. Beginning in the 1994–95 season, regulations restricting the entry of others in the domestic marketing and processing of cotton and cotton products have been relaxed (except for health, safety and environmental reasons), effectively eliminating the monopoly of the CMB. With effect from 1994–5, sunflowers are no longer controlled crops, together with soyabeans and groundnuts. Private traders are now free to compete, while the GMB continues to be a buyer of last resort, setting its own prices. Similarly, the pricing and marketing of beef has been liberalized. Subject to conforming to stipulated hygiene and public health standards, private traders are now allowed to market beef and the slaughter quotas have been removed at all abbatoirs. Similar measures have been adopted in the dairy industry. Since 1994–5, responsibilities for the licensing of dairy enterprises has shifted from the DMB to the Ministry of Lands, Agriculture and Water

---

[3]In particular, finished goods attract lower duties relative to imported intermediate inputs, making it difficult for local producers to compete against imported finished goods. The tariff regime has subsequently been revised.

Development. New entrants are now permitted in the processing, marketing and exporting of dairy products.

The financial sector reforms included liberalization of interest rates and relaxation of regulations governing entry into the sector. Interest-rate liberalization entailed a shift towards market-determined rates that reflect the real cost of funds. Interest-rate liberalization was designed to generate additional domestic and foreign resources through positive real deposit rates, which were expected to attract savings. Furthermore, by increasing domestic interest rates relative to foreign ones, it was expected that this would attract capital inflows, which would augment domestic savings, thereby raising the pool of loanable resources. This increase in savings is expected, all other things remaining equal, to lead to increased investment. In addition, the liberalization of interest rates is expected to favour more labour-intensive techniques. Higher interest rates raise the cost of capital relative to labour, thus encouraging firms to switch production techniques in favour of the more abundant and relatively cheaper factor, labour. Overall, by raising interest rates, it is hoped that this will raise the average efficiency and quality of investment.

Regulations governing entry of new players were relaxed as part of the financial sector reforms. Two new commercial banks have been allowed to operate, the number of merchant banks has risen from 4 to 10, 3 new discount houses have set up, a fourth building society is operational and a number of unit trusts have started operations. Six stockbroking firms have been established following the liberalization of rules governing the Zimbabwe Stock Exchange. Such liberalization of the financial sector is expected to broaden the range of financial products and services. Competition is expected to result in dynamic efficiency as financial intermediaries are forced to undertake innovations that benefit the consumer.

An important component of domestic deregulation was the liberalization of the labour market. Labour market reforms were geared towards the decentralization of regulations pertaining to the terms and conditions of employment.[4] In line with the adoption of a market-driven strategy, the law applying to retrenchments was changed through Statutory Instrument 404 of 1990. This provides that any employer wishing to retrench should give written notice of his/her intention (i) to the works council established for his/her undertaking or (ii), if there is no works council or if the majority of the workers concerned agree to such a course, to the employment council or employment board.[5] In his/her letter of notice, the employer is expected to give details of every employee affected and the reasons for the proposed retrenchment. A copy of the notice should be send to the Retrenchment Committee. If the matter is not resolved within a month, the issue is referred to this Committee.

Sweeping changes were also made to the law governing dismissals and disputes. Through Statutory Instrument 379 of 1990, workplaces and employment councils/ employment boards were given the task of establishing employment codes (codes of conduct). Once an employment code is registered with the Ministry of Public Service, Labour and Social Welfare, Statutory Instrument 371 of 1985 would cease to

---

[4]The previous employment regulations were indeed onerous, requiring Ministerial approval for retrenchments. This had an adverse effect on employment (Fallon and Lucas, 1993). The dispute procedure was long and cumbersome, resulting in inordinate delays in dealing with grievances (see Kanyenze, 1993).

[5]A works council is a decision-making body at the shopfloor level comprising equal representation of workers and management. All Employment Boards have now been abolished; all sectors which had boards therefore have to form employment councils.

apply. However, Statutory Instrument 379 remained ambiguous in terms of what happens should both a workplace and an employment council register an employment code. This issue was clarified through Statutory Instrument 356 of 1993 whereby a works council was allowed to register a code, notwithstanding that an employment council had applied or proposed to apply for the registration of a code. In the event that both registered codes, the statutory instrument makes the code registered by the works council binding, implying that the shopfloor-level arrangement supersedes any arrangement at the industrial level.[6]

Other important changes arising from the 1992 amendments to the Labour Relations Act included the streamlining of the dispute procedure, allowing for the formation of committees for managerial employees, abolition of the principle of 'one industry one union or employers association' and minor amendments to the provisions on maternity leave. The cumbersome dispute procedures were amended to allow for quick decision-making, with the number of stages to be followed in resolving a dispute substantially reduced. The new structure is such that, from the workplace, an appeal can be made to the employment council, from where the dispute may be taken to the Labour Relations Tribunal (which was made full-time), and finally to the Supreme Court. Time limits were also set for handling cases at all stages, in order to speed up the resolution of disputes.

These changes had the overall effect of transferring decision-making powers from the Minister of Labour to the workplace.[7] Both the Zimbabwe Congress of Trade Unions (ZCTU) and the Employers Confederation of Zimbabwe (EMCOZ) felt that by vesting decision-making powers in the works council, the amendments overlooked and undermined the already established structures at the industrial level (employment councils).[8] Elevating works councils to the extent that they compete with the employment councils weakens the incentive to join unions or employers' associations. The ZCTU in particular was worried that shifting decision-making powers to the works council would weaken unions. The ZCTU's fears were also based on the perception that workers at the plant level are ill-organized and vulnerable to manipulation by the employer. These fears appear to have been vindicated: following the harsh effects of the drought and recession of 1992, a flurry of retrenchments occurred. Concerned about the frequency and apparent inadequacies in terms of the period of notice served on workers and the absence of compensation, the Minister of Labour intervened by invoking a long forgotten section 25 subsections 2 and 3 of the Labour Relations Act. These provisions empower the Minister to intervene where a collective bargaining agreement negotiated by a workers' committee contains provisions: (a) inconsistent with those of the Act; (b) inequitable to consumers or to the members of the public generally or to any party to the agreement; or (c) unreasonable or unfair, having regard to the respective rights of the parties. In such cases the Minister can order the parties to renegotiate an amendment to the agreement. Retrenchment characterized by lack of proper packages was one of the issues raised by President Mugabe during the March 1996 Presidential elections. The then Minister of Public Service, Labour and Social Welfare, Nathan Shamuyarira, announced at the 1996 May Day rally that, henceforth, all retrenchments had been suspended. However, this pronouncement had no legal basis, and hence could not be implemented. The new Minister of Labour, Florence Chitauro, has also taken up the issue of retrenchments,

---

[6]These changes are formally incorporated in the amendments to the Labour Relations Act of 1992.

[7]More generally, both ZCTU and EMCOZ welcomed the streamlining of the cumbersome dispute procedures and the move towards freer collective bargaining.

[8]The institutional impact of the economic reforms is the subject of a separate paper (see Mashakada, 1996).

and warned that her Ministry would like to vet retrenchments to see whether they are justifiable, implying that, in certain instances, they may be unwarranted.

Institutional reforms

Though much progress has been achieved with respect to competition-enhancing policy reforms, there has been little real progress regarding institutional reforms, encompassing public sector and public enterprises reforms. The main objective of fiscal reform was to reduce the budget deficit from 10.6 per cent of GDP in 1990–91 to 5 per cent by 1994–5. This was expected to be achieved partly by reducing recurrent expenditures. The civil service wage bill was to be reduced from 16.5 per cent of GDP in 1990–1 to 12.9 per cent by 1994–5, by reducing the number of civil servants (excluding health and education) by 25 per cent (23,000 posts) and implementing wage restraint.[9] In view of Zimbabwe's high tax ratio, it was envisaged that most of the budget-reducing measures would focus on cutting expenditures (GoZ, 1991a). Most importantly, it was resolved that, with the re-emergence of external imbalances since 1988 and accelerating inflation, fiscal adjustment would be front-loaded. This was intended to release resources early in the programme in order to support the restructuring of production in the private sector (*ibid.*). It was also envisaged that ministries would be encouraged, through efficiency units, to streamline their structures by identifying areas of redundancy and duplication. It was hoped that such reforms would deliver an efficient, and effective, leaner and well remunerated civil service. Cost-recovery measures were also to be introduced as a way of reducing public sector expenditures. In addition, expenditures would be reduced through subcontracting and commercializing some government activities.

Public enterprise reform aimed at reducing the level of direct subsidies and transfers from around Z$629 million in 1990–91 to a maximum of Z$40 million by 1994–5. Much of this reduction was expected to occur during the first two years, when the subsidy was expected to fall to about Z$360 million in 1991–2 and Z$130 million in 1992–3. For the purpose of the reforms, all public enterprises were classified according to the action to be taken. Public service monopolies were to remain in government control; however, these would be rehabilitated to run as commercially viable enterprises. Viable commercial entities were to be operated on a commercial basis, while non-viable commercial or industrial entities were targeted for liquidation. Those entities with a social role duplicating that of another body would be closed or merged. Entities with a valid social role were to be maintained under the government, but any remaining subsidy was to be small and made transparent.

The objective of reducing the budget deficit from 10.4 per cent of GDP in 1990–91 to 5 per cent by 1994–5 has not been achieved. On the contrary, the deficit increased to 13.4 per cent of GDP in 1994–5. In fact, the problem of reducing the deficit has been further exacerbated by the decline in tax revenues, while recurrent expenditures have continued to rise. The tax ratio declined from 39 per cent of GDP in 1990 to 28 per cent in 1995. This resulted from the reduction in income tax from a top marginal rate of 60 per cent in 1990 to 40 per cent by 1995, with the company tax falling from 50 to 37.5 per cent during the same period, and the drought and recession of 1992 causing the closing of companies.

Reforms in the civil service have led to the reduction of more than 20,000 posts (Table 7.1) which, coupled with wage restraint, reduced the wage bill as a proportion of GDP from 16.5 per cent in 1990–91 to 12.6 per cent by 1995–6.

---

[9]According to GoZ (1991a) average salaries in the public sector were to be allowed to fall in real terms.

Table 7.1   *Civil service reform, Zimbabwe*

Indicator	No.
Size of service before reform	192,000
Size of service in 1994/5	171,472
Exempted posts in the Ministry of Education	10,000
Exempted posts in the Ministry of Health	90,000
Posts subject to 25% reduction	92,000
Target posts to be reduced	23,000
Cumulative abolished posts as at June 1995	21,547
Balance of posts to be abolished	1,453

Source: Ministry of Finance.

However, a major criticism of civil service reform is that:

> ... budget cutting appears to have been an end in itself (with a focus on numerical targets, such as a 25 percent reduction in the number of civil service posts), without a systematic assessment of the structural changes needed to improve efficiency and effectiveness. In the case of civil service reform, this has resulted in few efficiency gains and has encouraged the exodus of key civil servants, already disgruntled with severe salary compressions. The widely reported 'brain drain' of experienced teachers and health workers in the public sector, despite no official retrenchments in these areas, has been particularly worrisome (World Bank, 1995c: 9).

Furthermore, the civil service reforms became an impediment to the implementation of the adjustment programme since:

> ... insufficient attention has been paid to skills requirements and too much reliance has been placed on overburdened staff and existing institutional structures to implement the reforms (*ibid.*).

As for public enterprise reforms:

> ... progress until now has mainly consisted of the introduction of financial measures, in the form of tariff increases and price adjustments, to reduce operating losses. However, the point is rapidly being reached where such increases are becoming a constraint on growth and affecting the competitive position of Zimbabwe's economy. Parastatals need to be weaned away from 'cost plus' pricing and forced to pursue greater internal efficiency in order to enable them to maintain a degree of price stability (World Bank, 1993: 10).

Even though the government established a cabinet committee on commercialization and privatization in October 1994, little progress has been made on this front. However, problems with civil service and public enterprises reforms are not confined to Zimbabwe. Various commentators have observed that such reforms have been politically difficult to implement, in part owing to the systems of patronage that had been created prior to the reforms (Harvey, 1996; van Ginneken, 1990; Lindauer and Nunberg, 1994).

In order to finance the high budget deficit the government resorted to extensive borrowing. As a result, debt outstanding disbursed rose sharply from 42.5 per cent of GDP in 1990, peaking at 82.6 per cent in 1993 before declining to a projected 66.9 per cent in 1995. Reduction of the debt-service ratio to below 20 per cent was the target of debt policy during the reform period. However, the ratio has averaged 27.5 per cent during 1991 to 1995.[10] Whereas interest payments accounted for 12 per cent of government expenditure in 1990/91, the share had risen to 22 per cent by 1995/6. This has had the effect of constraining the government's discretionary expenditure, resulting in real declines in social expenditure, especially on health and education.

---

[10]Based on projections that the debt-service ratio for 1995 was 21.5 per cent (RBZ, 1996).

The combined effect of high budget deficits, a depreciating exchange rate, decontrol of prices, removal of subsidies and poor supply response due to drought delivered high levels of inflation. Inflation rose from 15.5 per cent in 1990, peaking at 42.1 per cent in 1992, before falling to 22.3 and 22.5 per cent in 1994 and 1995 respectively. These high levels of inflation, in the face of loose fiscal policy, have necessitated the maintenance of excessively high interest rates, which remain above 30 per cent. Thus, lack of progress on civil service and parastatal reforms remained a major area of weakness. As the IMF put it: 'a strengthening of fiscal policy, combined with an acceleration of public enterprise reforms, were prerequisites for Zimbabwe's return to its targeted adjustment path and continuation of Fund support' (1993: 1). Therefore, following lack of real progress in this key area, the IMF suspended disbursement of funds under the Enhanced Structural Adjustment Facility (ESAF) in September 1995 and put Zimbabwe on a shadow programme for the next 6 months. The *Financial Gazette* of 16 May 1996 reported that the IMF had cancelled disbursement of Z$1 billion (US$100 million) owing to failure by the Zimbabwean Government to meet unspecified targets. The IMF was reportedly unhappy with the government's failure to reduce the deficit and its continued financing of loss-making parastatals.[11]

The Social Dimensions of Adjustment Programme

To protect the poor during the adjustment programme, the government created a Social Developments Fund (SDF) within the Social Dimensions of Adjustment Programme. The SDF programme had the following four components:

(i)   an employment and training programme, including support for informal small-scale enterprises and public works;
(ii) targeting of food subsidies;
(iii) provision for exemption from cost-recovery measures for vulnerable groups; and
(iv) monitoring and evaluation of developments.

It is widely agreed that the Social Dimensions of Adjustment Programme has failed to cushion vulnerable groups from the social costs of adjustment.[12] To begin with, whereas the government had indicated that the programme would be given high priority and established urgently, a co-ordinator was appointed only in March 1993, well after the adjustment programme had started and its social costs were already being felt. Moreover, the employment and training component of the SDF focused entirely on retraining retrenchees. These retrenchees were offered a 5-day business course on 'how to start and run your own business', after which they were to apply for project funding through their training agency. By the end of 1994, only 8,809 retrenchees had been retrained, representing 28 per cent of retrenchees (using official statistics).[13] However, in view of the fact that official statistics grossly underestimate private sector retrenchments, the proportion of retrenchees retrained is much lower.[14] A total of 1,195 projects worth Z$89 million were approved by the end

---

[11]The IMF had approved a US$400 million (Z$4 billion) loan facility to be disbursed in tranches over a three-year period. When the three-year programme expired in 1995, the IMF withheld disbursement of the remaining US$100 million because the budget deficit was double the agreed target and parastatal reforms had not yet materialized.

[12]These social costs of adjustment were aggravated by the severe drought of 1991–2.

[13]Of these, 5,605 were from the private sector, while 3,204 were from the public sector.

[14]For instance, the official statistics suggest that only 59 workers were retrenched in the textiles industry in 1994, and yet the widely publicized closure of Cone Textiles alone affected 6000 workers.

of January 1995. These were expected to create 5,032 jobs, implying that only 16 per cent of retrenchees were redeployed (according to official data).

The ILO (1993) estimated that the SDF component assisting those unable to pay school fees covered only one-eighth to one-tenth of the target group. The assistance for cost recovery in the health sector was not as well developed as that for education. Thus, targeted assistance with respect to food money, school and examination fees and health care encountered administrative problems and a general failure to reach the targeted groups.

The failure to mitigate the social costs of adjustment through training programmes has been attributed to cumbersome procedures, and to the narrow focus of the training component on retrenchees to the exclusion of school-leavers, the existing unemployed, and the existing poor, who are even worse-off. Furthermore, a 5-day training course is too short to be effective. Moreover, not all retrenchees are suited to running businesses and it might have been better to provide more suitable skills retraining; given the high failure rate of existing business, little employment may be created on a sustainable basis. In general, the programmes had a small coverage and those eligible had little knowledge about the programme, which was centrally managed (based in Harare) with a very small staff complement only of people at the level of project analyst and above (ILO, 1993; Chisvo and Munro, 1994).

Somewhat paradoxically, the SDF was allocated only US$50m in the 1995–6 fiscal year (compared with US$100m in 1994–5). Given these weaknesses, compounded by the lack of proper funding, the Poverty Alleviation Act Plan, which succeeded the SDF after the end of the first phase of the ESAP in June 1995 and is far more ambitious, is unlikely to succeed in cushioning the poor.

The next section will therefore examine the labour market implications of the adjustment reforms, with specific reference to wages and employment. The interaction between measures embodied in SAPs, on the one hand, and the labour market outcome (real wages and employment), on the other, largely determines the sustainability of the programme (Toye, 1995). This is so, given that the poverty implications of the reforms are mediated through the labour market (Ghani, 1984).

Adjustment and the labour market: The orthodox adjustment framework

At the heart of structural adjustment programmes is the desire to shift the composition of national output towards the production of tradeable goods (both exportables and importables). To achieve such expenditure and production switching, adjustment programmes typically include policies of fiscal and monetary restraint and exchange-rate depreciation. The World Bank advocates exchange-rate devaluation, arguing that 'devaluation is a powerful tool for restructuring relative prices and incentives ... Devaluation combined with tariff reduction or relaxation of import restrictions, enables the full effect of the exchange rate change to be concentrated on exports' (1981: 30). Thus, a successful devaluation is expected to change relative prices in favour of the tradeable (T) sector, which in turn induces expenditure and production switching from the non-tradeable (NT) sector to the T sector. In this regard the labour market is expected to play a central allocative role 'since the achievement of a devaluation demands both real wage flexibility and intersectoral labour mobility' (Fallon and Riveros, 1989: 1).

In order to understand the interface between adjustment and the labour market, orthodox adjustment theory specifies an analytical framework. In this framework, based on a small, open dependent model (the standard Australian open macro-economy model), the following assumptions are made:

(i)   the relative price of importables to exportables remains constant; hence, a composite good, 'tradeable', whose price is determined in the world market, is used in the analysis;

(ii) prices of non-tradeable goods are determined by supply and demand in the domestic market;

(iii) tradeables and non-tradeables are final consumption goods and therefore intermediate goods do not appear in the analysis;

(iv) only two factors (labour and capital) exist and these are treated as homogeneous (see Toye, 1995 and 1996).

The labour market outcome typically depends on these assumptions. In particular, the impact on the labour market critically depends on the timeframe of the analysis. Three periods are distinguished: immediate impact, short-run and long-run. The immediate impact period is characterized by complete factor immobility. What distinguishes these periods are the assumptions made regarding the degree of factor mobility. In the short run, only labour is mobile, whereas in the long run, all factors are mobile. In addition, the economy is assumed to be operating at full employment (Addison and Demery, 1994).

In the 'impact period', theory predicts that a devaluation raises net incomes of producers of tradeables and lowers those of producers of non-tradeables. In the short-run period, with only one mobile factor, labour, and capital locked in its specific sector, an increase in incomes in the T sector induces only labour to switch sectors. Given that, following devaluation, the terms of trade are such that the price of tradeables (Pt) rises relative to that of non-tradeables (P), the real product wage declines in the T sector and rises in the NT sector.[15] All other things remaining equal, the tradeable goods sector becomes more profitable relative to the non-tradeable goods sector. Production switching occurs as labour shifts from the declining NT sector to the T sector. Output rises in the T sector relative to that in the NT sector. From the perspective of poverty, what is important is what happens to the real consumption wage. The net effect on the real consumption wage is ambiguous depending on the relative weights of T sector and NT sector goods in the worker's consumption basket. If the average propensity to consume T sector goods is high, then devaluation leads to a decline in workers' standard of living. Conversely, should the average propensity to consume NT sector goods be high, theory postulates a short-run improvement in the standard of living (provided the price of NT sector goods falls with a decline in demand).

In the long run, with both factors mobile, production switching induced by devaluation redistributes income in favour of the factors intensively used in the T sector. This arises from the intra-sectoral competition for factors of production in a situation characterized by intra-sectoral factor mobility (Ghani, 1984). Without knowing *a priori* which factor is intensively utilized in the T sector, then the predictions of theory with respect to real wages and employment become ambiguous (see Kanyenze, 1993).

---

[15]The real product wage is defined as the nominal wage in a particular sector deflated by the corresponding output price. On the other hand, the real consumption wage is derived by dividing the nominal wage by the overall consumer price index.

So far, the interface between adjustment and the labour market has been based on the assumption of market clearing. In this case, unemployment is seen as search unemployment only (Toye, 1995). Naturally, the model has been criticized as unrealistic especially when applied in developing countries. Relying on such models can result 'in serious policy mis-specifications' (Addison and Demery, 1994). These authors discuss the outcomes with unemployment in the initial position.

With Keynesian unemployment, where the goods sector is quantity-constrained (the N sector is in excess supply), devaluation is still expected to lower the real product wage in the T sector, thereby inducing employment growth as the profitability of the T sector rises, resulting in increased demand in both sectors. Thus, the increase in income in the T sector, unlike under full employment conditions, does not disadvantage the N sector. Income in both sectors rises as a result of expansion in employment. The net effect depends on the trade-off between the gains accruing through increased employment and the extent of the decline in real wages, the relationship being measured by the real wage elasticity of demand for labour. Thus, with unemployment in the initial position, the real product wage in the T goods sector is expected to fall relative to that in the NT sector, resulting in the former sector becoming more profitable than the latter. Assuming all other things remain equal, the change in the rate of growth of output in the T sector is expected to be higher than in the NT sector. In addition, the relative labour cost advantage of the T sector is expected, all things being equal, to result in a faster rate of growth of employment in the T sector compared to the NT sector. It is attempted in the remainder of this section to determine whether these postulates of orthodox theory occurred with respect to Zimbabwe's ESAP.

Trends in relative prices of tradeable and non-tradeable goods
A successful devaluation is expected, all other things remaining equal, to shift terms of trade such that the price of tradeable relative to non-tradeable goods rises. In fact, the ratio of tradeable to non-tradeable goods prices is an alternative definition of the real exchange rate. This definition of the real exchange rate measures the internal competitiveness of tradeable to non-tradeable goods in the home country. For the purposes of analysis, as suggested in theory, the formal sector will be divided into tradeable and non-tradeable sectors. Tradeable goods are defined as those commodities which may cross international frontiers and whose prices are determined by world markets. Non-tradeable goods are taken as all the goods and services whose prices are insulated from world markets (the prices are determined by domestic supply and demand conditions). However, the classification of commodities according to whether they cross international frontiers or not encounters both conceptual and empirical problems. To begin with, commodities can switch categories in response to policy changes. Secondly, commodity classifications can change geographically. For instance, a commodity may be an importable at or near the port of entry, but as transport costs rise, in remoter areas its price may be insulated from world markets. In this respect, it has been suggested that, in practice, it is better to rank commodities in terms of their 'tradeability'. In addition, some sectors, such as electricity and water, have aspects that are traded (electricity) and others that are non-traded (water). Besides, tradeable and non-tradeable goods can be produced as joint products. In such cases, the Central Statistical Office classifies activities on the basis of the dominant activity.

The overall sectoral classification is therefore only a crude indicator of whether a sector is a tradeable or a non-tradeable one. Furthermore, considering that tradeable goods sectors can also use non-tradeable inputs, and that non-tradeable goods sectors can also source tradeable inputs, the overall price movements are interrelated. Given the conceptual and practical problems discussed above, it is necessary to adopt a broader definition of a tradeable good. In this case, a commodity is treated as a tradeable good if it is capable of entering into international trade (Killick, 1994). The concept of 'tradeability' becomes a matter of degree. The tradeables sector comprises mining (which includes quarrying), agriculture (which includes forestry) and manufacturing; while all services are treated as non-tradeables.

Table 7.2 traces the trends in the prices of tradeable and non-tradeable goods for the period before the ESAP (1981–90) and the ESAP period (1991–4). The implicit GDP deflators were used to obtain relative prices.

Table 7.2   *Trends in relative prices of tradeable and non-tradeable goods, Zimbabwe 1981–94 (annual average % change)*

Sector	1981–4	1985–90	1991–4
Tradeables	12.4	15.6	33.5
Non-tradeables 1	12.3	11.7	20.3
Non-tradeables 2	12.6	11.3	28.8

Notes: Non-tradeables 1 includes public administration, education, health, domestic services and other sectors, while non-tradeables 2 excludes these sectors.

Clearly, during the period of economic reform (1991–4), prices rose much faster than during the pre-reform era. In line with theoretical predictions, prices of tradeable goods, on average, rose much faster than those of non-tradeable goods. In this regard, terms of trade shifted in favour of tradeable relative to non-tradeable goods and services.

Trends in real product wages
Table 7.3 shows the trends in real product earnings. Average real product earnings for each sector were obtained by deflating the average annual earnings by the implied GDP deflator.[16] Average real product earnings appear to have behaved in line with theoretical predictions.

Table 7.3   *Trends in real product earnings, Zimbabwe, 1981–94 (annual average % change)*

Sector	1981–4	1985–90	1991–4
Tradeables, *of which:*	8.5	−2.1	−12.4
Agriculture	14.9	−6.2	6.0
Mining and quarrying	24.1	−0.1	−8.8
Manufacturing	0.3		−18.1
Non-tradeables, *of which:*	1.1	0.3	−7.6
Electricity	5.1	8.6	1.0
Construction	−3.3	−6.9	−4.5
Finance and distribution	1.3	−0.5	2.1
Distribution	−4.8	4.0	−9.8
Transport and communications	−7.1	2.0	−0.2

Source: Calculated from *Quarterly Digest of Statistics*, various issues.

[16]Earnings data include all cash wages and salaries, allowances, commissions and bonuses, employers' contributions in respect of employees (pensions, provident and holiday funds and medical aid contributions) and payment in kind.

The rate of growth of real product earnings declined sharply from an average annual rate of 8.5 per cent during the period before ESAP (1981–4) (–2.1 per cent 1985–90) to a negative rate of 12.4 per cent during the ESAP period (1990–96). In the non-tradeable goods sector, the rate of growth in average real product earnings decelerated from an average rate of 1.1 per cent during 1981–4 (0.3 per cent 1985–90) to a negative rate of 7.6 per cent during the period of reform (1991–4). The rate of decline in the growth of average real product earnings of 15.6 percentage points in the tradeables sector is much steeper than the 8.3 percentage points experienced by the non-tradeables sector during the period of the ESAP.

Thus, as predicted in theory, the tradeable goods sector experienced a comparative labour cost advantage compared to the non-tradeables sector during the period of economic reforms. In line with theoretical expectations such a trend is expected to be associated with a faster rate of employment creation in the tradeable relative to the non-tradeable goods sector. As Collier argued:

> Certainly, inflation has been faster during the liberalization than prior to it, and so it is reasonable to conclude that the liberalization has contributed to the decline in real unskilled wages. Note that this is not a decline in the equilibrium real wage, but rather an acceleration in what was already a gradual adjustment to the equilibrium. Such an adjustment raises employment. The transfer from wages to profits may also raise savings (1995: 5).

In terms of which sector benefits most, Collier boldly predicts that 'both of these effects happen to benefit the import-substitute sector (which is largely coincident with manufacturing), because it is more intensive than other sectors in imported inputs, and because it is more subject to disequilibrium wages for unskilled workers than other sectors' (ibid.). Table 7.3 suggests that the sharpest decline in real product earnings occurred in the manufacturing sector, where real product earnings declined by 18.1 percentage points following the introduction of economic reforms. Against such bold predictions, one would therefore expect a strong performance by the tradeable and, in particular, the manufacturing sector.

However, before analyzing the effect of these changes on output and employment, it is necessary to examine the movement of real consumption wages. From the point of view of poverty, trends in the real consumption wages become more important than those of the real product wages, which are more important to the employer than to the employee.[17] Thus, the movement of real consumption wages has welfare implications (Ghani, 1984; Addison and Demery, 1994).

Trends in real consumption wages
As indicated above, orthodox theory is agnostic in predicting the direction of change with respect to real consumption wages following the depreciation of the exchange rate, the final outcome being dependent on the workers' average propensity to consume tradeable and non-tradeable goods. If the average propensity to consume tradeables is high, then devaluation leads to a decline in workers' standard of living and vice versa.

Table 7.4 traces the movement in real consumption earnings for the period prior to the reforms and during the ESAP.

Because theory does not predict which way consumption wages move, the aggregation of sectors into tradeables and non-tradeables may not be essential here – in which case, the analysis looks at all the sectors, including those involving non-market transactions. Table 7.4 shows that, in virtually all sectors, real average

---

[17]The real product wage measures what the firm pays the worker relative to output price. If the real product wage is rising, to the employer this signifies falling profitability and vice versa.

Table 7.4　*Trends in average real annual consumption earnings, Zimbabwe 1980–94 (1980=100)*

Sector	1980	1982	1984	1986	1988	1990	1992	1994
Agriculture	100.0	160.3	138.6	130.4	130.3	130.1	69.7	76.0
Mining	100.0	127.2	108.5	110.0	112.5	116.6	97.3	89.4
Manufacturing	100.0	113.7	98.2	97.4	101.2	102.9	82.8	89.6
Electricity	100.0	104.5	95.6	95.3	97.1	95.2	82.8	89.6
Construction	100.0	114.5	104.1	93.4	83.6	77.0	56.2	47.5
Finance	100.0	101.7	83.9	88.0	92.9	94.5	92.2	80.1
Distribution	100.0	116.6	89.3	88.7	88.0	84.1	70.0	57.6
Transport	100.0	107.4	77.6	77.8	81.1	91.2	66.7	61.2
Public administration	100.0	87.4	64.1	60.3	62.1	60.5	41.2	34.9
Education	100.0	85.8	66.8	69.8	76.9	81.8	64.2	48.5
Health	100.0	100.2	77.0	81.3	80.8	89.8	67.8	55.7
Domestics	100.0	111.8	79.7	94.8	91.6	81.6	48.2	30.9
Other services	100.0	104.5	82.9	76.9	75.7	80.0	61.5	55.0
Total	100.0	119.7	97.5	97.4	100.8	102.9	78.0	67.4

Source: Calculated from *Quarterly Digest of Statistics*, various issues.

consumption earnings have declined substantially over time. Thus, real wage rigidity, which is often blamed for unemployment (see IMF, 1993), did not exist in the case of Zimbabwe. Orthodox theory sees such an adjustment in real wages as a good thing, reflecting labour market flexibility. As the World Bank commented with respect to the collapse in real wages in sub-Saharan Africa, such a trend represents 'a brutal but necessary adjustment to reflect a labour force that has outstripped job creation and the need to become internationally competitive' (1989: 29).

What is important, therefore, is to check whether such an adjustment, as argued in orthodox theory, raises employment. Before examining the employment response, it is necessary to discuss the output response, because the demand for factor inputs, including labour, is derived from the demand for output.

Trends in real output

Table 7.5 shows trends in real output (GDP) for the tradeable and non-tradeable goods sectors for the period before and during the economic reforms (1981–94).

Contrary to theoretical expectations, the tradeable and non-tradeable goods sectors did not perform better during the period of economic reforms. The non-tradeables sector experienced a decline in the rate of growth of real output of 4.4 percentage points during the period of economic reform. Within the tradeable goods sub-sectors, agriculture and mining experienced a higher rate of growth in

Table 7.5　*Real GDP growth for tradeable and non-tradeable goods sectors, Zimbabwe, 1981–94 (%)*

Source	1981–4	1985–90	1991–4
Tradeables, *of which*:	1.1	3.8	1.1
Agriculture	3.6	2.9	5.7
Mining	0.6	1.1	2.1
Manufacturing	0.4	5.6	–0.8
Non-tradeables, *of which*:	–0.6	4.4	0.0
Electricity	0.2	13.6	–3.3
Construction	–1.0	–6.0	10.6
Finance	5.7	3.4	–1.1
Distribution	–4.9	5.8	–0.3
Transport and communications	1.8	2.9	1.8

Source: Calculated from *Quarterly Digest of Statistics*, various issues.

real output during the period of reforms compared to the pre-reform period, in line with theoretical expectations. It is, however, the performance of the manufacturing sector that raises serious concerns. In this sector, the rate of growth of real output decelerated from an average annual rate of growth of 3 per cent during 1981–90 to a negative 0.8 per cent during 1991–4.

Indeed, the severe droughts of 1992 and 1994 had an adverse effect on economic performance. Given that there were also periods of severe drought in the pre-reform period, such as that of 1982–3, drought alone cannot fully account for such a dismal performance, especially from the sector predicted to benefit the most from reforms (Collier, 1995). The reasons for such poor performance are discussed below.

Trends in real labour productivity

Orthodox theory predicts that following the 'capital shallowing' arising from the substitution of capital for labour as a result of the reform-induced rise in the cost of capital relative to labour, the productivity of labour falls.[18] This occurs as the average worker finds him/herself with less capital to work with and hence he/she produces less (Collier, 1995).[19]

Table 7.6 traces the movement in real output per employee (real productivity) for both the period before and during the economic reforms.

In both the tradeable and non-tradeable goods sectors, real labour productivity declined during the period of economic reform, in line with theoretical predictions. At sub-sectoral level, real labour productivity appears to have risen, on average, in the construction sector, owing mainly to a faster rate of real output relative to employment growth. With respect to the employment sector he analysed, Collier argues that:

> ... this conjunction of falling labour productivity and low investment in the manufacturing sector may superficially appear disturbing, but it is a sign of health as long as it is in the context of growing overall employment. The crucial failure of the manufacturing sector prior to liberal-ization was to provide satisfactory dynamism for employment opportunities. The former incentive regime diverted national resources into capital formation which replaced jobs. Under the new incentive regime those resources are released and production is achieved by increased employment (Collier, 1995: 11).

Table 7.6 *Trends in real labour productivity before and during economic reforms, Zimbabwe 1981–94 (%)*

Sector	1981–4	1985–90	1991–4
Tradeables, *of which:*	4.0	2.2	0.7
Agriculture	8.5	1.5	2.4
Mining	5.8	2.2	1.5
Manufacturing	−0.8	2.7	−1.4
Non-tradeables, *of which:*	−3.8	0.4	−2.1
Electricity	−2.0	10.3	−3.1
Construction	−3.0	−14.0	7.1
Finance	−1.9	1.5	−6.4
Distribution	−8.1	2.7	−2.8
Transport	−0.6	1.9	2.0

Source: Calculated from *Quarterly Digest of Statistics*, various issues.

---

[18]Labour productivity is defined as 'real value added per employee at constant 1980 prices'.
[19]Falling labour productivity is therefore used as an indicator of the substitution of capital for labour.

The next sub-section checks whether, in response to these developments, an employment response occurred as predicted in orthodox theory.

Trends in employment

According to orthodox theory, the combined effect of real exchange-rate depreciation and trade liberalization is to promote the expansion of labour-intensive relative to import-intensive production and such changes should favour the employment of unskilled labour. As the price of labour (the real product wage) falls, this is expected to encourage a favourable quantity (employment) response. In addition, the rising cost of capital relative to labour resulting from both high interest rates and real exchange-rate depreciation should encourage the promotion of labour-intensive production. In this regard, orthodox theory expresses no concern about falling real wages and real labour productivity, as these are expected to be more than compensated for through rising employment. It is therefore particularly interesting to know that the ESAP was adopted mainly to resolve the unemployment crisis (Government of Zimbabwe, 1991b).

Table 7.7 shows the trends in employment growth rates following the adoption of economic reforms in 1991.[20]

In line with theoretical predictions, the rate of growth in employment in the tradeable goods sector accelerated from an annual average of –0.7 per cent during the pre-reform period 1981–90, to an average rate of growth of 1.7 per cent during the reform period 1991–4. However, the rate of growth in employment changed by only 2.4 percentage points comparing 1981–90 with 1991–94. At sub-sectoral level, while the rate of growth of employment accelerated during the period of ESAP compared with that prior to the reforms, that in the manufacturing sector decelerated from an annual average growth rate of 2.1 per cent during 1981–90 to 0.4 per cent during 1991–4. This raises serious concern, especially in view of the fact that the manufacturing sector was, according to Collier (1995), expected to benefit most from

Table 7.7 *Trends in rates of employment growth before and during economic reforms, Zimbabwe, 1981–94*

Sector	1981–4	1985–90	1991–4
Tradeables, *of which:*	–2.9	1.5	1.7
Agriculture	–4.5	1.2	2.8
Mining	–4.6	–0.9	0.7
Manufacturing	1.2	2.9	0.4
Non-tradeables, *of which:*	3.0	4.0	2.1
Electricity	2.2	3.0	–0.1
Construction	2.1	9.2	3.2
Finance	5.9	2.0	5.7
Distribution	3.4	3.1	2.4
Transport and communications	2.4	1.0	–0.2
Other sectors			
Public administration	7.1	0.8	–4.6
Education	–2.4	4.3	1.1
Health	6.0	3.9	0.9
Domestics	0.7	0.7	0.0
Other services	–2.9	5.1	5.8
Total	3.0	2.4	1.4

Source: Calculated from *Quarterly Digest of Statistics*, various issues.

---

[20]An employee is defined by the Central Statistical Office as a person who works for a public or private employer for more than 30 hours per week (this includes owners of private liability companies).

the removal of market distortions. In the non-tradeable sector, at both aggregate and sub-sectoral levels, the rate of growth of employment appears, on average, to have decelerated during the period of the reforms.

When other sectors that do not respond to market signals are included, total employment decelerated from an average growth rate of 2.7 per cent during 1981–90 to 1.4 per cent during 1991–4. The observed fall in real labour productivity arose not as a result of growing employment, but rather due to falling real output. The conjunction of falling labour productivity and low investment is in this regard a cause for concern. As Toye observed, 'if a pervasive impact of adjustment policies is a reduction in the real wage, then, unless labour-intensive employment expands strongly, income distribution is likely to worsen' (1995: vii). Thus, with as many as 200–300,000 school-leavers joining the labour market each year, and the economy creating on average only 16,375 new jobs between 1981 and 1991, unemployment was set to rise, notwithstanding the liberalization of markets.[21]

In this context of falling real wages, falling labour productivity and marginal rises in employment, the welfare implications are indeed adverse. Using the 1990/91 *Income, Consumption and Expenditure Survey* (ICES), the World Bank (1995a and 1995b) estimated that 25 per cent of Zimbabwe's population is poor, with 7 per cent of the population considered very poor.[22] The incidence of poverty was found to be higher in the rural areas, where 31 per cent of the rural population was estimated as poor (the rural areas account for 71 per cent of the total population).

Around 88 per cent of the total poor (2.2 million people) and 92 per cent of those considered to be very poor (650,000 people) lived in the rural areas in 1991. Although the incidence of poverty is much lower in the urban areas (12 per cent of the poor in 1991), it is estimated that during the 1990s (period of ESAP), the number of urban poor has grown faster than in the rural areas, mainly as a result of economic contraction and insecurity of employment in the formal sector (World Bank, 1996). In terms of gender, the World Bank study (1995a and 1995b) found that female-headed families were no poorer than male-headed ones in rural areas.[23] In urban areas, female-headed families, which accounted for 20 per cent of all urban households in 1992, had on average incomes 20 per cent lower than those in male-headed families (World Bank, 1995a; 1995b; 1996).

The 1995 *Poverty Assessment Study Survey* carried out by the Ministry of Public Service, Labour and Social Welfare's Social Development Fund Unit shed much more light on the incidence of poverty in Zimbabwe (Government of Zimbabwe, 1996). The study calculated two poverty lines, namely, the food poverty line (FPL) and the total consumption poverty line (TCPL). The FPL was defined as the amount of income required to buy a basket of basic food needs for an average person for a year, while the TPCL was seen as the level of income necessary to purchase a basket of food and non-food needs. Those whose incomes are above the FPL and below the TCPL were defined as 'poor'. Using a national FPL of Z$1,331.87 and a TCPL of Z$2,213.28, the study found that 62 per cent of the population are poor (incomes below the basic needs threshold, the TCPL). The 'very poor', whose incomes are below the FPL, constitute 46 per cent of the population. Rural poverty accounts for 72 per cent of the rural population, while 46 per cent of urban households are

---

[21]The rate of unemployment is currently estimated at around 44 per cent (ZCTU, 1996).

[22]The World Bank study (1996) argues that the ICES underestimated the incidence of poverty in Zimbabwe.

[23]This rather surprising finding is accounted for by the definition of household used in the survey, whereby as long as the male head was working in urban areas, the rural family was seen as female-headed. In this case remittances from urban areas accounted for the higher incomes accruing to female-headed families in rural areas

considered poor, with incomes below the TCPL. Although, due to methodological differences, the World Bank estimates cannot be compared with the government study, there is general agreement that the incidence of poverty has risen in the 1990s. Of relevance to policy are the reasons given for rising poverty. In the government study (GoZ, 1996), the main cause of poverty was identified as unemployment or retrenchment, accounting for 38 per cent of the responses, followed by drought at 29 per cent and low pay at 12 per cent. Predominantly urban areas ranked unemployment and retrenchment as the major causes of poverty, followed by low pay and inflation. The predominantly rural areas quoted drought as the main cause, with unemployment and retrenchment as the other dominant factors.

The importance of the informal sector has grown during the period of the ESAP. This growth reflects both a change in official policy towards the sector and its residual role. The deregulation of the legal environment affecting the sector acted as an impetus for the growth of this non-formal sector. It is estimated that, between 1991 and 1993, the informal sector grew by 14 per cent, with those sectors directly affected by the policy changes, such as transport, benefiting most. The transport and trading sub-sectors grew by 35 per cent and 23 per cent respectively during 1991–3. Unfortunately, much of this growth has occurred in low-profit activities. In some areas such as transport, the growth has been demand-driven, while in most cases it has been characterized by supply-led survivalist strategies. As expected, the proportion of women working in the informal sector increased from 68 per cent of all informal sector proprietors in 1991 to 71 per cent by 1993 (*ibid.*). The combination of falling purchasing power and increased competition in the informal sector has effectively condemned participants in this sector into the low productivity, low profit trap. Without a clearly defined strategy to develop the positive and dynamic aspects of this sector, it is difficult to raise its productivity in a manner that is welfare-enhancing.

Why ESAP failed to deliver

The performance of the economy before ESAP was, on average, much better than during the reform period. Comparing the outcome during the reform period with the ESAP targets suggests that most of the targets were not met. For instance, the objective of ESAP was to achieve an average annual growth rate of 5 per cent during the period of reform, and yet the outcome was an average growth rate of only 0.7 per cent during 1991–5. Inflation was expected to decline to 10 per cent by 1995, and yet by that time it was 22.5 per cent. The budget deficit, which had been projected to fall from an average of 10.4 per cent of GDP before the reforms to 5 per cent by 1995, is still double that figure. Investment, averaging 15.8 per cent of GDP during the first two years of the reforms, is well below the expected level of 25 per cent of GDP by 1995. Exports, which had been expected to grow at an annual average rate of 9 per cent during the reform period, experienced on average a rate of growth of 4.3 per cent. Social conditions deteriorated further during the period of reforms as employment, on average, declined and real incomes collapsed (see Table 7.8 below).

Although the severe drought of 1992 had a contractionary effect on the economy, it is generally agreed that drought alone cannot account for the lacklustre performance of the economy during ESAP (see World Bank, 1996; 1995c; ZCTU, 1996). The failure to create macroeconomic stability played a major part in holding back growth. The incidence of high inflation, resulting from excessive government borrowing largely to finance recurrent expenditure, delivered high interest rates

Table 7.8   *Economic performance before and during ESAP, Zimbabwe 1980–95 (annual average % change)*

Economic indicator	Pre-ESAP period (1980–90)	Pre-ESAP period (1985–90)	ESAP period (1991–5)
Real GDP (factor cost)	3.7	3.9	0.7
Inflation (CPI)	13.4	11.3	27.6
Budget deficit/GDP	9.6	10.3	10.9
Investment/GDP	14.2	15.7	15.8[a]
Debt service ratio	22.1	26.6	26.1
DOD/GDP	41.3	49.9	73.1
Employment	1.7	2.4	1.3[b]
Real average earnings	0.5	1.2	−9.9[b]

Notes: [a]denotes 1991–2, [b]implies 1991–4, DOD stands for debt outstanding disbursed.

Source: Calculated from *Quarterly Digest of Statistics*, various issues.

well in excess of 30 per cent. Such punitive interest rates discouraged borrowing, resulting in economic contraction. Macroeconomic instability dampened manufacturing activity and, following trade liberalization, a number of firms (especially in the textiles and clothing sectors) were forced to close down. For instance, the number of clothing firms registered with the CZI declined by 21.4 per cent from 280 in 1991 to 220 by 1995 (ZCTU, 1996: ch. 3).

Trade liberalization together with high interest rates have been blamed for much of the retrenchment. As a result, fears of deindustrialization have been raised. The Economist Intelligence Unit (EIU) observed that 'the situation is certainly worrying, and those analysts who saw liberalization as a solution to the industry's former problems now look very foolish' (EIU, 1996). As Gunning and Mbengegwi (1995) found, ESAP did not raise capacity utilization following the increased availability of imports. They found that firms operated at around 65 per cent of capacity. The situation was further exarcebated by the impasse in the bilateral trade agreement with South Africa following the expiry of the earlier agreement in 1992. In addition, the removal of the export incentives, which many analysts believe accounted for export growth prior to the reforms, further worsened the situation (see Muzulu, 1993; ZCTU, 1996).

The adverse effects of trade liberalization have now led to calls for protection, especially with respect to South Africa. This raises an important question with regard to the sequencing of reforms. Toye (1995) rightly observes that, although economic theory does not offer an optimal sequencing path, the sequencing of reforms should encourage the complementarity of measures, which the 'Big Bang' approach adopted in Zimbabwe does not encourage. As he comments,

> ... to embark on a radical programme of economic liberalization and de-regulation before taking measures to stabilize macroeconomic imbalances is an incorrect sequence which will not produce the desired welfare results (Toye, 1995: 72).

In fact, he suggests the importance of providing:

> a clear advance warning before liberalizing the trade current account. This gives a limited time to firms operating in protected industries either to improve their competitiveness, or to diversify their assets into other activities that will not be damaged by the removal of protection (*ibid.*: 72–3).

More importantly, ESAP failed because it did not bring benefits to the majority of the people. According to the World Bank (1995c: 18):

> unless the programme is seen to be generating benefits for everybody in Zimbabwe, it might not be possible to follow through with and maintain the momentum of many of the recent policy

changes. This will require dealing more effectively with poverty and with the social dimensions of adjustment.[24]

The failure of ESAP to redress the inequalities inherent in the economy means the majority of the people cannot take advantage of the opportunities offered. This constitutes a major impediment to the success of reforms. 'Trickle-down', often argued to be the route through which the majority will benefit from reforms, has not occurred in a manner that raises the welfare of Zimbabweans (see ZCTU, 1996: ch. 1).

Interestingly, a recent World Bank 'performance audit' of ESAP concedes that,

> ... the concerns, however, go beyond the issues of pace and design: the comprehensiveness of the program seems a fundamental issue, especially given the objective of reducing poverty. Given the highly dualistic nature of Zimbabwe's economy (where the white majority dominates formal sector economic activity and owns two-thirds of high potential land, and the black majority is concentrated in rural, communal areas and the urban informal sector), it would appear that some basic questions were not explicitly addressed at the outset. First, would ESAP, predicted on the formal sector acting as an engine of growth, create sufficient jobs, quickly enough, to address the serious problems of employment? ... Even realization of the most optimistic scenarios for formal sector growth will not provide a quick solution to the unemployment problem (World Bank, 1995c: 11).

As the ZCTU (1996) rightly observed, by focusing exclusively on the formal sector as the engine of growth, ESAP neglected the sectors with greatest potential for employment creation – the informal, small and medium-sized enterprises. It is estimated that the cost of creating a formal sector job is Z$80–100,000 while that of creating a job in the small and medium-scale enterprises (SMEs) is only Z$10,000. In addition, these sectors, apart from being labour-intensive, make small demands on high cost imported inputs.

The reforms were largely expected to raise exports to finance the programme. Available data suggest that exports declined by 19.2 per cent in 1991, rose to 12.8 per cent in 1992, and declined substantially to 1.8 per cent in 1993. For the period 1991–3, exports declined at an annual rate of 1.5 per cent per annum. If these figures are projected in real terms, then exports fell markedly. The failure of the supply response suggests that, while getting prices right is necessary, it is insufficient. Studies on successful exporting point to the importance of non-price factors such as incentives, infrastructural development, building up technological capabilities, of which marketing and development of human capital are central (Lall, 1993; Toye, 1995). The removal of export incentives at a time when other regional economies are maintaining them contributed to the poor performance of exports. Furthermore, the emphasis on static comparative advantage inherent in World Bank advice that Zimbabwe should focus on being 'a supplier to industrialized economies, based on its resource base and low labour costs' (1995a: 133), is misplaced. The experience of successful exporters in South East Asia suggests that these completely ignored their areas of existing comparative advantage and developed output in areas where the world market was growing fastest (Amsden, 1993). These analysts therefore emphasize that the state has an important strategic role to play in building these technological capabilities (see ZCTU, 1996).

---

[24]Already, the government has announced that laws pertaining to retrenchment will soon be tightened further; and that public sector employment may have to be raised, contrary to ESAP prescriptions; and that calls for protecting local firms are rising.

Is labour market flexibility a good thing?

The radical extent to which Zimbabwe deregulated its labour market was discussed above. The theoretical objective with labour market deregulation has been the creation of a 'flexible' and 'efficient' labour market. The 'flexibility' or 'efficiency' is measured in terms of the speed with which quantities (employment) adjust to changes in prices (real wages) (for a further definition, see Standing, 1986). The foregoing discussion has shown that real wages (whether production or consumption) were indeed flexible. There has also been a marked tendency towards 'casualization' and informalization of employment (see ILO, 1993; World Bank, 1995a; and ZCTU, 1996).

Considering that wages have various important roles, such as being a reward for labour services, an instrument for allocating human resources across sectors, regions and occupations, and an inducement for greater effort and productivity, falling real wages may have adverse, unintended effects. Falling real wages, especially in government, have often triggered adverse adjustments that negate efficiency, thus hindering the recovery process. Such adverse reactions include moonlighting, declining morale, shirking, absenteeism, high labour turnover and outright corruption.[25] The often quoted case in this respect is the extreme example from Uganda, where civil servants are reported as having spent only a third or half their normal working time on government duty. The Public Salaries Review Commission in 1982 established that 'the civil servant had either to survive by lowering his standard of ethics, performance and dutifulness, or remain upright and perish. He chose to survive,' (quoted in Schiller, 1990: 85). In this regard, Singer contends that: 'it does not follow that squeezing wages is the best way of getting labour out of non-tradeables and low productivity sectors ... exploitation wages must themselves be treated as a labour market "distortion"' (1992: 34). A recent study of labour markets and adjustment by the World Bank came to a similar conclusion, observing that: 'beyond a certain point the macroeconomic consequences of real wage declines may lead to an additional cost of adjustment that relies too heavily on labour markets' (Horton *et. al*, 1991: 5).

In Zimbabwe, the projected employment response did not occur, effectively adding to the social costs of adjustment. However, this lack of employment response is not unique to Zimbabwe, as it has been found elsewhere where such programmes have been applied (see Turnham, 1993). In fact, the expected switch from capital intensity to labour intensity may not occur due to the fact that firms had already adjusted to the absolute shortage of foreign exchange in Zimbabwe by employing an 'optimal' workforce. Any further shifts towards labour intensity would adversely affect the quality of products (see Muzulu, 1993). In any event, promoting the extensive use of unskilled labour is no longer suitable in a world economy where competition is increasingly skill-driven (Lall, 1990). Thus, sustained growth is increasingly associated with the building of technological capabilities, the provision of incentives especially for research and development, and the establishment of requisite institutions.[26] Within the current division of labour, the location of production is influenced much more by the level of technological capacity existing, and in particular the level of human resource development. In this context,

---

[25]The Public Service Review Commission of 1989 found that these reactions already exist in the public service in Zimbabwe (see Kanyenze, 1993).

[26]These involve human skills – entrepreneurial, managerial and technical – required to operate industries efficiently (Lall, 1990).

'labour tends to be seen as much as an innovatory resource whose potential has to be maximized than as a factor whose cost should be minimized' (Kaplinsky and Posthuma, 1993: 1).

Recognizing that pursuing such an approach entails promoting capital/technology-intensive production which may not be labour-intensive, the ZCTU (1996) advocated a strategy that stands on two legs. The first leg involves adopting the technology-intensive techniques essential for international competition in the formal sector, while at the same time promoting labour-intensive informal, small and medium-scale enterprises in both the rural and urban areas. Appendix 7.1 summarizes the ZCTU's recommendations on labour market policies, as set out in the document *Beyond ESAP.*

Conclusions

Orthodox adjustment theory places emphasis on the role of the labour market in ensuring that resources switch from the production of non-tradeables towards the production of tradeable goods. This expenditure and production switching is induced by incentives generated by the real depreciation of the exchange rate, trade liberalization and restrictive monetary and fiscal policy. The real product wage in the tradeable goods sector is expected, all other things remaining equal, to fall relative to that in the non-tradeable goods sector. In this regard, income redistribution occurs, away from workers who are argued to have a high propensity to consume, in favour of capital recipients, who have a high propensity to save and invest (Ghani, 1984).

All things remaining equal, these incentives should make the tradeables sector more profitable relative to the non-tradeables sector, resulting in higher investment and consequently higher output levels. As a result of these adjustments, employment is expected to rise faster in the tradeable relative to the non-tradeable goods sector. It is important to recall that the welfare-enhancing effect of reforms is expected to come from rising employment such that the decline in real wages is more than compensated for.

It was shown that, in spite of its failure to implement fiscal reforms, Zimbabwe has come a long way in liberalizing its economy. The analysis also suggests that the predicted fall in real product wages did not occur, implying that real wage rigidity, often blamed for hindering employment creation, did not exist in Zimbabwe. Indeed, real consumption wages fell dramatically, especially during the period of the economic reforms. The fall in real consumption wages had major adverse effects on demand and productivity, thus contributing to economic contraction.

Contrary to theoretical expectations, the tradeable and non-tradeable goods sectors did not perform better during the period of economic reform. Real labour productivity behaved in line with theoretical predictions. However, the observed fall in real labour productivity was not induced by the substitution of labour for capital, implying increased employment. This fall in real labour productivity was caused by falling real output, with minor changes in employment. The expected employment response did not occur. Employment in the tradeable goods sector accelerated from an average annual rate of growth of 1.5 per cent during the period before the reforms (1985–90) to an average rate of 1.7 per cent during the period of reform, 1991–4.

The simultaneity of declining real wages and employment implies rising poverty. In order to survive, those adversely affected by the social costs of adjustment resorted to survivalist strategies in the informal sector. The lack of a coherent strategy on the informal sector means that, with increasing competition in the sector, participants will be locked in a low productivity and low profit trap. Given that women are among the most affected, this implies that there is no way they participate meaningfully in the development process. As the World Bank observed, 'the SDF appeared to have been tacked on to ESAP more as an afterthought than as an integral part of the overall program' (1995c: 23). In this context, the social costs of adjustment were not mitigated at all. In the apt words of the World Bank itself, the ESAP 'entailed considerable pain but little visible gain' (*ibid.*: 10).

Of importance therefore is to trace the causes of the failure of ESAP. The severe drought of 1992, and to an extent that of 1994, contributed to economic contraction. However, drought alone cannot account for the failure of ESAP. A number of weaknesses have been identified concerning the design of the programme. The World Bank's *Performance Audit Report* provides an interesting self-examination when it contends that

> ... The Bank's overall performance was satisfactory, but its shortcomings were in focusing, almost exclusively, on policies and targets. In retrospect, it is clear that the Government needed assistance in formulating specific action plans, as well as institutional strengthening to enable it to carry out in particular successful fiscal and parastatal reform and an effective program to alleviate the burden of adjustment on the poor (1995c: 10).

The lack of institutional capacity, and absence of strategic planning, with so much emphasis on meeting numerical (quantitative) targets, meant that the goal of achieving development was lost. The World Bank makes a pertinent observation:

> the arbitrary decision to retrench 25 per cent of the civil service is a meaningless exercise. The civil service – and the parastatals – need root-and-branch reform, not just number shedding. It means starting by asking what services do we want and what resources are needed to satisfy them. Then – and only then – can we say how many public servants are needed in each department. Cutting numbers is not the problem. It is a culture problem, an attitude problem – a matter of getting people to understand that they are there to provide a service, not to obscure and obstruct. It's a qualitative issue, not a quantitative one (World Bank, 1995c: 50).

Quantitative targets should therefore be a means to attaining a desired objective, and not the end themselves. In this regard, the audit notes that, 'Given the weak implementation capacity in African economies, ... structural adjustment programs, in general, have unrealistic expectations about how fast adjustment can occur; consequently, the political costs of speedier implementation are also often underestimated' (*ibid.*: 3).

This introduces the important dimension of the sequencing of reforms. Toye (1995) argues that for reforms to be sustainable, they must begin with those areas that promise the greatest benefits. Thus, before liberalizing the trade regime, the financial sector should be able to provide credit at affordable rates so as to broaden the economic base. Because this did not occur in the case of Zimbabwe, the absence of an enabling macroeconomic environment meant that it was more profitable to 'park resources in the money market or engage in trading speculation, rather than manufacturing, resulting in a destruction over time of the productive sectors in the economy' (World Bank, 1995c). The speedy liberalization of the trade regime did not give local industries sufficient time to adjust, resulting in deindustrialization (*ibid.*). Given, then, that issues of capacity and infrastructural development are medium-long-term issues, the sequencing of reforms becomes of crucial importance.

The emphasis of the ESAP, as in other SAPs, was on 'getting prices right' and hence over-reliance on 'free markets'. However, successful exporting requires 'the upgrading of export infrastructure, the provision of export finance, and the development of market intelligence' (*ibid*.: 4). Industrial development, as the lessons from South-East Asia suggest, requires a strategic role for the state in guiding and leading the market through the provision of incentives to those productive sectors offering the best returns.

More importantly, the failure to consult other social partners hindered progress. In the words of the World Bank, 'the Zimbabwe case demonstrates the importance of popular ownership and participation throughout the process of adjustment. An open, transparent dialogue can help generate realistic expectations, reduce uncertainty, and contribute to a unified sense of national ownership for reforms' (World Bank, 1995c). Thus, as the World Bank (1996) found, the shortcomings of ESAP in this regard made it highly unpopular.

References

Addison, T. and L. Demery (1994) 'The Poverty Effects of Adjustment with Labour Market Imperfections', in Horton *et al.*
Amsden, A. (1989) *Asia's Next Giant: South Korea's Late Industrialisation*. Oxford: Oxford University Press.
Chisvo, M. and L. Munro (1994) *A Review of Social Dimensions of Adjustment in Zimbabwe, 1990–94*. Harare: UNICEF.
Collier, P. (1995) 'Resource Allocation and Credibility', in *Regional Trade and Trade Liberalization in Sub-Saharan Africa*. Nairobi: AERC.
Economic Intelligence Unit (1996) *Zimbabwe Country Report*. London: EIU.
Fallon, P.R. and R.E.B. Lucas (1993) 'Job Security Regulations and the Dynamic Demand for Industrial Labour in India and Zimbabwe', *Journal of Development Economics*, No. 40.
—— and L.A. Riveros (1989) *Adjustment and the Labor Market*. World Bank WPS 214. Washington, DC: World Bank.
Ghani, E. (1984) *The Effects of Devaluation on Employment and Poverty in Developing Countries*. World Employment Programme Working Paper WEP 2–32-WP 57. Geneva: ILO.
van Ginneken, W. (1990) 'Labour Adjustment in the Public Sector: Policy Issues for Developing Countries', *International Labour Review*, Vol. 129, No. 4.
Government of Zimbabwe (1990) *Manpower Review, 1980s*. Harare: Ministry of Higher Education.
—— (1991a) *Framework for Economic Reform, 1991–95*. Harare: Government Printers.
—— (1991b) *Human Resource Development Plan 1991–1995*. Harare: Ministry of Higher Education.
—— (1996) *1995 Poverty Assessment Study Survey*. Harare: Ministry of Public Services, Labour and Social Welfare.
Gunning, J. W. and C. Mbengegwi (eds) (1995) *The Manufacturing Sector in Zimbabwe: Industrial Change Under Structural Adjustment*. University of Zimbabwe/University of Amsterdam.
Harvey, C. (ed.) (1996) *Constraints on the Success of Structural Adjustment Programmes in Africa*. London: Macmillan.
Horton, S., R. Kanbur and D. Mazumdar (ed.) (1994) *Labour Markets in An Era of Adjustment: An Overview*. PRE Working Paper Series WFS 694. Washington, DC: World Bank.
ILO (1993) *Structural Change and Adjustment in Zimbabwe*. Geneva: ILO.
IMF (1993) *Annual Report*. Washington, DC: IMF.
Kanyenze, G. (1993) 'The Impact of Economic Stabilization on the Wage Structure in Zimbabwe'. Unpublished DPhil. Thesis, University of Sussex, UK.
Kaplinsky, R. and A. Posthuma (1993) 'Organizational Change in Zimbabwean Manufacturing' (mimeo).
Killick, T. (ed.) (1994) *The Flexible Economy: Causes and Consequences of the Adaptability of National Economies*. London: Routledge.
Lall, S. (1990) *Building Industrial Competitiveness in Developing Countries*. Paris: OECD.
—— (1993) 'Trade Policies for Development: A Policy Prescription for Africa', *Development Policy Review*, Vol. 11, No. 1.
Lindauer, D.L. and B. Nunberg (eds.) (1994) *Rehabilitating Government: Pay and Employment Reform in Africa*. World Bank Regional and Sectoral Studies. Washington, DC: World Bank.
Mashakada, T. (1996) 'The Institutional Impact of ESAP in Zimbabwe', draft.

Mudenge, I.S.G. (1994) 'Closing Remarks Delivered by the Minister of Higher Education', Fourth Annual NAMACO Conference, Elephant Hills Hotel, Victoria Falls, 31 July to 3 August.

Muzulu, J. (1993) 'Exchange Rate Depreciation and Structural Adjustment: The Case of the Manufacturing Sector in Zimbabwe, 1980–91', unpublished D.Phil Thesis, University of Sussex, UK.

Raftopoulos, B. (1986) 'Human Resources Development and the Problem of Labour Utilization', in I. Mandaza (ed.) *The Political Economy of Transition, 1980–1986*, Dakar: CODESRIA.

Reserve Bank of Zimbabwe (1996) *Quarterly Digest of Statistics.* Harare: Government Printers.

Schiller, C. (1990). 'Government Pay Policies and Structural Adjustment', *African Development Review,* Vol. 2, No. 1 (African Development Bank).

Singer, H. (1992) *Research of the World Employment Programme: Future Priorities and Selective Assessment.* Geneva: World Employment Programme, ILO.

Standing, G. (1986) *Aspects of Labour Market Analysis: Labour Flexibility: Towards A Research Agenda.* Geneva: World Employment Programme, ILO.

Stoneman, C. (1995) *Trade and Trade Policy*, background paper for the ZCTU 'Beyond ESAP' project.

Toye, J. (1995) *Structural Adjustment and Employment Policy: Issues and Experiences.* Geneva: ILO.

Turnham, D. (1993) *Employment and Development: A New Review of Evidence*, Development Centre Studies. Paris: OECD.

World Bank (1981) *Accelerated Development in Sub-Saharan Africa: An Agenda For Action.* Washington, DC: World Bank.

—— (1987) *Zimbabwe: An Industrial Sector Memorandum.* Harare: World Bank.

—— (1989) *Sub-Saharan Africa: From Crisis to Sustainable Growth.* Washington, DC: World Bank.

—— (1993) 'Zimbabwe: Economic Update'. Paper prepared for the Consultative Group Meeting for Zimbabwe, Paris, 13–14 December.

—— (1995a) *Zimbabwe: Achieving Shared Growth.* Country Economic Memorandum (Vol. 1). Harare: World Bank.

—— (1995b) *The Public Sector and Poverty Reduction Options.* Discussion/Background Paper, Country Economic Memorandum. Harare: World Bank.

—— (1995c) *Performance Audit Report: Zimbabwe Structural Adjustment Program.* Washington, DC: World Bank, Operations Evaluation Department, June.

—— (1995d) *World Development Report: Workers in An Integrating World.* New York: Oxford University Press.

—— (1996) 'Current Knowledge About Poverty in Zimbabwe'. Washington, DC: World Bank (mimeo).

ZCTU (1995) *Beyond the Economic Structural Adjustment Programme (ESAP): Framework For a Long-Term Development Strategy In Zimbabwe.* Pilot study. Harare: ZCTU.

—— (1996) *Beyond ESAP.* Harare: ZCTU.

Appendix 7.1: Beyond ESAP: ZCTU Recommendations on Labour Market Policies

It has been argued that ESAP promotes a passive labour market policy, with a strong emphasis on creating a highly flexible labour market. Concentrating exclusively on the formal sector will only further entrench the inherited enclave and dualistic structure of the economy. In the process, the underdevelopment of the non-formal sectors of the economy is sustained, to the detriment of the majority of Zimbabweans. A policy document *Beyond ESAP* (ZCTU, 1996) suggests the adoption of a two-pronged approach involving both a top-down, formal sector-driven strategy and a bottom-up transformation of the non-formal sectors. Such an approach provides the most realistic way of resolving the enclave and dualistic legacy of the past, which has been further reinforced under ESAP. To achieve this two-pronged strategy therefore requires the adoption of a proactive labour market policy.

In this regard, it is important to distinguish those elements of such a strategy that are general and apply to both formal and non-formal sectors and those that are specific to each sector.

General elements of the strategy

(a) Labour market administration
To ensure proper co-ordination and harmony of labour market policies, it is essential that a Labour Market Commission (LMC) be established. The Commission should be tripartite in nature and have an autonomous existence so that it can reach decisions and respond quickly to changes on the labour market. Because of its tripartite nature, labour market administration will therefore be based on the close and active participation of the social partners. The direct involvement of the social partners is essential for swift decision-making and smooth implementation. When labour market policy falls under one authority, it is easier to create conditions for co-ordinated effort and develop a common vision. The involvement of workers and employers creates a culture of joint responsibility, which promotes a long-term commitment to problem-solving.

To formulate policies, up-to-date labour market information should be collected to make the labour market more efficient and demand-oriented.

(b) Strengthening the capacity for policy analysis, formulation and implementation
Human resource development in Zimbabwe has hitherto proceeded with little data on the skill requirements of industry or far from comprehensive data on the wage structure and changes thereto. This appendix summarizes the recommendations of *Beyond ESAP* (ZCTU, 1996: 73–8).

Given the limited capacity of government departments in providing timely, detailed data on occupational structures and tracer studies on the effectiveness of training, it is essential that other organizations be involved. In this case, it is particularly interesting to note that the Institute of Mining Research carried out a detailed study of skills distribution in the mining sector covering the period 1981–93. The pharmaceutical industry has also recently completed a study on skills in that industry. It is recommended that National Employment Councils, which cover all sectors of the economy, should provide detailed information on occupational and wage structures, and skill distribution and requirements on a regular basis. With such a detailed data system, it would be possible to redesign the curriculum and adapt the education and training system to meet the specific and changing needs of industry and the informal, small and medium-scale and rural sectors of the economy.

The goal of attaining full employment must be integrated into all labour market programmes.

(c) Pursuing an employment-intensive growth strategy

Beyond ESAP, the employment strategy should have the following elements: increasing capacity utilization of existing industries; development of new industries, especially small and medium-scale enterprises; promotion of the urban informal sector; creating employment through land reform and raising the productivity of the rural non-farming sector, especially through promoting labour-intensive, community-based works programmes.[27] Other ways of encouraging extensive use of labour, such as through wage subsidies, should be explored.

Employment-intensive growth strategies could easily be pursued within the framework of the indigenization programme. Government agencies that seek to promote SMEs, such as SEDCO, Zimbabwe Development Bank and the Venture Capital Company of Zimbabwe, need to be adequately financed.

(d) Developing an education and training system geared towards employment creation

The present education and training systems are designed to satisfy the human resource requirements of the formal sector. With high unemployment rates, the phenomenon of discouraged job-seekers is on the rise. Underutilization of skilled human resources has become common (with even engineers teaching). Formal sector enterprises are becoming more capital-intensive as they re-equip and update obsolete equipment so as to become internationally competitive.

All this calls for the reorientation of the education and training systems which are mainly geared towards credentials. Those who may not be good enough to obtain the necessary qualifications are doomed. In this regard, a parallel system that promotes the acquisition of practical skills should be developed. This way, the inefficiencies associated with academic education, where thousands of students have to re-take examinations to attain the required qualifications, will be avoided.

Curricula have to be redefined so as to meet the specific demands of the informal and small-scale sectors. Skill requirements of the small-scale enterprises and informal sectors should be addressed within the formal education and training systems. A culture of entrepreneurship needs to be inculcated from an early stage of a child's education (as in countries like Mauritius). This implies that changes are needed in attitudes at home (parental guidance) and through labour market counselling.

(e) Creating flexibility through decentralization and semi-autonomous institutions

For the curricula to be sufficiently flexible to adapt to the changing skill requirements, it is essential that the gap between policy-makers and 'users' of trained personnel be reduced. This can be promoted by involving the stakeholders (workers

---

[27]In many African countries, small and medium-scale enterprises account for in excess of 80 per cent of manufacturing employment. In Zimbabwe, they account for less than 10 per cent, suggesting that they have great potential.

and employers) in the running of training institutions. In this regard, training institutions should be accorded a semi-autonomous existence to enable them to react quickly and promptly to changing skill requirements. National Employment Councils, which are composed of both worker and employer organizations, should play a more active role in designing training curricula for their specific sectors. They should take over the recruitment of apprentices, so as to encourage the participation of enterprises.

In addition, given the failure of the Department of Employment Development (DEED) to provide an efficient and effective job placement service, and in view of the urgency of rationalizing government expenditures, job placement, career guidance and counselling services should be provided by National Employment Councils.

(f) Role of private versus public sector training institutions
Considering the limited financial resources within the public sector, and in line with current international trends, the private sector should be encouraged to participate more in human resource development. Given the prevalence of market failures in human resource development, government should put in place a transparent incentive system to promote private sector participation, especially in the provision of firm-specific skills.

(g) Review of the Manpower Planning and Development Act, 1984
As currently constituted, the Manpower Planning and Development Act of 1984 will not promote flexible adaptation to the changing technological needs of industry and commerce. The centralization of apprenticeship training constrains training. Employers have withdrawn from participating, resulting in inadequate output. Equity concerns can be catered for by allowing National Employment Councils (bipartite bodies of workers and employers) to take over the recruitment and running of the apprenticeship training scheme, with government retaining the supervisory functions.

In addition, rather than restrict coverage to a narrow range of formal sector employers, employers in the informal and small-scale sector should also be involved. In view of the dwindling resources of the Zimbabwe Development Resources Fund (ZIMDEF), it is necessary to implement the recommendations of the National Manpower Council. ZIMDEF should only be used for its core function, training. The use of ZIMDEF funds to upgrade infrastructure, to pay salaries, to acquire equipment, etc. should be phased out. This is particularly important in view of the difficulties with raising the 1 per cent levy on the wage bill. To encourage flexibility, ZIMDEF should be made semi-autonomous.

Elements specific to the formal sector

(a) Guidelines on retrenchments, retraining and redeployment
The tripartite Retrenchment Committee should design national guidelines on retrenchments, retraining and redeployment of retrenchees in order to minimize the social costs involved. Assistance for those experiencing hardship should be provided under the Poverty Alleviation Action Plan.

(b) Technological capacity-building
At international level, consensus has now emerged on the importance of reorganizing the industrial structure towards technology-intensive production techniques.

In terms of human resource development, this entails introducing new courses at tertiary level with a bias towards product design, quality control and marketing. Workers are required to acquire multi-skills so that they can perform several tasks.

Recent studies show that new techniques require radical changes in management attitudes. Within the framework of the fashionable Japanese approaches, firms are shifting from the traditional vertical organizational structure towards a horizontal one, with emphasis on team work.

(c) Consolidating the institutional framework
Zimbabwe has an already developed educational and institutional capacity, but some of these institutions are operating under capacity due to shortages of lecturers and equipment. Enrolments at some institutions could easily be increased by 70 per cent without any additional capacity being installed. In this regard, priority should be given to improving technologies currently in use in technical colleges. These were found to be out-of-date with respect to technologies currently in use in industry, which in turn lag behind international trends. New equipment, text books and other resources have to be acquired and the curricula redesigned so that the training will meet today's requirements. Working conditions have declined in public sector institutions, so mechanisms have to be developed to improve these conditions, thereby enhancing productivity.

Elements specific to the non-formal sectors

In order to achieve the required shift in resources towards promoting the non-formal sectors, detailed studies of the different needs of these sectors should be undertaken. These studies should, among other things, examine the existing institutions to determine whether they could be reoriented to serve the non-formal sectors as well.

Affirmative action, especially in recruiting disadvantaged groups with weak links to the labour market (such as women, the disabled and young people), needs to be intensified. Incentives (such as tax refunds) should be used to encourage the employment of these disadvantaged groups. Everyone has the right to work, including the disabled. Labour market policy must entrench this right in a manner that involves workplace adaptation and other measures which enhance their employability. Sweden has developed Employability Institutes for such purposes. Special public sector enterprises, which could fall under the Industrial Development Corporation, should be established to encourage private sector participation in employing disabled people.

8 Malawi

EPHRAIM CHIRWA & WYCLIFFE CHILOWA

Introduction

The Malawi economy is largely dominated by the agriculture sector in terms of output, foreign-exchange earnings and employment. Agriculture accounts for about 35 per cent of gross domestic product (GDP), more than 90 per cent of the country's foreign-exchange earnings and provides paid and self-employment to 92 per cent of the rural population. Malawi is one of the poorest countries in the world. In 1994, nominal per capita income was estimated at US$140 and Malawi is ranked as 157th out of 174 countries in terms of human development (UNDP, 1996). The economy is further characterized by rapid population growth and a narrow resource base. These are some of the challenges the country is attempting to address in the long term.

The performance of the Malawi economy after independence in 1964 until the late 1970s was relatively encouraging, registering high growth rates in economic activities and a favourable balance-of-payment position. After the oil shock of 1979 and the intensification of the Mozambican civil war, the economy manifested structural weaknesses. Economic growth in 1980 was negative for the first time since independence and there was slack in the productivity of the estate-led agricultural sector. Harrigan (1991) argues that many of the structural weaknesses were by-products of Malawi's post-independence development strategy and the associated political economy. The economic difficulties of 1979 and 1980 led the government to adopt and implement IMF-sponsored stabilization programmes and World Bank-sponsored Structural Adjustment Programmes (SAPs). Since then, the economy has gone through turbulent times without a clear trend in long-term growth. Malawi was amongst the first African countries to adopt SAPs and it has pursued these policies for a fairly long period, but the benefits are minimal and uncertain while the social costs, especially the effects on the poor and the resource constraint on women and children, are enormous and evident.

This chapter reviews the performance of the economy under SAPs since the 1980s, with particular emphasis on the labour market and trade liberalization, the main objective being to evaluate the economic and social impact of the SAPs. The chapter is organized as follows. The next section describes the economic situation prior to the SAPs, identifying the factors that led to their adoption. The major policy reforms and the process of negotiations among the various stakeholders are then outlined, followed by an assessment of the economic and social impact of the SAPs. The concluding section focuses on alternative policies for sustainable economic growth and development in Malawi.

Background to structural adjustment programmes

Since independence in 1964, Malawi's economic performance has varied, with a good performance record in the 1970s but deteriorating economic conditions since 1980. It took about eight years after independence for Malawi to formulate a coherent economic plan. The first statement of strategies and policies for development was produced in 1971 and covered the period 1971–80 (Government of Malawi, 1971). The focus of the first Statement of Development Policies (DEVPOL I) was on the pursuance of a limited import-substitution industrial strategy and the role of the agricultural sector in economic development. The large-scale agricultural sub-sector was designed to commercialize agriculture for export expansion, while the smallholder sub-sector was designed to perform the dual task of ensuring domestic food self-sufficiency and limited exports of cash crops. Moreover, DEVPOL I aimed at achieving an economic growth rate of 8 per cent per annum and a rapid increase in agricultural productivity as a means of raising both rural incomes and foreign-exchange earnings. In any case, the export-oriented agro-based expansion, with import-substituting industrialization playing only a secondary role, was restricted to a narrow range of consumer goods. The trade regime in the post-independence period was primarily determined by the over-riding aim of stimulating agricultural exports (Harrigan, 1991). In this respect, the economy was relatively open and tariffs were generally low and direct restrictions on imports minimal. In addition, wages and incomes policies were important aspects of public sector wage restraint to contain public sector expenditure and mitigate wage-led inflation and rural-urban migration.

This open regime paid dividends, and the performance of the economy was impressive in the 1970s. Real GDP grew by 8.03 per cent per annum between 1970 and 1979. The agricultural sector remained the dominant contributor to GDP at 40 per cent, while the manufacturing sector only contributed 12 per cent. Exports grew by an impressive 21.1 per cent per annum, while imports grew by 17.4 per cent per annum; nevertheless, given the initial imbalance, the trade deficit grew by 33.6 per cent. Employment in the formal sector increased by 9.5 per cent per annum between 1971 and 1979, with private sector employment growing by 11.5 per cent compared with 3.7 per cent per annum in the government sector.

However, this economic expansion was short-lived. The progress of the 1970s was interrupted in 1979 when Malawi experienced a sharp reduction in growth, deteriorating financial positions of public and private enterprises and rapid exacerbation of balance-of-payment pressures for three years (Government of Malawi, 1987).[1] In 1979, Malawi was hit for the first time by its major problem of land-lockedness through the closure of the Beira route to the Indian Ocean as a result of the intensification of the civil war in Mozambique. The economy was in crisis, which was manifested in the early 1980s by deteriorating terms of trade, transport bottlenecks, the rising cost of fuel, adverse weather conditions and weakening internal demand.[2] The real growth rate of GDP fell from 8.3 per cent in 1978 to 3.9 per cent in 1979 and for the first time negative growth rates of –1.1 per cent in 1980 and –4.7 per cent in 1981 were registered. The mixed economy development

---

[1] This was the background to the second Statement of Development Policies (DEVPOL II) resulting in the introduction of a market-led economy.

[2] Kaluwa *et al.* (1992) and Mhone (1992) give a detailed analysis of the emergence of the economic crisis which led to the adoption of SAPs in Malawi.

strategy pursued since independence failed to bring the economy back to the performance of the 1970s.

According to Mhone (1992) and Kaluwa *et al.* (1992), the balance-of-payments pressure experienced between 1979 and 1980 drove Malawi to adopt World Bank structural adjustment programmes and IMF stabilization measures. An in-depth analysis of the growth period in the 1970s revealed that the economy suffered from structural rigidities that required restructuring to allow the efficient operation of the market mechanism. Other studies have observed that the agricultural-led growth of the economy was based on the estate sub-sector which never ploughed back profits into the smallholder agriculture sector (Kydd and Christiansen, 1982). According to Harrigan (1991), preparatory work for the first Structural Adjustment Loan (SAL) identified six structural weaknesses in the economy: the slow growth of smallholder exports; the narrowness of the export base and increased reliance on tobacco; dependence on imported fuel and on a declining stock of domestic fuelwood; the rapid deterioration of parastatal finances; the increasing budget deficits of the late 1970s, and the inflexible system of government-administered prices and wages. These structural weaknesses were reinforced by the exogenous shocks of the late 1970s related to oil price hikes which meant a dramatic worsening of the terms of trade; a sharp rise in international interest rates; drought conditions in 1979–80; and disruption to Malawi's traditional trade route to the sea due to the civil war in Mozambique.

Structural adustment programmes in Malawi

Structural adjustment loans
Ever since the economic crisis that manifested itself in the late 1970s, Malawi has tapped resources from the World Bank in the form of structural adjustment loans (SALs) and sectoral credit. These have been supplemented by short-term IMF stabilization facilities, mainly to address balance-of-payments problems. A summary of structural adjustment loans and sector credits is given in Appendix Table 8.1 at the end of this chapter.

The first structural adjustment loan, SAL I, was implemented in the 1981 fiscal year. The World Bank made US$45 million available to the government. The major objectives under SAL I were to diversify the export base; encourage efficient import substitution; ensure an appropriate prices and incomes policy; improve the public sector's financial performance; and strengthen the government's economic planning and monitoring capabilities. The policy instruments involved devaluation of the Malawi Kwacha (by 15 per cent in 1982, 12 per cent in 1983 and 3 per cent in 1984), increases in smallholder producer prices, increase in tax rates, increased budgetary allocation to the agricultural sector, increased tariffs of public utilities, adjustments in interest rates and restructuring of public enterprises. SAL I was supported by three IMF Stand-by facilities which aimed at reversing the unfavourable balance-of-payments trends and reducing the fiscal imbalance.[3] SAL I was reinforced by SAL II involving US$55 million from the World Bank in 1984. The policy objectives and policy measures were the same as in SAL I. However, under SAL II prices for most industrial goods were decontrolled and a further two devaluations were carried out (15 per cent in 1985 and 9.5 per cent in 1986).

---

[3] For a discussion of IMF stabilization facilities see Kaluwa *et al.* (1992).

SAL III which was implemented in 1986 focused on the same policy objectives as the first two SALs. Smallholder producer prices and interest rates continued to be periodically adjusted; some of ADMARC's investments unrelated to marketing activities were divested; most prices on industrial products were decontrolled except for petrol, beef, fertilizers, sugar and vehicle spare parts; and some taxes on selected items were raised. Supplementary resources to support SAL III were made available in 1987 with the additional objective of expanding the role of the private sector in the marketing of smallholder crops and improving the financial performance and operational efficiency of ADMARC. Following this a further 15 per cent devaluation was effected; marketing of smallholder crops was liberalized except for tobacco and cotton; and there was further divestiture of ADMARC investments.

In addition to the three SALs, the World Bank also financed four sectoral credit facilities. First, the Industry and Trade Policy Adjustment Credit (ITPAC) was implemented in 1988 to consolidated the existing reforms (World Bank, 1988 and 1993). The main objective was to improve the policy environment for the manufacturing sector in order to increase the efficiency of resource use including imports, and to expand exports. The policy actions included a further devaluation of 7 per cent in 1990, decontrol of beef prices, elimination of industrial monopoly rights, revision of the tax system, reduction of the scope of export licensing, removal of prior foreign-exchange allocation by the Reserve Bank and revision of legislation affecting the financial sector.

Second, the Agriculture Sector Adjustment Credit (ASAC) was made available in 1990. While continuing the principles of the previous loans, the main objectives of ASAC were to increase the efficiency and improve the incomes of smallholder farmers, increase efficiency of land use and protect the environment, and improve the macroeconomic environment through further import liberalization and public expenditure restructuring (World Bank, 1990). The policy instruments involved under ASAC include smallholder price adjustments, liberalization of fertilizer marketing, removal of fertilizer subsidies, liberalization of burley tobacco farming, and adjustments of estate land rents. In addition to ASAC, in 1990 the government started the implementation of the programme on Social Dimensions of Adjustment (SDA), a project aimed at minimizing the adverse effects of SAPs on the vulnerable groups in Malawian society and strengthening the capacity for the integration of the poor into the national development planning process.

Thirdly, in response to the drought that hit Southern Africa in the 1991/2 season, the Entrepreneurship Development and Drought Recovery Programme (EDDRP) was instituted in 1992, providing US$210 million worth of financial resources to the government (World Bank, 1992). This was augmented by supplementary resources in 1995. The EDDRP aimed at supporting: an improved environment for entrepreneurial activities and investment in labour-intensive activities, the adoption of policies aimed at deepening financial markets, the reorientation of fiscal and labour policies towards human capital development, reduction in balance-of-payments pressure due to drought-related imports, and alleviation of the impact of drought. Several policies were pursued to achieve these objectives. The Kwacha was finally floated in 1994 after another two devaluations of 15 per cent in June and 22 per cent in July 1992. The policy instruments used, *inter alia*, included a review of labour market imperfections and policy, a budgetary allocation to education of at least 15 per cent of total expenditure, an increase in the share of health in the overall budget, increases in the surtax rate on public utilities, reduction in the surtax base rate to 30 per cent, decreases in corporate and income taxes, elimination of direct credit control, and liberalization of interest rates.

Finally, the Fiscal Restructuring and Deregulation Programme (FRDP) began in 1996. Its first aim was to prioritize, protect and expand inter- and intra-sectoral allocations to the social sectors. Secondly, FRDP aimed at accelerating the consolidation of the structural measures under previous adjustment facilities including the complete removal of the remaining pricing and marketing constraints on small-holder agriculture, and removal of binding constraints to broad-based private sector entry and development. Other major objectives were restructuring the civil service to improve efficiency and control the growth of civil service wages and salaries, the development of land policy, and the rationalization of tariffs and surtax. As a result, there was increased allocation of public spending to pro-poor areas, introduction of a cash budget system, retrenchment of temporary workers in the civil service, adoption of a privatization policy, and removal of laws discriminating against race.

In essence, the SAPs were designed to provide incentives for the production of tradeables, to rationalize government taxes and expenditure, and to strengthen key sectors and institutions with a view to setting the stage for sustainable macroeconomic growth. As Lensink (1996) argues, the task of the World Bank became much wider than that of the IMF.[4] Traditionally, the World Bank mainly concentrated on financing projects. Chipeta (1996) argues that the shift from the World Bank's project lending to funding policy reforms has *not* enhanced the productive capacity of the poor nations. The specific major policy measures, their timing and the resultant economic and social impact on different groups in the case of Malawi are highlighted in the following sections.

Timing and implementation of policy reforms

Trade and investment liberalization Trade liberalization has been a major tenet of SAPs for Malawi both in the external and the domestic sectors as a means of diversifying the export base and encouraging efficient import-substitution industrialization. Trade-related liberalization measures may be divided into external trade policies, domestic trade policies and policies to facilitate foreign investment.

External trade policies in Malawi have consisted of tariff adjustments and removal of non-tariff barriers such as export and import controls. Under SALs I–III the tax base was expanded and tax rates increased, and the buoyancy of the tax system was improved. However, under the EDDRP (FY92) the base surtax rate was reduced to 30 per cent and there were downward revisions in tariffs. Between 1973 and 1979, the average tariff was 15.4 per cent with a standard deviation of 18.1 per cent, compared with an average tariff of 26 per cent with a standard deviation of 32.3 per cent between 1980 and 1990. The World Bank argued that the period 1973–9 was one of substantially free international trade with virtually unimpeded movement of goods (World Bank, 1989). However, beginning in 1980 due to balance-of-payments and fiscal problems, the government adopted policies which resulted in a gradual closure of the economy. It has been argued that the rise in tariffs was necessitated by revenue needs to support internal imbalances. Under ITPAC (1988–9), policy centred on the removal of non-tariff barriers to trade and administration of export-related tax incentives. The scope of

---

[4]The IMF was founded in order to promote international monetary co-operation and stabilization of exchange rates. Its primary role is therefore to create a climate in which governments are forced to dismantle restrictions on foreign-exchange dealings and to promote free trade in goods and capital. Lensink (1996) further argues that SAPs are designed in such a way as to minimize the growth of income and demand, but that economic developments in the 1970s and early 1980s, in particular the debt crisis, prompted the World Bank to undertake a major policy review with respect to developing countries. Financing of projects proved to be unsustainable to combat the stagnating growth.

export licensing was reduced and import licensing requirements were reduced to only 19 products by 1996.

Several policy measures have been implemented to facilitate domestic trade under various SALs. Since 1981, there have been periodic adjustments in small-holder producer prices, particularly for maize. Under ASAC, started in 1990, the marketing of fertilizers was liberalized by allowing other agents, the economic subsidy on fertilizer was reduced, smallholders were allowed to grow burley tobacco, and estate land rents were adjusted more frequently. In 1995, the system of fixed producer prices for smallholder agricultural products was replaced by a price band within which the actual price fluctuates. ADMARC now defends only the gazetted floor and ceiling prices. Private traders have been allowed to buy small-holder produce since 1987 and in 1996 the legal instrument granting monopsony power to ADMARC to purchase smallholder cotton and other crops was repealed.

Prior to SAPs, domestic trade in industrial products was constrained by price controls prescribed under the Control of Goods Act, 1968. By 1983, there were 43 commodities under formal price control and many more in the informal control system (Khan *et al.*, 1989). Under the SAPs, the Control of Goods Act has been amended several times and prices were decontrolled in phases. Of the 43 controlled commodities, 13, 20 and 6 commodities were decontrolled in 1983, 1984 and 1986 respectively, under SALs I–III. By 1996, only petroleum products and motor vehicle spare parts were subject to price controls.

In terms of domestic and foreign investments, liberalization has entailed simplifi-cation of procedures. Entry into the manufacturing sector was governed by the Industrial Development Act of 1966 whereby all manufacturing investments were required to be licensed between 1964 and 1990. In addition the Act also provided exclusive monopoly rights to large enterprises with a potential for the exploitation of economies of scale. However, under ITPAC and EDDRP the scope of industrial licensing was reduced, exclusive product rights were eliminated in 1988 and the Industrial Development Act was replaced by the Industrial Licensing Act of 1991 which eliminated the industrial licensing process for investments, except for a short negative list.

An explicit policy on foreign investment was introduced in 1991 in the Investment Promotion Act of 1991 which led to the establishment of the one-stop investment centre, the Malawi Investment Promotion Agency (MIPA). These efforts were supported under EDDRP. In 1995 the government enacted the Export Processing Zones Act which was implemented in 1996 as an institutional framework for the promotion of both domestic and foreign investment.

Exchange-rate policy reforms Exchange-rate adjustment played a critical role in facilitating domestic and external trade. Malawi adopted a fixed exchange-rate regime at independence and the Malawi Kwacha was pegged to the British pound until 1973 when it was pegged to the dollar-pound basket. Later, between 1975 and 1984, it was pegged to the Special Drawing Right (SDR) and thereafter to a basket of seven currencies taking into account Malawi's trading position (Silumbu, 1992).

During the structural adjustment programmes, an activist and flexible exchange-rate stance was adopted, with eleven devaluations announced between 1982 and 1992, leading to the cumulative devaluation of the kwacha in nominal terms by 131 per cent. The devaluations were mainly effected under SALs I–III, with one under ITPAC and two under EDDRP. At the beginning of 1994, the government opted for the flotation of the Kwacha which led to its depreciation against the US dollar by about 300 per cent by the end of the year.

Financial sector policy reforms The financial system in Malawi is highly oligo-polistic, dominated by two financial institutions offering standard banking services. Monetary policy was characterized by interest-rate controls, credit ceilings and foreign-exchange rationing. During the first few years of adjustment, financial reforms involved the periodic adjustment of interest rates. In fact, under SALs I–III interest-rate adjustment was the only financial reform. Lending interest rates were increased from 11.5 to 16.7 per cent in 1980 and to 18.5 per cent in 1981 and 1982. Between 1979 and 1987, lending and deposit rates increased by 74 and 105 per cent, respectively. Under ITPAC and ASAC there was gradual liberalization of interest rates and under EDDRP the monetary authorities eliminated direct credit control and prior foreign-exchange control and interest rates were fully liberalized.

Institutional changes in terms of revision of the Reserve Bank Act and Banking Act were effected under ITPAC, and the Capital Market Development Act under EDDRP. The new Banking Act of 1989 opened up the financial system to new competition. Under the Banking Act three existing institutions and four new entrants were granted commercial banking licences. This resulted in a decline in monopoly power of the two established commercial banks (Chirwa, 1996). The index of market concentration, as measured by the Hirschmann-Herfindahl index, fell by 20 per cent between 1987 and 1994. Furthermore, bank capitalization and savings mobilization increased while financial intermediation costs declined. Bank profitability improved and there has been a sectoral shift in credit towards the trading and manufacturing sectors away from the favoured agricultural sector. As a result of granting commercial banking licences to the non-bank financial institutions, the financial interrelations ratio (the ratio of NBFI deposits to commercial bank deposits) increased significantly.

Privatization of state-owned enterprises Privatization of state-owned enterprises (SOEs) has been an integral part of the SAPs. In essence, Malawi has been characterized by two waves of privatization as part of structural adjustment programmes. The first occurred between 1987 and 1990 in ADMARC's divestiture programme. This privatization aimed at restructuring ADMARC's portfolio and refocusing its activities in the promotion of agricultural development through its marketing activities. Furthermore, the programme had a distributive objective of dispersing ownership of productive assets to the general public. Under the ADMARC Divestiture Programme, several enterprises which were wholly or partly owned by ADMARC were offered to the private sector between 1987 and 1990 (see Chirwa,1994). The major divestiture activities under ADMARC's Divestiture Programme have involved PEW Limited, National Seed Company, National Oil Industries Limited, ADMARC Canning Limited, Grain and Milling Limited and Auction Holdings Limited.

The second wave of privatization, which started in 1994, is fairly recent although the groundwork started a long time ago. Privatization became institutionalized in 1996 in the Public Enterprises (Privatization) Act and is encompassing targeting reforms in the whole SOE sector. According to the Privatization Act of 1996, the objectives of privatization in Malawi include promotion of economic efficiency, facilitation of competition, promotion of public share ownership and raising government revenue. Under this programme Wood Industries Corporation (WICO) and the National Insurance Company have been the first enterprises to be sold to the private sector. Many more enterprises have been earmarked for partial or wholesale privatization. Under the FRDP (FY96) a Privatization Commission was established and a number of public enterprises have been earmarked for liquidation, divestiture and integration into line ministries (World Bank, 1996b).

Civil service reform The civil service reform programme in Malawi started fairly late in the adjustment sequence and is being implemented under the FRDP line of credit from the World Bank. According to the World Bank (1996b) the civil service reform is critical for containing the overall wage bill to achieve fiscal stabilization and restructuring of expenditures in order to increase the efficiency of public service delivery. As a precondition for negotiating the FRDP, the government retrenched about 20,000 employees in non-established and temporary positions in non-priority areas during the first nine months of 1995. Furthermore, a Civil Service Census was conducted. According to the census results (Government of Malawi, 1996), the size of the civil service stood at 112,975 civil servants in 1995, only 25 per cent of whom were women. The Census results were to be a basis for further retrenchment and restructuring of government departments and sections, foreseen to take place throughout the 1990s.

Labour market reforms Reforms in the labour market have been undertaken rather late. The SAPs were not designed to reform the labour markets, hence the reforms have been pursued internally in line with the democratization process that has taken place since 1992. According to Banda *et al.* (1996), Malawi has never had a comprehensive labour and employment policy. However, the government had piecemeal policies which have guided the operation of the labour market. Two related policies inherited from the colonial government have been central. First, the Wage Restraint Policy required the employer to seek approval from the Minister of Labour and Manpower Development for salary increases in excess of 5 per cent. It is argued that, by 1972, the Wages Restraint Policy had been successful in increasing formal employment and minimizing inflation and rural-urban income differentials (*ibid.*). Secondly, the Regulation of Minimum Wages and Conditions of Employment Act stipulated minimum wages that ensured employees a living wage. However, the minimum wage adjustments were very infrequent, and with increases in the price level, this has implied that real wages have fallen. For instance, between 1965 and 1992 minimum wages were reviewed 9 times with a maximum 7-year interval.

Reforms in the labour market have taken the form of reviewing the basis for minimum wage-fixing from static and ad hoc reviews to wage indexation. In this respect, minimum wage reviews will be called for either when the cumulative retail price index measured by the Consumer Price Index (CPI) reaches 20 per cent or at least every two years. As a results of riots in 1992, the government has since institutionalized collective bargaining through the promotion and strengthening of trade unions and employers' organizations. This has resulted in the formation of new trade unions. Furthermore, the Malawi Congress of Trade Unions has been actively involved in adjustment programmes, especially those that have implications for employment.

The negotiation process of SAPs

The process of design, negotiation and implementation of SAPs is one of stages. The first activity is the preparation of a Country Economic Memorandum by World Bank/IMF staff in consultation with the government. The Country Economic Memorandum is essentially a situation analysis of the economy. Secondly, sector studies culminating in a Policy Framework Paper follow to identify sector-specific issues and constraints. Concepts aimed at addressing the issues are developed at this stage. Thirdly, a World Bank appraisal mission leads to the preparation of a white-cover Memorandum of the President and Staff Appraisal Report. The Memorandum summarizes how funds are to be utilized. This is given to the government in draft form to agree or disagree with its contents. It is also discussed thoroughly by World Bank staff.

Fourthly, a yellow-cover Memorandum of the President is prepared by the World Bank and sent to the government for review in consultation with the various stakeholders in the country. This is a critical stage in the design of structural adjustment programmes, as the government can reject some of the policies and conditionalities according to the views of stakeholders in the market economy. This yellow-cover document is the basis for negotiations.

Fifthly, after review of the yellow-cover Memorandum of the President, the government requests funding for the Programme in a Draft Letter of Development Policy from the Minister of Finance to the President of the International Development Association. This leads to the preparation of the green-cover Report and Recommendation of the President of IDA to the Executive Directors. The preparation of the green-cover document means that the World Bank and the government have effectively agreed on the policies, conditionalities and disbursement of resources, together with deadlines of implementation. Finally, the document is then changed to a grey cover, whose circulation is limited.

However, experience has shown that, prior to the agreement about adjustment programmes where wider consultations with stakeholders are expected, things have tended to go wrong in Malawi. The government negotiating team draws staff from three key departments: the Ministry of Finance, the Ministry of Economic Planning and Development and the Reserve Bank of Malawi. Information and interviews with decision-makers from these key institutions revealed institutional constraints on effective discussion of the document. First, the grey-cover document is not circulated internally for discussions within departments. Secondly, there is no common understanding of the programmes among the three institutions in the government's negotiating team. Thirdly, the negotiating teams lack the skills to develop alternative programmes and to make a critical policy analysis of the World Bank-sponsored adjustment programmes. For example, the Policy Framework Papers which review the economic and policy environment are prepared by World Bank and IMF staff, with government economists being mere providers of information.

In addition, line ministries, departments and the private sector which are directly involved in implementation of the programme are not consulted. For example, there is no effective forum for consultation with the private sector and trade unions on SAPs prior to their implementation. According to the Malawi Chamber of Commerce and Industry, consultations only occur after the programmes have been implemented and when their negative effects have been felt by the business community. In some cases, these consultations present problems for the government because the private sector sometimes demands policy reversals. The other problem with the existing government-private sector consultation is that government representation is sometimes at a lower level and resolutions at the meetings are inconclusive. In effect, over the years these consultations have been ad hoc and have become less frequent (Ministry of Commerce and Industry, 1995). As a result, the few government officials involved in the negotiations panic when they receive the yellow document and agree to it without really appreciating the policies and conditionalities. This creates resistance in other ministries to implementing policies which effectively conflict with their priorities.

However, quite apart from institutional constraints, the World Bank (1996b) argues that there has been lack of clear and unequivocal political commitment to poverty alleviation, liberalization in smallholder agriculture, and broad-based private sector development. In addition, there have been delays in acting on agreed measures, and this underscores the weak administrative and institutional base and lack of adequate consultation with the various stakeholders in the economy.

Economic impact of structural adjustment

Structure of production and economic growth

Agriculture has been and remains the mainstay of the economy, accounting for more than a third of GDP and 90 per cent of export earnings. As noted above, structural adjustment programmes were designed to create incentives that would alter the structure of production. However, the policies seem to have limited effects on altering the composition of GDP. For instance, in the period prior to SAPs, the agricultural sector contributed 40 per cent to GDP. This share only fell to 36 per cent in the adjustment period. What seems to have changed significantly is the relative importance of the estate and the smallholder sub-sectors. In the pre-adjustment period the smallholder sub-sector produced 84 per cent of agricultural production, while the estate sub-sector contributed only 16 per cent. However, in the adjustment period the share of smallholder agriculture declined to 76 per cent while that of the estate sub-sector increased to 24 per cent. Table 8.1 shows the structure of production and growth in economic activities.

Similarly, the share of the manufacturing sector has not changed significantly. At independence, the manufacturing sector accounted for only 8 per cent of GDP, but improved to 12 per cent in the 1970s and remained stable at 13 per cent in the adjustment period. The distribution and service sectors have remained stable, contributing 34 per cent to GDP in the pre-adjustment and adjustment periods. However, the share of central government in GDP increased from 9.4 per cent in the pre-adjustment period to 14 per cent in the adjustment period.

Structural adjustment programmes have not only failed to alter the structure of production, but economic growth has also been erratic. The economy achieved high growth rates in the 1970s, growing by 5.9 per cent per annum in the pre-adjustment period compared with an average annual growth rate of 1.5 per cent. For the first time the economy experienced negative growth in 1980 and 1981 of –1.7 and –5.2 per cent, respectively. As observed by Kaluwa *et al.* (1992), after 1982 the economy began to regain positive growth but it has experienced several negative growth

Table 8.1   *Distribution and growth of GDP by sector of origin, Malawi, 1973–94 (at factor cost, in %)*

Sector of origin	Average composition			Average growth rate		
	1973–9	1980–89	1990–94	1973–9	1980–89	1990–94
Agriculture, forestry, fishing	39.6	36.6	33.4	5.4	0.8	2.1
Manufacturing	11.9	12.4	13.4	6.7	2.9	2.0
Electricity and water	1.6	2.0	2.6	8.4	4.6	7.2
Building and construction	5.4	4.4	4.2	7.4	0.3	–0.3
Distribution	14.1	12.9	12.3	6.4	0.7	0.5
Transport and communications	6.6	6.1	5.7	6.0	0.5	–0.5
Financial and professional services	5.3	6.4	6.8	14.8	1.8	1.1
Ownership of dwellings	3.8	4.3	4.4	7.5	2.6	2.5
Private social services	4.1	4.3	4.4	1.7	3.9	2.5
Government	9.4	13.2	15.0	6.0	7.1	0.6
Unallocable finance charges	–1.8	–2.6	–2.1	22.5	1.1	–1.6
GDP at 1978 factor cost	100.0	100.0	100.0	5.9	2.0	0.6

Source: GoM *Economic Report* (various)

rates within the adjustment period. Notably, real GDP fell by 3.3, 7.9 and 12.4 per cent in 1988, 1991 and 1994, respectively. Overall, performance in terms of expansion of the national cake has worsened in the adjustment period compared with the growth in GDP in the pre-adjustment period.

It is not known definitely whether the meagre growth in GDP which Malawi has achieved has been fairly distributed. Data are not available to reflect differences in poverty and income distribution in the pre-adjustment and adjustment periods. Using per capita GDP measures, nominal GDP per capita increased from 9.2 per cent per annum in the pre-adjustment era to 20 per cent in the adjustment era. However, real per capita GDP shows a decline between the two periods, with an average growth in the pre-adjustment period of 5.2 per cent per annum, declining at an average rate of 1.5 per cent per annum since SAPs began to be implemented in 1980 (see Appendix Figure A8.1).

Price stability
Inflation is one of the macroeconomic variables that is vital in maintaining purchasing power. However, SAPs have been characterized by high price instability. Using the changes in the composite retail price index, in the pre-adjustment period inflation averaged about 8 per cent per annum, the lowest rate being 3.6 per cent in 1972 and the highest 15.5 per cent in 1975. It is worth noting that the Mozambican civil war started around this period, and this created insecurity in the use of the shortest route to the sea for both exports and imports.

The period of SAPs has been characterized by high macroeconomic instability in terms of inflation. Figure 8.1 shows the trend in the inflation level in Malawi since

Figure 8.1   *Price stability and inflation, Malawi, 1970–94 (%)*

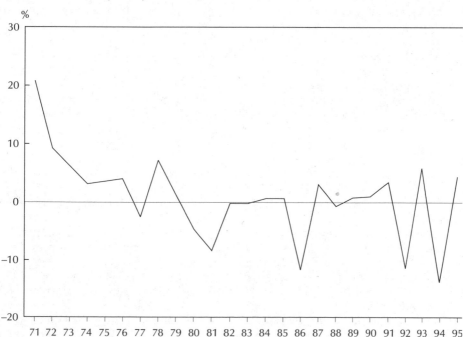

1970. Inflation in the pre-adjustment period was moderate compared with the period under structural adjustment. The average annual rate of inflation in the pre-adjustment period was 8.4 per cent, while in the adjustment period inflation averaged 22.0 per cent per annum. Another observation is that inflation was rarely double-digit in the 1970s, while in the adjustment period it was normally double-digit.

During the adjustment period, three phases can be identified. First, the period between 1982 and 1988 was characterized by increasing inflation from less than 10 to 32 per cent. This period was also characterized by high and increasing government deficit spending, a cumulative devaluation of the Malawi Kwacha of about 99.5 per cent, price decontrol and the 1988 drought. The second phase is the period between 1988 and 1991 when inflation fell from 32 to 8 per cent. Factors that can be attributed to the downward trend in inflation during this period include less devaluation, good weather conditions and moderate government deficit spending. In fact, only one devaluation of 7 per cent occurred in 1990 and this did not exert much pressure on the price level. The third phase, 1991–5, is a period of increasing and high inflation. Inflation increased from below 10 per cent in 1991 to the highest recorded level of 83 per cent in 1995. Many factors can be blamed for the rising trend in inflation within this phase, including drought in 1992 and 1994, suspension of donor aid pending political changes in 1992, devaluation of the Kwacha by 37 per cent in 1992 and its subsequent flotation in 1994 and increasing government deficit spending, especially since 1994. In all these phases, the closure and ineffectiveness of the shortest route to the sea can be identified as a common cost-push factor.

Consumption and investment performance

Private and public sector consumption Overall consumption expenditure takes up a high proportion of GDP and ranged from 49 to 90 per cent between 1970 and 1995. Private consumption accounts for about 80 per cent of total consumption expenditure. In real terms, total consumption expenditure grew by 12.4 per cent in the pre-adjustment period, but the growth rate fell to 5.2 per cent per annum in the adjustment period. However, growth in real per capita consumption fell between the two periods; it was 9.4 per cent per annum in the pre-adjustment period, but fell to 1.5 per cent per annum in the adjustment period. The fall was more significant in private than in public per capita consumption. Growth in real private consumption fell from an average of 11.3 per cent per annum to 1.9 per cent, while growth in per capita government consumption fell from 5.5 to 1.5 per cent per annum. However, real per capita consumption has increased from an average of K93 in the pre-adjustment period to K114 in the adjustment period. Real per capita private consumption also increased from K74 to K92 (the trend is illustrated in Appendix Figure A8.2).

The trends in consumption show that the SAPs have had a significant impact on overall consumption, and private consumption in particular. The real figures show that the increases would have been substantial if inflation had been kept under control. Hence, the inflationary pressures, especially in the 1990s, have eroded the benefits that the population would have reaped as a result of structural adjustment.

Private and public sector investments Gross investment has been dominated by the public sector which accounted for about 51 per cent in the 1970s and 52 per cent in the adjustment period. In nominal terms, total investment grew in both the pre-adjustment and adjustment periods. The private sector has reacted favourably to adjustment programmes. However, its growth rates are likely to be low if inflation is taken into account. There has also been an increase in the growth rates of domestic investment in the public sector in nominal terms. As a share of GDP, gross domestic investment was about 27 per cent in the pre-adjustment period but fell significantly to 18.2 per cent in the adjustment period (as illustrated in Appendix Figure A8.3).

Table 8.2 presents the composition and growth of manufacturing investment by sub-sector. It shows a marked shift of investments from agro-based traditional industries to sectors with a potential for higher value-added. Similarly, investment in the manufacturing sector was highly concentrated in a few agro-processing activities, prior to the SAPs. Food processing, beverages, tobacco and textile manufacturing activities accounted for two-thirds of manufacturing investment in the 1970s. However, the share of these sub-sectors declined to 59.2 per cent in the 1980s.

In terms of growth, there were greater incentives for manufacturing investment during the adjustment period, compared with the pre-adjustment period. Overall, investment in manufacturing grew by 22.2 per cent in the adjustment period, while it grew by only 4.6 per cent per annum in the 1970s (nominal terms). Furthermore, most sub-sectors demonstrated high growth rates in the adjustment period, with sawmill products, textiles and machinery taking a leading role.

There are several explanations, linked to the SAPs, for the growth in private sector and manufacturing sector investment. First, fiscal policy reforms which led to reduction in the deficit minimized the crowding-out effects. During the adjustment period credit from the financial system to the private sector increased, thus increasing the availability of resources to the private sector. Secondly, price decontrols, exchange-rate adjustments and elimination of foreign-exchange rationing facilitated the operation of the market system. As Khan *et al.* (1989) observed, average profitability, which is the main source of investment financing in Malawi, improved after most prices were decontrolled. Thirdly, trade liberalization also facilitated the importation of capital equipment and raw materials and this partly led to a fuller utilization of production capacity. Furthermore, trade liberalization led to a boom in micro, small and medium-scale enterprises with a potential contribution to private investment.

Table 8.2 *Investment in manufacturing production by industrial sector, Malawi, 1973–9 to 1980–88 (%)*

	Composition	
Industrial sector	1973–9	1980–88
Food processing, including sugar	27.4	10.8
Tea manufacture	6.7	13.5
Beverages	8.6	9.5
Tobacco manufacture	6.4	8.5
Textiles, netting and blankets	18.5	16.9
Clothing, leather goods, footwear	2.0	2.7
Sawmill and wood products	2.5	5.1
Packaging, printing, publishing	8.0	6.9
Chemicals and fertilizers	2.5	1.1
Pharmaceuticals, paints, soaps and cooking oils	3.0	5.4
Tyre retreading and plastic products	3.0	3.1
Non-metallic mineral products	5.7	7.0
Metal products other than machinery	3.4	3.9
Machinery and motor vehicle assembly	0.6	2.7
All other manufactures	1.8	2.8

Source: National Statistical Office, *Annual Economic Survey* (Large Establishments) (various)

Domestic and foreign trade performance

Domestic trade Adjustment programmes have impacted favourably on the efficiency of domestic trade in a number of ways. First, the decontrol of prices for most industrial products enabled firms to determine the price level freely and the average profitability of firms has increased. The decontrol programme did not significantly increase pressure on the domestic price level. Secondly, trade liberalization has increased competition in trading activities, especially from the booming micro, small and medium enterprises. This has broadened the supply base of domestic and imported products and hence has widened consumer choice.

Another aspect of adjustment in domestic trade is the deregulation of trading activities which were hitherto monopolized by the state-owned enterprises. For instance, private traders were allowed to conduct trade in agricultural inputs and in the purchase of smallholder agricultural output, dismantling the monopoly power of state-owned ADMARC. However, private traders have not been very effective, due to various constraints such as lack of storage facilities, poor transportation and lack of credit to facilitate the purchase of produce from smallholder farmers. Furthermore, deregulation of trade led to the closure of ADMARC's less viable markets which were mostly in the remote rural areas. Private traders cannot access these areas, and hence smallholder farmers have had problems in marketing their agricultural produce. Following the liberalization of agricultural trading activities in 1987, ADMARC closed about 125 markets on the basis of marketed volume (Christiansen and Stackhouse, 1989). In terms of income, most smallholder farmers have gained through increases in produce prices offered by private traders, since ADMARC is just a buyer of last resort at a guaranteed market price.

External trade sector: a) visible trade balance One measure of assessing the effectiveness of trade liberalization and exchange-rate adjustments is the trend in the trade balance calculated as the difference between exports and imports. Figure 8.2 indicates the relative shares of imports and exports (including non-factor services) in GDP. It is evident that imports as a proportion of GDP have been higher than the export/GDP ratio, except in 1984. Exports as a proportion of GDP have been following an upward trend, particularly since 1985, while the import-GDP ratio has been increasing. In fact, the export-GDP ratio averaged 18.1 per cent in the 1970s but increased to 21 per cent in the adjustment period. On the other hand, the import-GDP ratio was 32 per cent in the 1970s and fell to 27.9 per cent in the adjustment period.

The overall trend in the balance of trade is depicted in Table 8.3 and Appendix Figure A8.4. The trade balance has continued to be adverse since the 1970s, and the trade gap has progressively widened during the adjustment period. Imports increased from K177.4 million in the 1970s to K2.6 billion in the 1990s, while exports increased from K112.6 million in the 1970s to K1.6 billion in the 1990s. On average,

Table 8.3   *Value of visible trade balance, Malawi, 1970–94*

	Value (million Kwacha)		
	1971–9	1980–89	1990–94
Exports (f.o.b)	112.6	444.6	1,622.8
Domestic	102.8	434.1	1,578.2
Re-exports	9.8	10.5	44.6
Imports (c.i.f.)	177.4	585.4	2,563.0
Visible trade balance	−64.8	−140.7	−940.1

Source: Reserve Bank of Malawi, *Financial and Economic Review* (various)

Figure 8.2   *Imports and exports as a ratio of GDP, Malawi, 1970–95 (%)*

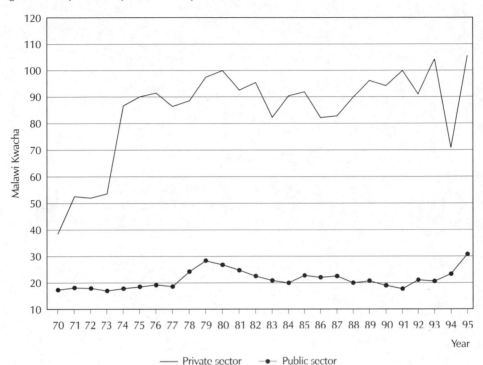

the trade deficit was K64.8 million in the 1970s and increased to K940.1 million in the 1990s. Although imports have increased in absolute terms compared to GDP, in terms of growth imports grew by 17.6 per cent and exports by 16.7 per cent in the 1970s. However, in the 1990s growth in exports was higher than growth in imports and consequently the growth in the trade deficit has fallen.

This shows that liberalization measures, in terms of opening up the market combined with devaluation of the Kwacha, arrested the growth of imports and encouraged export trade especially in the 1990s, as there were short-term losses in the 1980s.

(b) Import performance A similar trend is obtained when imports are analyzed by end-use between 1970 and 1989. Table 8.4 presents the composition and growth of imports by end-use. Imports of merchandise are dominated by basic and auxiliary materials for industry, plant, machinery and equipment and commodities for intermediate and final consumption. These sub-sectors accounted for 61.2 and 69.5 per cent of imports in the 1970s and 1980s, respectively. Consumer goods accounted for 15.3 per cent of imports in the 1970s but the ratio fell to 12 per cent in the adjustment period.

(c) Export performance More than 60 per cent of Malawi's export earnings in the 1990s originated from tobacco exports alone, reflecting the very limited export diversification. In essence, the traditional exports of tobacco, tea and sugar contributed about 85 per cent of the value of total export earnings in 1994. Table 8.5 shows the composition and growth of exports by main commodities between 1970 and 1994. Tobacco exports dominated in the share of export earnings. It is apparent

Table 8.4   *Composition of imports by end-use sub-sector, Malawi, 1970–89 (%)*

Sub-sector	Average composition	
	1971–9	1980–89
Consumer goods	15.3	12.0
Plant, machinery and equipment	13.9	13.8
Transport means	14.2	12.1
Materials for building and construction	8.5	6.0
Basic auxiliary materials for industry	33.7	39.9
Goods for intermediate and final consumption	13.6	15.8
Miscellaneous transactions	0.8	0.5

Note: Data for imports by end-use not available for the 1990s

Source: Reserve Bank of Malawi, *Financial and Economic Review* (various)

from the data that the share of tobacco exports has increased over time from 47.7 per cent in the 1970s to 68.7 per cent in the 1990s, while the shares of other exports have declined.

Table 8.5   *Composition of exports by main commodity, Malawi, 1970–94 (%)*

Commodity	Average composition		
	1970–79	1980–89	1990–94
Tobacco	47.7	54.0	68.7
Tea	21.2	16.3	9.6
Groundnuts	7.7	2.5	0.0
Cotton	2.9	1.0	1.0
Sugar	7.2	11.7	6.5
Other	13.3	14.5	14.1

Source: *ibid.*

Exports of cotton which account for only 1 per cent of export earnings experienced a temporary boom in the 1970s. The growth rate in other exports including manu-factured goods has been impressive particularly in the 1990s. In general, exports have grown substantially from 18.5 per cent of GDP in the 1970s to 28.4 per cent in the 1990s (see Figure 8.2). It seems, therefore, that liberalization measures provided a temporary disincentive to export trade in most commodities in the 1980s, but the sectors responded favourably in the 1990s. The likely explanation lies in the imple-mentation of ITPAC and EDDRP in the late 1980s and early 1990s. These programmes had more far-reaching reforms in the trade sector than earlier programmes.

Labour market and social impacts of structural adjustment

As noted above, there have been very limited adjustments in the labour market, the reason being that there were very few controls in the labour market in Malawi. Apart from the minimum wage legislation, the private sector was free to determine wages and salaries of unskilled labour. And the salaries and wages of skilled labour have been flexible. However, the SAPs have affected the labour market directly and indirectly.

Employment trends under adjustment

The population of Malawi was estimated at 4.44 million in 1971; it increased to 6 million in 1980 and 8.8 million in 1990. According to Banda *et al.* (1996), in 1980 the total labour force was estimated at 2.8 million, 44 per cent of it female, but it almost doubled to 4.1 million in 1990 with the per cent of females declining to 41 per cent. Formal employment covers only a small proportion of this labour force. In 1971 only 172,273 people were employed in the formal sector, with the private sector accounting for 69 per cent, and 33 per cent were employed in the agricultural sector. In 1980 only 359,825 people out of a labour force of 2.8 million were employed in the formal sector, with the private sector accounting for about 80 per cent. Similarly in 1990, the formal sector employed only about 11.6 per cent of the total labour force. Table 8.6 shows the composition and growth of employment in the formal sector under adjustment.

Table 8.6 *Composition and growth of formal employment by sector of economic activity, Malawi, 1971–90 (%)*

Sector of economic activity	Composition	
	1971–9	1980–90
Agriculture, forestry, fishing	40.61	47.26
Mining and quarrying	0.29	0.11
Manufacturing	11.87	12.42
Building and construction	9.22	7.59
Electricity and water	1.11	1.18
Transport and communications	5.09	5.48
Wholesale, retail and hotels	8.05	7.30
Financial and business services	1.38	3.13
Community and personnel services	22.36	15.53
Growth rate		
All industries	9.45	2.96
Private sector	11.54	2.88
Public sector	3.68	3.69

Source: RBM, *Financial and Economic Review* (various)

Formal employment increased at 9.45 per cent per annum between 1971 and 1979, reflecting a net generation of 179,990 jobs. However, the rate at which the formal sector generated employment opportunities declined to 2.96 per cent per annum in the adjustment period. The data show that most sectors, except for community and personal services, experienced a decline in the growth rate. Between 1980 and 1990, there were only 113,264 new jobs. Private sector employment experienced a decline in the growth rate from 11.54 per cent per annum in the pre-adjustment period to 2.88 per cent in the adjustment period, while growth in formal employment in the public sector remained more less stable at 3.7 per cent per annum.

Assessment of the impact of adjustment programmes on informal employment is difficult because of data unavailability for such enterprises. However, given that the formal sector employs only about 10 per cent of the total labour force, a much larger proportion was employed in the informal sector. Daniels and Ngwira (1992) estimated that in 1992 Malawi had 570,000 micro, small and medium-sized enterprises in the informal sector and employed over 1 million people. Activities in the informal sector have increased in the adjustment period either as a survival mechanism or as a result of trade liberalization. The impact of the growth of informal activities on employment cannot be understated.

Real wage developments under adjustment
Although nominal average monthly earnings in the formal sector show increases in the adjustment period, due to increases in the general price level, real wages experienced a downward trend. In the pre-adjustment period nominal monthly

earnings were on average K30.90 and they increased significantly to K72.51 in the adjustment period. Minimum wages increased from K11.87 in the pre-adjustment period to K33.41 in the adjustment period. However, as Table 8.7 shows, average monthly earnings and minimum wages in real terms show that real wages have declined within the adjustment period compared with the pre-adjustment period. Real monthly earnings fell from K51.87 in the pre-adjustment period to K38.17 in

Table 8.7   *Average monthly earnings and minimum wages by sector of economic activity, Malawi, 1971–9 and 1980–90 (at 1980 prices, Malawi Kwacha)*

Sector of economic activity	1971–9	1980–90
Agriculture, forestry and fishing	18.81	13.84
Mining and quarrying	42.12	25.69
Manufacturing	64.73	50.59
Building and construction	53.19	30.60
Electricity and water	73.55	56.14
Transport and communications	101.69	56.24
Wholesale, retail and hotels	75.76	60.78
Financial and business services	208.89	221.72
Community and personnel services	74.54	52.95
All industries	51.87	38.17
Private sector	48.28	34.03
Public sector	62.21	54.11
Statutory minimum wages	20.26	15.99

Source: ibid.

Figure 8.3   *Manufacturing/agricultural wage ratio, Malawi, 1971–90*

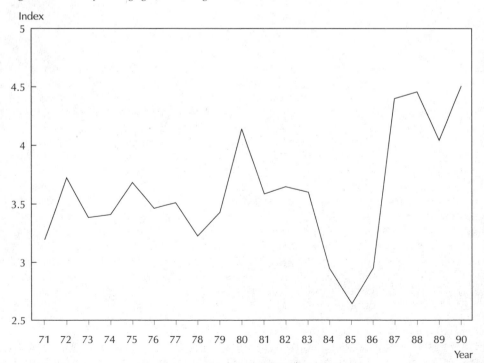

Manufacturing/agricultural wage

the adjustment period. The decline is largely attributed to a decline in real wages in the private sector from K48.28 in the 1970s to K34.03 in the adjustment era. Similarly, real statutory minimum wages have fallen from K20.26 to K15.99 between the two periods. The decline in public sector real wages was not substantial. The trend in average monthly earnings and statutory minimum real wages as illustrated in Appendix Figure A8.5, shows that structural reforms, via their influence on the price level, have led to a persistent decline in real wages since 1980.

The other aspect of wages development in the adjustment period is the movement in the ratio of the manufacturing to the agricultural wage. This gives an indication of the rural-urban wage gap, since most formal agricultural activities are in the rural areas whereas manufacturing activities are in the urban areas. In the 1970s the real manufacturing wage was 3.44 times the agricultural sector wage, but this increased to 3.74 times in the adjustment period.

Figure 8.3 illustrates the urban-rural wage differentials. The data point to the fact that SAPs have not been able to eliminate the wage gap between the urban and rural areas. The figure shows that, between 1971 and 1978, the ratio of the manufacturing to the agricultural wage was more stable, hovering at about 3.5 times. However, it increased to more than 4 times in 1981. The wage gap showed a declining trend between 1982 and 1985, when the ratio reached its lowest level, but started to increase sharply thereafter to a ratio above the 1970s levels since 1986.

Structural adjustment and labour market institutions
There are several institutions involved in labour issues in Malawi, namely, the government through the Ministry of Labour and Manpower Development, the Employers' Consultative Association of Malawi (ECAM) and the Trade Union Congress of Malawi (TUCM). Structural changes in labour market institutions have occurred as a result of SAPs and the democratization; they were never a part of a policy package. Tripartite negotiations have always taken place between employers, employees and the government on labour relations, minimum wages and the economic situation in the country. However, the trade union movement, prior to adjustment, was very weak and negotiations were merely on a case-by-case basis. The democratization movement has changed this situation quite considerably.

The main provision for the formation of trade unions was contained in the Trade Union Act of 1965, which is basically derived from ILO Convention No.98 on the Right to Organize and Collective Bargaining, 1948. The government ratified this Convention as early as 1965. The Act provides a channel of communication between workers and employers with a view to enabling the two parties to negotiate on wages and terms and conditions of employment. However, despite the provisions in the Act, for over 30 years after independence and prior to the democratization of the early 1990s, the trade union movement was dormant. According to Banda *et al.* (1996), after independence government policy was to consolidate its political power and to stifle the labour movement and trade union activities as well as meaningful collective bargaining. As a result the majority of trade unions were systematically eliminated, leaving only five in the services, agriculture, transport and building and construction sectors. These unions, through their umbrella organization, the Trade Union Congress of Malawi, were affiliated to the ruling Malawi Congress Party and in essence were co-opted to government rule.

This obviously resulted in the ineffectiveness of trade unions in influencing labour relations. According to the Ministry of Labour and Manpower Development, unionization was very low, standing at 56,000 out of the 488,000 paid employees in 1991. The demise of effective trade union activities was partially strategic in the implementation of the government's Wages and Incomes Policy which essentially focused on minimizing labour costs.

In contrast to other African countries, the social impact of the economic reforms and the democratization led to the rebirth of active trade union movements. Under the SAPs, through increases in the price level via the devaluation of the Malawi currency, public deficit spending and transport bottlenecks, the purchasing power of many workers had dwindled. In 1992, most employees were on strike and in some cases this resulted in riots. The positive outcomes that resulted from negotiations between employee representatives and employers encouraged the formation of trade unions. Some 12 unions, Transport and General Workers Union, Railways Workers Union, Local Government Employees Union, Tea and Plantation Workers Union, Teachers Union of Malawi, Commercial Insurance Union, Building and Construction Workers Union, Textile, Leather and Garments Union, Hotels, Food and Catering Union, Civil Servants Union, Customs Union and Sugar Employees Union, have held elections and are affiliated to the Trade Union Congress of Malawi. Apart from these, many employees have standing representatives to bargain wage increases with their employers.

On the demand side, the Employers' Consultative Association of Malawi (ECAM) was formed in 1963 to promote private sector interests and as a channel for business consultation with the government. It has a membership of individual companies and associations of companies, and is involved in tripartite negotiations between employees, employers and the government on labour relations and wage policies. Consultation between the government and ECAM was very strong and this resulted in the marginalization of the weak and ineffective trade unions. However, the emerging effectiveness and political clout of trade unions during the 1990s imply a promising balance of power between employers and employees. Unions are participating in almost all issues that affect them in tripartite fora organized by the government.

Other social effects of adjustment

Public expenditure reforms and social sectors Structural adjustment policies have invariably involved reductions in government expenditure. The emphasis has been on improving the efficiency of the public sector, reduction of the budget deficit and the removal of subsidies. According to World Bank (1992), fiscal policy under the SAPs established fiscal discipline and resulted in substantial reduction in the central government budget deficit and enabled resources to be channelled to the private sector. The deficit declined from 16 per cent in 1980/81 to 5 per cent in 1991/2. These reductions in the government deficit have had different implications in the sectoral allocation of resources to the social sectors. In some studies, SAPs have demonstrated a negative impact on sectoral allocations of public resources, especially in the education and health sectors. In yet others, there have been significant increases (Cornia et al., 1987). Kaluwa et al. (1992) have argued that improvements in the macroeconomic balance (both external and internal) have been caused mainly through the contraction of domestic demand rather than a change in the structure of the economy, hence expenditure reduction rather than expenditure switching.

According to Chilowa and Chirwa (1997), the share of the social sectors in recurrent expenditure has hovered between 17.5 and 24.4 per cent in the 1990s. Per capita social expenditures measured at 1990 prices were between K30.30 and K39.60 in the 1990s. In terms of share of GDP, government recurrent expenditure significantly increased from 14.7 per cent in the pre-adjustment period to 23.9 per cent in the adjustment period. The shares of education, health, and community and social

development in GDP also rose from 2.3, 0.96 and 0.07 per cent in the pre-adju
period to 2.38, 1.47 and 0.16 per cent in the adjustment period, respe
However, the increase was only statistically significant with respect to the s
health and community and social development expenditures in GDP. Pe
expenditures for all social sectors increased significantly between the two
What worries many people in Malawi is the increase in public debt charge:
expenditure on defence, which increased both as a share of GDP and as pe
expenditure. Debt servicing more than doubled as a share of government
diture, increasing from 17 per cent in 1977 to 36 per cent in 1986 and 39 per
1989 (Chilowa, 1991; Kandoole, 1990). However, since 1991 debt servicing h
falling as a share of recurrent expenditure. In 1994 and 1995, public debt
were 13.7 and 21.3 per cent of recurrent expenditure, respectively.
payments on external debt amounted to MK105.9 million and MK134.4 m
1992 and 1993, respectively. It is apparent from the time series trend that th
debt burden has increased in the adjustment period.

The shares of education and health expenditures in total government re
expenditure fell, while that of community and social development inc
Chilowa and Chirwa (1997) found that the share of education expendit
significantly from 15.5 per cent in the pre-adjustment period to 10.05 per cer
adjustment period. The share of health expenditure fell from 6.53 per cen
pre-adjustment period to 6.17 per cent in the adjustment period, while the :
community and social development expenditure increased, though these
were very limited. In the adjustment period the share of the social
(education, health, community and social development) in government re
expenditure fell as low as 13.6 per cent in 1990, but picked up thereafter to r
per cent. In essence, there was a sharp decline in resource allocation to th
sectors, especially in the 1980s. However, the government did not react qu
the worsening trend in resource allocation. It was only in 1991 that it
addressing the bias against the social sectors. Since then, there has been a de
policy to ensure that at least 20 per cent of government recurrent expe
should be allocated to the education and health sectors. However, this
mended target was not achieved until 1995.

According to the World Bank (1996a), public recurrent spending on ed
more than tripled in real terms between 1990/91 and 1994/5 fiscal years, but
against primary education persists. One positive development in the ed
system has been the introduction of free primary school education since 19
increased the primary school enrolment from 1.9 million in July 1994 to 3.2
in September the same year. However, the increased enrolment has put
strains on available resources such as classrooms, teachers' houses and inst
materials. In 1995, the government estimated that the country had a shor
38,000 classrooms and 30,000 teachers' houses (MEPD, 1995). In reaction
increase in the enrolment rate, the government recruited 19,000 more te
15,000 of whom were untrained. The poor learning environment has led to
drop-out rate, in spite of free education. The increased employment of unq
teachers has meant that the quality of education has declined.

Furthermore, according to the World Bank (1996b) public spending wit
social sectors has been skewed towards higher levels of service, which are th
least likely to benefit the poor. Proportional allocations to primary-level s
which is the level most likely to benefit the poor, are among the lowest
country. For instance, the poorest income quintile received only 10 per cer
public education spending, while the share going to the richest income quin

38 per cent, in 1990/91. However, the introduction of free primary education in 1994/5 has substantially reduced this inequality to 16 and 25 per cent in the poorest and richest income quintiles, respectively. In the health sector, intra-sectoral allocations have favoured services at central hospitals *vis-à-vis* health centres. Arguably, accessibility to these central services at regional and district levels mostly caters for people who are not poor. Such biases have limited the availability of drugs and personnel at health centres.

Public sector restructuring and state-owned enterprise reforms Public sector restructuring and privatization are associated with various economic and social costs and benefits.[5] The social aspects of privatization include the unequal share of benefits and costs that follow from economic growth as a result of private sector-led growth; distributional effects such as widening and deepening ownership of enterprises, and broadening and democratizing the ownership of productive sectors; promoting decentralization and rural development; creation and loss of employment and business opportunities; transferring property rights to sections of the population hitherto deprived of them; use of privatization proceeds in the provision of social services; promotion of labour movements; and creation of freedom of choice (see UNCTAD, 1995). All these dimensions affect social and human development. This section analyzes how privatization in Malawi has affected the quality of life of the population.

(a) Public sector reforms and employment According to UNCTAD (1995), employment is perhaps the most visible and sensitive social aspect affected by public sector reforms and privatization in many countries. The employment impact of privatization has varied across countries. For instance, Haskel and Szymanski (1994) contend that the greatest impact of privatization in the United Kingdom has been in the labour market, and they estimated that employment fell by 26 per cent in industries due to privatization between 1980 and 1988. In contrast, Hachette and Luders (1993) contend that privatization as a means of divestiture does not seem to have had negative effects on persons employed in Chile. Their analysis revealed that the trend in employment level in Chile was similar in public, privatized and private firms. Overall they show that the level of employment increased in privatized firms, and more so in the manufacturing sector.

Any analysis of the impact of privatization in Malawi is severely constrained by data availability. As mentioned above, in the civil service reform programme, the government had retrenched about 20,000 civil servants in 1995 in non-established and temporary positions in non-priority areas such as unskilled labourers, cooks, gardeners, bricklayers, plumbers, drivers, messengers and janitors (World Bank, 1996b). The restructuring of Malawi Railways Limited involved a loss of employment for 1,083 workers. In addition, the government also privatized the Wood and Industry Corporation and Malawi Book Service in 1995. In the case of Malawi Book Service, all employees lost their jobs as a result of outright liquidation of the enterprise.

Privatization in Malawi has focused more on economic aspects as compared with its social dimensions. Several issues may be raised in this respect. First, there have been delays in paying retrenchment benefits; Malawi Railways workers had to march to the President demanding prompt payment of their retrenchment benefits. This creates hardship for the retrenched workers and their families, espe-

---

[5]Hachette and Luders (1993) and Bishop *et al.* (1994) present rigorous economic analysis of privatization in Chile and the United Kingdom, respectively.

cially those who do not immediately find new jobs. Secondly, there seems to be very limited provision for social protection in the design and implementation of the privatization programme. In fact, the Public Enterprises (Privatization) Act does not make any provision for the protection of workers. This is the foremost reason why the trade unions have opposed rapid privatization. In other countries such as Malaysia, Pakistan and Sri Lanka, the policy decision to protect employment offers a proviso that no staff of privatized firms may be retrenched within the first five years of privatization; staff redundancy is to be resolved through normal attrition; affected personnel upon privatization are offered a package of employment benefits on no less favourable terms and conditions of service than those they enjoyed while in government service; entitlement to unemployment benefits for two years; and provision of training and soft loans to support their self-employment.[6]

(b) **Public sector reforms and ownership structure** Widening and deepening the ownership of enterprises has been key amongst the objectives of privatization both in ADMARC's Divestiture Programme and in the Privatization Act of 1996. This was to facilitate the redistribution of wealth and productive assets.[7]

The case of Malawian privatization does not seem to have achieved the wider share ownership objective, especially in ADMARC's Divestiture Programme. As Chirwa (1994, 1997) argues, most enterprises in ADMARC's divestiture were sold to existing shareholders who had pre-emptive rights and large international and domestic conglomerates with interlocking ownership/directorships in various sectors of the economy. Only the estates were sold to private individuals, albeit only to those in the political elite group. The Employee Share Ownership Scheme was used only in the partial divestiture of Stagecoach Limited, where ADMARC sold 15 per cent of its shareholding to employees. The first wave therefore did not have a significant impact on social and human development with respect to ownership of productive assets. The first wave was marked by poor design and asymmetric information. Divestiture offers were not open to public information and enterprises were sold through negotiated bids in a less than transparent manner. This contributed to the reinforcement of the ownership position of existing shareholders and the political and business elites.

The Public Enterprises (Privatization) Act of 1996 lays emphasis on local participation by providing a loan fund for ordinary Malawians to buy shares at preferential prices. For instance, in the divestiture of the National Insurance Company, 15 million shares were offered. About 7 million and 5 million shares were offered to the general public and Malawian citizens, respectively. This offer has resulted in 2,272 individual new shareholders, the implementation of an employee share ownership scheme and mobilization of foreign resources to the tune of US$75,000 in the form of foreign investment. Furthermore, the divestiture of the remaining ADMARC shareholding in Auction Holdings has resulted in the dispersion of shares to ordinary and progressive tobacco farmers.

---

[6]UNCTAD (1995) provides many country examples of social provisions of privatization.

[7]The development of wider share ownership has been a key social principle in the privatization programme in the United Kingdom. UNCTAD (1995) reports that individual share ownership in the UK rose from 3 million in 1979 to 10 million in 1992, representing 7 and 22 per cent of the adult population, respectively (see Bishop and Kay (1989); Vickers and Yarrow (1989) and Grout (1994) for further exposition). In Latin America most governments made deliberate efforts to widen share ownership, by offering shares at preferential rates to employees to be purchased by severance payments (Glade, 1991).

Malawi's experience with structural adjustment: problems and constraints

Malawi was the first country in Southern Africa to adopt World Bank/IMF-sponsored structural adjustment programmes. However, our analysis shows that after this long history of structural adjustment most of the objectives set under different structural adjustment loans are far from being achieved. The economy requires a continuous dosage of financial resources. In most sectors the reforms seem to be complete but the economy's performance has been characterized by macroeconomic instability. Hence, the economy has not performed to the expectations of the designers or the implementors of the programmes. Indeed, both World Bank and government officials have conceded that to a great extent SAPs have not been successful in Malawi, yet they have continued to be implemented based on the same principles. According to the officials, their effective implementation has been constrained in several ways, which have eventually led to a failure to yield tangible benefits to the economy.

First, there has been a misconception in the adjustment process. SAPs are perceived as World Bank conditionalities for financial assistance rather than as what the World Bank/IMF think should be done to resolve the external and internal imbalances in order to improve the economic situation of the country. This has resulted in resistance on the part of interest groups to accepting and implementing the programmes.

Secondly, there has been a lack of government commitment to implement the agreed SAP measures completely. This has resulted in policy reversals and delaying the implementation of complementary measures. For example, the removal of the fertilizer subsidy was halted under SAL II in 1985, as the government's response to the fall in the utilization of fertilizers among smallholder farmers. The subsidy was completely removed only in 1994 and this created problems of timing because most farmers had inadequate resources to purchase inputs as a result of the drought. Furthermore, there has long been resistance to reducing the size of the civil service and the parastatal sector as strategies for reducing government deficit spending.

Thirdly, there have been serious problems of sequencing of SAPs. This has impacted adversely on the operation of the market mechanism. For instance, as Kaluwa (1992) observed, whereas the price decontrol programme was completed in 1985, monopoly rights in the industrial sector were abolished in 1988 and entry into manufacturing activities was still regulated until 1992. Hence, the price incentive created by price liberalization did not facilitate the development of the private sector and the inflow of capital from foreign investors. In another instance, the government liberalized the exchange-rate system in 1994 amidst problems of agricultural production resulting from a drought and at a time when the country had inadequate foreign-exchange reserves.

Fourthly, both the government and the World Bank rush through the process of design and implementation of SAPs. The government, which is usually in dire need of the financial resources, readily accepts the design of the adjustment and then fails later on to implement the agreed measures. Apart from the need to have immediate access to financial resources from the World Bank, there are institutional and human resource constraints in the government machinery. Officials in key positions do not have adequate skills to analyze technical World Bank documents. As a result, the government team lacks the skills to negotiate with the World Bank team and relies heavily on World Bank analysis of the situation. To make matters worse, the government negotiating team fails to present approaches of structural reforms designed by Malawians. In addition, the documents are always confidential and there is no consultation within the key ministries and departments, nor between the government and the private sector, the trade unions and other non-governmental organizations. This results in accepting conditions and policies that become practically or politically difficult to implement and hence lead to serious delays in implementation.

However, a more serious institutional and human resource constraint is the inability of the government economists to prepare their own thorough analysis of the economy in general, and vital sectors in particular. The Policy Framework Papers are prepared by World Bank missions who spend a few days in the country and later compile a report for Malawi. As the World Bank (1996b) acknowledges, this has resulted in reduced rigour in economic and sector analyses which could have resulted in enhancing the performance of SAPs.

Fifthly, there is a lack of political commitment to undertake SAPs. According to the World Bank (1996b), a review of previous adjustment operations revealed that the most important obstacle to sustainable growth and reform has been the lack of clear and unequivical political commitment to poverty alleviation, liberalization of the smallholder sector, and broad-based private sector development. At the same time, the World Bank acknowledges that the autocratic leadership style of the one-party regime, combined with the pragmatic economic policies, had some success, more particularly in areas where the vested interests of political elites were not compromised, but failed to achieve a broad-based transformation of the economy. This implies that, in the multi-party government era, SAPs are politically sensitive and wider consultations will have to be undertaken to institute measures that may go against vested interests.

Finally, but by no means least important, the implementation of SAPs has been affected by external factors over which Malawi had no control. As the World Bank (1996b) acknowledges, recurrent and external shocks have hampered the effectiveness of the policy measures. These shocks include adverse terms of trade, high interest rates in the international financial markets, continued closure of Malawi's shortest external transport link through Mozambique, and natural factors such as drought. This has led to policy reversals that involved short-term solutions to the shocks and delays in the implementation and sequencing of policy measures. Consequently, it resulted in the diversion of policy-makers' attention from medium-term and long-term strategies, thus pushing the adjustment process off track.

In spite of the structural reforms in Malawi, the evidence in this chapter shows that the policies that have been implemented have not taken the economy back to the pre-adjustment performance levels. International and domestic trade liberalization, agricultural sector reforms, public sector restructuring and privatization, and financial sector reforms are some of the reforms that have been adequately implemented. Reforms in the labour market are recent and minimal and have largely been prompted by the democratization process in the transition from a one-party to a multi-party state. On the whole, the benefits of SAPs in Malawi have been less tangible and have mostly resulted in a decline in the social well-being of the population. Overall, there has been a decline in real per capita GDP, and economic growth has been erratic, registering three down-swings within the adjustment period.

Adjustment programmes have created limited employment opportunities. In fact, the rate at which the economy absorbs the growing labour force has fallen by 69 per cent between the pre-adjustment and adjustment periods. Due to high rates of inflation, real wages have also fallen within the adjustment period. Nonetheless, labour market institutions have flourished and have become very proactive as a result of the SAPs and the democratic environment.

Because of rapid population growth and declining land holding sizes, more people will have to find gainful employment outside of agriculture. The promotion of small and medium-scale enterprises will be the key to this. There is a need to remove all unnecessary restrictions that hinder the growth of small and medium enterprises and other informal sector activities. Human resources development has been neglected in the past in favour of the so-called 'productive' sector. Efforts that the present government is making in allocating more resources appear to be discriminatory, for instance in the case of the allocation of resources to primary education alone without commensurate allocation to the other parts of the education sector which are also beneficial to the country's development process. There is a need for the government to incorporate social provisions in both civil service reform and privatization programmes to include: efficiency in redundancy or severance payments; retraining or vocational training; promotion of income-generating activities; phased approach to retrenchment; negotiations with prospective buyers of state-owned enterprises to restrain immediate retrenchment. These could lessen the problems of the retrenched workers and contribute to the country's social and human development.

The SAPs are not adequately discussed in Malawi and the government negoti-ating team lacks the skills and analytical ability to discuss things in depth with the World Bank team. This has tended to create problems of implementation of some of the measures in accordance with the agreements. Donors should give adequate time and resources for the designing of country-specific interventions and a thorough analysis of the likely impact of each reform policy should be undertaken prior to any intervention. There should also be adequate consultation with various stakeholders such as trade unions and employers' organizations in the negotiation, design and implementation of SAPs and less reliance on the IMF and World Bank in diagnosing the problems of the economy. It is the government's role to build the capacity to analyze economic reform processes which can be used by social partners in consultations at national and sectoral level.

References

Banda, A.L. *et al.* (1996) 'Labour Market and Employment Policy in Malawi'. Paper presented at the Regional Workshop on Labour Market and Employment Policy in Southern and Eastern Africa, Lusaka, Zambia.

Bishop, M.R. and J.A. Kay (1989) 'Privatisation in the United Kingdom: Lessons from Experience', *World Development*, Vol. 17, No. 5.

Bishop, M.R., J. Kay and C. Mayes (eds) (1984) *Privatisation and Economic Performance*. Oxford: Oxford University Press.

Chilowa, W.R. (1991) *Structural Adjustment and Poverty: The Case of Malawi*. CMI Working Paper. Bergen: Christian Michelsen Institute.

—— and E.W. Chirwa (1997) 'The Impact of Structural Adjustment Programmes on Social and Human Development in Malawi', *Bwalo*, Vol. 1, No. 1.

Chipeta, C. (1996) 'An Alternative View of SAPs', *Southern Africa Political and Economic Monthly* (SAPEM), 9 (12), pp. 9–11.

Chirwa, E.W. (1994) 'Privatisation and Divestiture: The Case of Malawi'. Paper presented at the University Research and Publications Committee Conference, Mangochi.

—— (1996) 'Market Structure, Liberalisation and Performance in the Malawian Banking Industry'. Draft final report presented at the AERC Economic Research Workshop, Nairobi.

—— (1997) 'State Divestiture and Private Sector Development in Malawi: Lessons from ADMARC's Divestiture Programme', paper to be presented at the AERC Biennial Conference on Rekindling Sustainable Development in Africa: Agenda for the 21st Century, Cotonou, Benin, 27–30 January.

Christiansen, R.E. and L.A. Stackhouse (1989) 'The Privatisation of Agricultural Trading in Malawi', *World Development*, Vol. 17, No. 5.

Cornia, G.A., R. Jolly and F. Stewart (1987) *Adjustment with a Human Face*. Oxford: Oxford University Press for UNICEF.

Daniels, L. and A. Ngwira (1993) *Results of a Nation-wide Survey on Micro, Small and Medium Enterprises in Malawi*. GEMINI Technical Report No. 53. Lilongwe: World Bank.

Glade, W. (1991) *Privatisation of Public Enterprises in Latin America*. San Francisco: ICS Press.

Government of Malawi (1971) *Statement of Development Policies 1971–1979*. Zomba: Government Printer.

—— (1987) *Statement of Development Policies 1987–1996*. Zomba: Government Printer.

—— (1996) *Malawi Civil Service Census Results*, Lilongwe: Office of the President and Cabinet.

Grout, P. (1994) 'Popular Capitalism' in Bishop *et al.*

Hachette, D. and R. Luders (1993) *Privatisation in Chile: An Economic Appraisal*. San Francisco: ICS Press.

Harrigan, J. (1991) 'Malawi', in P. Mosley, J. Harrigan and J. Toye (eds) *Aid and Power: The World Bank and Policy-based Lending*, Volume 2, Case Studies. London: Routledge.

Haskel, J. and S. Szymanski (1994) 'Privatisation and the Labour Market: Facts, Theory, and Evidence' in Bishop *et al.*

Kaluwa, B.M. (1992) 'Malawi Industry: Policies, Performance and Problems', in G.C.Z. Mhone (ed) *Malawi at the Crossroads: The Post-Colonial Political Economy*. Harare: SAPES Books.

Kaluwa, B.M., E. Silumbu, Banda E. Ngalande and W. Chilowa (1992) *The Structural Adjustment Programme in Malawi: A Case for Successful Adjustment?* Monograph Series No. 3. Harare: SAPES Books.

Kandoole, B.F. (1990) 'Structural Adjustment in Malawi: Short-term Gains and Long-term Losses', in, G. Roe (ed) *The Effects of Structural Adjustment Programme in Malawi*. Zomba: Centre for Social Research.

Khan, S., B. Kaluwa and Spooner (1989) *The Impact of Malawi's Industrial Price Decontrol* (Washington, DC: World Bank.

Kydd, J. and R.E. Christiansen (1982) 'Structural Change in Malawi Since Independence: Consequences of a Development Strategy Based on Large-Scale Agriculture', *World Development*, Vol. 10, No. 5.

Lensink, R. (1996) *Structural Adjustment in Sub-Saharan Africa*. London: Longman Group.

Mhone, G. (1992) 'The Political Economy of Malawi – An Overview', in G.C.Z. Mhone (ed.) *Malawi at the Crossroads: The Post-Colonial Political Economy*. Harare: SAPES Books.

Ministry of Commerce and Industry (1995) *Situation Analysis for Trade and Industry Policy*, UNDP/Malawi Government Report.

Ministry of Economic Planning and Development (MEPD) (1995) *Economic Report 1995*. Zomba: Government Printer.

Silumbu, E.B.D. (1992) 'Foreign Trade Policies and Performance in Malawi 1965–1990', in G.C. Mhone (ed) *Malawi at the Crossroads: The Post-Colonial Political Economy*. Harare: SAPES Books.

UNCTAD (1995) *Comparative Experiences with Privatisation: Policy Insights and Lessons Learned*. Geneva: United Nations.

UNDP (1996) *Human Development Report 1996*. Oxford: Oxford University Press.

Vickers, J and G. Yarrow (1989) 'Privatization in Britain' in P. MacAvoy (ed.) *Privatization and State Owned Enterprises*. London: Kluwer Academic Press.

World Bank (1988) *Malawi: Industry and Trade Policy Adjustment Credit (ITPAC)*. Washington, DC: World Bank.

—— (1989) *Malawi: Industrial Sector Memorandum*. Washington, DC: World Bank.

—— (1990) *Malawi: Agriculture Sector Adjustment Credit*. Washington, DC: World Bank.

—— (1992) *Malawi: Entrepreneurship Development and Drought Recovery Programme*. Washington, DC: World Bank.

—— (1993) *Malawi: Industry and Trade Policy Adjustment Credit (ITPAC) – Completion of Project Report*. Washington, DC: World Bank.

—— (1996a) Malawi: Human Resources and Poverty – Profile and Priorities for Action. Washington, DC: World Bank.

—— (1996b) *Malawi: Fiscal Restructuring and Deregulation Program*. Washington, DC: World Bank.

Appendix 8.1

Table A8.1   *Structural adjustment loans and sectoral credit, Malawi*

Loan/year (funds)	Main objectives	Main actions taken
SAL I FY81 (IDA $45m)	Diversify export base Encourage efficient import substitution Ensure appropriate price and income policy Improve public sector's financial performance Strengthen government's economic planning and monitoring capabilities	Periodic adjustment of the exchange rate (devaluation): April 1982 15%; Sept. 1983 12%; Jan. 1984 3%. Annual increase of smallholder producer prices, notably for maize Expansion of tax base and increasing tax rates Strengthening government's capability for macro and sectoral planning, and public debt monitoring and management Increased recurrent budget allocation for agriculture and other key economic and social sectors Improved financial structure of MDC and Press Holdings Increased tariffs of public facilities, for MR and MHC Periodic adjustment of interest rates
SAL II FY84 (IDA $55m)	Diversify export base Encourage efficient import substitution Ensure adequate incentives Improve public sector's financial performance Strengthen policy-making capabilities	Periodic exchange-rate adjustments (devaluations): April 1985 15%; Jan. 1986 9.5%. Smallholder producer prices increased ADMARC's financial management capabilities strengthened Industry Price Decontrol (41% of items) Improved buoyancy of tax system Increased non-tax revenues from higher fees and levies Preparation of 3-year PSIP Strengthening of government's planning capability with emphasis on formulation of medium-term strategy, project identification, evaluation and monitoring Recurrent budget to key economic and social sectors increased Financial restructuring of ADMARC, MDC and Press Adjustment of tariffs for public utilities Periodic adjustments of interest rates
SAL III FY86 IDA $30m African Facility $40m. Financing $29m Total $99m.	Diversify export base Promote exports Strengthen policy-making capabilities Improve performance of development institutions	Periodic exchange-rate adjustments (devaluations): Aug. 1986 10%; Feb. 1987 20% Smallholder producer prices increased Postponement of elimination of fertilizer subsidies to 1989/90 Divestiture of ADMARC's investments unrelated to marketing activities

Table A8.1 *continued*

Loan/year (funds)	Main objectives	Main actions taken
		Industry Price Decontrol, except for petrol, low-grade beef, fertilizers, sugar, vehicle spare parts Preparation for an export promotion strategy Establishment of export financing facility Tax increases on selected items Adjustment of tax system to improve efficiency and incentives Preparation of 3-year PSIP Strengthening of government's policy-making and economic analysis capability Introduction of a programmatic budget system Restructuring of ADMARC, MDC and Press Periodic adjustments of interest rates
SAL III Supplement FY87 IDA $10.0m SJF $30.0m USAID $15.0m Total $55.0m	Expand role of private sector in marketing of smallholder crops Improve financial performance and operational efficiency of ADMARC Strengthen government's policy-making capability	Periodic exchange-rate adjustments (devaluations): Jan. 1988 15% Intra-regional differentiated producer and consumer maize prices implemented to expand role of private sector in marketing smallholder crops except tobacco and cotton Government took over financing of strategic grain reserves from ADMARC Divestiture of ADMARC's investments unrelated to marketing activities Periodic adjustment of interest rates
ITPAC FY88 IDA $79.0m Japan $25.0m EEC $15.0m ADF $17.2m USAID $35.2m Germany $10.2m Netherl. $3.9m Total $186.5m	Improve policy environment for manufacturing sector to increase efficiency of resource use including imports and expand exports	Periodic exchange-rate adjustments (devaluations): March 1990 7% Beef prices decontrolled Reduction of scope of industrial licensing requirements, and elimination of authority to grant exclusive product rights Reduction of scope of export licensing Revision of duty drawback system Introduction of surtax credit system Reduction of financial deficit Preparation of 3-year rolling PSIP Expansion of excise tax base and move to ad valorem rate Introduction of current payment system for corporate income tax Removal of requirement for prior allocation by Reserve Bank for 65% of all imports Revision of Reserve Bank Act Revision of Banking Act
ASAC FY90	Increase efficiency and improve incomes of smallholders	Continued monitoring of exchange rate Smallholder price adjustment

Table A8.1   *continued*

Loan/year (funds)	Main objectives	Main actions taken
IDA $79.0m UK $25.0m Netherl. $10.6m Germany $9.0m Total $123.6	Increase efficiency of land use and protect environment Improve macroeconomic environment through further import liberalization and public expenditure restructuring	Introduction of two-payment price system for smallholder tobacco Other agents allowed to market fertilizer Improved cash flow management for FFRFM Removal of fertilizer subsidies Rationalization and government financing of ADMARC development functions Smallholders allowed to grow burley tobacco Maize research shifted to develop high-yielding flint varieties Estate land rents adjusted more frequently; rent raised in 1990/91 and 1992/3 to real 1985 level Transfer of land from customary to estates halted except in low population density areas Enforcement of woodlot environmental covenants strengthened Preparation of 3-year rolling PSIP, and maintenance of satisfactory fiscal deficit Removal of prior foreign-exchange control except for small negative list
EDDRP FY92 IDA $120.0m Japan $70.0m ADF $20.0m Total $210.0m	Support improved environment for entrepreneurial activity and investment in labour-intensive activities Support adoption of policies aimed at deepening financial markets Support reorientation of fiscal and labour policy towards human capital development Help alleviate impact of drought	Maintaining exchange rate at a level consistent with external competitiveness in line with trade liberalization; devaluation of Kwacha: June 1992 15%; July 1992 22%; Feb. 1994 Flotation of Kwacha Expansion of smallholder access to burley tobacco production Issuance of Investment Policy Statement Legislation for establishment of MIPA Revision of policy directives so that business registration and incorporation of companies consist of one step with Registrar General Replacement of Industrial Development Act with Industrial Licensing Act so as to eliminate industrial licensing process for investments except for a short list Review of labour market imperfections and policy options including minimum wage policy Budgetary allocation to education of at least 15% and 15.5% of total expenditure in 1992/93 and 1993/94, respectively Introduction of budgetary system for separating allocation and control of individual districts and peripheral health care services in Ministry of Health Revenue Budget Increase in peripheral services' share of health Revenue Budget

Table A8.1 *continued*

Loan/year (funds)	Main objectives	Main actions taken
		Expansion of surtax base to electricity and telephone as well as certain other services
		Increase in surtax rate on electricity and telephone services to not less than 10%
		Identification of target base surtax rate, review of increase in surtax rate on services already taxed to that rate, and review of expansion of surtax base to further services
		Reduction of base surtax rate to 30%
		Review of further decreases in corporate and personal income tax rates
		Elimination of surtax exemption for domestically produced goods
		Consolidation of protective effect of domestic surtax exemption into existing tariff system
		Limiting resulting consolidated tariff rates to maximum of 75%
		Implementation of major tariff schedule revisions
		Establishment of a Capital Market Department at Reserve Bank of Malawi to conduct periodic auctions for issuance of RBM bills
		Elimination of direct bank credit controls
		Maintenance of free determination of interest rates
		Continuing to actively seek applications from sound international and regional banks
		Preparation of a bank restructuring programme
EDDRP Supplement FY95 IDA $40.0m	Help reduce balance of payments pressure due to drought-related imports	
FRDP FY96 IDA $106.4m	Prioritize, protect and expand inter- and intra- sectoral allocations to social sectors on sustainable basis Accelerate consolidation of structural measures under previous adjustment including complete removal of remaining pricing and marketing constraints on smallholder agriculture, and removal of binding constraints to broad-based private sector entry and development Improve expenditure control Restructure civil service to	Reorientation of public spending to pro-poor areas Introduction of cash budgeting system Completion of civil service census Retrenchment of about 25,000 temporary workers Pre-Shipment Inspection strengthened Improved duty drawback system Implementation of EPZ Act Increased land rents Amended Land Act All constraints on smallholder access to burley lifted Replacement of fixed producer/consumer price system for maize with price band Approved removal of licensing and registration procedures for private

Table A8.1   *continued*

Loan/year (funds)	Main objectives	Main actions taken
	improve efficiency and control growth of wages and salaries Rationalize tariffs and surtax and improve tax administration to increase efficiency and protect revenue collection	traders in seed and fertilizer marketing Removal of all restrictions on second-hand imports of trucks and spare parts Removal of minimum freight tariff Approved Privatization Bill Adoption of transparent Privatization Policy Increased availability of suitable industrial land Repeal of laws that discriminate against race

Notes: ADMARC = Agricultural Development and Marketing Corporation, ASAC = Agriculture Sector Adjustment Credit, EDDRP = Entrepreneurship Development and Drought Recovery Programme, FRDP = Fiscal Restructuring and Deregulation Programme, IDA = International Development Association, ITPAC = Industry and Trade Policy Adjustment Credit, MDC = Malawi Development Corporation, MR = Malawi Railways, PSIP = Public Sector Investment Programme, SAL = Structural Adjustment Loan, SJF = Special Joint Facility

Source: World Bank (1996b)

Figure A8.1   *Growth in real per capita GDP, Malawi, 1971–95 (%)*

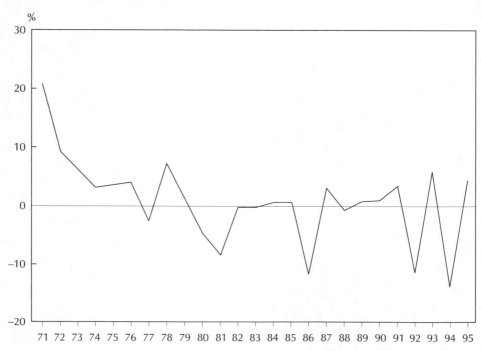

Figure A8.2   *Real consumption per capita, Malawi, 1970–95 (Kwacha)*

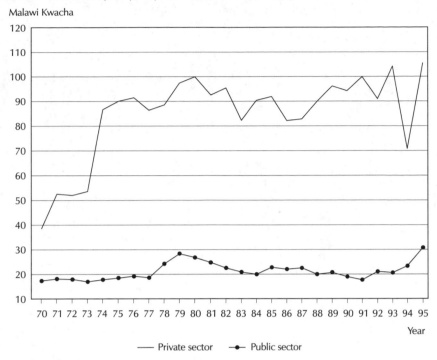

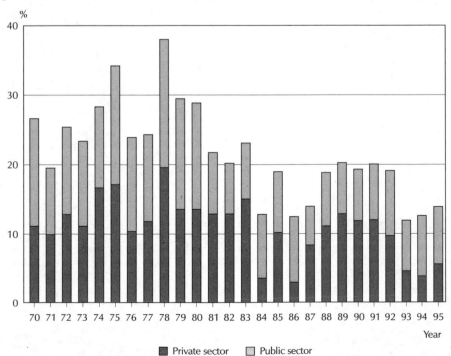

Figure A8.3   *Gross domestic investment, Malawi, 1970–95 (% of GDP)*

Figure A8.4   *Trade deficit as ratio of GDP, Malawi, 1970–95 (%)*

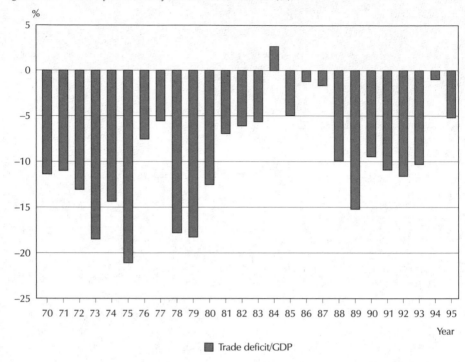

■ Trade deficit/GDP

Figure A8.5   *Real wage developments, Malawi, 1971–90 (1980 prices)*

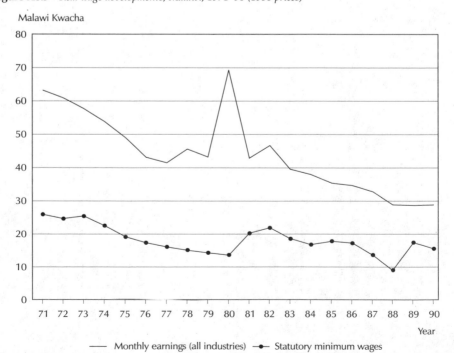

—— Monthly earnings (all industries)   —●— Statutory minimum wages

Index

Note: Figures and tables are indicated by *italic* page numbers, significant text sections by **bold** numbers.